MANUAL ON THE USE OF THE
DEWEY DECIMAL CLASSIFICATION

Manual on the Use of the DEWEY Decimal Classification: Edition 19

Prepared by

John P. Comaromi, Editor
DEWEY Decimal Classification

and

Margaret J. Warren, Assistant Editor
DEWEY Decimal Classification

with the assistance of

Winton E. Matthews, Jr.
Gregory R. New
Robert R. Trotter
Benjamin A. Custer

FOREST PRESS
A Division of
Lake Placid Education Foundation

85 Watervliet Avenue
Albany, N.Y. 12206 U.S.A.
1982

Library of Congress Cataloging in Publication Data

Manual on the use of the Dewey decimal classification.
  Includes index.

  1. Classification, Dewey decimal—Handbooks, manuals, etc.   I.   Comaromi, John Phillip, 1937-
  II.   Warren, Margaret J.   III.   Dewey, Melvil, 1851-1931.   Decimal classification and relativ index.

Z696.D7M36   025.4′31   82-1516
ISBN 0-910608-32-6   AACR2

Contents

Publisher's Foreword

In 1962 a *Guide to Use of Dewey Decimal Classification* was prepared by the Decimal Classification Office at the Library of Congress, based on the 16th Edition of the DEWEY Decimal Classification as it was applied by the staff of that office. Since that time, the Classification system has become more comprehensive and complex, reflecting, as it must, the ever increasing growth and interdependence of knowledge. In order to help classifiers use the current edition of the DDC, the Forest Press Division of the Lake Placid Education Foundation, publisher of the Classification, approved the preparation of this new and updated *Manual.* The Press believes that such a work will bring about more efficient and effective use of the Classification, which in turn will provide greater standardization of application as well as help advance universal bibliographic control.

The urgent need for an up-to-date manual first came clearly to the fore in 1975 during the gathering of data for and the preparation of the *Survey of the Use of the DDC in the United States and Canada,* a study sponsored by Forest Press. Librarians reported that the 1962 *Guide* had been rendered obsolete for the most part by topical and structural changes that had taken place in the Classification in Editions 17 and 18 and that were about to be included in Edition 19. Feeling the need for guidance in the application of the Classification, many librarians participating in the survey requested a new and updated guide or manual. This *Manual on the Use of the Dewey Decimal Classification* therefore serves a long-standing need for classifiers who have experienced certain difficulties with the substantial expansions and resulting complexities of the DDC. It should provide practicing classifiers with information enabling them to apply the Classification in greater conformity to that which takes place within the office of the Decimal Classification Division itself.

Preparation of the *Manual* was begun in 1978 by John P. Comaromi, then Associate Professor, Graduate School of Library and Information Science, University of California at Los Angeles, with the assistance of Catherine Hall, a graduate student. In 1980, Dr. Comaromi was appointed Editor of the DEWEY Decimal Classification and Chief of the Decimal Classification Division of the Library of Congress, at which time Margaret J. Warren, Assistant Editor of the Classification, was given major responsibility for working with him on the *Manual.* Her knowledge of the Classification and her editorial skills proved invaluable. Winton E. Matthews, Jr. and Gregory R. New, Decimal Classification Specialists at the Decimal Classification Division of the Library of Congress, contributed many sections to the *Manual.*

Robert R. Trotter, Head, Dewey Decimal Classification Section, Bibliographic Services Division, The British Library, worked closely with the authors of the *Manual,* providing them with useful guidance. Benjamin A. Custer, who retired as Editor of the Classification early in 1980, reviewed the manuscript for editorial accuracy and made helpful suggestions. The Press is grateful for the dedication and service of these individuals.

Other members of the Decimal Classification Division staff also contributed to the *Manual* project. Forest Press acknowledges with gratitude the work of the following Division staff members: Melba D. Adams, Assistant Chief; Decimal Classification Specialists: Julianne Beall, Frances A. Bold, Michael B. Cantlon, Rosalee Connor, Eve M. Dickey, William S. Hwang, Letitia J. Reigle, Virginia Anne Schoepf, Emily K. Spears, and Cosmo D. Tassone; Marisa C. Vandenbosch, Editorial Reviser; Marcellus S. Todd, Library Materials Distributor; and the late Idalia V. Fuentes.

Two experts in classification generally and in the DDC in particular provided useful and objective assistance in critiquing the manuscript in its developing stages. Forest Press is indebted to Irma R. Tomberlin, Boyd Professor, School of Library Science, The University of Oklahoma at Norman, and Sarah K. Vann, Professor, Graduate School of Library Studies, University of Hawaii at Manoa.

The Decimal Classification Editorial Policy Committee enthusiastically supported the preparation of this *Manual.* Members of the EPC also gave of their time to read and react to the manuscript. The Press extends its thanks and appreciation to former and current members: Lizbeth J. Bishoff, Director, Ela Area Public Library and representative of the American Library Association; Barbara Branson, Principal Cataloger, Duke University Library; Lois M. Chan, Professor, College of Library Science, University of Kentucky; Margaret E. Cockshutt, Associate Professor, Faculty of Library Science, University of Toronto; Betty M. E. Croft, Technical Services Librarian, Northwest Missouri State University Library; Joel C. Downing, former Director of Copyright and English Language Services, Bibliographic Services Division, The British Library; Frances Hinton, Chief of the Processing Division, The Free Library of Philadelphia; Joseph H. Howard, Assistant Librarian for Processing Services, Library of Congress; Donald J. Lehnus, Associate Professor, Graduate School of Library and Information Science, The University of Mississippi; Clare E. Ryan, Head of Technical Processing, New Hampshire State Library, and former representative of the American Library Association; Marietta D. Shepard, former Chief of the Library Development Program, Organization of American States.

The Forest Press Committee authorized publication of the *Manual* and also supported it throughout its preparation. Members, both former and current, who were involved in the *Manual* project include: Henry M. Bonner, present representative on the Forest Press Committee of the Board of Trustees of the Lake Placid Education Foundation; Calvert H. Crary, former Committee representative of the Board of Trustees of the Lake Placid Education Foundation; Walter W. Curley, Chairman, formerly President of Gaylord Bros., Inc.; Richard K. Gardner, Professor, Graduate School of Library and Information Science, University of California at Los Angeles; J. Michael O'Brien, Head Librarian, Oak Lawn Public Library, Illinois; and Thomas E. Sullivan, Associate Director of Indexing Services, The H. W. Wilson Company.

The Forest Press staff, Judith Kramer-Greene, Forest Press Editor; Mildred Gipp-Dugan, Administrative Assistant; and Dorothy W. Ryan, Accountant, contributed substantially to the editorial, production, and distribution process of the *Manual.* It is fitting to take note of their special competencies in helping complete this work.

Finally, the cooperation of the University of Maryland Department of Geography and Urban Studies in the preparation of the Area Maps for Table 2 is gratefully acknowledged.

John A. Humphry
EXECUTIVE DIRECTOR
Forest Press Division
Lake Placid Education Foundation

January 14, 1982

Introduction

The *Manual on the Use of the DEWEY Decimal Classification* is intended to serve practicing classifiers and students. Since members of these groups are familiar with the DDC and have studied its Introduction in one or more of its recent editions, there is little to be gained by restating the Introduction to Edition 19 or by repeating the notes in the Schedules and Tables. Nevertheless, redundancy has its virtues, and certain troublesome problems receive attention in both the *Manual* and the Introduction to Edition 19.

The *Manual* consists of three parts: (1) general principles of library classification and of the DDC; (2) a discussion in schedule order of the structure of the Tables and Schedules, accompanied by guidance in classifying items in difficult areas, and including outline maps which provide a display of key area numbers from Table 2; and (3) two indexes (DDC numbers referred to and topics discussed). In order to hold the *Manual* to a manageable size, each entry's usefulness to classifiers has been considered carefully. Though its contents are selective, the *Manual* will aid in the solution of many problems through the use of analogy and through the application of general principles.

The *Manual* is intended in the main to be pragmatic. It is theoretical only when theory explains practice or policy, and historical only when knowledge of the past explains the present or is a guide to the future. If the *Manual* can assist classifiers whose libraries are using earlier editions, we shall be gratified. The discussion presented herein, however, pertains specifically to Edition 19.

The Nature of Library Classification

The overall goal of organizing a library is to store and retrieve information effectively and efficiently. Among the means of organizing a library, a classification system plays several roles:

(1) Usually it organizes the collection of books and other materials along disciplinary lines so that works most often used together are found together in groupings meaningful to the user in his field of study.

(2) It provides an order for the shelf list.

(3) In some subject catalogs (classed, or classified, catalogs), the classification organizes the entries for items along disciplinary lines so that users may peruse a file of entries to discover what a library possesses in a given field and on a topic in the field without having to inspect the collection itself and without fear of missing what might be absent from the shelf.

A classification scheme is used most productively in those libraries where the larger segments of works are analyzed and a class number is assigned to each (i.e., subject analytics are organized by means of the classification), which is the practice, of course, of the classed catalog. Where the classification is used for shelf arrangement only, the shelf list becomes the nearest substitute for a classed catalog, and eventually the classification becomes merely the means to supply an address for an item rather than a means to organize and gather works on a particular topic or category within a particular field of study.

Precoordinate vs. Postcoordinate Indexing Systems

Like the Library of Congress Classification and the subject heading lists of the Library of Congress and Sears, the DDC is a precoordinate indexing system. In such systems the terms that describe the contents of a work are set down in a specified order at the time of indexing rather than at the time of searching. For instance, in the DDC the order of the primary categories of a collection of works of literature is language, literary form, literary period, and topic. The order of the categories is invariable: the language in which the works were written plus the form in which they were written (e.g., drama, fiction) plus the period in which they were written plus their topic if one is discernible. If a patron wishes to find Victorian fiction that deals with ghosts, he must first go to 82 (English), on to 823 (English fiction), on to 823.8 (Victorian fiction), to 823.808 (collections of Victorian fiction), to 823.8080375 (collections of Victorian fiction in which ghosts, ogres, fairies, and vampires figure prominently). There the indexing ends. (Other than for novels the DDC does not allow both period and kind of fiction to be indicated.)

When using a precoordinate indexing system, one must know the principles and rules of application appropriate to it in order to retrieve material through it effectively. One must know the order in which the elements of a class number or a subject heading fall. Precoordinate systems have several strengths. They are usually predictable and they allow for browsing, vocabulary control, and economy in number of entries. Their weaknesses are the need to know the system well, a slow response to new terminology and subjects, and an inflexible order of elements.

In postcoordinate indexing systems, the elements of an entry are coordinated or combined at the time of searching rather than at the time of indexing. For instance, a subject cataloger would assign to our collection of Victorian fiction in which ghosts figure prominently the terms English, Fiction, Victorian period, and Ghosts (if these were permissible terms, which they probably would be), listing or coding the four terms on the record for the item. When patrons wish to retrieve the works that are defined precisely by the four terms, they would make their request by asking the system to indicate the records of all works to which the given terms had been assigned. It does not matter in what order the terms are put to the system; the list of works will be the same.

When using a postcoordinate system, one need only know the names by which subjects are called. The strengths of such systems are their response to new terminology and their ability to list all aspects of a work in any order. Problems in vocabulary control are their primary weakness.

Citation Order in the DDC

Each main class, division, and subdivision of the DDC is made up of categories that are combined in a certain order. Success in assigning DDC numbers and in using the Classification for retrieval purposes requires knowing which categories exist and being able to determine the citation order within the various classes. Citation order is the order in which the various categories or elements that constitute a class are combined.

Many of the categories of the classes of the DDC are facets. A facet is a category that represents one characteristic of division. Note, however, that many of the categories of the classes are not facets. For instance, Physical anthropology 573 is not a facet of Biology 570, and 573.5 Pigmentation is not a facet of Physical anthropology. The point is that classes, whether large or small, are not subdivided by facets solely.

Though it usually provides a number for every category that is an essential part of a class, the DDC does not always recognize all categories pertaining to the class. Nor are all those recognized necessarily specified in the notation for a particular work. For instance, a work on cataloging prints for university libraries treats a library process or operation (cataloging), a library material (prints), and a library type or kind (university). At 025.34 Cataloging, classification, indexing of special materials, the DDC directs the classifier to cite the material after the process. Thus, 025.34 (cataloging of special materials) + 71 (the number for prints that has been derived from 025.1771) = 025.3471, which is the full number. We can build no further, as permission is not given to specify the library type. We see here that no provision exists to specify library type, a recognized facet in library and information science.

The failure to cite the known categories of a class exhaustively is normal in the DDC and in other precoordinate indexing systems. Length of notation is undoubtedly behind the decision to eschew exhaustivity. Of course, in the DDC, as in any precoordinate indexing system, a gain in brevity of notation inevitably entails a loss of information. For instance, 641.5972 indicates Mexican cookery. If the full number is used, all works on Mexican cookery are gathered in one place on the shelf. Reduce the number to 641.597 and one gathers cookery of North America. Reduce the number to 641.59 and one gathers ethnic cookery and cookery by place. Each digit deleted is information lost. To be sure, Mexican cookery can be found at 641.5, 641.59, or 641.597, but then all works on the subject will not be found together, and each patron has to provide the effort to gather the works he or she seeks because the library has decided not to expend the effort required to provide the one digit, or two, or three that would gather the works in one place.

Situations arise in which topics can legitimately be classed in two or more places. Tables of precedence and class notes inform the classifier which characteristic is to be preferred. When using these devices, the classifier must be certain that the work actually treats each of the characteristics equally, because in many works one or more characteristics are only incidental. The following examples illustrate the problem:

(1) The classifier using the table of precedence at 362 in Edition 19 would class a work discussing the social welfare problems of black women in 362.83, not 362.8496. If, when examining the work, the classifier should find that the majority of the black women studied are also members of the working class, but that this characteristic is not considered by the author, the classifier would correctly class the work in 362.83, not 362.85, even though laboring classes come before women in the table of precedence.

(2) In classing a work on the murals of the Sistine Chapel, the classifier must make sure whether or not the religious subjects of the murals are discussed in the book. The note at 751.7 in Edition 19, "Class specific subjects in specific forms in 753-758," indicates that if the work discusses the religious aspects of the murals, it should be classed in 755.20945634. If, however, it mentions the religious subjects only in order to indicate which murals are being discussed, the note should be ignored and the work classed in 751.730945634.

To prevent cross classification, the classifier is directed to the correct citation order by tables of precedence, notes, and conventions regarding the use of zeros in the notation. Cross classification occurs when items compounded of two or more characteristics are classed with one characteristic taking precedence part of the time and other characteristics taking precedence the rest of the time. In the example of the prints for university libraries, cross classification would occur if some works on the subject were classed at 025.3471 (cataloging prints), others at 025.1771 (prints). Such systemless distribution defeats the objective of bringing works on a subject into a useful grouping in the class in which the subject is found.

Notes instruct directly. When the classifier reads at 025.34: "Add to base number 025.34 the numbers following 025.17 in 025.171–025.179, e.g., cataloging, classification, indexing of maps 025.346," the citation order is being laid down; it is process before material.

Zeros instruct by their number. Normally the fewer the zeros the more specific the subject represented by the notation. As specificity is a general desideratum in classification, the notation with the fewest zeros is preferred if there is a question of precedence. For example, a dictionary of the history of Rome during the Renaissance is classed in 945.0503 since period takes precedence over dictionary.

Tables of precedence (actually a special kind of note) are the most easily grasped of the instruments that delineate order. They are common in the DDC and in the *Manual*. For an example, see Edition 19, Vol. 2, p. 75.

Citation order of the classes and subclasses of the DDC is most often derived from the many notes scattered throughout the Classification. Bear in mind that all characteristics or categories that are apparent in the work being classified may not be embodied in the class number. Characteristics beyond the first allowed are expressed only when there are specific directions for synthesis, or when they are embodied in the standard subdivision table. (There are, of course, many directions in the standard subdivision table for further synthesis.)

Procedure for Assigning a DDC Number to a Work

Concept Analysis

A classifier or subject cataloger examines the title page, table of contents, preface, index, text, and any other internal or external source of information regarding the intellectual content of a work in order to determine the concepts treated in it so that they may be indicated and used subsequently in the retrieval of the work. The process is called concept analysis. It entails essentially determining the subject or topic involved, the field of study in which it is treated or for which it is intended, and the point of view of the author. Concept analysis is no easy task.

(1) *Determine what the work is about:* What a work is about is not the author's purpose, his thesis, or his theme. What a work is about is the focus of the author's attention, what he describes and discusses. For instance, John Steinbeck's *Travels with Charley* is a description and discussion of what Steinbeck saw as he traveled about the United States with his dog. His ostensible purpose can be seen in the subtitle: *In Search of America.* His other purposes we can only surmise. None of his purposes is the subject. Nor is his thesis—which, let us say for the sake of argument, is that the United States was and is a good place to live but that it is changing and becoming another place whose quality of life only time will reveal—the subject. Nor are his themes, the chords that one hears again and again in the work, such as death, regeneration, and the stable nature of the American character, the subject.

The Library of Congress subject heading for *Travels with Charley* is UNITED STATES—DESCRIPTION AND TRAVEL—1961–. The DDC class number for it is 917.304921. Note that each indexing system deals with the same concepts: travel in the United States during a specific period. The DDC places the work in the travel class (91), Library of Congress Subject Headings (LCSH) place it in the subject (United States). Here you see that even though the systems use the same concepts to describe the content of a work, each has a fundamentally different approach to the information: the DDC by class, LCSH by topic. LCSH tells the user directly what the work is *about*; the

DDC tells the user directly into what class the work falls, later telling him what the topic is.

(2) *Determine the proper field of study or discipline:* Certain terms are frequently used interchangeably with respect to discipline; they are "aspect" and "field of study."

The basis of organization of the DDC is the belief that a work belongs in the discipline that produced it or to which it is directed or with which it is most closely associated. By making discipline the primary consideration in classing a work, classifiers provide for the systematic gathering of the works of a library on its shelves and for the arrangement of the records of the works in its catalog (when a classified catalog is used). Thus works that will be used together or studied within the boundaries of a given discipline will be found together on the shelf; their records will be found together in the classified catalog.

Works without a discernible focus are likely to belong to the general division for a specific class, e.g., in 370 for a general work on education, in 600 for a work on new technologies.

(3) *Consider the point of view taken by the author:* Point of view, though it may sound as if it could be used interchangeably with aspect, discipline, or field of study, has a meaning not shared by the other terms. A point of view is the body of principles, beliefs, and rules associated with a particular class of persons, usually within a particular field of study: for example, within religion the point of view of Methodists, within literature the point of view of Marxists, within evolution the point of view of Darwinians.

The point of view of an author is regarded when it transcends the topic discussed. That is, a work on evolution is classed in 575 whether written by a biologist or by a member of a fundamentalist Christian sect so long as the topic is the sole focus of the work and the idea of evolution is argued on its own merits. If, however, the member of the sect is trying to show that the view of evolution held by his group is sanctified and that of the scientists sinful, then the work is classed in 200.

A work by a person having a unique point of view is usually not classed in a discipline. For example, a theory that humanity is descended from scorpions would be classed in 001.9, not 575.

(4) *Consult the schedules:* A classifier versed in the structure of the DDC can go directly to the vicinity of the appropriate class. Few classifiers are capable of doing so in all areas, of course. Most must decide into which of the main classes a work should go, then into which division, then into which section, and so on until the right class is reached.

(5) *Use the index when all else fails:* When no amount of thought can reveal the class or division into which a topic should be classed, the index may be consulted. It is a backup tool, not a tool of first resort.

The nature of the index is such that it delineates alphabetically the various aspects of a particular topic. It does not always indicate directly, for it frequently sends the classifier to an entry that in turn requires further searching elsewhere. The index entry for "Moon" exemplifies this process:

Moon
  astronomy
    description   523.3
     theory   521.62
    regional sub. trmt.   *area*–991
    other aspects see Celestial bodies
  s.a. Lunar

The moon has its own number only in astronomy and Table 2 Areas, thus only those numbers are given in the index. Upward references lead us to other numbers where a discussion of the moon may occur, e.g., Celestial bodies, the class to which the moon belongs. (There is also a reference to phrases beginning with "Lunar," a reference we will not consider here.) At the entry for "Celestial bodies" we find:

Celestial
  bodies
    astronomy
      description   523
      theory   521.5
     internat. law   341.47
    lit. & stage trmt.
     folk lit. soc.   398.362
      other aspects see Natural phenomena
    magnetism *see* Geomagnetism
    s.a. spec. celestial bodies, e.g., Stars

By having followed the upward reference, we now discover that 398.362 is likely to be the proper number for a work on the moon in folklore, and 341.47 the proper number for a treatise on international law relating to the use of the resources of the moon. If the reader verifies the index numbers in the schedules, which should always be done, he will find them to be correct.

  Note that at the subentry "lit. & stage trmt." we are instructed to turn to Natural phenomena for still other aspects of celestial bodies. At Natural phenomena we learn that all anthologies of world literature written in a variety of forms with the moon as the organizing element are classed at 808.8036.

  The reader has probably noticed that most entry words in the index have no number assigned them. The reason for this practice is the intent of the editors to indicate to the classifier that the index subentries are *not* the only possible locations for the topic in the Classification. They are, however, the only instances of the topic that are actually specified in the Classification. Even though a topic is implied at a given number, but is not listed there, a work written upon the topic in that field of study will still be classed there. Though all aspects of a topic are not indicated at the index entry for the specific topic, the upward references offer advice on further avenues of approach, and these in turn may reveal yet other avenues.

Using the Schedules and Tables

Having arrived at the appropriate class, the classifier must check the numbers above and below the class that he has tentatively chosen. This should be done for two reasons:

(1) The work should be placed in a class that is coextensive with the subject of the work. A class broader or narrower than the appropriate one should not be used; such practices mislead the user. There are times, of course, when a broader class is all that is available.

(2) The note system is so structured that certain notes located at a broader class are applicable to the narrower class appropriate for a work.

The classifier needs to make the effort necessary to grasp the significance of the various kinds of notes. The notes that are frequently misunderstood are these:

(1) *Definition notes:* These limit the coverage of a number by enumerating the specific qualifications applicable to the number and its subdivisions. For instance, at 633 Field crops is the definition note "Large-scale production of crops, except fruit, intended for agricultural purposes and industrial processing other than preservation." This means that small-scale production of crops cannot be classed in this number or any of its subdivisions.

(2) *Including notes:* Topics found here are classed at the number, not at any of the subdivisions of the number. Standard subdivisions may not be added for these topics because the topics do not approximate the whole of the number.

(3) *Class here notes:* Topics found here are either broader than the class (or overlap it in some respect) or are applicable to the subdivisions of the class. In the second situation, for instance, one sees at 642.1–642.5 Meals: "Class here menus, meal planning, comprehensive works on meals and table service in specific situations." This means that if the classifier has before him a collection of menus for meals while camping, it is classed in 642.3 Meals for camp, picnic, travel.

Two kinds of references are used in the DDC to lead the classifier from one number or topic to another. One of these is the "class elsewhere" note in the following form (seen at 364.6 Penology): "Class welfare services to prisoners in 365.66, reform of penal institutions in 365.7." The other is the "cross reference" proper, which is a note in italics following all other notes, indented under them, in the following form (again seen at 364.6): "*For penal institutions, see 365; treatment of discharged offenders, 364.8.*" In the following discussion "cross reference" refers to the latter kind of note.

Cross references are used for one purpose only, to lead from the point where comprehensive works on a topic are classed to actual parts of that topic that are to be classed in numbers other than the number referred from or direct subdivisions thereof. All other uses are taken care of by class elsewhere notes.

For instance, main class 700, entitled in part The Arts, has a cross reference *"For . . . literature, [see] 800."* This is because literature is a legitimate part of the arts, but is not itself classed in 700 or any subdivision thereof. Therefore, comprehensive works on the arts, including literature, are classed at 700, but literature alone at 800. Cross references have hierarchical force, which means that this cross reference applies to every subdivision of 700. For example, music and drama treated together are classed in 782, but drama alone in appropriate subdivisions of 800, e.g., French drama 842.

Whenever, therefore, a cross reference appears, this is a signal to the classifier that here is the place for comprehensive works on the topic under consideration, *including* the topic mentioned in the cross reference. Works on the topic mentioned in the cross reference alone are classed at the point referred *to.*

Usually the cross reference applies to the heading; sometimes, however, it applies to a note under that heading. For example, at 342 Constitutional and administrative law appears the note, "Class here comprehensive works on public law." The cross references then lead to branches of public law at 343, 344, and 345. An example of both types together occurs at 581.1 Physiology of plants, which is followed by a note, "Class here comprehensive works on physiology and anatomy." The cross reference reads *"For . . . development and maturation, see 581.3* [part of the topic mentioned in the heading]; *anatomy, 581.4* [part of the combined topic mentioned in the note]."

It should be noted that under certain circumstances the class elsewhere note is used in place of the cross reference and has the same force, notably when the reference is "blind" or when the topics referred to are in numerous scattered locations. The opposite situation never occurs, however; the cross reference is not used for any of the numerous uses of the class elsewhere note and thus the cross reference always signals the presence of comprehensive works.

Centered Entries

Be particularly careful when dealing with a centered entry (an entry for a concept that has no specific number of its own, but covers a span of numbers). The notes governing the class will be found at both the centered entry itself and at superordinate positions in the hierarchy of classes. For instance, a classifier faced with a work on public regulation of the marketing of agricultural products in the international market has to deal with the notes at several centered entries and at the division number. To begin, he will probably arrive at 382 International commerce, and then at 382.41 Products of agriculture, either entry being governed by a note at a centered entry. The first centered entry 382.41–382.43 Products of primary (extractive) industries, has no special information to help the classifier. The second, 381–382 General internal and international commerce (Trade), has the important information that marketing is classed in these numbers. Since the note is a class here note, marketing is pervasive throughout 381–382, e.g., the marketing of a specific product will be classed with the product. The classifier should take one more step, however, and see whether any information at 380 may guide him in the choice of the appropriate number. There he reads "Class regulation and control in 351.8." The appropriate number, therefore, is 351.8233.

More Than One Discipline or Subject

Frequently a work will deal with more than one subject. When this occurs, either a relationship between the subjects is being discussed (complex) or the treatment of each subject stands alone even though the subjects may belong to the same class (compound).

Compound: If there are two subjects, class with the subject receiving fuller treatment, but if the subjects receive roughly equal treatment, class the work in the class coming first in the DDC. If three or more subjects are treated in the same work, class the work in the broader class that contains them, e.g., class at 200 a work on Buddhism, Christianity, and Islam when each is treated more or less equally and separately.

Complex: Class with the subject emphasized. If emphasis is equal, class with the subject being affected, e.g., class at 381.41 the effect of superhighways on the marketing of farm produce. (*See also* Citation order in the DDC.)

Unless otherwise instructed, class an interdisciplinary work with the discipline receiving most emphasis. If emphasis is equal, class with the discipline coming first in the schedules; or, in the case of several disciplines falling within a class and others scattered throughout the Classification, class with the discipline coming first in the preponderant class, e.g., an interdisciplinary work on divorce from religious (200), social (301–307), legal (340), welfare (360), medical (610), and personal life (640) aspects is classed at 306.89.

Rules of Inclusion in the *Manual*

The rules of inclusion for specific numbers and topics follow:

(1) Numbers and topics are included that have been developed since the deadlines for various segments of the Classification were established. Some deadlines go back as far as 1973. The publication of Edition 19 was, of course, 1979.

(2) Numbers and topics are included that require clarification because of their difficulty or because of a lack of direction in the Classification.

(3) Still other numbers and topics are included that present persistent problems in the application of the Classification, especially in the case of interdisciplinary or comprehensive works.

(4) Also included are the practices and policies of the Decimal Classification Division of the Library of Congress that heretofore have not been made public or have not been clearly explained.

Since the *Manual* reflects the practices of the Decimal Classification Division, it excludes options (except in Law 340) authorized by the Introduction, Schedules, and Tables of Edition 19 as well as the vast number of variations that have been adopted by libraries to meet the needs of their clienteles. The topics it includes are dealt with according to the preferred practices of Edition 19.

The problems discussed in the *Manual* are generally of three types:

(1) Problems of choice of discipline or field of study: works on the borderline between two disciplines (e.g., physical chemistry vs. chemical physics), and frankly interdisciplinary works (e.g., the legal, administrative, economic, and social aspects of environmental protection).

(2) Problems of precedence and citation order:

    a. Which one of several facets to choose: Are wages of handicapped women classed with wages of women or with wages of the handicapped?

    b. The order in which to set forth the elements when it is possible to express more than one: In international relations between two countries, which country should be cited first?

(3) Specific topics for which placement is not obvious: Where, for instance, should embryo transplants be classed?

Format of the *Manual*

The *Manual* is arranged in the numerical order of the Tables and Schedules in Edition 19. Within each main class, division, section, or subsection for which an entry is given, one or more of the following may be found, usually in this sequence:

(1) An introduction, often giving a general citation order.

(2) General problems applicable to the whole segment: how to distinguish between the class and a closely related one, e.g., 600 vs. 300, or an explanation of a major change in the Schedules (as at 658). (The generalities section in each segment may be long or short, depending on the difficulties involved in the area.)

(3) Problems involving specific subdivisions of the segment in question.

Certain conventions have been adopted for conveying information expeditiously and accurately:

(1) *Boldface entries:* Instructions at boldface entries apply to the number and all its subdivisions.

(2) *Centered boldface headings:* These are used to indicate notable topics related to the number at which they are discussed.

(3) *Bracketed headings:* These are used in the *Manual* to represent headings that exist only by implication in the Schedules or Tables. They are provided to show the meaning of the number. For example: 378.198 [The student in higher education].

(4) *Bracketed portions of headings:* These have been supplied to give sense to a heading that is given in the *Manual* out of its schedule context. For example: 371.77 Safety programs [for students].

(5) *At vs. In:* When an instruction directs the classifier to class a topic *in* a number, it means that the topic is to be classed at the number itself and at any appropriate subdivisions of the number, e.g., the instruction "Class tabular statistics of accidents in 312.4" means that tabular statistics are also classed at 312.45. When the instruction directs the classifier to class a topic *at* a number, it means that the topic goes at that number only and not in any of its subdivisions (except standard subdivisions), e.g., the instruction "If a religion not named in the schedule claims to be Christian, class it at 289.9 even if it is unorthodox or syncretistic" means that the subdivisions of 289.9 cannot be used for that particular topic; the work classed stays at 289.9.

(6) *Numbers or instructions referred to in Edition 19:* These are accompanied by the phrase "in Edition 19." Numbers or instructions referred to in the *Manual* have no further identification.

Terminology of the *Manual*

For the sake of economy, the *Manual* uses certain expressions as a form of shorthand to describe recurring problems and situations. Definitions of the most common of these follow:

(1) *Approximate the whole.* This rule applies when the subject of a given work is approximately coextensive with the topic expressed by the heading of the number in which the work is classed, e.g., 620.17, 769.567. *See also* Standing room, Unitary term.

(2) *At* [*the number*]. *See above* at **Format of the *Manual*** (5).

(3) *Cognate numbers (also called parallel numbers).* This term is used when numbers in two different segments of the Classification have exactly the same set of endings (frequently, but not always, the result of an add note at one place or the other). Note that the final 2 in each of the following class numbers expresses the idea of respiration: 574.12 respiration in general biology, 581.12 respiration in plants, 591.12 respiration in animals, 611.2 anatomy of human respiratory organs, 612.2 physiology of human respiration, 616.2 diseases of human respiratory organs. These are all cognate numbers. *See also* Related numbers.

(4) *First of two rule.* This rule is applied when a work dealing with two topics is classed with the topic whose number comes first in the schedules. If the work contains more than two topics, it is classed with the narrowest or "most specific" number that will contain all of them. Thus, if a work deals with military mobilization of both raw material and industrial resources, it is classed in 355.24 Raw materials, not 355.26 Industrial resources. If, however, the work also contains material on mobilization of transportation and communication facilities, it is classed in 355.2 Military resources. If a work covers both railroad transportation (385) and ocean transportation (387.5), it is classed in 380.5, the number for comprehensive works on transportation. This rule has many exceptions, numerous examples of which are noted in the *Manual.*

(5) *In [the number].* See above at **Format of the *Manual*** (5).

(6) *Other.* In general, the word "other" means all topics other than those already named or implied in prior numbers. If a class called "Other" is accompanied by a note saying either "examples" or "including," it may be used for other topics not named in either the note or subdivisions, if any. In the absence of either "examples" or "including," unnamed "others" are to be given standing room in the next higher number.

Examples: 636.0889 [Animals] For other purposes
That is, purposes not named in 636.0881–636.0888. If a work is received on a purpose not named in 636.0881– 636.08899, e.g., for production of fertilizer, class it at 636.088, where it will have standing room until such time as a new subdivision is established, e.g., 636.08895.

636.6869 Other cage and aviary birds
Here the word "examples" in the note indicates that works on other unnamed birds may be classed here, e.g., hummingbirds.

663.59   Other [distilled liquors]
Note that here the absence of the word "examples" or the word "including" indicates that only the kinds of distilled liquors named are to be classed here; all others should be classed in standing room at 663.5.

In the absence of a subdivision for "other" topics, class a specific topic not provided for in the subdivisions by name or clear implication in the encompassing general number, where it has standing room until such time as the editors make specific provision, e.g., if a work is received on the culture of betel nuts, class it in 633.7 Alkaloidal crops.

(7) *Parallel numbers. See Cognate numbers.*

(8) *Related numbers.* This term is used to indicate numbers (neither cognate nor parallel) expressing the same topic in two or more different contexts. 351.74 is the number for police agencies in central government, 352.2 for police agencies in local governments. *See also Cognate numbers.*

(9) *Standing room.* This term is used when the subject of a given work is less extensive than the topic expressed by the heading for the most specific number available. Works classed in such a number are said to be in standing room. Standard subdivisions are not added to class numbers for such works. *See also Approximate the whole.*

(10) *Unitary term.* According to the general rules for classing works as set forth in the Editor's Introduction to Edition 19, 8.711, especially the last paragraph, standard subdivisions are not added to the number for a work whose subject does not approximate the whole of the subject represented by the number. In deciding when a work approximates the whole, the expression "unitary term" is frequently used.

Many headings contain two or more parts joined by the word "and." Sometimes the two words thus joined are so close in meaning that they are unlikely ever to be separated. These constitute a unitary term. When dealing with a unitary term, standard subdivisions may be added even when the work in hand uses only one of the terms. Examples of both unitary and nonunitary terms follow:

Unitary terms

268	Religious training and instruction
271	Religious congregations and orders
332.8	Interest and discount
338.9	Economic development and growth
341.5	Disputes and conflicts between states
351.8642	Highways and roads
362.2	Mental and emotional illnesses
371.26	Educational tests and measurements
725.81	Music and concert buildings

Nonunitary terms

306	Culture and institutions
306.8	Marriage and family
312.5	On marriage and divorce
535	Visible light and paraphotic phemonena

Underused General Numbers

In certain instances subclasses in Edition 19 have been defined so broadly that each covers almost all the material in the class of which it is a part. In such cases the *Manual* will provide instructions as to which number to use, the broad one or the narrow one. *See Dominant subdivisions under 500 for examples.*

*   *   *

With these general remarks in mind, the classifier is now ready to use the *Manual*. It is hoped that the *Manual* will assist classifiers in applying Edition 19 of the DEWEY Decimal Classification more accurately, efficiently, and with greater ease, thus creating a greater consistency in its application.

John P. Comaromi
EDITOR, DEWEY DECIMAL CLASSIFICATION

Margaret J. Warren
ASSISTANT EDITOR,
DEWEY DECIMAL CLASSIFICATION

Winton E. Matthews, Jr.
DECIMAL CLASSIFICATION SPECIALIST

December 9, 1981

Index to Introduction

Tables

Table 1. Standard Subdivisions

Standard subdivisions are so called because they are applicable to virtually all classes regardless of their nature. There are several kinds of standard subdivisions:

(1) Subdivisions for the bibliographic forms that records may take (external forms), e.g., dictionaries, periodicals, catalogs.

(2) Subdivisions for modes of treatment of the subject (internal forms), e.g., history, philosophy and theory, study and teaching, humorous treatment.

(3) Subdivisions not fitting categories 1 and 2. Some represent techniques or processes applied to the subject. Others are indicators to which other numbers are attached; for example, the intended audience of a chemistry textbook for nurses is indicated by —024 plus the number for nurses from Table 7 Persons: 540.24613.

The entire array of subdivisions at the two-digit level is spelled out for every main class but not necessarily elsewhere, for this would lead to unneeded repetition. When a few standard subdivisions are given under a number, those subdivisions have meanings or notations that have been modified in some way for the unit in question. The rest of the standard subdivisions under that number (those not given) are to be understood and used with their normal meanings as given in this table. For example, in the standard subdivision position for 370 Education the classifier sees only 370.1 and 370.7, which have been given modified meanings, and 370.68, which is not used. 370.2–370.6 and 370.8–370.9 are there with their normal meanings, but only conceptually, not visibly.

At the beginning of Table 1 there is a table of precedence that informs the classifier which standard subdivision to choose when more than one is applicable, e.g., the techniques of performing a specific operation in Great Britain take —028 rather than —0941, but techniques employed by a specific person in performing the operation take —0924 rather than —028.

When two or more standard subdivisions are applicable to a work, usually only one is to be used. Note that —09 by itself comes near the bottom of the order, just before —05 Serial publications. *See —074 and —075 for exceptions.*

Standard subdivisions may be added to:

(1) Apparent standard subdivisions that are not truly so because of specially changed or extended meanings, e.g., periodicals on educational psychology 370.1505, on nursing 610.7305, on political situations and conditions 320.9005; but on the history of political science 320.09.

(2) Standard subdivision concepts displaced to non–0 numbers, e.g., periodicals on crime in the United States 364.97305, on penal institutions in the United States 365.97305; but periodicals on criminology in the United States 364.0973.

(3) Standard subdivision —04, which is actually not a standard subdivision, but a device to permit the further subdivision of a class.

Take care in using standard subdivisions when the number to which the standard subdivision is to be attached is itself the result of synthesis. The standard subdivision applies to the entire number that has been synthesized, not to any of its elements. Take for instance the following: 687.05 means a periodical on clothing manufacture. 380.145 is trade in products of secondary industries and services. 380.145687 is trade in clothing. When —05 is added to 380.14687, it does not produce the same result as when added to 687 alone. To assume that it does would be to produce something of an absurdity, i.e., trade in periodicals dealing with manufacture of clothing. While this is a possible combination, it is not a likely one. The —05 should be considered as modifying the combination 380.145687 (everything before the —05). We then have a periodical dealing with trade in clothing, a much more likely combination.

The determination of the number of zeros to be used is fairly straightforward. If there is no indication to the contrary and conditions permit, use one zero, e.g., history of radiobroadcasting 384.5409. The following instructions indicate the number of zeros (other than one) that are to be used:

(1) In the number column: For example, history of engineering 620.009.

(2) Standard subdivision note: For example, at 371.2 Educational administration is found the instruction to use 371.2001–371.2009 for standard subdivisions. Thus, the number for the history of educational administration is 371.2009.

Table 1. Standard Subdivisions

(3) Footnotes to add notes: For example, a portion of the add note under 327.3–327.9 sends the classifier to a footnote that instructs him to use extra zeros and to consult the instructions at the beginning of Table 1. Thus, the history of the foreign policy of the United Kingdom is 327.41009, not 327.4109.

(4) Instructions to add from a table at which the number of zeros is stipulated: For example, a special table at 784.1–784.7 indicates 001–009 for standard subdivisions. At 784.623 the heading *High school songs is governed by a note that says to add as instructed under 784.1–784.7. Thus, the history of high school songs is 784.623009, not 784.62309.

(5) Instructions found in the second paragraph of Table 1: If at any given number there are subdivisions having a notation beginning with 0 for a special purpose, use 001–009 for standard subdivisions; if notations beginning with 0 and 00 both have special purposes, use 0001–0009 for standard subdivisions.

A displaced standard subdivision (one that has been moved away from most of the standard subdivisions for a number) may be subdivided as shown in Table 1, except for standard subdivisions or sections of them that have been given a changed or extended meaning (as at 370.71). For example, 340.1 Philosophy and theory of law may be subdivided to yield 340.14 for legal language and communication (most standard subdivisions for 340 are located at 340.02–340.09). Similarly, 910.01 Philosophy and theory of general geography, displaced from 910.1, may be subdivided to yield 910.016 for indexes of general geography.

See also Introduction: Unitary term pp. xxiv–xxv.

—01　　　**Philosophy and theory**

Most of the subdivisions of —01 are easy to understand and apply; —01 by itself can present problems. The term "philosophy and theory" here is considered to be unitary. It covers the general or abstract principles applied to a sphere of activity or thought such as science or art. It is, however, to be used with caution. At times, theory is the actual subject matter of the discipline; the theory of electrons (539.72112) is simply about electrons and does not take —01. If, however, the work is discussing the discipline itself as a discipline rather than discussing the subject matter of the discipline, it is a likely candidate for the use of —01.

The following subjects (unless otherwise provided for) are likely to be indicated by —01:

(1) The boundaries and limits of the field of study: What is art? What is science?

(2) Schools of thought within a discipline: Although the actual development is at 150.19 rather than at 150.1, the listing of schools of psychological thought at 150.19 is a good example of the kind of work that falls in this category.

(3) The ideal state of the discipline, and how far it can be expected to reach its goal: How close can science come to the absolute truth?

Use —01 of the techniques of criticism in a specific field, but not for the criticism itself. Class criticism with the work or works criticized without further subdivsion, or use s.s. 092, e.g., a criticism of Browning's poetry 821.8, the effect of Frank Lloyd Wright on architecture 720.924. *For an exception, see criticism of musical composition in 780, e.g., 782.1 analysis of opera.*

—014   **Languages (Terminology) and communication**

Class here works about the terminology of a subject, i.e., systems of terms, etymology of terms used, abbreviations. Class in —03 systematically arranged lists of words with their meanings.

—0141   Communication

Including content analysis, a research technique involving the quantitative study of the substantive content of communication.

—0147   Nonlinguistic communication

If the communication can be broken down into words or smaller units, this standard subdivision is not to be used. Thus, flags standing for a whole concept take this standard subdivision; semaphoric signaling that can be broken down into words or letters does not.

—016   Indexes

Some "indexes" are actually bibliographies and are classed in 010. For example, an "index" to the contents of a number of periodicals, e.g., *Readers' Guide to Periodical Literature,* is classed at 011.34; an index to engineering periodicals is classed at 016.62.

—0202   Synopses, outlines, manuals

Note that many works using one of these words in the title are actually quite full treatments of the subject. Use —0202 only for genuinely condensed and abbreviated treatment.

Table 1. Standard Subdivisions

—0207   Humorous treatment

     Use with caution: a writer making a serious contribution may write in a jocular or humorous manner. In such cases do not use —0207.

—0212   Tables, formulas, specifications, statistics

     Use this standard subdivision only for tabulated statistics, not for analysis of statistics.

—0228   Models and miniatures

     Note that "miniatures" has been added to the heading at this number.

—024   **Works for specific types of users**

     Be alert to the difference between works dealing with the subject *for* a specific type of person and works *about* that type of person. The two categories may carry similar sounding titles. For example, a work called "health for mothers" may deal with the health of mothers. On the other hand, it may be about the health of children and be written for the use of a mother in caring for her children. It is the latter type of work for which —024 is used.

     Use caution also in adding —024 where there is little adaptation of the content of the work for the named class of users. For example, a work on cardiology for nurses might be just as suitable for patients, parents, or general readers as for nurses. In such cases the standard subdivision not only may double the length of the number but also imply a limitation on the usefulness of the work. Therefore, in this case, prefer 616.12 over 616.12024613 unless the work emphasizes special instructions for nurses that general readers would not find helpful.

     Do not use —024 if it is redundant. For example, do not use 620.002462 for engineering for engineers, but engineering for architects is correctly classed in 620.002472.

     Do not use —024 for works written for students.

     The Decimal Classification Division has not used —024 to gather works written for children. All juvenile works are currently classed from the full edition with the exception of fiction and "easy" books, which are not classed.

—025   **Directories of persons and organizations**

     Class here membership lists containing directory information. However, if a list contains biographical information, use —0922. If the work includes a description or listing of products for sale, use —0294 whether or not the arrangement is by company.

—0275   Trademarks and service marks

Class interdisciplinary works on trademarks and service marks at 929.9, works on trademarks in technological fields at 602.75.

—028   **Techniques, procedures, apparatus, equipment, materials**

See —072 vs. —028.

—0287   Testing and measurement

Class here research on testing, but class the use of tests in research in —072. If in doubt, prefer —0287.

Class educational testing at —076.

—0289   Safety measures

Use for safety technology only. Class safety management in —068, social services with respect to safety in 363. Do not use —0289 in the 300s except as instructed at 351.783 and 352.3 in Edition 19. *See also 363.1 Safety management.*

—0294   Price lists and trade catalogs

See discussion at —025.

—032–039   **[Dictionaries, encyclopedias, concordances] By language**

Class with the preferred language. *For guidance as to precedence see the directions at Lang. Sub. 32–39, Table 4, in Edition 19 for the treatment of bilingual dictionaries.*

—06   **Organizations and management**

Class here membership lists. However, if a list contains directory information, use —025; if it contains biographical information, use —092.

Note that —06 is not used unless the scope of the organization is approximately the same in extent as the subject that the number represents, e.g., the Cataloging and Classification Section of the American Library Association 025.306073, a workshop on the main entry rules for corporate bodies of the second edition of the *Anglo-American Cataloging Rules* held in Boston 025.322.

In adding to —060 as instructed at —0603–9 in Edition 19 use notation for the area covered by the membership. If this cannot be determined, or if the organization is an institution or foundation without membership as such, use the place of the headquarters. Class a conference, seminar, workshop, or other meeting at the place where it was held.

Class local branches of an organization with the parent organization; student organizations at 371.83.

Table 1. Standard Subdivisions

—068   Management of enterprises engaged in specific fields of activity, of specific kinds of enterprises

> *See 658 for a detailed treatment of —068 in conjunction with cognate number in 658; 363.1 Safety management.*

—0683   Personnel management [in enterprises engaged in specific fields of activity, in specific kinds of enterprises]

> *See 331.255 for management of employee benefits in specific industries.*

—07   **Study and teaching**

Class here training of teachers to teach a specific subject, and practice teaching in a specific subject. Class here also financial support of education in a specific field, e.g., support of schools —071, of research —072, of museums —074.

Do not use —07 for textbooks. Textbooks are treated like any other treatise and are classed with the subject with which they deal. The only exception to this is programmed textbooks, which are classed in —077, e.g., programmed texts in mathematics 510.77.

—0712   Secondary schools

Use with caution for secondary schools in a specific subject. Many vocational secondary schools offer a somewhat broader program with emphasis on vocational training. Class such schools in 373.243–373.246.

—072   **Research**

Class here methods of research, plans and projects for research, surveys of the work being done in a field. Do not use —072 for the results of the research.

—072 vs.   **Research vs. Techniques, procedures, apparatus, equipment, materials**
—028

Use —028 for methods of performing work in a specific field, how to go about accomplishing some specific task. Do not use —028 for investigation, research, exploration, or study. Techniques of investigation, research, exploration, and study are classed in —072. For example, techniques of performing dental work are classed at 617.60028, methods of studying dentistry at 617.60072.

—0723   Descriptive research

Use this standard subdivision for works on the methods of doing surveys in a specific subject area, including the statistical methods involved in so doing. (It should be noted that statistical methods are also applicable to —072 in general and to its other subdivisions.) Class interdisciplinary works on descriptive research at 001.433, interdisciplinary works on statistical methods in 001.422.

—074   **Museums, collections, exhibits**

Class a historic building that has become a historical museum with the history of the place whose history is exemplified, e.g., a museum of Michigan history 977.40074, but a museum of general history in Detroit 907.4017434.

Do not use for lists of works by individual artists.

—074 and   **Museums, collections, exhibits [and] Collecting objects**
—075

These standard subdivisions may be added to other standard subdivisions, —09 being the one to which they are most frequently added. Examples follow:

(1) An exhibition of French costume held in New York City: 391 (costume) plus 00944 (of France) plus 074 (an exhibition) plus 0 (from instructions at —07401–09) plus 1471 (in New York City) equals 391.0094407401471. Note that the area number following —0740 is taken from the development at 708.1–708.9, not directly from Table 2 Areas.

(2) Collecting English glass in the United States: 748.29 (historical and geographical treatment of glassware) plus 2 (of England) plus —075 (collecting) plus 09 (from the instructions at —07509) plus 73 (United States) equals 748.2920750973.

—077   Programmed texts

Note that this is the sole exception to the rule that textbooks do not take s.s. —07. The art of creating a programmed text and the teaching methods to be used with such texts are indicated by —07 undivided.

—079   Competitions and awards

Including orders or societies whose main purpose is to grant awards in a specific subject field. Class interdisciplinary works on awards at 929.81.

—08   **History and description of the subject with respect to groups of persons**

Until Edition 19, —08 was used to indicate collections of works. As these are usually of a comprehensive nature, —08 actually separated general works on a subject. It was, therefore, decided that, except in the 800s, —08 would no longer be used with its original meaning.

At the same time, the need for an indicator providing for the specification of groups of persons in relation to a subject became evident. The now vacant —08 was chosen, —088 being designated as the indicator for groups of persons primarily defined by the

Table 1. Standard Subdivisions

structure of the Classification (to which a number from Table 7 will be attached), and —089 being assigned to racial, ethnic, and national groups (to which a number from Table 5 will be attached).

Since the publication of Edition 19 the heading for —08 has been slightly modified: "among groups of persons" has been changed to "with respect to groups of persons." The intention in so doing was to make the use of this standard subdivision a little more flexible. The subdivisions of —08 can be used for the subject among a group of persons, e.g., drug abuse among young adults 362.2932088055. It can be used for works about various groups of people in connection with the subject, e.g., life insurance rates for older people 368.30110880565. It can be used for even looser relationships such as doctors and religion 200.88616.

See also –024.

—08 vs. **—09**	**History and description of the subject with respect to persons vs. Historical and geographical treatment**

The groups designated by —088 and —089 all have some factor in common other than the subject to which they are related through the use of —08. All are doctors, all are women, all are young, or all are members of a racial group. If there is no such common denominator, or if the relation to the subject is more significant than the common denominator, use —0922. For example, handicrafts among American native races 745.508997, but a group of artists (no common factor) producing handicrafts 745.50922. Do not use —08 for individual members of any of these groups; use —0924.

Note that each racial, ethnic, or national group almost without exception is predominant in one or more geographic locations. For this reason a work dealing with a subject as it relates to such a group in a particular geographic area where it predominates is classed, not as treatment of the subject with respect to members of the group in —089, but as geographic treatment of the subject in —09, e.g., the subject with respect to Frenchmen in Paris —0944361, not 08941; with respect to Caucasoids in Europe —094, not —089034; with respect to Arabs in regions where Arabs predominate —09174927, not —089927.

On the other hand, class the subject with respect to a racial, ethnic, or national group in general, or in a place where the group is not dominant in —089, e.g., the subject with respect to Germans in Brazil —08931081, with respect to Chinese in Europe —08995104, with respect to Arabs in London —0899270421, with respect to Swedes in regions where Arabs predominate —0893970174927.

With groups other than racial, ethnic, or national the situation is different. Predominance in an area is not a factor. —088 is used whether or not the group predominates in its area (although in most cases there is no question of this). For example, use —08822 for the subject in relation to Roman Catholics even in an area where they predominate, e.g., Spain.

Use —09 and its geographical subdivisions to identify distinguishing characteristics of a subject rather than —089. For example, class Arab art in 709.174927, not 704.03927 (in lieu of 708.9927 which has been preempted for other purposes); Islamic art 709.17671, not 704.2971 (in lieu of 708.82971 which has been preempted).

If in doubt, prefer —09 to —08.

—088 **[History and description of the subject with respect to groups of specific kinds of persons]**

Do not use —08804–08808 for certain age, sex, or handicapped groups under numbers where such groups have been otherwise provided for in Edition 19, e.g., age and sex groups at 613.04; the handicapped, men, women, and children at 646.31–646.36 and cognate numbers in 646.4–646.7; the handicapped and infirm at 720.42–720.43 and cognate numbers in 721–729.

See also —08 vs. —09.

—088056 [History and description of the subject with respect to adults]

As may readily be seen, this standard subdivision will seldom be used, since most persons connected with any subject are adults. Use it only when stress is laid on the fact that adults are being discussed as against any other age group. However, use —0880565 for older adults.

—089 [History and description of the subject with respect to specific racial, ethnic, national groups]

See —08 vs. —09.

—09 **Historical and geographical treatment**

Note that there is a difference between the historical and geographical treatment of a subject and the historical and geographical treatment of the discipline within which the subject is treated. For example, 598.29 is for the geographic treatment of birds: where the birds appear, how they are distributed, their migration paths, the kinds of birds common to certain areas. 598.09, on the other hand, is the historical and geographical treatment of ornithology; it is not about birds but about people who study them and the

Table 1. Standard Subdivisions

methods they employ in doing so. More often than not, the two subjects are covered by the same number. When they are not, directions to that effect will be given, e.g., in Edition 19 at 320.09 Historical and geographical treatment of political science appears the note "Class historical and geographical treatment of politics and government in 320.9."

See also —08 vs. —09.

—0901
–0905 **Historical periods**

Use these subdivisions with caution at all times; seldom are the epochs of the history of any subject as neat, precise, and symmetrical as the periods given here suggest. Do not use the subdivisions for subjects that have existed only during the period indicated, e.g., the history of railroads 385.09, not 385.0903, but the history of railroads in 19th century 385.09034. In order to take these subdivisions a subject has to have existed for a substantial length of time over several periods. If in doubt, do not use periods.

—092 **Persons associated with the subject**

The remarks here apply also to area —2 from Table 2. Area —2 is used instead of —092 when area notations are added directly to a number without the intervention of —09.

—092 is to be used only when the focus of the work is on one or more persons, on his or their work in relation to the subject.

In some instances the history of a subject (especially in the arts) is elucidated through the study of representative people of the period or place. When this is the case use —09 plus the notation for period or place rather than —0922 or —0924. Reserve —092 for genuine biography or criticism.

A work dealing with portions of a person's life that precede the activity with which he is chiefly associated is classed in the general biography number for the person, e.g., the childhood of Abraham Lincoln 973.70924; but if the work has a specific focus of its own, class it with the subject focused on, e.g., the period of Justice Byron White's life when he was an All–American football player 796.3320924. *See discussion of public figures below.*

Class a history of the family of a famous person in the biography number for that person if the work strongly emphasizes the famous person. The same treatment is accorded the life of a relative of a famous person. However, if the famous person is not strongly featured, class a family history at 929.2, the life of a relative in the appropriate period of history or with whatever subject is warranted by the life of the relative. For example, a biography of Ruth Carter Stapleton that mentions Jimmy Carter only incidentally is classed at 269.20924.

Biographies of statesmen, politicians, and public administrators are treated in the following ways:

(1) Presidents, kings, prime ministers, vice-presidents, and defeated candidates who were their party's nominees, heads of state in 930–990. (Note that premiers and prime ministers are not usually heads of state.)

(2) Cabinet members, administrators in 353–354.

(3) Legislators in 328.4–328.9.

(4) Ambassadors and other diplomats in 327.

A difficulty frequently confronting the classifier is that many public figures have filled more than one of the above positions at one time or other. To decide which is the most significant for classification purposes is a difficult task, and rules to handle the various combinations create more problems than they solve. Nevertheless, several guidelines may be found useful. Bear in mind that the focus is general biographies.

(1) Biographies of a particular part of a public person's life are classed with the subject, e.g., Jimmy Carter as governor of Georgia 975.80430924, John F. Kennedy in World War 2 940.5459730924, Gerald R. Ford as minority leader of the U.S. House of Representatives 328.7307620924. *See also paragraph 4 of this discussion.*

(2) Give weight to the designation that appears first in entries in biographical dictionaries.

(3) Give weight to federal or national office over state or local office.

(4) Give greatest weight to the highest office reached. All other things being equal, apply the following table of precedence:

(a) Heads of state or government, or their deputies
(b) Unsuccessful party nominees for the above
(c) Ambassadors
(d) Cabinet members
(e) Legislators
(f) Diplomats below the level of ambassador
(g) Administrators
(h) Persons holding any other position in government.

Do not use —092 if redundant, e.g., Muhammad 297.63.

Table 1. Standard Subdivisions

—0922   Collected [persons associated with the subject]

Class here biographies of two people engaged in the same field of work, e.g., the Wright brothers, Pierre and Marie Curie. However, if the focus is strongly on one of the two, use —0924.

—0926   Case histories

Use this standard subdivision for accounts of persons treated as illustrations of the subject. If, however, a work is simply an account of one or more persons' experiences with a certain subject or condition, use —0922 or —0924.

Table 2. Areas

—1   **Areas, regions, places in general**

Subdivisions of —1 are used only for areas, regions, and places that overlap more than one continent (considering Oceania as a continent), e.g., urban regions of the United States, Europe, and Japan —1732. Such regions within one continent but covering several countries are classed with the number for the continent in combination with the appropriate subdivision of —1, e.g., urban regions of Europe —4009732, of North America —70009732.

Within a single country or place these general regions are classed in the general number for the country or place; then, in the disciplines of geography and history, the appropriate subdivisions of —1 are added, e.g., a history of the urban regions of England 942.009732, geography of the urban regions of England 914.2009732. However, in all other disciplines this is done only as an option that will not be followed by the Decimal Classification Division.

Note the reverse citation order (third note at —1 in Edition 19) that, in case of conflict, gives the preference to the later subdivision, e.g., cities on tropical islands —1732 for cities rather than —142 for islands or —13 for tropics.

See also —2 vs. —1, —3–9.

—163–165   **[Atlantic, Pacific, Indian Oceans]**

This table follows the latest thinking of geographers in dividing the world ocean into three parts—Atlantic, Indian, and Pacific Oceans. The "Arctic Ocean" is considered a sea of the Atlantic. There is no Antarctic Ocean, but provision is made in —167 for the extreme southern portions of the three oceans.

Divisions between the oceans are considered to be as follows:

Atlantic-Pacific: north, Bering Strait; south, a line drawn southeasterly from Cape Horn to the northern tip of Palmer Peninsula, Antarctica.

Pacific-Indian: north, a line from Melville Island to Timor, thence through the islands of Indonesia to Singapore Strait; south, a line drawn south from Cape Howe, Victoria, Australia, on the 150° east meridian.

Indian-Atlantic: north, Suez Canal; south, a line drawn south from Cape Agulhas, South Africa, on the 20° east meridian.

Notes and references throughout show where to class connecting bodies of water, e.g., Bering Strait —16451, not —16325 or —16327.

Table 2. Areas

—163–165 vs. —182	**[Atlantic, Pacific, Indian Oceans] vs. Ocean and sea basins**

Note that —163–165 deal with the oceans and seas themselves, i.e., their waters. Specific lands are classed in —3–9, while the total lands around an ocean or sea or surrounded by an ocean or sea are classed in the appropriate subdivision of —182.

—172 **[Socioeconomic regions characterized] By degree of economic development**

Regions of high economic development are those independent of aid from other regions except in case of disaster. Regions of medium economic development are those needing aid from other regions only for special projects. Regions of low economic development are those dependent on other regions for many types of aid.

—1812 Western [Hemisphere]

Use —7 for works emphasizing North and South America. In all cases class history of Western Hemisphere in 970, geography of Western Hemisphere in 917.

—182 **Ocean and sea basins**

See —163–165 vs. —182.

—1821 Atlantic region   Occident

Note that, while the Occident is classed here, the Orient is classed at —5 with Asia.

—19 vs. —99 Space vs. **Extraterrestrial worlds**

Class in —19 only space itself. The various bodies of the universe moving through space are classed in —99, e.g., moon rocks 552.09991. The anticipated use of —19 is not great.

—2 **Persons regardless of area, region, place**

This "area" notation is an anomaly. Obviously persons are not areas, at least not large ones nor fixed. However, the notation is needed for description, critical appraisal of the work, biography, and the like of persons in class numbers to which area numbers are added directly instead of after s.s. 09.

—2 vs. —1, —3–9 **Persons regardless of area, region, place vs. Areas, regions, places in general [and] Specific continents, countries, localities**

Observe carefully that the heading of —2 says "regardless of area, region, place"; this means that persons are classed here, not in area —1 or in areas —3–9. This parallels similar instructions in Table 1 for preferring s.s. 092 over s.s. 091 or s.s. 093–099.

—3–9 **Specific continents, countries, localities; extraterrestrial worlds**

Class with a specific place a specific instance of the subject occurring in that place, e.g., Christian church buildings in New York City 726.5097471, the Riverside Church building in New York City 726.5097471.

Note that the subdivisions of —1 *may* be added as an option to any area number in —3–9 (through the use of 009), but that they *are* to be added to the area numbers for the continents. *(See in the text of Edition 19 —4009, —5009, —6009, —70009, and —80009.)* In addition, under —66 West Africa, numbers are to be added from —1 for Anglophone and Francophone West Africa.

See also —163–165 vs. —182; —2 vs. —1, —3–9.

—3 **The ancient world**

The arrangement under —3 follows no particular pattern, but was orginally established, presumably, to maintain a certain mnemonic standard: China —31 and —51, Egypt —32 and —62, India —34 and —54.

—3 vs. **The ancient world vs. The modern world**
—4–9

Under —3 "The ancient world" are gathered those parts of the world more or less known *to* classical antiquity, and considered only during the period of "ancient history." The same areas in later times, as well as other areas such as America in both ancient and later times, are classed in —4–9. Examples: ancient China —31, later China —51; ancient Palestine —33, later Palestine —5694; ancient Gaul —364, France —44; Yucatan, both ancient and later, —7265. The approximate date of demarcation between "ancient" and "later" varies from place to place and may be determined by examination of the terminal dates in classes 931–939, e.g., 931 China to 420 A.D., 933 Palestine to 70 A.D., 936.4 Celtic regions to 486 A.D.

Works comprehensive of both ancient and later times are classed in —4–9, e.g., history of science in ancient Egypt 509.32, in medieval and modern Egypt 509.62, in both ancient and later Egypt 509.62.

Table 2. Areas

—**4–9**   **The modern world; extraterrestrial worlds**

As in —3, the arrangement of countries in —4–9 follows no special pattern, except perhaps to emphasize the places of greatest concern to 19th-century America, and even this does not account for the progression from Canada to Mexico, Central America, the Antilles, and then back to the United States and its parts.

However, within each country there is usually a pattern, e.g., in France where the arrangement is from the northwest eastward, south to the central portion of the country and back west, south again and again east thus:

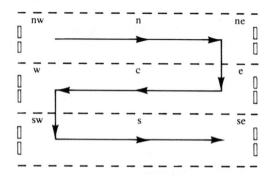

This is not always the case, as for example, India, though even in that country there is a rather vague progression from east to northeast and counterclockwise around to the south with numerous inexplicable side trips. In the United States the pattern, beginning at the eastern seaboard, is roughly north to south to north to south rather than east to west or west to east.

See also —3 vs. —4–9.

Physiographic regions and features

Careful study of the second note at —4–9 in Edition 19 on the treatment of physiographic features will be worthwhile. For features not named in the area table, class one wholly or almost wholly contained within a political or administrative unit with the unit, e.g., Mount Washington, New Hampshire —7421; Lake Moultrie, South Carolina —75793. Class a river with the unit where its mouth is located, e.g., Escanaba River, Michigan —77494. However, if the upper part of the stream is definitely more important politically, economically, or culturally, class the river with that part, e.g., Tigris and Euphrates Rivers —5674 rather than —5675.

Physiographic features named in Table 2 that are marked with asterisks are to be treated as though they approximate the whole content of the numbers where they are named. This means that standard subdivisions may be used (as well as other applicable subdivisions from the tables at 913.1–913.9, 914–919, and 930–990) for works on these features, e.g., periodicals on the history of the Mississippi Valley 977.005.

Cities, towns, villages

Class unnamed cities, towns, and villages with the narrowest political or administrative units that contain them. With certain exceptions, cities are not named in the area table. The exceptions include:

(1) the capital and largest city of each state of the United States, e.g., Pierre and Sioux Falls, South Dakota, at —78329 and —783371 respectively;

(2) major world cities, usually with their own numbers, e.g., Athens at —49512 and Calcutta included at —5414;

(3) smaller cities given their own numbers in early editions of the DDC when spare numbers were available, e.g., Guelph, Ontario —71343; Grand Rapids, Michigan —77456;

(4) independent cities, e.g., Alexandria, Virginia —755296;

(5) cities having the same name as the units containing them (much more frequent in the Old World than in the New), e.g., Geneva, Zurich, Bern at —4945;

(6) United States cities coextensive with their counties (or parishes), e.g., Philadelphia —74811, San Francisco —79461;

(7) cities, towns, and villages named to help define the boundaries between numbers where none exist in law or on maps, e.g., throughout Australia —94 and the western provinces of Canada —711–712;

(8) in the United Kingdom —41–42 where a new administrative alignment in recent years has not yet been reflected in large numbers of redrawn maps and revised gazetteers. It is probable that the next edition of the Dewey Decimal Classification will not need to name so many villages under each administrative unit, since, by then, standard reference tools will be available.

Table 2. Areas

The foregoing will explain why many large cities are not named, while many much smaller and less important ones are.

Class a metropolitan area with the central city, using standard subdivisions as needed, e.g., Chicago —77311.

Changes in geographical concepts

Note that some geographical concepts of an earlier day have been divided by the whims of history. Many such concepts are given special notes to show where comprehensive works are to be classed, e.g., Armenia as a whole and Turkish Armenia at —5662, Soviet Armenia at —4792.

However, in many cases adjustments have been made between recent editions of the DDC to conform to historical changes. For example, Finland, which before World War 1 was part of the Russian empire, was placed by Melvil Dewey in —471, as the first subdivision of Russia. It was not until recently that the DDC relocated works on Finland to —4897, thus removing the block of material that had separated comprehensive works on Russia and the Soviet Union in —47 from works on their various parts in —472–479. Also, works on the part of Turkey that is located in Europe have been relocated from —4961 to —562–563 with the major, Asian, part of Turkey; in spite of this, Cyprus remains in —5645 where it separates works on the parts of Turkey.

On the other hand, Hawaii, which is not part of North America, is classed in —969 under Oceania, separated from the rest of the United States in —73–79; and the Asian parts of the U.S.S.R. are classed in —57–58, quite apart from the European portion of the U.S.S.R. in —47.

—41 vs. —42   **British Isles vs. England and Wales**

In the early 1970s, when it became necessary to make provision for the many new local administrative subdivisions of the United Kingdom, it was decided to correct a poor arrangement that existed since Melvil Dewey's time, i.e., to relocate comprehensive works on the British Isles, United Kingdom, and Great Britain from —42, a number that they had traditionally shared with England and Wales, to —41, where they logically precede their parts, Scotland, Ireland, England, and Wales.

—42   **England and Wales**

See —41 vs. —42.

—5   **Asia   Orient   Far East**

For Occident, see —1821.

—7   **North America**

See —1812.

—70009   Regional treatment [of North America]

Note the third zero as compared with —4009 *et al.*

—71339   Niagara Falls

This is the number for comprehensive works on Niagara Falls; compare with the text at —74799 in Edition 19. The indexes of Editions 18 and 19 are both wrong; those of Editions 16 and 17 are correct.

—74799   Niagara Falls in New York

See —71399.

—8   **South America**

See —1812.

—80009   Regional treatment [of South America]

Note the third zero as compared with —4009 *et al.*

–99   **Extraterrestrial worlds**

See —19 vs. —99.

Maps

Maps

The following outline maps provide a display of key area numbers from Table 2. With the exception of island nations lying beyond the continental maps used, the maps indicate the Dewey Decimal Classification area numbers of members of the United Nations and comparable states. Sub-national areas are shown for the United States, Canada, the British Isles, and Australia.

While DDC area numbers are largely hierarchical, be sure to check Table 2 before using a number for part of a given area. In some instances (as illustrated here with the United States), the numbers for the parts are built on a base other than that of the area as a whole.

Note that certain major regional concepts which do not correspond to delineated areas are listed in the margins.

OCEANS AND CONTINENTS

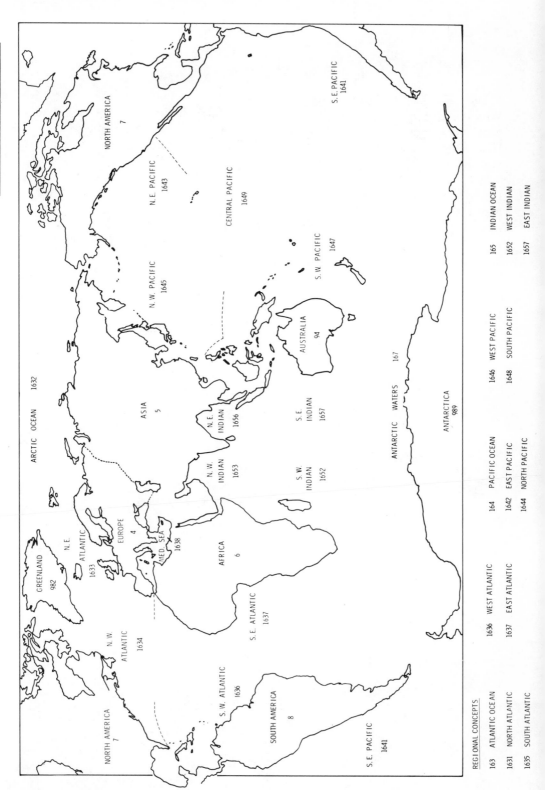

NORTH AMERICA
7

S. E. PACIFIC
1641

N. E. PACIFIC
1643

CENTRAL PACIFIC
1649

S. W. PACIFIC
1647

N. W. PACIFIC
1645

AUSTRALIA
94

ARCTIC OCEAN   1632

ASIA
5

N. E.
INDIAN
1656

S. E.
INDIAN
1657

ANTARCTIC WATERS   167

ANTARCTICA
989

N. W.
INDIAN
1653

S. W.
INDIAN
1652

GREENLAND
982

N. E.
ATLANTIC
1633

EUROPE
4

MED. SEA
1638

AFRICA
6

N. W.
ATLANTIC
1634

S. E. ATLANTIC
1637

S. W. ATLANTIC
1636

NORTH AMERICA
7

SOUTH AMERICA
8

S. E. PACIFIC
1641

REGIONAL CONCEPTS

163	ATLANTIC OCEAN	164	PACIFIC OCEAN	165	INDIAN OCEAN
1631	NORTH ATLANTIC	1642	EAST PACIFIC	1652	WEST INDIAN
1635	SOUTH ATLANTIC	1644	NORTH PACIFIC	1657	EAST INDIAN
1636	WEST ATLANTIC	1646	WEST PACIFIC		
1637	EAST ATLANTIC	1648	SOUTH PACIFIC		

EUROPE

ICELAND
4912

FINLAND
4897

SOVIET UNION
47

NORWAY
481

SWEDEN
485

DENMARK
489

EIRE
417

UNITED
KINGDOM
41

NETHERLANDS
492

BELORUSSIA
4765

BELGIUM
493

WEST
GERMANY
43

EAST
GERMANY
431

POLAND
438

UKRAINE
4771

LUX.
4935

CZECHOSLOVAKIA
437

FRANCE
44

SWITZ.
491

AUSTRIA
436

HUNGARY
439

ROMANIA
498

PORTUGAL
469

SPAIN
46

ITALY
45

YUGOSLAVIA
497

BULGARIA
4977

ALBANIA
4965

GREECE
495

TURKEY
561

MOROCCO
64

ALGERIA
65

TUNISIA
611

MALTA
4585

LIBYA
612

EGYPT
62

REGIONAL CONCEPTS

4	WESTERN EUROPE	43	CENTRAL EUROPE	48	NORTHERN EUROPE, SCANDINAVIA
42	ENGLAND AND WALES	47	EASTERN EUROPE	496	BALKAN PENINSULA

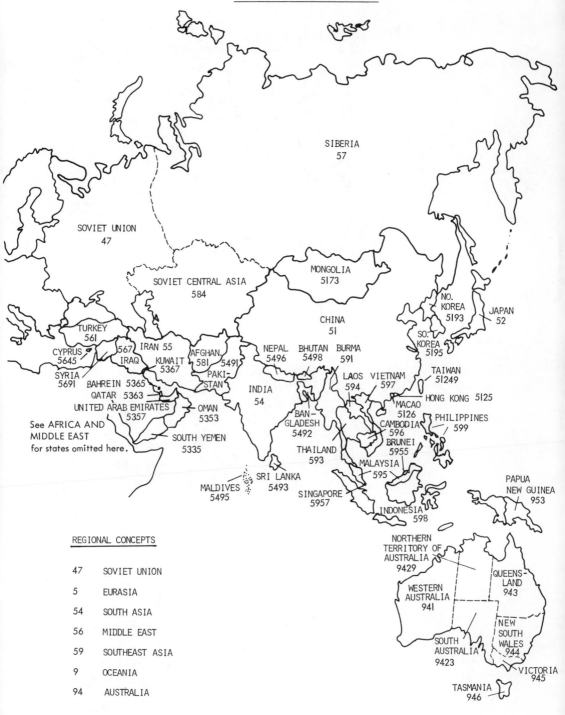

ASIA AND AUSTRALIA

SIBERIA
57

SOVIET UNION
47

SOVIET CENTRAL ASIA
584

MONGOLIA
5173

CHINA
51

NO.
KOREA
5193

JAPAN
52

SO.
KOREA
5195

TURKEY
561

CYPRUS
5645

IRAN 55

IRAQ

SYRIA
5691

KUWAIT
5367

AFGHAN.
581   5491

PAKI-
STAN

NEPAL
5496

BHUTAN
5498

BURMA
591

567

BAHREIN 5365

QATAR 5363

UNITED ARAB EMIRATES
5357

OMAN
5353

INDIA
54

LAOS
594

VIETNAM
597

TAIWAN
51249

HONG KONG 5125

MACAO
5126

PHILIPPINES
599

See AFRICA AND
MIDDLE EAST
for states omitted here.

SOUTH YEMEN
5335

BAN-
GLADESH
5492

THAILAND
593

CAMBODIA
596

BRUNEI
5955

MALAYSIA
595

PAPUA
NEW GUINEA
953

MALDIVES
5495

SRI LANKA
5493

SINGAPORE
5957

INDONESIA
598

REGIONAL CONCEPTS

47	SOVIET UNION
5	EURASIA
54	SOUTH ASIA
56	MIDDLE EAST
59	SOUTHEAST ASIA
9	OCEANIA
94	AUSTRALIA

NORTHERN
TERRITORY OF
AUSTRALIA
9429

WESTERN
AUSTRALIA
941

QUEENS-
LAND
943

SOUTH
AUSTRALIA
9423

NEW
SOUTH
WALES
944

VICTORIA
945

TASMANIA
946

AFRICA AND MIDDLE EAST

TURKEY 561

CYPRUS 5645

MALTA 4585

TUNISIA 611

LEBANON 5692

ISRAEL 5694

SYRIA 5691

IRAQ 567

IRAN 55

JORDAN 5695

MOROCCO 64

CANARY ISLANDS 649

ALGERIA 65

LIBYA 612

EGYPT 62

SAUDI ARABIA 538

OMAN 5353

SAHARA 648

MAURITANIA 661

MALI 6623

NIGER 6626

CHAD 6743

SUDAN 624

YEMEN 5332

SOUTH YEMEN 5335

DJIBOUTI 6771

ETHIOPIA 63

SOMALIA 6773

SENEGAL 663

GAMBIA 6651

GUINEA REP. 6652

GUINEA BISSAU 6657

UPPER VOLTA 6625

NIGERIA 669

SIERRA LEONE 664

IVORY COAST 6668

GHANA 667

TOGO 6681

BENIN 6683

CAMEROON 6711

CENTRAL AFRICAN REPUBLIC 6741

UGANDA 6761

KENYA 6762

LIBERIA 6662

EQUATORIAL GUINEA 6718

SAO TOME 66994

GABON 6721

CONGO 6724

ZAIRE 6751

RWANDA 67571

BURUNDI 67572

TANZANIA 678

COMOROS 694

ST. HELENA 973

ANGOLA 673

MALAWI 6897

MOZAMBIQUE 679

MADAGASCAR 691

ZAMBIA 6894

ZIMBABWE 6891

NAMIBIA 688

BOTSWANA 6811

SWAZILAND 6813

SOUTH AFRICA 68

LESOTHO 6816

REGIONAL CONCEPTS

61	NORTH AFRICA
62	NILE VALLEY
624	THE SUDAN
66	WEST AFRICA, SAHARA DESERT
67	AFRICA SOUTH OF THE SAHARA, BLACK AFRICA, CENTRAL AFRICA
676	EAST AFRICA
68	SOUTHERN AFRICA
69	SOUTH INDIAN OCEAN ISLANDS

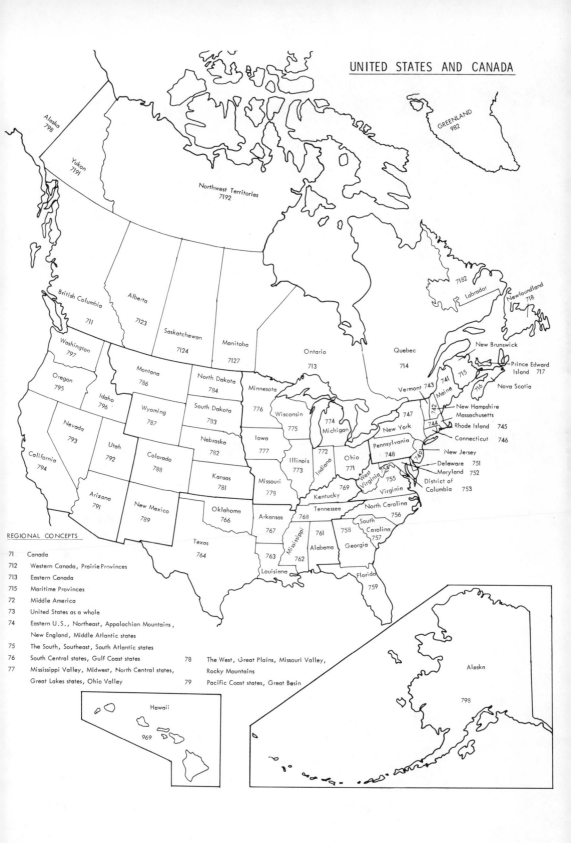

UNITED STATES AND CANADA

Alaska 798

Yukon 7191

Northwest Territories 7192

GREENLAND 982

British Columbia 711

Alberta 7123

Saskatchewan 7124

Manitoba 7127

Ontario 713

Quebec 714

7182

Labrador

Newfoundland 718

New Brunswick

Prince Edward Island 717

Nova Scotia

716

715

Washington 797

Montana 786

North Dakota 784

Minnesota 776

Wisconsin 774

Vermont 743

741

Maine 742

New Hampshire

Massachusetts 744

Rhode Island 745

Connecticut 746

Oregon 795

Idaho 796

Wyoming 787

South Dakota 793

Iowa 777

Michigan 775

New York 747

Nevada 793

Utah 792

Colorado 788

Nebraska 782

Illinois 773

Indiana 772

Ohio 771

Pennsylvania 748

749

California 794

Arizona 791

New Mexico 789

Kansas 781

Missouri 778

Kentucky 769

West Virginia 754

New Jersey

Delaware 751

Maryland 752

District of Columbia 753

Virginia 755

North Carolina 756

Oklahoma 766

Arkansas 767

Tennessee 768

Texas 764

Mississippi 762

Alabama 761

Georgia 758

South Carolina 757

Louisiana 763

Florida 759

REGIONAL CONCEPTS

71   Canada

712   Western Canada, Prairie Provinces

713   Eastern Canada

715   Maritime Provinces

72   Middle America

73   United States as a whole

74   Eastern U.S., Northeast, Appalachian Mountains, New England, Middle Atlantic states

75   The South, Southeast, South Atlantic states

76   South Central states, Gulf Coast states

77   Mississippi Valley, Midwest, North Central states, Great Lakes states, Ohio Valley

78   The West, Great Plains, Missouri Valley, Rocky Mountains

79   Pacific Coast states, Great Basin

Hawaii 969

Alaska 798

SOUTH AMERICA

VENEZUELA 87

GUYANA

COLOMBIA 861

GUYANE

SURINAM

881 883 882

ECUADOR

866

BRAZIL 81

PERU 85

BOLIVIA 84

CHILE

892

PARAGUAY

83

ARGENTINA 82

895

URAGUAY

REGIONAL CONCEPTS

8   LATIN AMERICA, SPANISH AMERICA, SOUTH AMERICA, ANDES

86   NORTHWESTERN SOUTH AMERICA

88   GUIANAS

9711

FALKLANDS/MALVINAS

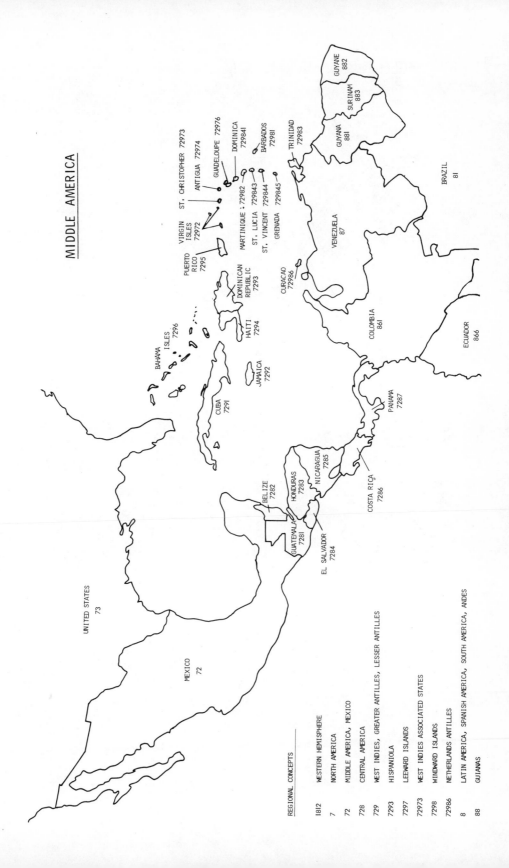

MIDDLE AMERICA

UNITED STATES
73

MEXICO
72

BELIZE
7282

GUATEMALA
7281

EL SALVADOR
7284

HONDURAS
7283

NICARAGUA
7285

COSTA RICA
7286

PANAMA
7287

CUBA
7291

BAHAMA
ISLES
7296

JAMAICA
7292

HAITI
7294

DOMINICAN
REPUBLIC
7293

PUERTO
RICO
7295

VIRGIN
ISLES
7972

ST. CHRISTOPHER 72973

ANTIGUA 72974

GUADELOUPE 72976

DOMINICA
72984I

MARTINIQUE: 72982

ST. LUCIA 729843

ST. VINCENT 729844

GRENADA 729845

BARBADOS
7298I

TRINIDAD
72983

CURACAO
72986

COLOMBIA
861

VENEZUELA
87

GUYANA
881

SURINAM
883

GUYANE
882

BRAZIL
81

ECUADOR
866

REGIONAL CONCEPTS

18I2	WESTERN HEMISPHERE
7	NORTH AMERICA
72	MIDDLE AMERICA, MEXICO
728	CENTRAL AMERICA
729	WEST INDIES, GREATER ANTILLES, LESSER ANTILLES
7293	HISPANIOLA
7297	LEEWARD ISLANDS
72973	WEST INDIES ASSOCIATED STATES
7298	WINDWARD ISLANDS
72986	NETHERLANDS ANTILLES
8	LATIN AMERICA, SPANISH AMERICA, SOUTH AMERICA, ANDES
88	GUIANAS

BRITISH ISLES

Orkney
41132

Western Isles
4114

Highland
4115

Grampian
4121

Tayside
4125

Fife
4129

Central
4131

Lothian
4132

Strathclyde
4141

Borders
4137

Dumfries and Galloway
4147

Northumberland
4288

Tyne and Wear
4287

Cleveland
4285

Durham
4286

Cumbria
4278

North Yorkshire
4284

Humberside
4283

Isle of Man
4279

Lancashire
4276

West Yorkshire
4281

Merseyside
4275

Greater Manchester
4273

South Yorkshire
4282

Lincolnshire
4253

Cheshire
4271

Derbyshire
4251

Nottinghamshire
4252

Norfolk
4261

Clwyd
4293

Staffordshire
4246

Leicestershire
4254

Gwynedd
4292

Shropshire
4245

West Midlands
4249

Cambridgeshire
4265

Suffolk
4264

Powys
4295

Warwickshire
4248

Northamptonshire
4255

Bedfordshire
4256

Hereford and Worcester
4244

Buckinghamshire

Hertfordshire
4258

Essex
4267

Dyfed
4296

Gloucestershire
4241

Gwent
4299

Oxfordshire
4257

Greater London
421

Berkshire
4229

West Glamorgan
42981

Avon
4239

Wiltshire
4231

Surrey
4221

Kent
4223

Mid Glamorgan
4297

South Glamorgan
42986

Somerset
4238

Hampshire
4227

West Sussex
4226

East Sussex
4225

Devon
4235

Dorset
4233

Isle of Wight
4228

Cornwall
4237

Scilly Isles
42379

Donegal
41693

Northern Ireland
416

Sligo
4172

Monaghan

Leitrim
4176

Louth
41825

Mayo
4173

Cavan
41698

Roscommon
4175

Longford
41812

Meath
41822

Westmeath

Dublin
4183

Galway
4174

Offaly
4186

Kildare
4185

Laois
4187

Wicklow
4184

Clare
4193

Tipperary
4192

Carlow
41882

Limerick
4194

Kilkenny
4189

Wexford
41885

Kerry
4196

Waterford
4191

Cork
4195

Table 3.
Subdivisions of Individual Literatures

For a schematization of the procedures for building numbers in the literatures of specific languages, see Number building *under 800.*

—102 Dramatic [poetry]

  Example: dramatic monologues.

—103 Narrative [poetry]

  The heading at this number has been broadened (*see DC&*, Vol. 4, No. 1, p. 10). Subdivisions may be added for epic poetry alone.

—104 Lyric and balladic [poetry]

  Including haiku, troubadour poetry.

—108 Light and ephemeral verse

  Class satirical and humorous light verse at —107.

—2 **Drama**

  Class here dialogues; however, if they are meant to serve as expositions of some subject, class them with the subject, e.g., Plato's dialogues in philosophy 184.

—2051 Tragedy and serious drama

  Including Noh plays.

—2052 Comedy and melodrama

  Including interludes.

—20523 Comedy

  Including farces.

—2057 Variety and miscellaneous [drama]

  Including comedy sketches, Punch and Judy shows.

—3081 Historical and period [fiction]

  See discussion of the nonfiction novel in the last paragraph of Form *under 800.*

—4 **Essays**

  See Form *under 800.*

—5 **Speeches**

See Form *under 800.*

—504 Recitations

Class here collections of recitations containing more than one literary form meant to be read aloud. If limited to one form, class with that form, e.g., poetry recitations —1.

—6 **Letters**

See Form *under 800.*

—7 **Satire and humor**

Inasmuch as every other form takes precedence over it, e.g., humorous poetry —1, humorous fiction —3, —7 is used only for collections in several literary forms and for critical works about literary works in several forms that are admittedly satire or humor.

—803 and   Diaries, journals, reminiscences
—8 + 03
Including literary notebooks (journal jottings as source material for an author's writing).

This section includes diaries of literary authors not identified with a specific form of literature, in which the life of the author or authors as such is of key interest. If the author or authors are identified with a specific form, class the diary or diaries with that form. However, the diaries of literary authors in which not so much the life of the author or authors in general, but rather some other subject, is of key interest are classed with the subject of interest. For example, the diary of an author compiled while in a prison camp in World War 2 is classed in 940.5472.

Class diaries of nonliterary authors with the appropriate subject, e.g., the diary of an astronomer 520.924.

Class collections of diaries involving several disciplines in 900.

—807 and   Experimental and nonformalized works
—8 + 07
Class here modern original fables if they are in the prose mode; class in poetry —1 if in the poetic mode.

Class here joke books and other humorous works by individual authors if the telling is not anecdotal; if anecdotal, class at —802 or —8 + 02.

Table 3. Subdivisions of Individual Literatures

—808 and   Prose literature
—8 + 08

      Note that a collection of prose containing the form with which the author is chiefly identified is classed with that form, e.g., a collection of stories, essays, and letters by a contemporary American writer of fiction 813.54; but a collection of short stories, essays, and letters by a contemporary American poet 818.5408.

Table 3–A   Notations to be added where instructed throughout Table 3

1   Literature displaying specific qualities

      Including irony, expressionism, surrealism, radical writing, primitivism, dadaism.

12   Realism and naturalism [in literature]

      Including determinism.

14   Classicism and romanticism [in literature]

      Including pastoral literature.

15   Symbolism, allegory, fantasy [in literature]

      Including myth.

17   Comedy

      Including textbooks and teaching collections showing the development of manifestations of comedy in literature of various forms; class collections of humor read for pleasure in —7 in Table 3.

27   Characters [in literature]

      Including the "double" in literature.

32   **Places [in literature]**

      Examples: Midwestern life 3277, the sea 32162, California 32794, rural villages 321734.

35   **Humanity and human existence [in literature]**

      Class here works dealing with dreams, contemporary perspectives.

352   Specific kinds of persons [in literature]

      Including heroes, rebels, fools or jesters, gentlemen, barbarians.

353   Human psychological and moral qualities and activities [in literature]

      Further examples: melancholy, heroism, personal beauty, justice, sentiment, honor, snobbishness.

355   Social themes [in literature]

Further examples: costume or dress, college years, sports, drugs, school, dancing, travel.

37   The supernatural, mythological, legendary [in literature]

Including white magic, spiritualism, witchcraft.

372   [Supernatural, mythological, legendary] Places [in literature]

Further example: utopia, hell. Class religious treatment of hell at 382 in this table.

375   [Supernatural, mythological, legendary] Beings [in literature]

Further example: undines.

382   Religious concepts [in literature]

Further examples: the devil, hell.

Class persons connected with religion in 351 in this table, e.g., Buddha.

384   Philosophic concepts [in literature]

Further examples: transcendentalism, conscience, self-knowledge.

93–99   [Literature] For and by persons resident in specific continents, countries, localities

Do not use for individual authors. Use for:

(1) Literature in a language by nonnative residents of a specific country, e.g., a collection of English literature by non-Japanese residents of Japan 820.80952.

(2) Literature in a language by persons from a certain area within a country, e.g., a collection of American literature by residents of Illinois 810.809773.

(3) Literature in a language by residents of several countries on the same continent from more than one period, e.g., French literature by residents of France, Switzerland, Belgium, etc. 840.8094.

(4) Affiliated literatures, e.g., a collection of French poetry by Swiss authors of the later 19th century 841.80809494.

Table 4.
Subdivisions of Individual Languages

Note that standard subdivisions may be added to the notations listed when appropriate, e.g., —3028 techniques of making dictionaries.

—042   **Bilingualism**

This is a new entry that has been promulgated in *DC&*, Vol. 4, No. 1, p. 11.

Add "Languages" notation 2–9 from Table 6 to base number —042 for the language that is not dominant in the country in which the linguistic interaction occurs, e.g., works dealing with the dominant language and English —04221.

See also 404.2.

—07   Study and teaching

Class in —8 textbooks for learning the fundamentals of using a language.

—1–5   Description and analysis of the standard form of the language

With the exception of —3 Dictionaries, these numbers are limited to the history, development, and description of a language. Use of a language is classed in —8.

—11   Notation

Including transliteration into other systems of notation, e.g., of the Cyrillic alphabet into the Roman alphabet.

—15   **Phonology**

See —5.

—152   Spelling and pronunciation

Class here orthography, and the description and analysis of the nature, history, and function of pronunciation; but class training in pronunciation and usage in —81–83. Class in 808.5 speech training for public speaking, debating, and conversation.

—16   Intonation

See —5.

—3028   [Techniques of making dictionaries]

Including lexicography.

—31   Specialized [dictionaries of the standard form of the language]

Examples: reverse dictionaries; crossword puzzle dictionaries; dictionaries of clichés, idioms, eponyms, paronyms, puns, collective nouns.

—32–39   **[Bilingual dictionaries of the standard form of the language]**

A method other than that set forth in Edition 19 for determining the more useful language if the entries are in both languages is to class the dictionary with the language in which the introduction is not written. If the introduction is written in both languages, class with the language coming later in the sequence 420–490.

See also 410.

—5   Structural system (Grammar) of the standard form of the language

Morphology (the patterns of word formation) and syntax (the patterns of sentence formation) do not necessarily constitute all of grammar. Often works on grammar include as well material on sounding and intonation. When dealt with separately, phonology and intonation are provided for at —15 and —16 respectively; but works that treat the two topics within a broader grammatical framework are classed here.

—7   Nonstandard forms of the language

When topics forming the subdivisions of —8, e.g., pronunciation (—81), are applied to nonstandard forms of the language, they are classed here.

Note that subdivisions of —7 are spelled out under individual languages where their use is recommended.

—709   [Modern nonregional variations]

Do not use unless specifically spelled out in 420–490.

—8   **Standard usage of the language (Applied (Prescriptive) linguistics)**

Class here the study of linguistic elements and patterns used in conveying meaning through language. Class here also prescriptive grammar, works on a language for those who are not native speakers, and works intended for native speakers who are learning the acceptable patterns of their language.

Class purely descriptive grammar at —5, topics of —8 applied to nonstandard forms of the language in —7.

—81   Words

Class at —81 the proper spelling and pronunciation of words in the language, wordbooks arranged by subject or any other approach intended to be used for pedagogical purposes.

Class at —152 the principles governing spelling in a language and the rules and methods of pronunciation.

—**82**   **Structural approach to expression**

Class here verb tables and inflectional schemata designed for use as aids in learning a language.

—**83**   **Audio-lingual approach to expression**

Class here the "hear-speak" school of learning a language, bilingual phrase books.

—86   Readers

When the text is devoted primarily to practice in reading a language, class it here.

—864   [Readers] For those whose native language is different

Class at —864 readers for nonnative speakers intended to instill a knowledge of the special vocabulary of a specific subject or discipline, e.g., science readers. Note, however, that works on the vocabulary of a specific subject or discipline without regard to the language status of the reader are classed in the number for the subject or discipline followed by s.s. 014.

Table 5.
Racial, Ethnic, National Groups

It will be seen at once that Table 5 and Table 6 Languages are very similar and that they are based on the traditional sequence of languages in 420–490. Two tables have been developed, however, because language and race or nationality do not always match. Examples: there are Swiss people (—35 in Table 5) but no Swiss language; there is a Yiddish language (—37 in Table 6) but no Yiddish people.

Use the notation from each table where specified, and note that numbers from Table 5 can be added anywhere through the use of s.s. 089.

Table 6. Languages

As noted in the instructions at the head of this table in Edition 19, the notations in this table do not necessarily correspond with the numbers for individual languages in 420–490 and in 810–890. For example, although the base number for English is 42, the notation for English in Table 6 is —21, not —2. Thus, a bilingual French-English dictionary intended for French speakers is classed at 443.21. The correct number is not 443.2 as one might otherwise think.

See also Table 5.

Table 7. Persons

In a general way the notations from —1 through —9 have been developed from a reduction of numbers from the whole classification; however, the mnemonic matches are by no means perfect, and the table should not be used without consultation, e.g., local government personnel —354, not —352.

Changes in the general schedules between editions are not necessarily, or even likely to be, reflected by changes in this table.

Schedules

000 Generalities

Two categories of works fall within the Generalities class:

(1) Works in the "umbrella" disciplines, i.e., works in such fields of endeavor as communication, information, and data processing (001–003); bibliography (010 and 090); library and information sciences (020); museology (069); and publishing (070). Some of the umbrella disciplines may be directly related to other disciplines through subdivision, i.e., attaching a number from the 001–999 span, resulting in such topics as 016.54 bibliographies of chemistry, 026.61 medical libraries.

(2) Multidisciplinary works, e.g., general encyclopedias (030), general periodicals (050), general collections (080).

There are corresponding and often parallel standard subdivisions for many of the instances of these various types, making possible the expression of these forms in connection with specific subjects:

030 General encyclopedic works
s.s. 03 Dictionaries, encyclopedias, concordances

050 General serial publications and their indexes
s.s. 05 Serial publications

060 General organizations . . .
s.s. 06 Organizations . . .

001   Knowledge

Discussion of ideas from many fields; intellectual history.

Class a compilation of knowledge in a specific form with the form, e.g., encyclopedias 030.

001.4　　　Research

Class here works discussing what research is and how it is done.

Class works embodying the results of research in the number for the subject of the research, e.g., research in chemistry 540. Do not use s.s. 072 in such instances.

001.422　　**Statistical method**

See 519.5 vs. 001.422.

001.4225　Analysis of data

Class here works discussing how the nature of the problem governs which mathematical techniques are used.

Class works discussing how to perform the mathematical techniques in 519.5.

001.44　　Support of and incentives for research

Class awards for general achievements in 929.81; awards granted in a specific discipline with the discipline, using s.s. 079, e.g., honors in elementary teaching 372.079.

001.51　　Communication

Including semiotics, the science whose object is the study of messages and the sign systems that underlie them.

Class here interdisciplinary works on mass media, on communication: works dealing with communication among humans, between humans and other creatures, among nonhuman creatures.

Class semiotics in a philosophical context at 101.41, in the context of culture or society at 302.2, in a linguistic context at 401.41, in terms of literary analysis at 808.00141, as a philosophical system at 149.946.

Class the psychology of communication at 153.6, the sociology of communication in 302.2, systems of communication in 383–384, animal communication at 591.59.

001.510999　[Communication with and among extraterrestrial worlds]

Class here interstellar communication.

Class communication with UFOs at 001.942.

001.534　　Perception theory

Including perceptrons.

001.54　　Communication through language

Class language in 400.

001.543   Written communication

Class here the study of the processes of written communication, e.g., writing from left to right or top to bottom.

Class composition in 808; penmanship, typing, and related techniques in 652; the communications themselves with the specific subject, e.g., newspapers 070–079.

Class graffiti in general in 080; graffiti on a specific subject with the subject, e.g., on women 305.4; general compilations of graffiti illustrative of civilization in a given place in 930–990; a general compilation assembled for literary quality in 800.

001.55   Communication through records

The use of various physical forms of records as mediums of communication.

Class a specific aspect of a specific medium with the subject, e.g., motion picture production 791.43.

001.56   Nonlinguistic (Nonstructured) communication

Including flower language.

See also s.s. 0147.

001.61   Systems analysis

Class here systems analysis in data processing.

Class interdisciplinary works on systems analysis at 003.

001.64   Electronic [data processing]

Class interdisciplinary works on computer simulation at 001.434; computer simulation in a specific discipline or subject with the discipline or subject, using s.s. 0724, e.g., computer simulation in military operations 355.40724.

001.644   Input, storage, output [in electronic data processing]

Class engineering aspects and description of the equipment in 621.38195.

001.6443   Output [in electronic data processing]

Class various forms of output applied to a specific subject with the subject, e.g., computer graphics as a physical medium of communication 001.55.

001.9   **Controversial knowledge**

This number and the 130s both pertain to topics in the twilight realms of half-knowledge, topics that refuse either to be disproved or to be brought into the realm of certain and verifiable knowledge. Certain recognizable characteristics of a work are good indicators that they belong either here or in 130:

(1) a claim of access to secret or occult sources;

(2) rejection of established authority;

(3) a pronounced reverence for iconoclasts, for laymen-become-experts;

(4) an uncritical acceptance of lay observation of striking phenomena;

(5) a fixation on the unexplained, the enigmatic, the mysterious;

(6) a confidence verging on certainty in the existence of conspiracies and in the working of malevolent forces;

(7) acknowledging the powers of extraterrestrial beings or intelligences (other than religious beings).

Class here unverified phenomena not related to the human mind, spirit, or body. Class those that are so related in 130.

Class specific alleged conspiracies and actual conspiracies either in 909 and 930–990 (e.g., an alleged conspiracy to assassinate John F. Kennedy 973.922) or with the specific subject of the conspiracy, e.g., criminal conspiracies 364.1.

Class specific curiosities, hoaxes, errors, or groupings of them that are treated as part of the history of a discipline with the discipline, e.g., Piltdown man 573.3.

Class controversial medical remedies at 615.856.

For works applying scientific principles to any of the topics in subdivisions of this number, use s.s. 015, whether the work is pro or con. Use s.s. 072 for techniques of research into these subjects, but not for the results of the research.

See also discussion at 133.

001.93   Curiosities

Do not confuse curiosities here with books of the curious and unusual, which are classed in 030, e.g., *Ripley's Believe It or Not* 031.02.

001.95   Deceptions and hoaxes

Class deceptions and hoaxes in occultism in 133; hoaxes that influenced history in 930–990, e.g., Pseudo-Demetrius 947.045.

001.96   Errors, delusions, superstitions

Class here superstitions in general.

Class superstitions about a specific subject with the subject, e.g., marriage superstitions 392.5.

010 Bibliography

A bibliography is a list of books, articles, visual or audiovisual media. Certain bibliographies are not classed in 010, however. Publishers' catalogs are classed in 070.50294. Catalogs and lists of art works are classed with the subject, using s.s. 074, e.g., a catalog of the prints found in the Library of Congress 760.0740153.

011.02   [Bibliographies] Of reference works

Class reviews of reference works at 028.12.

011.7   General bibliographies of works having specific kinds of content

Class here abstracts of dissertations, bibliographies of directories.

013   Bibliographies and catalogs of works by specific classes of writers

Class dissertations at 011.7.

016   Subject bibliographies and catalogs

These may be in either list or essay form.

Class biobibliographies with the biography of the subject, e.g., Donald L. Hixon's *Women in Music: A Biobibliography* 780.922.

020 Library and information sciences

SUMMARY

021   **Library relationships**
022   **Physical plant of libraries and information centers**
023   **Personnel and positions**
025   **Library operations**
026   **Libraries devoted to various specific disciplines and subjects**
027   **General libraries**
028   **Reading and use of information media**

The primary facets in library and information sciences in their order of precedence are as follows:

(1) Operations, such as technical services, e.g., acquisitions, cataloging; and readers' services, e.g., circulation, reference. But comprehensive works on operations in a specific kind of institution are classed with the kind of institution.

(2) Materials by subject, e.g., chemistry, or by format, e.g., serials.

(3) Special clientele: classes of users, such as children, the handicapped, engineers.

(4) Administration (governance, management).

(5) Institutions serving types of clientele other than special.

(6) Standard subdivisions.

Examples follow:

(1) Book selection in public libraries
Operation (book selection) + institution (public library)
025.218 + 74 (from 027.4) = 025.21874

(2) Directory of engineering libraries
Subject of material (engineering) + s.s. (directory)
026.62 + s.s. 025 = 026.6200025

(3) Circulation services for children
Operation (circulation) + special clientele (children)
025.6

(Note that special clientele [children] cannot be indicated in the number.)

(4) Selection and acquisition of chemistry serials for university libraries
Operation (selection and acquisition) + subject of material (chemistry) + format of material (serial) + institution (university library)
025.27 + 54 (from 540) = 025.2754

(Note that format of material [serial] and institution [university library] cannot be indicated in this number.)

(5) Cataloging of braille materials for school libraries
Operation (cataloging) + format of material (braille) + institution (school library)
025.34 + 92 (from 025.1792) = 025.3492

(Note that institution [school library] cannot be indicated in this number.)

020.9	Historical and geographical treatment [of library and information sciences]

Class here librarianship (what librarians do, not the buildings in which they do it).

Class historical and geographical treatment of libraries in 027.

021	Library relationships

Class instructional manuals on library use and library orientation in 025.56.

021.2	Libraries and community

Class instructional media centers in 027.

021.7	Promotion of libraries

Including public relations in libraries, regardless of kind.

022.9	Equipment, furniture, furnishings [in libraries]

Class comprehensive works on computers in libraries at 025.002854.

025.04	Information storage and retrieval systems

Class information services in 025.52.

025.26	Acquisition [of library materials] through exchange, gift, deposit

Including Universal Serials and Book Exchange.

027.625	[Libraries] For children

Including toy lending services in a library context.

027.663	Libraries for the handicapped

Class here mainstreaming (the provision of library services through regular channels to individuals with special needs).

030 General encyclopedic works

031.02	[American] Books of miscellaneous facts

Example: *World Almanac & Book of Facts*

032.02	[English] Books of miscellaneous facts

Example: *Whitaker's Almanack*

050 General serial publications and their indexes

Class bibliographies of general serial publications at 011.34, bibliographies of directories at 011.7, catalogs of general serial publications in 017–019.

Class periodical indexes on one subject selected from several periodicals in 016 plus the subject, e.g., an index to information on chemistry found in several periodicals 016.54.

060 General organizations and museology

Class organizations whose members are political states in 341, e.g., Arab League 341.2477.

060.42   General rules of order

Example: *Robert's Rules of Order*

Class conduct of the meetings of business organizations at 658.4563.

069.13   Circulation services [in museums]

Class lending and rental collections at 069.56.

069.51–.54   **General principles [of collections and exhibits of museum objects]**

See 702.87–.89.

069.53   Maintenance, preservation, display, arrangement, storage [of museum objects]

Including the preservation of monuments *in situ*.

Class historic preservation at 363.69.

069.56   Lending and rental collections [in museums]

Class circulation services in 069.13.

069.63   Personnel and positions [in museums]

Including in-service training, staff manuals

070 Journalism, publishing, newspapers

070   Journalism, publishing, newspapers

Class bibliographies of newspapers at 011.35.

070.1   News media

Class here journalism (as defined at 070.1–070.4 in Edition 19) applied to and practiced by various specific media.

Class ethics of journalism in 174.9097.

070.4   Various specific journalistic activities and types of journalism

Class journalists whose careers span many activities in 070.92; persons in a specific type of journalism with the subject, e.g., foreign correspondents 070.433, editors 070.41092.

070.44   Features and special topics [in journalism]

Techniques and procedures involved in the collecting, writing, and editing of reports, criticisms, opinions.

Class here journalists specializing in specific subjects, e.g., health columnists 070.444, sports announcers 070.449796092.

Class reports, criticisms, opinions on a specific subject with the subject, e.g., criticisms of theatrical productions 792.

070.5   **Publishing**

Class here publishers regardless of the field of their activity; book clubs, e.g., Book-of-the-Month Club.

070.52   Relations with authors

See 808.001–.7.

070.595   Governmental and intergovernmental [publishers]

Including the U.S. Government Printing Office.

Class management of the U.S. Government Printing Office at 353.00819.

070.92   Persons [connected with journalism] regardless of area, region, place

See 070.4.

080 General collections

To be classed here a work must contain a collection of writings, statements, or quotations on a variety of topics, e.g., selected articles of a general nature from one or more periodicals, such as "Adventures of the Mind" from the *Saturday Evening Post*. A collection of quotations by Winston Churchill on various topics is another example.

Class collections gathered for their literary quality in 808.88 and cognate numbers in 810–890.

090 Manuscripts and book rarities

Including broadsides.

Class a bibliography including both manuscripts and rare books at 011.31, of rare books alone at 011.44.

091 Manuscripts

Class a study of the illuminations in manuscripts in 745.67.

093 Incunabula

Class bibliographies of incunabula at 011.42.

095 Books notable for bindings

Class book binding in 686.3.

100 Philosophy and related disciplines

The main facets of philosophy are branch (field of study), viewpoint (school or system), place, time, and person. The major branches of philosophy are (1) logic (160), (2) epistemology (121), (3) metaphysics (110 and parts of 120), (4) ethics (170), and (5) aesthetics (111.85).

Psychology 150 and Paranormal phenomena and arts 130 comprise the study of mind and body, including their interaction, relationships, and character. Although they have a historical basis in philosophy, they are no longer considered to be a part of this discipline by most scholars. Psychology 150 is considered to be a behavioral science, while 130 Paranormal phenomena and arts is considered to be a congeries of unverifiable phenomena.

Ancient, medieval, and Oriental schools or systems (viewpoints) of philosophy are classed in 180, those of modern Western philosophy in 140. Modern Western philosophy of specific places or times and specific modern Western philosophers (collected works in two or more branches or subbranches, description and critical appraisal of works in general, and biography) are classed in 190. However, a specific school or system is classed with the school or system regardless of place or time, e.g., existentialism in France 142.780944. *See also 140.*

Class the philosophy of a discipline or subject with the discipline or subject, using s.s. 01, e.g., philosophy of history 901. However, class the ethics of a discipline in 172–179, e.g., philosophy of medicine 610.1, but the ethics of the medical professions 174.2.

100 vs. 200   Philosophy vs. Religion

Both philosophy and religion deal with the "ultimate nature of existences and relationships," but religion treats them "within the context of revelation, deity, worship," or, in the case of natural religion, at least within the context of deity. For instance, Natural religion 210 substitutes reason for revelation and does not involve worship.

Any work that emphasizes revelation, deity, or worship is classed in 200 even if it uses philosophical methods ("observation, speculation, reasoning, but not experimentation"), e.g., a philosophical proof of the existence of God 212.1. Similarly, a philosophy based on a religion is classed in 200 if it emphasizes deity, revelation, or worship. If it does not, it is classed in 100, e.g., the philosophy of Confucianism 181.09512. However, ethics based on a religion is classed in 200.

If in doubt, prefer 200.

100   Philosophy and related disciplines

Works to be classed here must include several periods of both Western and Oriental philosophy, or discuss the discipline of philosophy. Many introductory works take up the nature of philosophy as well as specific topics. Such works are classed here whether or not they include Oriental philosophy.

The comprehensive number for Western philosophy (including ancient and medieval Western philosophy) and for modern philosophy (including modern Oriental philosophy) is 190. *See also 190.*

101   Theory of philosophy

Class here works dealing with such topics as "the concept of philosophy," "the nature of the philosophical task."

Class schools of philosophical thought in 140 or 180.

See also s.s. 01.

101.41   [Communication aspects of philosophy]

Including semiotics. *See also 001.51.*

110 Metaphysics (Speculative philosophy)

Speculative philosophy is a term used in a variety of ways, and it can cover a wide variety of topics.

Class here only works dealing with topics listed in the subdivisions of this number.

111.85 Beauty

Class here comprehensive and interdisciplinary works on aesthetics.

Class aesthetics of a specific discipline or subject with the discipline or subject, e.g., aesthetics of the arts 700.1.

113 Cosmology (Philosophy of nature)

Class the cosmological argument for the existence of God in 212.1.

120 Epistemology, causation, humankind

121 Epistemology (Theory of knowledge)

Psychological topics listed in 153, such as Association of ideas 153.22, may be treated in works that are properly classed here, but such topics must be discussed in relation to the nature and derivation of knowledge, the scope of knowledge, or the validity of claims to knowledge.

126 The self

Including Atman (Indian philosophy) as applied to the individual.

128.2 Mind

See 153.

129 Origin and destiny of individual souls

Use this number with caution. Some works on this topic call themselves philosophical, but deal predominantly with occult or religious beliefs. (*See 133.9013.*) If in doubt, prefer 133 or 220–299.

130   Paranormal phenomena and arts

SUMMARY

131   **Parapsychological and occult techniques
for achievement of well-being, happiness, success**
133   **Parapsychology and occultism**
135   **Dreams and mysteries**
137   **Divinatory graphology**
138   **Physiognomy**
139   **Phrenology**

From the earliest years of the Dewey Decimal Classification, the 130s have provided places for works on the interplay of the spirit and the body, of the mind and the body, and of the body and mind with things external. When it is believed that such interplay can be studied and verified by the current rules of science, the subject discussed is classed in 150; when not verifiable, it is classed in 130, e.g., graphology when divining one's future 137, but analysis of character through handwriting 155.282.

150 Psychology was once limited strictly to faculty psychology, the study of the capabilities and functions of the mind. As psychology came more and more to study the physical and biological aspects of the nervous system as they affect the workings of the mind, the 130s began to lose much of their substance to the 150s. Today there is little left in 130 but topics that students of psychology believe to be illegitimate or unfruitful for scientific study.

Some subjects belonging to 130 have been classed in 001.9 Controversial knowledge, e.g., fire walking 001.93. However, 001.9 is normally to be used for unverified phenomena that do not deal with the relationship of the mind, spirit, and body of humankind. *See discussion of criteria for controversial knowledge at 001.9.*

Class works combining the topics of 130–139 and those of 001.9 in 001.9.

130   Paranormal phenomena and arts

   130 alone is seldom used; prefer 133 for comprehensive works.

131   Parapsychological and occult techniques for achievement of well-being, happiness, success

   Class use of specific techniques of parapsychology and occultism for achieving well-being with the subject in 130–139, e.g., spells and charms 133.44.

133   Parapsychology and occultism

   See 129.

133 vs. 200   Parapsychology and occultism vs. Religion

   The occult emphasizes claims to knowledge of the unknown, discloses that which is secret, uncovers that which is hidden, especially that which is still unknown, secret, or hidden to the uninitiated. If there is worship, it is usually of deities with names symbolic of evil, e.g., Satan, Beelzebub, and there are attempts at mechanistic manipulation of deities, spirits, and unknown forces.

Religion, on the other hand, emphasizes beliefs about the divine, and devotion to deities held to be moral and from whom humanity often attempts to win approval.

For instance, demonology, i.e., the worship of evil beings, which mocks pious religions, is classed in 133.42. However, a Satanic cult that holds that Satan is a maligned deity is classed in 299. Witchcraft practiced by those who claim to be adherents of an ancient religion and who consider certain positive beliefs about a deity to be central to their cult is classed in 299; witchcraft as a purely manipulative device is classed at 133.43.

Knowledge reputedly derived from secret and ancient religious texts but not applied for religious purposes is classed with the occult; however, class editions of the texts in religion, even if annotated from an occultist point of view, e.g., I Ching divination unrelated to the rest of the Confucian tradition 133.33, I Ching divination as a manifestation of the Confucian religion 299.51232, and texts of I Ching 299.51282.

133.1   Apparitions (Ghosts)

Class here accounts of ghosts that are not Folklore 398 or Literature 800.

133.3   Divinatory arts

Works on the divinatory arts are often limited to the symbolism involved and do not include divinatory techniques. Works on this symbolism are classed in this number and its subdivisions.

Class here comprehensive works on foretelling the future.

See 133.324.

133.3092   [Persons in the divinatory arts]

Class here persons known chiefly for their predictions rather than their techniques, e.g., Nostradamus (Michel de Notredame), Jeane Dixon.

133.324   Fortunetelling

Fortunetelling here is limited to the subjects listed in subdivisions of this number and to those listed in the cross references. Other kinds of fortunetelling are classed with the form, e.g., fortunetelling by astrology 133.5. Class comprehensive works on foretelling the future at 133.3.

133.4   Demonology and witchcraft

Class here works combining treatment of the black arts, divination, and astrology.

Class divination in 133.3, astrology in 133.5.

133.43	Magic and witchcraft

Class here accounts of witches that are clearly not Folklore 398 or Literature 800.

Class here, using s.s. 09 plus areas 3–9, works on a specific witch craze, unless the craze is discussed as an element in the civilization of the place or time. For example, class a work on the Salem witch craze that emphasizes its occult side at 133.43097445, one emphasizing its reflection of the social or cultural milieu at 974.4402. If in doubt, prefer 133.43.

Standard subdivisions may be added for either magic or witchcraft treated separately.

133.53	Planets

Including sun, moon; rulership, symbolism.

133.548	Horoscopes of individuals

Class horoscopes of individuals connected with specific topics in 133.58, e.g., horoscopes of national leaders 133.589 plus appropriate area numbers.

133.58	Application [of astrology] to specific topics

Add 64677 to base number 133.58 for astrological guides to personal sex life, 9 for astrological analysis and prediction regarding a country and its leaders, e.g., predictions concerning the United States 133.58973.

133.8	Psychic phenomena

Class here comprehensive works on extrasensory perception (ESP), spiritualism, and ghosts.

Class spiritualism in 133.9, ghosts in 133.1.

133.8015	[Scientific principles of psychic phenomena]

Use of scientific principles to support or attack the validity of psychic phenomena.

133.8072	[Research into psychic phenomena]

Methods of research.

Class here psychic research even if the work embraces topics outside of those in 133.8.

133.9	Spiritualism

Class spiritualism as a religious doctrine in 291.213 and cognate and related numbers in 292–299; a spiritualist sect under the appropriate religion, using the denomination and sect subdivisions, e.g., a spiritualist Christian sect 289.9; independent spiritualist religions in 299.

133.9013	Personal survival, nature of the spiritual world and life after death

Class here accounts of life after death from personal sources or from within the occult tradition.

Class philosophical discussions of personal survival and life after death at 129.

If in doubt, prefer 133.9013.

135.3	Dreams

See 154.63.

135.4	Esoteric and cabalistic traditions

Class Cabalah in the context of Judaism at 296.16.

137	Divinatory graphology

Class here graphology that attempts to predict the future of the person whose handwriting is being analyzed; however, class the use of graphology in analyzing character at 155.282.

Class handwriting analysis for the examination of evidence at 363.2565, for screening prospective employees at 658.3112.

138	Physiognomy

Class here comprehensive works on physical features in occultism.

Class palmistry in 133.6, phrenology at 139.

140 Specific philosophical viewpoints

Distinguish between viewpoints or schools of philosophy and topics or branches of philosophy. Topics or branches are questions that are studied by philosophy, such as the nature of knowledge (epistemology), the nature of existence (ontology), or the nature of the self. Viewpoints or schools of philosophy are a set of attitudes or presuppositions that a given philosopher or group of philosophers bring to the study of the various topics. Therefore, works written from a specific viewpoint on a specific topic are classed with the topic, e.g., an existentialist view of ontology 111, not 142.78.

Philosophical viewpoints in 140 and its subdivisions are modern and Western.

Class here works that discuss or represent a school or viewpoint as a whole, covering many branches or fields of philosophy.

Class ancient, medieval, Oriental viewpoints in 180, e.g., medieval nominalism 189, modern Western nominalism 149.1; Indian idealism 181.4, modern Western idealism 141.

Class collected works of an individual author (two or more works in two or more branches of philosophy) and criticism of his work in general in 180–190, even if his work falls entirely within one specific philosophical viewpoint or serves as the foundation of a school. However, class an individual philosopher's work on a specific topic with the topic, e.g., Bertrand Russell's *Human Knowledge, Its Scope and Limits* 121, his collected works 192.

When all of a philosopher's work deals with one subject, disregard the instructions at the first note under 180–190 in Edition 19 and class all works by or about him at the number for that subject, e.g., the biography of an epistemologist 121.092. If in doubt whether all of a philosopher's works deal with one subject, prefer 180–190.

146.32   Dialectical materialism

Class here works that treat this subject only in relation to philosophical issues.

Class comprehensive works on dialectical materialism at 335.4112.

150 Psychology

SUMMARY

152   Physiological psychology
153   Intelligence, intellectual and conscious mental processes
154   Subconscious states and altered states and processes (Depth psychology)
155   Differential and genetic psychology
156   Comparative psychology
157   Abnormal and clinical psychologies
158   Applied psychology
159   Other aspects

The many sources of influence upon the mind and brain create classification problems in the 150s and elsewhere in the DDC:

(1) The biological view claims that all things mental are physically determined.

(2) Others believe that society and the behavior of other individuals affect a mind's development and responses.

(3) Brain and mind may be one; that is, the brain and other elements of the nervous system may have developed as a response to the stimuli sent out by the universe, the stimuli being coherent and explicable.

Thus, psychology may be considered as a branch of biology, as a branch of the behavioral sciences, or as something that transcends both fields.

The chief classification problems in psychology involve making distinctions between it and the social sciences and between it and medicine, particularly 616.89 Psychiatric disorders and 612.8 Nervous and sensory functions.

The Decimal Classification Division of the Library of Congress considers psychology to be a branch of the behavioral sciences, most of which fall in the 300s. Social psychology (group dynamics, the structure of the group and pattern of interactions within it) is classed in 302 Social interaction. However, material that deals with the interaction of the individual and society is classed in psychology, e.g., interpersonal relations 158.2, the influence of the social environment upon an individual 155.92. A two-person group as a group is classed at 302.34, a person and a friend at 158.25, a friend's influence upon one at 155.925.

See also 155 Order of precedence.

Psychology vs. Other subjects

Application to a specific subject outside psychology takes precedence over any topic in psychology, s.s. 019 being used if appropriate. However, the application of social psychology to a subject is classed in the social sciences, most often in 302–307. For example, class the medical psychology of addictions at 616.860019, the social psychology of services to the addicted at 362.29, the social psychology of the drug culture at 306.1.

For an exception to this rule, see 153.94.

150 vs.   **Psychology vs. [social psychology]**
302–307
The question whether psychology or social psychology takes precedence is complicated: Individual reactions and group behavior
are taken to be primary phenomena in both disciplines, i.e., the
behavior of the individual and the influence upon him of group
behavior are the primary focuses of psychology; the interactions
of the group and the individual's role in it are the primary focus of
social psychology. In the absence of preponderance in works covering both the psychology and the social psychology of sex relations prefer 306.7019 over 155.34 since sexual relations are basically
social. A work dealing with both the psychological influence of the
community and the interactions of individuals in communities is
classed in 307 rather than 155.94 because the idea of community is
the more pervasive idea. In comprehensive works on conversation, individual behavior tends to be the focus of study. However,
in works on communication in large groups, individual cognition
plays a much less significant role. Thus 153.6 is preferred over
302.346 for conversation, 302.2 over 153.6 for works on communication where the scope of the communication is extended. Interdisciplinary works on communication, however, are classed at
001.51.

150 vs.   **Psychology vs. Psychiatric disorders**
616.89
Two major problems confront the classifier when attempting to
distinguish between psychology and psychiatry. The first involves
Psychoanalytic systems 150.195. These systems are the foundation
of much of the writing on psychiatric diseases (616.89), and are
also the bases of several schools of psychology. Complicating the
picture is the fact that many of the systems are focused on explaining the abnormal, and most of the authors are therapists. Only the
more theoretical discussions of the bases of abnormal conditions
are classed in 150, e.g., comprehensive works on Freud, Jung, and
others 150.195, applications of their ideas 616.8917. If in doubt,
prefer 616.89. The other major problem involves distinguishing
between abnormal psychology at 157 and psychiatric disorders at
616.89. When such a problem occurs, class the work in 616.89.

150.19   **Systems, schools, viewpoints [in psychology]**

Be careful not to class here works on the whole of psychology written according to a specific system, school, or viewpoint. The presence of chapters on the major topics in 152–158 signal the use of 150 rather than 150.19. Bear in mind, however, that certain schools and systems draw their fundamental principles from a few selected psychological topics. When such topics are used to illustrate a system, class with the system in 150.19, e.g., depth psychology (154) used to illustrate psychoanalytic principles 150.195.

150.1908   **[History and description of systems, viewpoints, schools, of psychology with respect to groups of persons]**

See discussion at s.s. 08 vs. s.s. 09.

150.194   **Reductionism**

Class here works combining treatment of reflexes (152.322) and reductionist methods of learning, e.g., operant conditioning (153.152), even though the topics are not being used to illustrate the system.

150.195   **Psychoanalytic systems**

Most of the founders of psychoanalytic systems were physicians, so material from psychiatry (616.89) is heavily used to illustrate the principles of the various psychoanalytic systems. Class comprehensive works on the founder of a system in 150.195, using s.s. 0924 when no number has been provided for the system. If in doubt as to whether a topic in psychiatry illustrates a system or the system is being applied to psychiatry, prefer 616.89 and related numbers, e.g., psychoanalysis 616.8917. Any emphasis on a healer-patient relationship or on the prognosis of a patient's condition points toward 616.89.

150.287   [Testing and measurement in psychology]

Be cautious in the use of this number. To be classed at 150.287, a work must discuss testing in physiological psychology (152.80287) and intelligence testing (153.93) as well as personality testing (155.28).

Class ethics of psychological testing in 174.915.

See also s.s. 0287.

150.724   [Experimental research in psychology]

Class here, not in 152, works on experimentation in psychology.

Class the ethics of research in psychology at 174.915.

See also 152.

150.8   **[History and description of psychology with respect to groups of persons]**

Note that 150.8 is limited to the discipline of psychology with respect to groups of persons not dominant in a place or not provided for according to the subject in which they find themselves. The psychology of specific kinds of groups is classed in 155 Differential and genetic psychology, e.g., specific racial, ethnic, national groups 155.84.

See also 150.1908.

150.93–.99   **[Treatment of psychology by specific countries, continents, localities]**

Class the national psychology of specific countries (i.e., their differential psychology) in 155.89.

See also 150.8.

152 vs. 612.8 Physiological psychology vs. [Physiology of] Nervous and sensory functions

The distinction between physiological psychology and psychophysiology is frequently difficult to make since psychologists write on physiology and physiologists on psychology. In general, works are classed in 152 if the emphasis is on awareness or on the sensations, actions, intentions, or meanings of the process, e.g., seeing red, feeling blue, reaching high. However, a discussion of the mechanisms and pathways of sensations or actions is classed in 612.8.

152   Physiological psychology

Note that "experimental psychology" in the first note in Edition 19 refers to the traditional, now nearly obsolete, name for this branch of psychology, a holdover from the period when it was the chief branch in which experimental research was applied. The second note in Edition 19 has been deleted (in *DC&*, Vol. 4, No. 1, p. 12) because virtually the whole of psychology can be regarded as an experimental science. If a work on experimental psychology transcends the subdivisions of 152, reaching into memory, subconscious states, ethnopsychology, it is classed at 150, using s.s. 0724 only if the method of experimental research is emphasized.

152.0287   [Testing and measurement in physiological psychology]

Do not use; class in 152.8.

152.0723   [Descriptive research in physiological psychology]

Do not use; class in 152.8.

152.1 **Sensory perception**

This subject is subordinate to 153.7 Perceptual processes. Abstractions regarding sensory perception are classed in 153.7, e.g., looking or listening 153.733. If in doubt whether to use a 152.1 subdivision or a 153.7 subdivision, prefer the 153.7 number, e.g., if in doubt regarding the number for perception of movement prefer 153.754 over 152.1425.

Note that the word "tests" in the second note in Edition 19 has been removed (in *DC&*, Vol. 4, No. 1, p. 12). Tests are now classed at 152.10287.

152.1423 Pattern perception

Including perception of form, shape, image. Note, however, that the abstract aspects of pattern perception are classed in 153.7, e.g., space perception (i.e., the space occupied by a pattern) 153.752.

152.322 **Reflexes**

See 150.194.

152.33 **Habits and habit formation**

Class here comprehensive works on habits.

Class intellectual, conscious mental habits in 153.

152.384 **Expressive movements**

Note that this subject must be limited to physiological psychology of movements, i.e., their strength, habituation, emotional content, etc. Class their meaning (as in body language) at 153.6. If in doubt, prefer 153.6.

152.4 **Emotions and feelings**

There being no provision for specific kinds of complexes of emotions and feelings, such as love, hate, and humor, such complexes and all affective states that can be called either emotions or feelings are classed at 152.4.

Class here aggressive emotions and feelings; however, class comprehensive works on aggression at 155.232.

152.5 Physiological drives

Class comprehensive works on drives in 153.8 Volition.

152.8 Quantitative psychology

Including testing and measurement and descriptive research in physiological psychology.

Class works applicable to psychology in general in 150 and consider s.s. 0287 for testing and s.s. 072 for research.

153   Intelligence, intellectual and conscious mental processes

Class works on the mind-body problem at 128.2 Mind. Since psychology grew from the branch of philosophy in which mind was studied, early works on mental processes may be classed in either 128.2 or 153. When dealing with works in this area, be guided by citations and by comparisons with the thoughts of other authors. If in doubt, prefer 153.

Class daydreams at 154.3, even when they are considered as conscious mental processes.

153.0287   [Testing and measurement of intelligence, of intellectual and conscious mental processes]

Do not use; class in 153.93.

153.12   **Memory processes**

Class here comprehensive works on memory.

Class memory with respect to a specific topic with the topic, e.g., memory and dreams 154.63.

153.15   **Learning**

Be careful to distinguish between studies that use students as subjects for research into the fundamental processes of learning, which are classed in 153.15 and related numbers, and studies on the application of learning to education, which are classed in 370.15 and related numbers.

Class a work on the learning psychology of students of a specific age bracket in 155.4–155.6 when this is actually the focus of the work. If the reference to age is vague or incidental, class the work in 153.15. If in doubt, prefer 155.4–155.6.

153.152   Methods [of learning]

Including operant learning, free recall; Pavlovian conditioning as a learning method.

See also 150.194.

153.24   Abstraction

Including the psychology of naming.

153.32   Imagery

The number and note for 153.32 Imagery, including visualization, inadvertently dropped in Edition 19, have been restored (in *DC&*, Vol. 4, No. 1, p. 12).

153.4 **Cognition (Knowledge)**

The terminology in this field is used in a variety of overlapping senses. Before using 153.4, check the table of contents of any work having cognition, thought and thinking, or reasoning in the title in order to be certain that it does not also cover such subjects as memory, communication, perception, motivation, and intelligence. Such a work is classed in 153.

Note that a work having the title "Cognitive Psychology" is more apt to belong at 153 rather than in 153.4.

If in doubt whether a work is on cognition or on intelligence, prefer 153.9 Intelligence and aptitudes.

153.40287 [Testing and measurement of cognition]

Do not use; class in 153.93 General intelligence tests.

153.43 **Reasoning**

Class here the psychology of reasoning and problem solving. The science of reasoning and problem solving, i.e., the processes considered apart from internal mental operations, is classed in Logic 160. If in doubt whether a work on reasoning is psychology or logic, prefer 160.

Class moral reasoning at 153.46 Judgment.

153.432 Inductive [reasoning]

Including inference.

153.46 Judgment

Including the psychology of moral judgment, moral reasoning.

153.6 Communication

Writers on psycholinguistics and the psychology of communication occasionally shift their emphasis from chapter to chapter, now using psychology to study the structure and function of language (401.9), now discussing language as it reveals internal mental processes (153.6). If in doubt, prefer 153.6.

Including body language.

Class comprehensive and interdisciplinary works on communication at 001.51, the social psychology of communication in 302.2.

153.733 Attention

Including vigilance, observation, orienting response.

153.75　　Types of perception

Including the perception of the feelings of others.

153.8　　Volition (Will)

Including self-control, intentionality.

Class here comprehensive works on drives.

Class physiological drives at 152.5.

153.85　　Modification of will

Class here behavior modification and attitude change when reference is to bending the will or changing conscious intents.

153.90287　[Testing and measurement of intelligence and aptitudes]

Do not use; class in 153.93 General intelligence tests.

153.93　　General intelligence tests

This is the comprehensive and interdisciplinary number for testing and measurement of intellectual and conscious mental processes, of cognition.

Class here the use of intelligence testing to determine low mental ability.

Class educational tests and measurements in 371.26; tests to diagnose medical conditions in 616.80475 and cognate numbers, e.g., diagnosis of retardation 616.8588075.

153.932　　Individual [intelligence tests]

These tests are individually administered tests in which there is interaction between tester and testee.

153.9323　[Individual] Verbal [intelligence tests]

Class comprehensive works on verbal intelligence tests at 153.9333.

153.9324　[Individual] Nonverbal [intelligence tests]

Class comprehensive works on nonverbal intelligence tests at 153.9334.

153.933　　Group [intelligence tests]

Most works on written tests will be classed here. Such tests are "group" tests even if the "group" consists of one person.

153.9333　Verbal [group intelligence tests]

Class here comprehensive works on verbal intelligence tests.

Class individual verbal tests at 153.9323.

153.9334   Nonverbal [group intelligence tests]

Class here comprehensive works on nonverbal intelligence tests.

Class individual nonverbal tests at 153.9324.

153.94   **Aptitude tests**

This is a number of convenience for a subject not limited to intelligence, or to intellectual and conscious mental processes, yet obviously partaking of all of these.

Class here the use of tests to determine aptitude in specific fields even if drawn from other branches of psychology, e.g., color matching tests for interior decorators 153.94747, personality tests for social workers 153.943613. This is an exception to the general order of precedence. (*See Psychology vs. Other subjects under 150.*) Note that the table of precedence at 150 in Edition 19 has been changed (in *DC&*, Vol. 4, No. 1, p. 12) to put 153.94 at the top.

Class here also vocational interest tests, aptitude tests, and testing limited to categories of persons defined in 155.3–155.9, e.g., vocational tests for adolescents 153.94, not 155.5.

Do not confuse aptitude tests with educational tests and measurements. Achievement tests in specific subjects can be regarded as an aspect of "review and exercise" and classed with the subject, using s.s. 076. For example, tests for engineering aptitude are classed at 155.9462, tests for engineering achievement and knowledge at 620.0076.

Do not use s.s. 08 with this number.

154   **Subconscious and altered states and processes (Depth psychology)**

See notes at 150.19 Systems, schools, viewpoints [in psychology] for systems derived in part from the study of subconscious states and processes.

154.3   Secondary consciousness

Including daydreams, fantasies, reveries, even if fully conscious. Class daydreams, fantasies, reveries considered as aspects of imagination in 153.3.

154.6 vs.   [**Psychology of**] **Sleep phenomena** vs. [Physiology of] Sleep phenomena
  612.821

The distinction between 154.6 and 612.821 for sleep phenomena is similar to that made at 152 vs. 612.8 above in the notes on physiological psychology vs. psychophysiology.

Class sleep phenomena here if the emphasis is on the overall state, on the effect of sleep on other psychological activity, or on dreams as phenomena that have meaning in themselves or in the life of the dreamer.

Class sleep phenomena at 612.821 if the emphasis is on the chain of bodily activities or on other physiological activity accompanying sleep or dreams, e.g., eye movements, breathing, brain waves. When both psychology and physiology are well represented, class the work at 612.821.

154.63   **Dreams**

Class the parapsychological aspects of dreams at 135.3. If in doubt whether a work is parapsychology or psychology, consider the indicators listed under 001.9 for treatment of specific topics of controversial knowledge. If still in doubt, prefer 154.63.

154.7   Hypnotism

Class medical applications of hypnotism at 615.8512 Hypnotherapy (Suggestion therapy) and related numbers in 616–618, using subdivision 06512 from the tables at 616.1–616.9, 617, and 618.1–618.8 for hypnotherapy for specific diseases and conditions.

Class hypnotism considered as psychic power at 133.8 or with the specific application in 133, e.g., in casting spells 133.44.

155   **Differential and genetic psychology**

Some works on topics in physiological psychology (152) and intellectual and conscious mental processes (153) analyze research based on persons belonging to one or several differential categories or subject to one or several environmental influences that are provided for in 155.3–155.9. If there is clearly little or no interest in the distinctiveness of the category or influence, class the work in 152–153. This guideline is particularly applicable to ethnic and national groups (155.8), adults (155.6), and social environment (155.92) where the researcher has simply reached out for convenient samples. It is also applicable to works on sex psychology, e.g., a study on sex psychology, drawing almost exclusively upon adult middle-class American whites, but showing only marginal interest in the class, nationality, or race of the respondents, is classed in 155.3. Discussion of the class, national, or ethnic bias of such research is classed with the research in 155.3 as the interest is on the validity of the findings about sex psychology.

Order of precedence

The second line in the table of precedence in Edition 19 at 155 for appraisals and tests has been deleted (in *DC&*, Vol. 4, No. 1, p. 12); do not treat 155.28 as an exception to 155.2 in the last line, e.g., personality tests of children 155.4180287, not 155.28.

As said above (at 153.94) the table of precedence at 150 in Edition 19 has been changed to put 153.94 first. Thus, aptitude tests for categories of persons identified under 155.3–155.9 are classed in 153.94, e.g., vocational tests for adolescents 153.94, not 155.5.

In those cases where notes at 155 in Edition 19 do not offer guidance see the tables at 155.42–155.45 and 155.9 in the *Manual.*

155.0287   [Testing and measurement in differential and genetic psychology]

Do not use; class in 155.28.

155.2   **Individual psychology**

Class general applications of the topics of individual psychology in 158, e.g., assertiveness training, self-improvement, fostering the development of individuality, all 158.1.

155.20287   [Testing and measurement of individual psychology]

Do not use; class in 155.28.

155.232   Specific traits [of character and personality]

Including attractiveness, "drive," extroversion, introversion, workaholism, comprehensive works on the psychology of aggression.

Class interdisciplinary works on aggression, aggressive social interactions at 302.54, aggressive emotions and feelings 152.4, aggressive drives and the motivation behind them in 153.8.

155.24   Adaptability

Including adjustment.

155.25   Character and personality development and modification

Note that the concept of developmental psychology (*see the note at 155.4–.6 in Edition 19*) is broader than 155.25. Comprehensive works on the topic are classed in 155.

Including maturity, development of self-control.

Class behavior modification and attitude change, when reference is to bending the will or changing conscious intent, in 153.85. If in doubt whether the emphasis is on modification of will or modification of personality, prefer 153.85.

155.28   **Appraisals and tests [of individual psychology]**

Class here testing and measurement in differential, genetic, and individual psychologies. Do not use either 155.0287 or 155.20287.

Class the use of personality tests to determine vocational aptitudes and interests in 153.94.

155.282   Diagnostic graphology

Note that the parapsychological aspects of graphology are classed at 137. If in doubt whether a work is parapsychological, first consider the indicators listed under 001.9 for treatment of controversial knowledge. If still in doubt, class the work at 155.282.

155.3   **Sex psychology and psychology of the sexes**

Note that the heading in Edition 19 has been broadened to include the psychology of the sexes. Sex psychology and psychology of specific sexes and ages are classed in 155.4–155.6, e.g., psychology of three-year-old girls 155.423. *However, see also the first note under 155.*

Class social psychology of sexual relations at 306.7019.

155.33   **Sex differences**

Masculinity at 155.332 refers to the sum total of the presumed distinctive characteristics of males, whether overtly sexual or not; and femininity at 155.333 to the sum total of presumed distinctive characteristics of females. Use each number regardless of which sex the characteristics are ascribed to, e.g., masculinity in females 155.332. Use 155.334 Bisexuality for cross matching of the characteristics in both sexes.

155.334   Bisexuality

Bisexuality here refers to the ambiguity of sexual orientation or the display of behavior characteristic of both sexes.

Class bisexuality in the sense of the psychology of sex relations with the same as well as with the opposite sex at 155.34 Sex relations.

155.34   Sex relations

Including heterosexual, homosexual, and bisexual relations.

Class comprehensive works on the psychology and social psychology of sex relations in 306.7019.

155.4   **Child psychology**

Class here and in the appropriate subdivisions works covering both child and adolescent psychology.

155.4120287 [Testing and measurement of physiological psychology of children]

> Class here aspects of quantitative psychology (152.8) that are properly regarded as testing and measurement.
>
> *See also 152.8.*

155.418 Personal-social behavior

> Including play; moral development; individual psychology (155.2) pertaining to children, e.g., personality development in children.

155.4180287 [Testing and measurement of personal-social behavior of children]

> Including personality tests for children.

155.42–.45 Specific groupings [of children]

> The following table of precedence is an expansion of the table of precedence at 155.42–155.45 in Edition 19:

Gifted children	155.455
Retarded children and slow learners	155.452
Emotionally disturbed children	155.454
Children with physical handicaps	155.451
With linguistic handicaps	155.4514
Crippled	155.4516
Blind and partially sighted	155.4511
Deaf and hard-of-hearing	155.4512
Socially and culturally deprived children	155.4567
Delinquent and problem children	155.453
Upper-class children	155.4562
Children of specific racial, ethnic, national origin	155.457
Institutionalized children	155.446
Siblings, twins, etc.	155.443–.444
Adopted and foster children	155.445
The only child	155.442
By age groups	155.42
By sex	155.43

155.422 Infants

> Class here comprehensive works on children from birth to age five. For works on wider age brackets, prefer 155.4, the appropriate subdivision in 155.41, or 155.43–155.45.

155.423 Preschool children

> Class here comprehensive works on children aged two to six or three to seven. For works on wider age brackets, prefer 155.4, the appropriate subdivision in 155.41, or 155.43–155.45.

155.424   School children

Class here comprehensive works on school-age children up to age 14. For works on wider age brackets, prefer 155.4, the appropriate subdivisions in 155.41, or 155.43–155.45.

155.43   **[Children] By sex**

Class here the sex psychology of children.

155.44   [Children] By class, type, relationship

Including the psychology of temporary or permanent separation from parents.

155.446   Institutionalized children

Including children raised in communes that serve as collective parents, e.g., kibbutz children.

155.4567   [Socially and culturally deprived children]

Including wildings ("wolf children").

Class psychoanalytic principles derived in part from the study of wildings in 150.195.

155.5   **Psychology of adolescents**

The age limits here may be stretched to include the early twenties if the work includes substantial material on the teens.

Class here without subdivision topics that are found in 155.4 or 155.6 when applied to adolescents. *But see note at 155.53.*

Prefer 155.6 for the psychology of persons of college age, of young adults, except for works that make clear that at least half their subjects are twenty or under. Also use 155.6 or other subdivisions of 155 as appropriate, for works covering both adolescents and adults.

Class vocational tests for adolescents in 153.94.

155.53   **[Adolescents] By sex**

Class here the sex psychology of adolescents.

See also 155.5.

155.6   **Psychology of adults**

The table of precedence at 155.42–155.45 in Edition 19 governs by analogy in 155.63–155.67, the missing categories having standing room at 155.6, e.g., young adult women under thirty 155.6 (there is no number for young adults, yet age takes precedence over sex); middle-aged mothers 155.6463 (there is no number for middle-aged people, but status, type, or relationship takes precedence over age and sex).

155.8 **Ethnopsychology and national psychology (Cross-cultural psychology)**

Class studies of cultural influence in 155.92.

See also 155 Order of precedence.

155.84 vs. **[Psychology of] Specific racial and ethnic groups vs. National psychology**
155.89

Class in 155.89 the psychology of nations taken as a whole, and the psychology of racial and ethnic groups that are predominant in an area constituting an independent nation. Class in 155.84 the psychology of racial and ethnic groups taken as a whole and the psychology of racial, ethnic, *and* national groups in areas where they are not predominant. For example, class the national psychology of Malaysia, or the psychology of Malays in Malaysia in 155.89595; but class the psychology of Malays taken as a whole in 155.84992, of Malays in Thailand in 155.849920593.

155.89 **National psychology**

See 155.84 vs. 155.89.

155.9 **Environmental psychology**

Unless other instructions are given, observe the following order of precedence, e.g., the influence of prisons upon persons who are deformed 155.962, not 155.916. In the subdivisions of each class, give precedence to the number coming last in the subdivision, e.g., housing influences upon persons living in rural communities 155.945, not 155.944.

Clothing	155.95
Specific situations	155.93
Restrictive environments	155.96
Deformities, injuries, diseases	155.916
Housing and community influences	155.94
Social environment	155.92
Physical environment and conditions	155.91 (except 155.916)

155.92 **Social environment**

The reference here is to the influence of family, friends, work associates, etc., upon a person's development. Class in 158.2 the art of getting along with them.

When a work treats both social interactions (302–307) and the psychology of social environments (155.92 or 155.94), prefer 302–307, e.g., the influences of a community on individuals and interactions within a rural community 307.72, not 155.944.

155.937 Imminence or approach of death

Class comprehensive and interdisciplinary works on death at 306.9.

155.94   **Housing and community influences**

See 155.92.

156   Comparative psychology

Class here comparative social psychology (sometimes called socio-biology or biosociology) when it is used to elucidate human psychological behavior. However, class works considering the social behavior of animals as a background to human social behavior or as a subject throwing light on human social interactions in the appropriate number in 302–307 Specific topics in sociology. If in doubt between 156 and 302–307, prefer 156.

Note that social psychology of humans is classed in 302 and related numbers, while animal social behavior is classed in 591.51 and cognate numbers.

157   **Abnormal and clinical psychologies**

Because there are few abnormal psychological conditions that are not considered medical problems except in their milder manifestations, 157 and 157.2–157.8 will rarely be used except for works with a high proportion of theory and no application to medical practice.

See also 150.195.

157.9   **Clinical psychology**

Use with caution. Whenever clinical psychology treats persons that a layman would think required "medical" attention class the work in 616.89, making no attempt to distinguish between psychologists and psychiatrists when they are treating the same kind of patients.

The use of clinical psychology in welfare and education settings is often connected with counseling programs, which have special numbers in 361–363 and in 370.

See also 158.3.

157.92   Psychodiagnoses

Prefer 616.89075 for diagnosis of psychiatric disorders and 155.28 for tests applicable to personality determination when psychiatric disorders are not suspected.

157.94   Rehabilitation

Rehabilitation is a medical and welfare concept. This number will almost never be used. Prefer 610 and 362.2.

158   **Applied psychology**

Class the application of a specific field of psychology with the field, e.g., how to be creative 153.35; however, the scope of Individual psychology 155.2 is so broad that its application is classed in 158.

The note in Edition 19 on classing application with the subject has one important exception: Class aptitude and vocational interest tests in 153.94 regardless of application whether or not applied to a subject.

158.1   **Personal improvement and analysis**

Note that "improvement" here can be stated indirectly, e.g., handling stress.

Class here works intended to make one a better person or to stave off failure, to solve problems or to adjust to a life that does not meet one's expectations.

Be alert for the distinction between this number and 158.9 for systems and schools of applied psychology. In general, works on specific systems written for persons who wish to be improved and analyzed are classed in 158.1, while those written for the advisors and counselors to help them assist others are classed at 158.9. Prefer 158.9 for works on the founders, noted teachers, or counselors of the various systems.

Class works on how to get along with others in 158.2. Works combining advice on how to better oneself and how to get along with others are classed in 158 and standard subdivisions may be added.

158.2   **Interpersonal relations**

Interpersonal relations refer to relationships between an individual and others, not the intrarelationships of groups. The latter are classed at 302.3.

Class here loneliness, intimacy, dominance; the applications of sensitivity training and transactional analysis.

158.3   Counseling and interviewing

Class here helping behavior.

Class helpfulness as a personality trait at 155.232, counseling in a specific subject with the subject.

Inasmuch as counseling in a specific subject usually encompasses the entire subject toward which the counseling is directed and not just the psychological aspect of the subject, be cautious about using s.s. 019 Psychological principles for counseling in a specific subject, e.g., investment counseling 332.6, not 332.6019. Note that counseling and interviewing in welfare are classed in 361.32 and often have specific provision in 362–363, using 86 from the table at 362–363, e.g., counseling and guidance of poor people 362.586. Guidance and counseling in education is classed in 371.4 and cognate numbers for specific levels of education.

158.4   Leadership

Be cautious about using s.s. 019 for psychological principles of leadership in a specific subject, for reasons explained at 158.7 vs. 650.

158.6   Vocational interests

Class aptitude in 153.9; testing for aptitudes and vocational interest for all occupations in 153.94.

158.60287   Vocational interests [tests]

Do not use; class in 153.94.

158.7 vs. 650   Industrial psychology vs. Management and auxiliary services

Before using 158.7 be sure the work is not limited to what would properly be classed in such a management number as 650.1 Personal success in business or 658.30019 psychological principles of personnel management. Similarly, in a specific industry make sure that s.s. 0683 Personnel management is not applicable before using s.s. 019 Psychological principles, e.g., a work on industrial psychology for construction supervisors 624.0683, but a work on industrial psychology for union organizers and shop stewards in the construction industry 624.019.

158.7   Industrial psychology

Including the psychology of work.

158.9   Systems and schools of applied psychology

See 158.1.

159   Other aspects

Do not use; class in 150.

160 Logic

Class here counterfactuals, modality, negation, question, reference.

Class symbolic (mathematical) logic in 511.3. If in doubt whether a work is about the science of reasoning or the psychology of reasoning, prefer 153.43.

170 Ethics (Moral philosophy)

SUMMARY

Class here the ethics of a discipline, e.g., ethics of the medical professions 174.2, not 610.1.

Class ethics based on a religion in 200.

170.202   Normative ethics for specific groups

Class comprehensive works on normative ethics in 170.44.

171   **Systems and doctrines**

Systems and doctrines at 171 is comparable to the 140s in that it deals with various specific ethical viewpoints. There is no provision for individual moral philosophers comparable to that for general philosophers at 180–190. The ethics of an individual philosopher are classed in 170, with the specific system he represents, if any. For example, a philosopher whose ethics are based on utilitarianism is classed at 171.5. The works of a philosopher writing on a specific subject in ethics are classed with the subject, regardless of viewpoint, e.g., works on political ethics from a utilitarian viewpoint 172, not 171.5. The biography of an ethical philosopher is classed according to the same principles, using s.s. 0924 where feasible. However, class in 180–190 the overall biography of a moral philosopher who is also a general philosopher, e.g., a general biography of John Stuart Mill 192.

Class here ancient, medieval, and Oriental doctrines as well as modern Western ones.

177   Ethics of social relations

Social relations is an ambiguous term with two separate meanings: (1) the interrelationships of society as a whole; and (2) what might be called "sociability," conversation, friendliness, social entertainments. In this section, most of the subdivisions refer to the second, narrower meaning. Since all of ethics deals with social relations in the broader sense, works classed here must deal only with topics actually listed in the subdivisions of this number.

179   Other ethical norms

Class here comprehensive works on cruelty.

Class specific instances of cruelty in 179.1–179.4.

179.8–.9   Vices, faults, failings; [and] Virtues

Interpret "not otherwise provided for" strictly. Except for cruelty (*see 179*) class here vices and virtues not named elsewhere either directly or by synonym.

179.9   Virtues

Further examples: sincerity, sympathy.

180–190   Historical and geographical treatment of philosophy

For individual philosophers:

(1) Class here single works without focus on a particular subject.

(2) Class here critical appraisal of an individual philosopher in general, but class with the branch or subbranch critical appraisals of the work of the philosopher in that branch or subbranch, e.g., Sartre's work on ontology 111; a critical appraisal of it 111; his life, ontological views, and their relationship 111.0924.

(3) If all of a philosopher's work deals with one subject, class all works by or about him in the number for that subject. If in doubt whether all his works fall in one subject, prefer 180–190.

(4) Never use s.s. 092 with these numbers. Most of the numbers are s.s. 09 concepts by virtue of time or place. *See also the discussion of s.s. 092 in both Edition 19 and this* Manual.

Do not add s.s. 09 to numbers that already express specific areas, e.g., twentieth-century philosophy of the British Isles 192, but twentieth-century Western philosophy 190.904.

180 Ancient, medieval, Oriental philosophy

181.04–.09   [Oriental philosophy] Based on specific religions

Though the distinction is difficult to draw, class here works dealing primarily with philosophical topics, not matters of faith. If in doubt, prefer 200–299. *See also 100 vs. 200.*

181.45   Yoga

Class here comprehensive works on the practice of yoga and on yoga as an Indian philosophical school.

Class bhakti and kundalini yoga in 294.543, karma yoga in 294.544, hatha yoga in 613.7046.

190 Modern Western philosophy

Because this is the comprehensive number for works on Christian philosophy, on modern philosophy, on Western philosophy, and on European philosophy, it is used more often than 100 for what appear to be general works on philosophy.

Note that modern Western philosophy may be considered to begin at approximately 1500 and to include the Renaissance period. Compare s.s. 0902–0903 in Edition 19. *See also 140.*

199   **Other geographical areas**

Class here modern philosophy of areas not provided for, even if not Western philosophy, e.g., traditional African philosophy 199.6.

200 Religion

SUMMARY

210   Natural religion
220   Bible
230   Christian theology   Christian doctrinal theology
240   Christian moral and devotional theology
250   Local Christian church and Christian religious orders
260   Christian social and ecclesiastical theology
270   History and geographical treatment of organized
       Christian church (Church history)
280   Denominations and sects of Christian church
290   Other religious and comparative religion

The allotment to Christianity of most of the notation in the 200s can be explained historically and, in many countries, can be justified by literary warrant, i.e., the large body of literature upon the subject. The lesser degree of expansion of the numbers for other religions is owing to (1) the fact that less literature on these religions arrives at the Decimal Classification Division, and (2) there is frequently a lack of agreement within these religions as to their essential structure.

Class here works on religion in general, religion as an intellectual topic.

Class comparative religion and comprehensive works on various specific religions in 291.

See also 100 vs. 200, and 133 vs. 200.

200.9   **Historical and geographical treatment of religion and religious thought**

Class here only works treating religion and religious thought in general.

Class comprehensive works on various specific religions in 291.

204.5   Christian mythology

Class mythology in the Bible at 220.68.

See also 398.2 vs. 291.13.

206   **Organizations of Christianity**

Class here societies dealing very broadly with the Christian religion as a whole.

Class societies for Christian work in 267.

207   **Study and teaching of Christianity**

Class here comprehensive works on the teaching of Christianity; works on the teaching of Christianity in secondary schools, in colleges, universities, and other specific institutions.

Class in 377 works that treat multiple aspects of schools supported by religious groups (including instruction in secular subjects) and that cover all levels or only the elementary level. Also class in 377 general treatment of the role of religious instruction in elementary schools, both sectarian and nonsectarian. Class specific discussion of curriculums and teaching methods for religion in elementary schools at 372.8. Class Christian religious instruction in Sunday schools, church schools, vacation Bible schools, other church auspices in 268; in the home at 649.7.

209   **Historical and geographical treatment of Christianity and Christian thought**
Works classed here must give as much emphasis to informal religious thought as to organized religion.

209.2   **[Biography of persons associated with Christianity and Christian thought]**
Use the following table of precedence for comprehensive biographies:

Jesus Christ, Mary, Joseph, Joachim, Anne, John the Baptist	232.9
Other persons in Bible	220
Founders of denominations	280
Founders of religious orders	271
Higher clergy	
Examples: popes, metropolitans, archbishops, bishops	
Prior to 1054	270–270.3
Subsequent to 1054	280
Theologians	230
Doctrinal theologians	230, 261
Moral theologians	241
Missionaries	266
Evangelists	269.2
Persons noted for participation in associations for religious work	267
Martyrs	272
Heretics	273
Saints	270
Prior to 1054	270–270.3
Subsequent to 1054	280
Mystics	248.22
Hymn writers	264.2

Sunday and Sabbath school teachers and superintendents	268
Members of religious orders	271
Clergymen (*See Higher clergy above*)	
Prior to 1054	270–270.3
Subsequent to 1054	280
Members of early church to 1054	270–270.3
Members of denominations	280
Including members of nondenominational and interdenominational churches	

Certain numbers in the range 210–269 other than those listed in the table of precedence above may be used for comprehensive biographies of persons with specialized religious careers, but are more commonly used for books treating only one aspect of a person's life and work, e.g., 220.0924 for a Biblical scholar.

This number (209.2) is the absolute last resort for Christian biography. Class here only biographies of persons known not to be a member of any church. This number may also be used when it has not been possible to make any determination as to whether there is church membership or not. Prefer a more specific number if at all possible.

Do not use 248.2 Religious experience or its subdivisions except 248.22 for comprehensive biographies, e.g., a biography of Charles W. Colson's religious life 286.1320924, not 248.2460924.

253, 255, and 262 are no longer used for biographies of the kinds of persons listed above in the table of precedence.

Class the comprehensive biography of a Biblical character with the book or books with which he is most closely associated. In many cases this is the historical part of the Bible in which persons' lives are narrated, e.g., Solomon, King of Israel, in 1st Kings 222.530924. His association with 223 Poetic books is weaker. However, some Biblical characters are more closely associated with nonhistorical books. For example, class Isaiah and Timothy with the books that bear their names. They appear briefly in historical narratives, but their lives are not narrated in full there. Class the apostles John, Peter, and Paul at 225.924 since each is associated with a number of books in the New Testament, but class the rest of the original Apostles, associated primarily with Gospels and Acts in 226.092.

Examples:

225.924	(New Testament biography) Paul, Saint, Apostle
230.20924	(Catholic theology) Thomas Aquinas, Saint, 1225?–1274
232.94	(John the Baptist) John the Baptist
266.20924	(Catholic missions) Francisco Xavier, Saint, 1506–1552
269.20924	(Evangelism) Graham, William Franklin (Billy), 1918–
271.125024	(Trappist order in church history) Raymond, Father, 1903– (*See instructions at 271*).
270.2	(Church history, 325–787) Gregory I, the Great, Pope, ca. 540–604
283.0924	(Anglican churches) Cranmer, Thomas, Abp. of Canterbury, 1489–1556
287.0924	(Methodist churches) Wesley, John, 1703–1791

See also 220.9505, 230.042–.044, 232, 253, 262.1, 270.

For non-Christian and comparative religious biographies, see 290.

210 Natural religion

Class here natural theology but not revealed theology. Revealed theology includes any theology based on a divine gift of knowledge to humanity (such as the Bible).

Class revealed theology in 291.2 and related numbers throughout the 200s, e.g., Judaic revealed theology 296.3; philosophical interpretation of any topic in revealed theology with that topic in 230 or 290.

212.1 Existence [of God]

Class proofs of the existence of God in the Christian religion in 231.042, of gods in other religions in 291.211 and cognate numbers in 292–299.

213 Creation

Class relation of scientific and revealed religious viewpoints on creation at 231.765, 291.24, and related numbers in 292–299.

215 **Science and religion**

Class antagonism and reconciliation of science and revealed religion in 261.55–261.56, 291.175, and related numbers in 292–299.

220 Bible

SUMMARY

Be wary of books purporting to treat Biblical theology. Such works, if presenting Biblical statements as the basis of Christian or Judaic theology, are classed in 230–260 or 296.3. However, "Biblical theology" may mean nothing more than an interpretation of the text itself, i.e., what the text means. Such works are classed in 220.6 and cognate numbers in 221–229. The key difference is whether the author adheres to the Biblical text and its meaning, or whether he uses the Biblical text as a springboard to the interpretation of the theological concepts themselves.

220.15   Biblical prophecy and prophecies

Class Judaic messianic and eschatological prophecies at 296.33.,

220.5   **Modern versions and translations [of the Bible]**

Class works containing translations in English and one other modern language with the other language in 220.53–220.59, in two modern languages other than English in 220.53–220.59 with the language coming later in Table 6, in more than two modern languages at 220.51.

220.5209   Private translations [of Bible]

"Private translations" means translations by individuals.

220.6   **Interpretation and criticism (Exegesis) [of Bible]**

Class Christian sermons based on the Bible in 252, material about the Bible intended for Christian preaching in 251; Judaic sermons based on the Bible and material about the Bible intended for Judaic preaching at 296.42. In case of doubt prefer 220.6 to either of these.

See also 242.5.

220.68	Mythological, allegorical, numerical, astronomical interpretations [of Bible]
	Including gematria.
220.9	**Geography, history, chronology, persons of Bible lands in Bible times**
	To be classed here these topics must be treated solely in relation to the Bible. Class these topics as general history in 933. Class a mixture according to the type of treatment that predominates. If in doubt, prefer history.
220.92	Collected persons [of Bible lands in Bible times]
	See 209.2.
220.9505	Bible stories retold
	Class biography in 220.92 or 232.9.
221.44	[Old Testament in Hebrew]
	Including Old Testament texts in Dead Sea Scrolls.
	Class pseudepigrapha in Dead Sea Scrolls at 229.918, comprehensive works on Dead Sea Scrolls at 296.155.
221.92	**Persons [in Old Testament]**
	See 209.2.
222–224	**Specific parts of Old Testament**
	Add as instructed under 222–224 in Edition 19 for portions of books, e.g., interpretation of Genesis 1–2 222.1106.
227.7	Ezra (Esdras 1)
	Class Esdras 1 (also called Esdras 3) of the Apocrypha at 229.1.
222.8	Nehemiah (Esdras 2, Nehemias)
	Class Esdras 2 (also called Esdras 4) of the Apocrypha at 229.1.
225.92	**[Persons in New Testament]**
	See 209.2.
225.9505	[New Testament stories retold]
	Gospel stories predominantly about Jesus, not constituting a biography, are classed in 226.09505.
226–229	**Specific parts of New Testament**
	Add as instructed under 222–224 in Edition 19 for portions of books, e.g., interpretation of Romans 9 227.106.

226   **Gospels and Acts**

Add as instructed under 222–224 in Edition 19 for a work that includes only the synoptic (first three) Gospels.

Class biographies of Jesus in 232.901, of Mary in 232.91, of Joseph in 232.932, of John the Baptist in 232.94.

226.06   **[Interpretation and criticism of Gospels and Acts]**

Class here Q document.

226.09505   [Gospel stories retold]

Class here stories predominantly about Jesus, not constituting a biography.

226.7–.8   **Miracles [and] parables [in Gospels and Acts]**

Class here texts and interpretations of New Testament passages about miracles and parables.

Class miracles and parables in context of Jesus' life in 232.954–232.955.

227   Epistles

Add as instructed under 222–224 in Edition 19 for a work that includes only the Pauline epistles.

229   Apocrypha, pseudepigrapha, intertestamental works

Add as instructed under 222–224 in Edition 19 for a work that includes only the Apocrypha.

229.1   [Apocryphal] Esdras 1 and 2

Also called Esdras 3 and 4.

Class nonapocryphal Esdras 1 at 222.7, nonapocryphal Esdras 2 at 222.8.

229.8–.9   **Pseudo gospels [and] Other pseudepigrapha**

Class here Jewish or Christian Gnostic pseudo gospels and pseudepigrapha, e.g., from Nag Hammadi Papyri; texts and interpretations of agrapha in pseudo gospels and pseudepigrapha.

Class agrapha in context of Jesus' life in 232.98.

230 Christian theology   Christian doctrinal theology

SUMMARY

231 **God**
232 **Jesus Christ and his family   Christology**
233 **Humankind**
234 **Salvation (Soteriology) and grace**
235 **Spiritual beings**
236 **Eschatology**
238 **Creeds, confessions of faith, covenants, catechisms**
239 **Apologetics and polemics**

See 220 for note on Biblical theology.

230.042–.044 Specific types of Christian theology

Class here collected and individual biography of theologians in one theological tradition or theologians important and influential enough to transcend their own denominations, e.g., Karl Barth, 230.0440924. *See also 209.2.*

230.1–.9   Doctrines of specific denominations and sects

Class here theology of several churches in one category, e.g., theology of Calvinistic and Reformed churches in Europe 230.42.

230.16–.2   [Doctrines of Roman Catholic Church, Eastern Orthodox Church, Oriental churches in communion with Rome]

Class here theology of these churches after 1054; for earlier theology use 230.11–230.14.

231.4   Attributes [of God]

Including transcendence of God.

231.73   Miracles

Class miracles of Jesus at 232.955, of Blessed Virgin Mary at 232.917.

232   Jesus and his family   Christology

Class doctrine and theories about Jesus Christ in 232.1–232.8, but class the events of Jesus' life in 232.9, e.g., the doctrine of the Resurrection 232.5, narration of the event of the Resurrection 232.97.

Use s.s. 092 for biography of Christologists (232.092) and Mariologists (232.91092), but not for biography of Jesus, Mary, Joseph, Joachim, Anne, or John the Baptist.

232.1   Incarnation and messiahship of Christ

         Class Immaculate Conception at 232.911.

232.3   Christ as Redeemer

         Class comprehensive works on the doctrine of redemption at 234.3.

232.6   Second Coming of Christ

         Class comprehensive works on the millenium at 236.3.

232.7   Judgment of Christ

         The doctrine that Jesus Christ at some time will pass judgment on men and their deeds.

         Class comprehensive works on the Last Judgment at 236.9.

232.8   Divinity and humanity of Christ

         Note that here "humanity" is used as the complement to "divinity."

         Class the human qualities of Jesus' character in 232.9.

232.901   Life of Jesus

         See 226.09505.

232.91   Mary, mother of Jesus

         See 232.

232.917   Miracles and apparitions [of Mary]

         Class here comprehensive works on shrines, miracles, apparitions.

         Class shrines to Mary in 263.042.

232.921   Nativity

         Including virgin birth.

232.954–.955 Teachings [and] Miracles [of Jesus]

         See 226.7–.8.

232.98   Agrapha

         See 229.8–.9.

234   Salvation (Soteriology) and grace

         Including merit, righteousness, holiness, universal priesthood, perfection of believers.

234.2   Faith and hope

         Class hope in the context of eschatology at 236, hope as a virtue at 241.4.

235.2   Saints

          Class miracles associated with saints in 231.73.

          See also 209.2 for biography of saints.

236   Eschatology

          Including rapture.

236.9   Last judgment

          See 232.7.

240 Christian moral and devotional theology

SUMMARY

      241   **Moral theology**
      242   **Devotional literature**
      243   **Evangelistic writings for individuals**
               and families
      245   **Hymns without music**
      246   **Art in Christianity**
      247   **Church furnishings and related articles**
      248   **Christian experience, practice, life**
      249   **Christian observances in family life**

241   **[Christian] Moral theology**

          See 261.8 vs. 241.

241.6   Specific [Christian] moral issues

          In adding as instructed at 241.6 in Edition 19, do not use 241.698–241.699; class vices and virtues "not otherwise provided for" in 241.3–241.4.

242   **Devotional literature**

          Class here religious poetry explicitly intended for devotional use. If not intended for such use, class religious poetry at 808.819382 and cognate numbers in 809–899. If in doubt, prefer the 800 numbers.

242.5   Prayers and meditations based on passages from Bible

          To be classed here, meditations based on Biblical passages must be intended for devotional use. If intended equally for devotion and study, class in 220.6 and cognate numbers in 221–229. If in doubt, prefer 220.6, 221–229.

242.801–.809 [Collections of prayers] **For specific denominations and sects**

Class here prayers by authors connected with specific denominations if such information is readily available in the work being classified.

246–247 vs. 700   **Art in Christianity** [and] **Church furnishings and related articles vs. The arts**

Class in 246–247 the religious use of art and art objects, their religious significance and symbolism, their purpose in the church service.

Class the creation, description, critical appraisal of such objects as art in 700.

Some discussion of religious use is typically included in a work intended primarily to describe and appraise religious art as art. Such treatment does not call for classing the work in 246–247. Class works treating religious and artistic aspects equally in 700. If in doubt, prefer 700.

248   **Christian experience, practice, life**

Except for biographies of persons chiefly noted as mystics (248.22092), do not class here comprehensive religious biographies.

248.48   **Guides to Christian life for specific denominations and sects**

Class here guides by authors connected with specific denominations if the information required is readily available in the work being classified.

250 Local Christian church and Christian religious orders

SUMMARY

251   Preaching (Homiletics)

See 220.6.

252   **Texts of sermons**

Class here sermons based on Biblical passages.

253   **Secular clergymen and pastoral duties (Pastoral theology)**

Class here works treating clergy and laity in relation to the work of the church at the local level.

Class works treating local clergy and laity in relation to the government, organization, and nature of the church as a whole in 262.1; role of clergy in religious training and instruction in 268; ordination of women at 262.14 (unless the work treats ordination of women only in relation to its effect on the local parish, in which case it is classed at 253.2).

Class biographies of clergymen in the period prior to 1054 in 270.1–270.3, in the period subsequent to 1054 in 280.

253.7   **Evangelistic methods**

Class here only evangelistic methods used in the context of the local church.

See also 269.2.

254   **Parish government and administration**

Class administration of the church at other than parish level in 260, of religious orders in 255. Use s.s. 068 if not redundant, e.g., financial administration of the Anglican church 262.030681, of the Jesuit order 255.5300681.

255   **Religious congregations and orders**

Class biography of members of religious orders in 271.

See also 254.

255.01–.09   **Specific kinds [of religious congregations and orders]**

Class here groups of orders of a particular kind, not single orders.

Class single orders in 255.1–255.9.

255.79   Other [Roman Catholic orders of men]

Including Knights Templar.

255.901–.909 **Specific kinds [of congregations and orders of women]**

Class here groups of orders of a particular kind, not single orders.

Class single orders in 255.91–255.98.

260 Christian social and ecclesiastical theology

SUMMARY

261   Social theology and interreligious relations and attitudes

Social theology is the study from the Christian viewpoint of the topics listed in the subdivisions of 261. Studies of the church and religion in relation to these topics treated from a frame of reference outside of a religious context is classed with the subject, e.g., church and state from the standpoint of political science 322.1.

It should be noted that Christianity and Christian church includes also those Christians not formally affiliated with organized bodies.

261.1   Role of Christian church in society

It should be emphasized that works classed here deal with the church's view of its own role, and how well it performs that role. Evaluations of the church's role in society from an outside viewpoint are classed with the discipline, e.g., sociology of religious institutions 306.6.

Class works on the role of the church with relation to specific topics in 261.2–261.8 with the subject, e.g., the church's role in international affairs 261.87. Class works on the relation of the church to topics not listed in 261.2–261.8 at 261, not 261.1.

261.5   **Christianity and secular disciplines**

Class here personal Christian views and church teachings about the discipline as a whole and its value, how seriously the Christian should take it, how far it should affect his faith. However, class Christian philosophy of a discipline or Christian theories within a discipline with the discipline, e.g., Christian philosophy of the arts 700.1. If in doubt, class with the secular discipline.

Class here works treating generally antagonism between and reconciliation of Christian belief and another discipline. Class antagonism of a specific Christian doctrine and another discipline with the doctrine in 231–239. For example, class relation between Christian doctrines in general and science at 261.55; but class relation between Christian doctrine on the soul and modern biology at 233.5.

261.7   **Christianity and political affairs**

Including civil war and revolution.

See also 322.1 vs. 261.7.

261.8   **Christianity and socioeconomic problems**

Class here comprehensive works on the Christian view of socioeconomic and political affairs.

Class Christianity and political affairs in 261.7.

261.8 vs. 241 **Christianity and socioeconomic problems vs. [Christian] Moral theology**

Note that some topics are covered in both moral and social theology, e.g., family relationships (241.63, 261.83587). Class in 241 works that focus on what conduct is right or wrong. Works classed in 261.8 may discuss right and wrong but in a broader context. They treat the topic as a problem in society and discuss Christian attitudes toward and influence on the problem. Class in 241 works that emphasize what the individual should do; class in 261.8 works that stress what the church's stance should be, or the church's view on problems transcending individual conduct. If in doubt, prefer 241.

262   **Ecclesiology**

See 254.

262.0011   Ecumenicalism

Class ecumenical movement in general church history, World Council of Churches at 270.82; history of relations among specific denominations at 280.042.

262.1 **Governing leaders of churches**

Class here the office of the leader and its role in church government and organization.

Class biography of bishops, archbishops, popes, patriarchs, metropolitans, local clergymen, and lay leaders before 1054 in 270.1–270.3, after 1054 in 280.

262.136 [Papal] Administration

Do not use s.s. 068 alone here, since the heading already specifies administration; however, s.s. 0681–0688 may be added for particular aspects of administration.

262.5 General councils

Class interdenominational councils at 262.0011.

262.91 Acts of the Holy See

Class nonbinding opinions of the Pope with the subject in religion, e.g., on the economic order 261.85.

263.042 **Holy places**

Class here shrines.

Class works treating holy places and miracles associated with them at 231.73, miracles of Mary and holy places associated with them at 232.917, miracles of Jesus and holy places associated with them at 232.955.

263.4 Sunday observance

Including works about labor or amusement on Sunday.

264.023 Texts of missals

Including sacramentaries.

264.1–.6 **[Specific elements of public worship]**

Class these specific topics when part of the Mass at 264.36, e.g., Eucharistic prayers.

264.1 Prayer

Class comprehensive works on public and private prayer at 248.32.

264.13 Texts of prayers

Class comprehensive collections of public and private prayers in 242.8.

264.36 Eucharist, Holy Communion, Lord's Supper, Mass

Including specific topics listed at 264.1–264.6 when part of the Mass, e.g., Eucharistic prayers. As part of the Mass these would not be classed in 264.1 Prayer.

266   **Missions**

Typically medical missions perform two functions: propagation of the faith and the provision of health services. Class here works that emphasize evangelization.

Class comprehensive works on medical missions in 362.1–362.4, on medical missionaries in 610.695.

See also 209.2, 253.7.

266.001   [Theory and philosophy of missions]

Including missiology.

267   **Associations for religious work**

See 209.2.

268   **Religious training and instruction**

See 207, 209.2.

269.2   Evangelism

Class here comprehensive works on evangelism.

Class witness bearing by individual lay Christians at 248.5, sermons for evangelistic meetings at 252.3, missionary evangelism in 266.

See also 209.2.

270 Historical and geographical treatment of organized Christian church (Church history)

SUMMARY

Use the following table of precedence for history of Christianity and Christian church (except for biography):

Specific topics	220–269
Persecutions in general church history	272
Doctrinal controversies and heresies in general church history	273
Religious congregations and orders in church history	271
Denominations and sects of Christian church. (Use 281.1–281.4 only for number building. *See 281.1–.4.*)	280, 281.5–289
Treatment of Christian church by continent, country, locality	274–279
General historical and geographical treatment of Christian church	270
Historical and geographical treatment of Christianity and Christian thought	209

For example, class Jesuit missions in India at 266.254, persecution of Jesuits by Elizabeth I and Anglicans at 272.7, Protestantism in France at 280.40944, the charismatic movement among Anglicans at 283.

For biography, see 209.2.

270.1–.3 [**Apostolic Church**]

Class here history of the Christian church prior to 1054.

See also 209.2.

270.4–.8 [Later periods of church history]

History of the Christian church as a whole subsequent to 1054.

Class history of specific denominations and sects in 280.

270.82 [**Historical and geographical treatment of Christian church in**] **20th century, 1900–**

Class theoretical works about ecumenicalism at 262.0011, pentecostal or charismatic movement within a specific denomination in 280, relations between denominations at 280.042.

271 **Religious congregations and orders in church history**

When using the add note for biography, add 22 or 24 from Table 2 to the 0, not s.s. 0922 or s.s. 0924, e.g., a biography of a Franciscan 271.3024, not 271.30924.

Another peculiarity of the add note at this number should be taken into consideration. Following the first clause (directing the addition to 271 of the numbers following 255) is a second clause directing the addition of 0 plus "Areas" notations 1–9 from Table 2. At 255, from which the digits to be added in the first clause are taken, there are also instructions for further addition. In this case the instructions at 255 are to be ignored, and the directions for further addition at 271 are to be used instead.

280 Denominations and sects of Christian church

SUMMARY

281 **Primitive and Oriental churches**
282 **Roman Catholic Church**
283 **Anglican churches**
284 **Protestant denominations of Continental origin and related bodies**
285 **Presbyterian, American Reformed, Congregational churches**
286 **Baptist, Disciples of Christ, Adventist churches**
287 **Methodist churches**
288 **Unitarianism**
289 **Other denominations and sects**

The kinds of biographies to be classed here are shown in the table of precedence for biographies under 209.2. Be as specific as possible in the assignment of the denominational number. However, biographies of religious figures frequently do not give exact information as to sect and branch. For instance, if it cannot be determined readily from the work itself or from common reference works whether the biographee is a Wesleyan Methodist or a United Methodist, class the work in 287. Similarly, if the denomination cannot be determined, but it is evident that the subject of the work is protestant, use 280.4. If all else fails, use 280 without subdivision. *See also 209.2.*

Class histories of specific denominations and sects subsequent to 1054 in 281.5–289 even if they contain some material on the period prior to 1054. *See also 270, 281.1–.4, and 289.9.*

280.042   Relations between denominations

Class here comprehensive works on relations between denominations.

Class relations between any two denominations or sects with the denomination or sect coming first in the schedules, e.g., relations between Roman Catholics and Lutherans 282, not 284.1. The same principle holds true for relations between branches of any one denomination or sect, e.g., relations between Freewill Baptists and Seventh-Day Baptists 286.2, not 286.3.

Class relations involving more than two denominations or sects (or branches thereof) as follows:

If one denomination is stressed (i.e., the relations of X with Y and Z), class with the denomination stressed, e.g., the relations of Anglicans with Roman Catholics and Presbyterians 283, not 282 or 285.

If there is no emphasis, and all are branches of one denomination, class with the denomination or sect, e.g., relations among Freewill Baptists, Seventh-Day Baptists, and Old School Baptists 286. If all are protestant, e.g., relations among Anglicans, Lutherans, Presbyterians, class at 280.4. If all are catholic, e.g., Roman Catholic, Eastern Orthodox, Nestorian churches, class at 280.2. If both protestant and catholic, e.g., Roman Catholic, Anglican, and Lutheran, class at 280.042.

Class theoretical works on ecumenicalism at 262.0011; discussions among denominations with respect to a specific subject with the subject, e.g., the Eucharist 264.36.

280.4   Protestantism

Including dissenters, nonconformists (British context).

281.1–.4   Early church

These numbers are not to be used directly. They are to be used only for number building.

Class history of Christian church prior to 1054 in 270–270.3.

281.5   Oriental churches

Including Catholics of the Byzantine rite.

282   **Roman Catholic Church**

Class here Catholic Traditionalist Movement.

283.3   Specific branches [of the Anglican Church]

Including the Church of South India.

284.8   Modern schisms in Roman Catholic Church

           Including Philippine Independent Church.

285.23   Specific denominations [of Presbyterian churches of British Commonwealth origin]

           Including Welsh Calvinistic Methodist Church (Presbyterian Church of Wales).

287.83   Specific denominations [of Black Methodist churches in United States]

           Local or branch churches of these denominations are sometimes located outside the United States. Class works about them at 287 without subdivision.

289.73   Specific branches [of Mennonite churches]

           Another example: Bruderhof Communities.

289.9   [Other denominations and sects of Christian church]

           Including Dukhobors, Evangelical Congregational Church, Evangelical Free Church of America, Messianic Judaism, Peoples Temple, Plymouth Brethren, Unification Church.

           Class nondenominational and interdenominational churches in 280 without subdivision or at 280.2 or 280.4 if limited to either catholic or protestant persuasions.

290 Other religions and comparative religion

SUMMARY

       291   **Comparative religion**
       292   **Classical (Greek and Roman) religion**
       293   **Germanic religion**
       294   **Religions of Indic origin**
       295   **Zoroastrianism (Mazdaism, Parseeism)**
       296   **Judaism**
       297   **Islam and religions derived from it**
       299   **Other religions**

290   Other religions and comparative religion

           290 by itself will never be used, since 291 has been designated as the number for comprehensive works on the non-Christian religions. (*See 292–299, second note, in Edition 19.*) 291 is also the comprehensive works number for Christian and non-Christian religions and the number for comparative religion.

291   **Comparative religion**

The subdivisions of the various religions in 292–299 are based on the subdivisions of 291. The order is sometimes different, but all topics in 291 are provided for either explicitly, by synthesis, or by implication under the separate religions included in 292–299. What is said here, therefore, will also be true of 292–299.

A comparison of the topics in 291 with the subdivisions of the Christian religion can sometimes be helpful in determining what goes where. A comparative list follows:

Social theologies	291.17...261
Doctrinal theologies	291.2.....230
Worship	291.3.....246–247, 263–265
Religious experience, life, practice	291.4.....242, 245, 248
Moral theology	291.5.....241
Leaders and organization	291.6.....250, 262, 267
Various religious activities	291.7.....266, 268
Sources	291.8.....220
Denominations, sects, reform movements	291.9.....280

For example, 291.211 (Gods, goddesses, other divinities and deities) includes those topics listed at 231 (God) which are not limited to the Christian religion: ways of knowing God, general concepts of God, attributes, providence, love and wisdom, relation to human experience, justice, and goodness.

Treat the early history of a specific religion before its division into sects as general history of the religion, but class a comprehensive survey of the various sects into which a religion may have divided in numbers analogous to 291.9. A work dealing with both early history and sects is, of course, classed in the general number for history of the religion.

Class the history of a specific congregation in the number for the sect to which it belongs, if this can be determined readily. (Congregation here refers to organizations in other religions analogous to the local church in Christianity, e.g., synagogues, mosques.) If the sect cannot be determined, class the work in numbers analogous to 291.9. In such a case do not add standard subdivisions.

Class religious orders at 291.65 and cognate numbers in 292–299, and not with any specific sect within the religion to which they may belong.

Biography

The following table of precedence applies to comprehensive biography only. Works dealing with only one specialized aspect of a person's career are classed with the aspect, e.g., Muhammad as a moral theologian 297.5, not 297.63. General discussions of the nature, role, and function of the various types of figures listed in 291.6 follow the order specified in the table of precedence under 291.61–291.64 in Edition 19.

Founders of religions	291.63
Founders of sects	291.9
Founders of religious orders	291.65
Religious leaders	
General	291.092
Sects	291.9
Theologians	291.64
Doctrinal theologians	291.2
Moral theologians	291.5
Missionaries	291.7
Martyrs, heretics, saints	
General	291.092
Sects	291.9
Teachers	291.7
Members of religious orders	291.65
Clergy	291.9
Members of sects and movements	291.9

Do not use s.s. 092 with numbers from 291.6 and its subdivisions.

291.13   Mythology and mythological foundations [of religions]

    See 398.2 vs. 291.13.

291.22   Humankind

    Creation of human beings only.

    Class creation in general at 291.24.

291.38   Rites and ceremonies

    Class offerings, sacrifices, penances at 291.34.

291.61–.65   **[Leaders of religious bodies]**

    Class here both concept and role of the leader but not necessarily biography. *See also 291: Biography.*

291.8 **Sources [of religious doctrine and practice]**

Class theology based on sacred scriptures with theology in 291.2 Doctrines, 291.17 social theology, 291.5 Moral theology. *See also 220.*

292–299 **Specific religions**

For each religion consult the general principles discussed at 291.

292–293 **Classical (Greek and Roman) religion [and] Germanic religion**

Class modern revivals of dead religions at 299 without subdivision.

See also instructions under 291.

292.13 [Classical mythology]

See 398.2 vs. 291.13.

293.13 [Teutonic mythology]

See 398.2 vs. 291.13.

294.3 **Buddhism**

See instructions under 291.

294.3421 [Objects of worship and veneration in Buddhism]

Including the concept Buddha.

Class biography of Gautama Buddha at 294.363.

294.3423 **[Eschatology in Buddhism]**

Class here karma.

294.35 Moral theology [in Buddhism]

Class karma in 294.3423.

294.363 [Divinely inspired persons in Buddhism]

See 294.3421.

294.382 Sacred books and scriptures (Tripitaka) [in Buddhism]

Class here Pali Tripitaka and other Hinayanist sacred texts that are also considered sacred by Mahayanist Buddhists. Most of them are accepted by both groups. Class here also works containing both Hinayanist and Mahayanist sacred texts, e.g., Chinese Tripitaka, Tibetan Kanjur and Tanjur.

Class Mahayanist sacred works at 294.385. The Hinayanists do not consider these sacred.

Note that Tipitika is a variant spelling form widely used.

294.3822 Vinayapitaka
    See 294.382.

294.3823 Suttapitaka
    Also spelled Sutrapitaka.
    See also 294.382.

294.3824 Abhidhammapitaka
    Also spelled Abhidharmapitaka.
    See also 294.382.

294.385 Sources of branches, sects, reform movements [in Buddhism]
    See 294.382.

294.391 Hinayana (Southern, Theravada) Buddhism
    Including Mahasamghika, Sarvastivada (Vaibhasika), Sautrantika schools.

294.392 Mahayana (Northern) Buddhism
    Including Madhyamika, Yogacara (Vijnanavada) schools.

294.3927 Zen
    Including Soto.

294.4   **Jainism**
    See instructions under 291.

294.5   **Hinduism**
    See instructions under 291.

294.523   **[Eschatology in Hinduism]**
    Class here karma.

294.543 [Worship in Hinduism]
    Including kundalini yoga, bhakti yoga, Narada's Bhakti Sutras.

294.548   **Moral theology [in Hinduism]**
    Class karma in 294.523.

294.55 [Hindu] Sects and reform movements
    Including Lingayats.

294.5512 Vishnuism
    Including Haridasas.
    Also spelled Vaisnavism, Vaishnavism.

294.5513	Shivaism
	Also spelled Saivism, Shaivism.
294.59	Sources [of Hinduism]
	Class Narada's Bhakti Sutras at 294.543.
294.592	**Sacred books and scriptures**
	Class at 294.595 works considered sacred by only a few sects.
294.5926	Dharmasastras
	Including Laws of Manu (Manusmrti).
294.6	**Sikhism**
	See instructions under 291.
294.682	[Sacred books and scriptures]
	Including Adi Granth (Guru Granth), Japji (Japuji).
295	**Zoroastrianism (Mazdaism, Parseeism)**
	See instructions under 291.
295.82	[Sacred books and scriptures]
	Including Avesta (Zend Avesta), Gathas.
296	**Judaism**
	See instructions under 291.
296.123	Mishnah
	Including Aboth (Avot or Pirke Abot).
296.142	**Haggadah**
	Class Passover Haggadah at 296.437.
296.16	Cabalistic literature
	Class here texts of the Zohar or other religious cabalistic literature even if the editor introduces and annotates it from an occult or Christian point of view; works that treat cabala in the context of the Jewish faith. Class Christian cabalism in 230–280, e.g., a work deriving Christian doctrines by cabalistic means 230. Class in 135.4 works that treat cabala as a source of occult knowledge without emphasizing its religious significance.
296.18	Halakah (Legal literature)
	Class Judaic law relating only to secular matters in 340.

296.19	Haggadah (Nonlegal literature)
	Class Passover Haggadah at 296.437, Midrashic Haggadah in 296.142.
296.3	**Doctrinal, moral, social theology [of Judaism]**
	Class here the Thirteen Articles of Faith.
	See also 220 for note on Biblical theology.
296.33	Eschatology
	Including Judaic messianic and eschatological prophecies.
296.4	Traditions, rites, public services
	Including rites of ancient Israel, e.g., sacrifice.
296.42	Sermons and homiletics
	See 220.6.
296.43	Festivals, holy days, fasts
	Including Sabbatical year, Jubilee.
296.437	Pesach (Passover)
	Including Passover Haggadah.
296.44	Rites and customs for specific occasions
	Including synagogue dedication.
296.65	Synagogues and congregations
	Class here the concept, principles, role of the synagogue.
	Class history of a specific synagogue with its sect in 296.8.
296.67	**Organization and organizations**
	Class here both theory and history for organizations other than synagogues and congregations; class these in 296.65.
296.71	Religious experience
	Class medieval mystical Judaism at 296.82, modern mystical Judaism at 296.833.
296.82	Medieval [sects and movements]
	Including medieval mysticism.
296.83	Modern [sects and movements]
	Including Musar movement.
297	**Islam and religions derived from it**
	See discussion under 291.

297.1228   Special subjects treated in Koran

Nonreligous subjects.

Class a religious subject treated in the Koran with the topic, e.g., Islamic theology 297.2.

297.4   **Islamic religious experience, life, practice**

Class here biography of Sufis, using s.s. 092.

Class specific aspects of Sufism in 297.1–297.7.

297.6   Islamic leaders and organization

Including ulama.

297.61   Functionaries

Class doctrines about the imamat at 297.24.

Standard subdivision 092 may be used for works that treat either muezzins or imams separately.

297.65   [Islamic] Organization and organizations

Class here the caliphate in relation to the organization of Islam, historical and biographical works about caliphates if they emphasize the religious role. Class doctrines about the caliphate at 297.24, historical aspects in 900.

297.8   Islamic sects and other religions derived from Islam

Including Khojas.

297.89   **Bahai faith**

See discussion under 291.

299   **Other religions**

Including religions not otherwise provided for.

If a religion not named in the schedule claims to be Christian, class it at 289.9 even if it is unorthodox or syncretistic.

Class in 291 syncretistic religious writings of individuals expressing personal views and not claiming to establish a new religion or to represent an old one.

299.1–.9   [Other specific religions]

Class modern revivals of dead religions listed here at 299 without subdivision.

299.512   **Confucianism**

See discussion under 291.

299.514   **Taoism**

     See discussion under 291.

299.54   Tibetan [religions]

     Class here Bon (a native, pre-Buddhist religion). Class Lamaism (Tibetan Buddhism) at 294.3923.

299.561   Shintoism

     Class here state Shinto.

     Class Shinto sects, e.g., Tenrikyo and Konkyo, at 299.5619.

     See also discussion under 291.

299.5619   [Sects and reform movements]

     See 299.561.

299.6   **[Religions] Of Black African and Negro origin**

     See discussion under 291.

299.67   Various specific cults [of religions of Black African and Negro origin]

     Class here Ras Tafari movement.

     Class voodooism focusing on witchcraft practices without regard to their religious significance in 133.4.

299.7   **[Religions] Of North American native origin**

     See discussion under 291.

299.92   [Religions] Of other ethnic origin

     Including religions originating with ethnic groups listed under 99 in Table 5 of Edition 19.

299.93   [Religions] Of miscellaneous origin

     Including Great White Brotherhood.

299.932   Gnosticism

     Class here comprehensive works on Gnosticism.

     Class Gnostic pseudo gospels or Biblical pseudepigrapha in 229, e.g., Gospel of Thomas 229.8; Gnostic Christian or Jewish texts with topic in Christianity or Judaism, e.g., Gnostic Christian theology 230.99. Consider a Gnostic text to be Christian or Jewish if it claims to be so or scholars consider it to be so. If in doubt, prefer 299.932.

     Class Gnosticism in 273.1 and Manicheism at 273.2 when these are treated as Christian heresies.

300 Social sciences

SUMMARY

301 Sociology
310 Statistics
320 Political science (Politics and government)
330 Economics
340 Law
350 Public administration   Executive branch of
     government   Military art and science
360 Social problems and services; association
370 Education
380 Commerce, communications, transportation
390 Customs, etiquette, folklore

The social sciences deal with the basic human structures and activities that enable people to live together and to produce the necessities and amenities of existence. They cover virtually every aspect of human activity except the technological and artistic. Even language 400 is sometimes considered to be a social science. Most of the social sciences are found in 300–399, but one of the most important, history, is found in 900 (considered by some to belong to the humanities). They are fluid and ever changing, the boundaries between one discipline and another are overlapping and far from clear. Without a doubt, the social sciences constitute the most difficult area in which to classify.

Sociology 301–307 is the study of the processes, interactions, groups, and institutions that give form and purpose to every society. Part of the subject matter of sociology is found in 390 Customs, etiquette, folklore.

Much of the raw data for the study of human society is found in 310 Statistics.

In order to maintain internal peace and safety from external threat, societies devise political processes and institutions such as the state and the government. These are dealt with in 320 Political science and in 350–354, which deal with the executive branch of government and public administration. The military arm of government is found in 355–359.

The production, distribution, and consumption of the goods and services needed to maintain society are dealt with in 330 Economics. Part of this discipline is also found in 380–382, that part which deals with commerce and trade. Also found in the 380s are two of the major auxiliaries to commerce, communication 383–384 and transportation 385–388.

Law 340 treats the codified social, political, and economic rules that society requires and by which its members agree to live.

No social structure, however good, is perfect, and social problems are inevitable. The nature of these problems, taken together with the services society performs to overcome them, are dealt with in the 360s.

Education 370 is the science and art through which society attempts to socialize the young and to prepare them for a useful role in the life of the society.

300 vs. 600   **Social sciences vs. Technology**

Many topics can be discussed from either a technological or a social point of view. Determining which point of view a work takes is sometimes difficult.

If a work discusses how to make, operate, maintain, or repair something, it is usually classed in technology. If, on the other hand, it discusses the social implications of a technological operation, it falls in the social sciences, e.g., the economic importance of lumbering 338.174982, not 634.982.

Class social utilization, social control, and the social effect of technology in 300. The distinction between social science and technology is especially difficult for works emphasizing the interface between technology and its use or control, works that fall somewhere along the continuum from technology at one end to social science at the other. This is particularly true of regulatory control (*see 363.1 Public safety programs and 363.7 Environmental problems and services*) and popular works (*see 385–388 Specific kinds of transportation*).

The following criteria will be useful in determining that material should be classed in 300 rather than in 600:

(1) When the emphasis is on social use rather than on operating or further processing, e.g., tea drinking in England 394.12, not 641.33720942 or 641.63720942.

(2) When the emphasis is on the overall perspective, e.g., the shift from coal to oil in American industry 333.82130973, not 621.4023.

(3) When the emphasis is on social control as opposed to the control exercised during the manufacturing process, e.g., standards of drug quality imposed by a government agency or a trade association 363.1946, not 615.19.

(4) When the raw statistics are cited, e.g., crop production, acreage, fertilizer use, farm size 338.1, not 631.

Technical reports

Many technical reports and research reports actually emphasize procedural technicalities and may refer to economic, legal, administrative, or regulatory complexities and should, therefore, be classed in the social sciences. In determining the classification of a report series, and of individual reports in a series, consider the mission of the agency authorizing the reports and the purpose of the writer. If the emphasis is on the exercise of social control over a process, the report is classed in 300, not with the process in technology which is being controlled. For example, water quality monitoring systems are more likely to be at 363.739463 than at 628.161. *See also notes on control of technology under 363, on safety regulations under 363.1, on water reports under 363.61.*

It cannot be stressed too strongly that many or most of the social sciences are involved in technological processes but are quite distinct from them. The classifier must go behind the technological vocabulary that often dominates title pages and tables of contents and analyze what is being described. A book on trains is not classed in 625.2 if it describes how railroads serve Argentina, but at 385.0982; and a report on fertilizer and rice is not classed at 633.18891 if it is studying production efficiency in developing countries, but at 338.162.

Interdisciplinary works

Generally speaking, the 300 number is the interdisciplinary number for a phenomenon of social significance; it is used as the place of last resort for general works on a subject lacking disciplinary focus, e.g., a work on industrial archaeology not emphasizing how things were made 338.47609 rather than 609. However, works that emphasize descriptions of products or structures, such as clocks, locomotives, windmills, are classed in technology.

Biography and company history

Works on artisans, engineers, and inventors are normally classed in technology. Works on artisans, engineers, and inventors who are of more interest as entrepreneurs are classed in 338.7, e.g., Henry Ford 338.762920924.

Many works on products concentrate on the products of specific companies, e.g., Seth Thomas clocks or Ferrari automobiles. So long as these works emphasize the description and design of the products, class them in technology (or art [700] if the interest is artistic). But as soon as the organization or history of the company receives significant attention, class in 338.7, e.g., Seth Thomas clocks 681.113097461, but the Seth Thomas Clock Company and its clocks 338.7681113097461.

301–307   Sociology [Expansion published February 1982]

Sociology is the description and analysis of social phenomena, i.e., of group behavior. Even if the social phenomena being studied take place in a special context, e.g., in a political or economic institution, the work is classed in 301–307. For instance, a descriptive work on the family patterns of members of the executive branch of government is classed at 306.87; on the social role of political institutions in Korea at 306.209519; on the use of power among committee chairmen of a national legislature at 306.23.

The description and analysis of the group behavior that occurs in a specific place is classed with the specific social behavior, if any, plus notation for any nondominant group rather than in the number for the place, e.g., patterns of mate selection among Jews in Los Angeles 306.82089924079494.

Sociology and anthropology

Sociology and anthropology cover much of the same territory and are classed in the same numbers. General works on anthropology are classed in 301. Different branches of anthropology are classed as follows: Physical anthropology is concerned with the biological aspects of being human and is classed in 573. Cultural and social anthropology deal with culture and institutions and are classed in 306. Criminal anthropology is classed in 364.2.

Structure of 301–307

All societies are composed of an environment that affects their development (304), of social processes that must be maintained so the society can continue to exist (303), of social groupings of persons that in one configuration or another carry on the processes that make society possible (305), of culture and institutions that are the framework (roles, functions, patterns) within which the groups carry on the processes (306), and of communities (307).

302 Social interaction contains basic forms of behavior between individuals in groups and between groups; these forms are basic to all other forms of social behavior.

Comprehensive works on all aspects of society are classed in 301.

Citation order

Unless otherwise instructed, e.g., at 305, when more than one topic is involved, class a work with the topic coming later in the schedule, e.g., the role of communication in economic institutions 306.3, not 302.2; the role of mass media in socializing Cuban immigrants 305.8687291, not 303.32 or 302.234. However, class the effect of one element upon another with the element affected, e.g., the effect of religious opinions on birth control practices among upper-class white women 304.66, not 305.4, 305.52, 305.8034, 303.38, or any number in the 200s; the effect of school desegregation patterns on housing patterns in three Eastern U.S. cities 307.336, not 370.19342 (there is a note to 370.19 from 306.4), and not 305.896073; effect of television violence on children 305.23, not 302.2345 or 302.24.

301–306 vs. 361–365   [Sociology] vs. Social problems and services

To be classed in 301–306 works on social phenomena must deal exclusively, or almost exclusively, with the phenomenon in its pure state, i.e., its social background, its role in the social structure, its effects on society, its innate characteristics and inner structure.

Consideration of social pathology apart from remedial measures is often found in 301–306, although social pathology is more likely to be found in the 361–365 span. The family as a social phenomenon is classed in 306.85. The dissolution of the family can be classed in either 306.88 or 362.82 depending on the focus of the work. A work discussing the effect of the changing social role of women in bringing about family dissolution is classed at 306.88. Once this topic begins to be considered as a problem about which something should be done, the work is classed in 362.82, e.g., what should be done to prevent family dissolution 362.827. The case for a 361–365 number is even stronger when remedial measures are considered, e.g., counseling services for families in trouble 362.8286.

It is even possible to find remedial measures discussed purely as social phenomena. Birth control, for example, can be discussed in terms of its prevalence in various social strata, in terms of its actual effect on population growth, in terms of public attitudes toward it. Such a discussion is classed at 304.66. However, the use of birth control as a social remedy is classed at 363.96. A work on remedial measures, of course, is even more likely to be found in applied than in pure sociology.

If in doubt, prefer 361–365. This means, of course, that 361–365 will be much more heavily used than 301–306. Many topics classed in 301 in Edition 18 and previous editions will now be classed in 361–365.

It should be noted that the above does not apply to criminology. Here both pure and applied sociology are to be classed in 364 as indicated by the note at 364.2 in Edition 19, "Class here criminal anthropology."

301.019   [Psychological principles of sociology]

Class social psychology in 302.

301.09   [Historical and geographical treatment of sociology]

Class here regional sociology.

302 vs. 150   [Social psychology] vs. Psychology

See discussion at 150 vs. 302–307.

302.24   Content [of communication]

Including censorship.

Class persuasion from the psychological standpoint at 153.852.

303.4   Social change

Class forecasting in 003.2; the effect of one aspect of change on another with the aspect being affected, e.g., social change brought about by change in climate 303.485, but the effect of human activities in changing the climate 304.25.

303.482   Contact between cultures

Class intercultural education in 370.196.

303.484   Purposefully induced change

Reform movements here are considered as a social phenomenon.

Class the political aspects of reform movements at 322.44, the role of reform movements in relation to a social problem in 361–365.

303.6 **Conflict**

Conflict as a social phenomenon.

Class the history of major conflicts in 900, e.g., the Miami race riot of 1980 975.9381063.

Class political aspects of conflicts in 320.

See also 322.4, 322.42.

304.2 **Human ecology**

The effect of natural factors on the social order in general, e.g., the role of such things as mountains, plains, tropical climate, prevailing winds, prevalence of volcanoes in shaping social activity, order, structure.

Class environmental policy at 363.70525.

304.28 Human activity [in relation to ecology]

Planning to combat pollution is classed with the problem at 363.73525.

304.6 **Population (Demography)**

Class statistics of population in 312.

304.66 Population control

Class programs and discussions of social policy at 363.96; personal practices and techniques of birth control in 613.94.

305 **Social stratification (Social structure)**

Social structure treats the division of society by kinds of people according to their age, sex, religion, language, race, or by any other characteristic that forms a definable grouping.

Frequently it will prove difficult to distinguish between a description of the social life of a group and a discussion of the institution of which the group is inextricably a part, e.g., slaves as a social grouping 305.567, slavery as an economic institution 306.362; soldiers as a social grouping 305.9355, military institutions 306.27. When related groups and institutions are discussed equally in a work, class the work in 306. If in doubt, prefer 306.

305.3 Men and women

Class relations between the sexes and within the sexes in 306.7–306.8, the relation of a specific sex to a specific subject with the subject, using s.s. 088041–088042, e.g., women in U.S. history 973.088042.

305.42 |Social role and status of women|

> Class here feminism as a social phenomenon. Class programs and policies to promote the welfare of women in 362.83.

305.43 |Occupations of women|

> Class here works that treat the sociological aspects of women's relation to labor, e.g., how work has affected the position and role of women in society, how jobs are changing so that women are being affected, how women regard work, and social views of women's occupations.

> Class economic aspects of the relation of women to labor in 331.4.

305.569   The impoverished

> Class problems of and services to the poor in 362.5.

305.8   **Racial, ethnic, national groups**

> Class here racial, ethnic, national groups only to illustrate their social behavior and the history of the behavior. Class works treating the history and civilization of such groups in 900, e.g., a history of the Australian aborigines 994.0049915, a history of their social behavior 306.0899915.

306   **Culture and institutions**

> The structural elements here are the functions performed rather than the kind of people involved; it is the framework within which the members of the various groups act.

> In the expansion of 301–307, 306.09 Historical and geographical treatment of culture and institutions was reinstated. This number is used for the anthropological and sociological works that deal with the social mechanics and social causation of the cultural and social life in a specific place. However, class the history of a particular group and its civilization in 909 or 930–990 when it is focusing on the social history of the place or the work is considered to be a contribution to the social history of the place. Thus ethnographic works can be classed in either 305–306 or 909, 930–990, depending upon the focus of the author, his field of study, and his intended audience. When in doubt, prefer 900.

The following table explains the distribution of works on social groups:

General anthropology	301
Physical anthropology	573
Criminal anthropology	364
Cultural and social anthropology	306
Cultural ethnology (culture of races in general)	306
Physical ethnology (physical characteristics of races)	572
Ethnography (cultural and social anthropology of specific groups)	
As a part of the general society of a place	305
Not as part of the general society of a place	306.089
Historical ethnography	909, 930–990
Civilization of any group	909, 930–990
Social conditions of a group	909, 930–990, 305

306.1   Subcultures

Including the drug culture: a subculture that shares the belief that the use of drugs is legitimate, a norm not approved by the dominant culture. Any emphasis on the problems the drug culture causes the larger society points to the use of 362.293, social problems and services connected with addiction.

306.3   Economic institutions

Class sociology of housing in 307.336.

306.6   Religious institutions

These must be treated from a secular, nonreligious viewpoint.

306.7   **Institutions pertaining to relations of the sexes**

Class here the sexual behavior and habits of a specific group, using s.s. 088, e.g., sexual behavior of adolescents 306.7088055.

Class sexual ethics in 176, problems and controversies concerning various relations in 363.4, sex offenses in 364.153, sexual customs at 392.6, sex hygiene in 613.95, manuals on sexual techniques at 613.96, sex practices viewed as treatable disorders in 616.8583.

306.74   Sexual services (Prostitution)

Class prostitution as an occupation at 331.76130674, as a social problem in 363.44, as a trade at 380.14530674; biographies of prostitutes, madams, and pimps in 306.74092.

306.85   The family

Class the psychology of family influences at 155.924. If in doubt regarding a work dealing with both the psychology of family influences and the patterns of family relationships, prefer 306.85.

307   Sociology of communities

This section is a combination of sociology and the applied social sciences. It includes works on the community as a social phenomenon and works on community planning and development. These terms are used here in their ordinary meaning to imply the planning for and development of the community as a whole. When specific subjects of community interest are addressed, the work is classed elsewhere in 300, e.g., economic development of the community 338.93–338.99, developing hospitals for the community 362.11, planning community housing 363.5525, planning the city water supply 363.61, planning the education system 379.4–379.9.

Class the psychology of community influences in 155.94. If in doubt whether a work should be classed in the psychology of community influences (155.94) or the social psychology of communities (307), prefer 307.

307 vs. 900   Sociology of communities vs. General geography and history and their auxiliaries

The description of such aspects of a community as population, size, residential patterns, kinds of neighborhoods is classed in 307, not in 900. For instance, urban renewal in London is classed at 307.3409421. However, when economic, political, and other social science aspects are included, such as are found in works on social situation and conditions, the work is classed in 900, e.g., London in the third quarter of the 20th century 942.1085.

307.72   Rural [communities]

Note that "rural" does not necessarily mean agricultural; it means here country rather than city environment.

Class villages in 307.762.

310 Statistics

Statistics here means statistics in tabulated form, not statistical analysis and comment, nor even tables accompanied by such analysis or comment.

Class comprehensive works on statistical analysis at 001.4225, statistical analysis on a specific subject with the subject outside 310 and its subdivisions. For example, statistical tables of crimes of violence in Virginia would be classed at 312.4609755; but an analysis of these statistics, discussing possible trends shown by the statistics, would be classed at 364.109755. Class techniques of presenting statistical data at 001.4226.

Except for 312 Statistics of populations and the subdivisions thereof, class statistics of a specific subject with the subject, using s.s. 0212, e.g., statistics of school libraries 027.80212.

312   **Statistics of populations (Demographic statistics)**

Class here censuses of populations compiled by governments. Add s.s. 09 plus the appropriate notation from Table 2 for the specific area covered. (Note that in some cases directions are given for adding the area number directly to the base number without the intervention of s.s. 09.)

Class census information published by genealogical organizations or by individuals for genealogical purposes in 929.3. (*See 929.3.*) Sociological studies of populations are classed in 304.6.

312.2   [Statistics] On deaths (Mortality)

Use 312.3 and its subdivisions for statistics combining death and illness, 312.4 and its subdivisions for statistics combining death and accidents, death and crimes of violence, or death and both accidents and crimes of violence.

312.3   **[Statistics] On illness (Morbidity)**

Class here combined statistics on death and illness.

312.3047   **[Statistics on surgical illnesses]**

Class here comprehensive works on the statistics of handicaps.

312.4   **[Statistics] On accidents and crimes of violence**

Class here combined statistics on death and accidents; on death and crimes of violence, on death and both accidents and crimes of violence.

312.6   [Statistics] On physical features and measurements (Somatology)

Examples: Statistics on vision, hearing, red blood cell counts, blood types, height, weight, eye color.

Class statistics on abnormal features and other illnesses and defects in 312.3, e.g., statistics on color blindness 312.3047759, on obesity 312.3398.

Do not add s.s. 09 for statistics of specific types of measurements.

312.8   [Statistics] On density, increase, decrease, movement of populations

Including statistical projections of population.

314–319   General statistics by specific continents, countries, localities in modern world

Do not add standard subdivision 09 after the area numbers.

320 Political science (Politics and government)

SUMMARY

321 **Kinds of government and states**
322 **Relation of state to organized social groups and their members**
323 **Relation of state to its residents**
324 **The political process**
325 **International migration**
326 **Slavery and emancipation**
327 **International relations**
328 **Legislation**

Political science is the study of the state, government, politics, and people either individually or in groups as related to the state. Politics (the political process) is concerned with the individuals and political parties that run or seek to run the government of a state. The government is not the state but rather the structure for maintaining the state; it represents the state in its relations with other states.

The state is the primary focus of 320. General considerations with respect to the state are dealt with in 320.1, forms of the state in 321.01–.09, its relationship to individual residents and groups of residents in 322–323 (citizenship being treated in 323.6), its relationship to people who are about to become residents or to cease being residents in 325, its relationship to other states in 327.

Government is a secondary focus of 320. General considerations are dealt with in 320.2–320.4, kinds of government in 321.1–321.9, the legislative branch of government in 328.

Politics (the political process) is still another focus of 320. It is dealt with theoretically in 320.5, and in general and in particular in 324, for instance, parties in particular places, e.g., the Conservative Party in New York 324.274703.

326 Slavery and emancipation is a holdover from a time when a large literature existed upon these topics.

The relationships of political science to other social sciences

Political science may be differentiated from the sociology of politics and government through the use of the following guidelines:

(1) Works dealing with political institutions and processes as a model of general social institutions or processes are classed in Sociology 301–307.

(2) Works that have an enlarged scope, not using the social environment as a background, but trying to find out the social sources (e.g., race, class, family) of political institutions and processes, or the impact these political institutions and processes have on the social environment, are classed in the sociology of politics and government 306.2.

(3) Works covering the major social institutions and processes in a society, not trying to present a total picture of the society, but to show how other social institutions and processes are related to and revolve around political ones are classed in Sociology 301–307.

(4) Descriptive, comparative, historical, and theoretical studies on politics and government, focusing on political institutions, ideologies, or processes (e.g., the structure, functions, and activities of government, political parties, campaigning, voting), using the social environment only as a background, are classed in Political science 320.

(5) If in doubt, prefer 301–307.

Political activities and issues relating to specific problems and organizations in other social sciences are classed with the other social science, e.g., the politics of public action in welfare 361.613, the political history of a banking system 332.1.

Most works on labor and labor movements are classed in 331. In a political context, class labor as a political entity at 322.2 Labor movements and groups, or, if working for wider objectives than those of the labor movement alone, in 322.4 Political action groups. Class labor as an unorganized social group in a state at 323.32 Socioeconomic classes, the labor movement in relation to political parties in 324.

Class the legal aspects of governmental and political institutions and processes in 340. For example, political works on elections are classed in 324.6, but laws, administrative regulations, and judicial decisions on the conduct of elections are classed in 342.07.

Governmental institutions and processes are usually divided among three functions: legislative, executive, judicial. In many societies, especially democratic ones, the three functions are performed by three separate branches of government. Only the legislative branch (328) is classed in the 320s. The executive branch is classed in 350–354, the judicial branch in 347, even though the works in question are political in nature. *For a fuller discussion of the relations between the 320s and 350–354, see 350 Branches of government.*

Works treating the effect of political events on events in general are classed in 900.

320.09 **Historical and geographical treatment of political science [as a discipline]**

See s.s. 09.

320.1 **The state**

Class here theoretical and general works.

Class specific kinds of states in 321.01–321.08.

320.12 vs. Territory vs. **Historical geography**
911
Class in 320.12 theoretical works on the role of territory in the nature and functioning of the state. Class the history of actual territorial changes in 911.

320.2–.4 **[Government]**

Class in these numbers the description of government as a whole.

320.3 Comparative government

Class a comparison of two governments, if neither area predominates, with the jurisdiction that comes first in the Area Table. Class a comparison of a specific subject in two or more jurisdictions with the subject, e.g., comparative political parties 324.2. If the jurisdictions compared are simply being used as models to study a specific topic, class the work with the topic being studied, e.g., a comparison of committee systems in various legislatures 328.365.

320.4 vs. **Structure, functions, activities of government vs. Political situation and**
320.9 **conditions**

Class in 320.4 works describing the structure and powers of governments. This should be interpreted quite narrowly. If the work also includes material (other than examples) describing the functioning of a government related to its current or past situation and problems, class the work in 320.9. If in doubt, prefer 320.9.

320.5   **Political theories and ideologies**

Standard subdivisions may be added with caution to the subdivisions of this number. For example: the theory of nationalism in Scotland 320.5409411, the theory of conservatism in the United States 320.520973. Be certain, however, that the work in question is not in fact discussing nationalism in the general political situation and conditions in the area. Such a work is classed in 320.9. For a work to be classed in 320.5 the focus must be on the ramifications of the particular ideology in that jurisdiction or region. If in doubt, prefer 320.9.

320.54   Nationalism

Nationalism applied to specific countries is not classed here, but in 320.9. Pan-nationalist movements (political movements crossing national boundaries) are classed here and may be divided by place; class Pan-Jewry as a nationalistic movement at 320.54095694. The history of Zionism is classed at 956.94001.

320.8   Local government

Class here the structure, functions, and activities of local government as a whole.

320.9   **Political situation and conditions**

Works classed here must discuss purely political events without regard for nonpolitical relationships, causes, and effects.

Class works dealing with a particular political ideology in an area in 320.5, with a particular form of government or state in an area in 321. *See also 320.5, 321.*

See also 320.4 vs. 320.9.

320.9 vs.   **Political situation and condition vs. History**
900
The relocation note at 320.9 shifting general political history to the 900s is intended to remedy a mistake in classification policy that became imbedded in earlier editions. The publicly expressed rule was that in order to be general history, a work must contain some material on the progress of civilization in general, including economics, technology, science, religion, the arts, and such topics. Purely political history was to be classed in 320.9.

The phrase "political history" is somewhat equivocal. It may mean a history of politics in the narrower sense: histories of changes in governmental forms, of the development of political institutions. Works of this sort are still to be classed in 320.9.

The phrase "general political history" is intended to designate the broader meaning of this term—what used to be called the "battles, kings, and dates" school of history. Thus, a history of England focusing on the various monarchs, their successions, depositions, usurpations, murders, intrigues, foreign relations, struggles with Parliament, etc., is general history even if it contains not one word about art, religion, sport, social stratification, or education and is therefore classed at 942. However, a work tracing the changes in the relationships of the branches of government is classed at 320.942.

321   **Kinds of governments and states**

The numbers in 321 are theoretical; however, class here these subjects in areas broader than a specific jurisdiction, e.g., city states in ancient Greece 321.060938.

Class a specific jurisdiction in 320.9, e.g., the city state of Athens 320.9385.

321.92   Communist [form of government]

Class the economic view of communism, communism considered as an economic system, comprehensive works on the political and economic aspects of communism in 335.43.

321.94   Fascist [form of government]

Class the economic view of fascism or fascism considered as an economic system at 335.6.

322.1 vs.   [Relation of state to] Religious bodies (State and church) vs. **Religious**
  200   **and political affairs**

The difference lies in the point of view taken. If the work in question is written from the standpoint of religion, the work is social theology and is classed in 261.7, 291.177, and cognate and related numbers in 292–299. A work written from a secular standpoint discussing the relation of church and state is classed in 322.1.

322.4   **Political action groups**

Class here a riot that is a confrontation of the constituted authority of a state with a particular social group.

Class the sociology of riots at 303.623, rioting as a crime at 364.143, riots as historical events in 904 and related numbers in 930–990, e.g., the Hindu-Muslim riots of 1947 954.04.

322.42   Revolutionary and subversive groups

Including promotion of revolution by a political group; terrorist groups and activities, e.g., Symbionese Liberation Army.

Class sociology of revolutions at 303.64, revolutions as historical events in 909 and 930–990.

Standard subdivisions may be added for a specific group, e.g., Ku Klux Klan 322.420973, Palestine Liberation Organization 322.42095694.

322.43–.44   Pressure groups [and] Protest and reform movements

Class here only comprehensive works on organized pressure groups and protest and reform movements.

Class works on groups organized for a specific purpose with the purpose, e.g., U.S. temperance movement 363.410973; woman-suffrage movement 324.623.

324.6 vs. 342.07   **Elections vs. Election law**

Manuals outlining procedures for the conduct of an election may be classed here with caution. If laws or administrative regulations for such conduct, or comments on such laws or regulations, are present to any significant degree, class the work in 342.07. If in doubt, prefer 342.07.

325   **International migration**

Class here only the political aspects of migration and colonization.

Class comprehensive and interdisciplinary works on migration in 304.8; on migration to, from, or within communities in 307.2.

325.3   **Colonization**

Class here the exercise of political domination over distant territories, even though colonization is not involved.

325.31 vs. 325.33–.39   **Colonial administration and policies vs. Colonization by specific countries**

Class in 325.33–325.39 the colonization policies of a nation as a whole—acquisition, administration, release of colonies. Class in 325.31 the administrative policies of a nation toward colonies already acquired, when considered from a political viewpoint. If in doubt, prefer 325.33–325.39. The working details of colonial administration are classed in 354.

325.33–.39   **Colonization by specific countries**

See 325.31 vs. 325.33–.39.

326   Slavery and emancipation

Political history of slavery only.

Class the social aspects of slavery at 305.567, as a system of labor at 306.362, the relation of the state to abolition groups and movements at 322.44, the relation of the state to slaves at 323.32, the legal aspects of slavery in 342.085, 342.087, or 346.013, the slave trade at 380.144 (and cognate numbers in 381 and 382), slavery as a cause of the U.S. Civil War in 973.711, religious views in regard to slavery as a social problem in 200, e.g., views of Christian church 261.8353.

327   International relations

Class foreign relations with respect to a specific subject with the subject, e.g., trade relations between the United Kingdom and the United States 382.0941073.

Class in 303.482 a combination of relations between nations, such as political, economic, cultural, and military.

See also 341 vs. 327.

327.09   Historical and geographical treatment [of international relations]

Class here comprehensive works on diplomatic history; also foreign relations in specific areas or blocs, e.g., foreign relations in the Middle East 327.0956, in the Communist bloc 327.091717.

Class diplomatic history of specific jurisdictions in 327.3–327.9.

327.11   International politics

Class here imperialism in the context of international relations.

Class the theoretical aspect of imperialism at 321.03, imperialism in relation to colonization at 325.32.

327.12   Espionage and subversion

Class here espionage and subversion outside of war, and comprehensive works on espionage and subversion. As a part of the military techniques for unconventional warfare, espionage and subversion are classed in 355.343.

Class espionage and subversion conducted by one country against another with the foreign relations between the two countries, e.g., subversion by Iceland in Lesotho 327.491206816.

327.14   Conduct of propaganda and psychological warfare

Including the Cold War as a practice in propaganda and psychological warfare in international relations.

Class propaganda and psychological warfare conducted by one country against another with the foreign relations between the two countries, e.g., psychological warfare conducted by Lesotho against Iceland 327.681604912.

327.174   Disarmament and arms control

Class here comprehensive works on disarmament and arms control, and works treating political aspects only.

Class legal aspects of disarmament and arms control in 341.73, military aspects in 355.03, the techniques of arms control and disarmament in 355.82.

327.2   Diplomacy

The art and science of conducting diplomatic relations.

Class comprehensive works on diplomatic history at 327.09, diplomatic history of specific countries in 327.3–327.9.

Class general registers of diplomatic personnel at 351.892. *See also 351.2.*

327.2092   **[Persons associated with diplomacy]**

Class here biographies of diplomats.

327.3–.9   **Foreign policies of and foreign relations between specific nations**

Class foreign policy with respect to a specific subject with the subject, e.g., export controls of Argentina 382.640982.

Class the foreign relations of a dependency with the dependency, not with the "mother country," e.g., British India's relations with the Kingdom of Nepal 327.5405496.

327.73   **[Foreign relations of the United States]**

Class here the activities of the U.S. Information Agency (USIA); however, class USIA libraries at 027.65.

328.33   Members and membership [of legislative branch of government]

Class in the cognate numbers under 328.4–328.9 membership directories of legislative bodies, e.g., the directory of the Oregon legislature 328.795073025.

328.346   Treaty and war powers [of legislative branch of government]

Class here legislative powers in the field of foreign policy.

328.361   Auxiliary organizations [of legislative branch of government]

Class here legislative councils.

Class a specific council with the jurisdiction to which it belongs in 328.4–328.9, using subdivision 0761 from the table at 328.4–328.9.

328.366   Discipline of members [of legislative branch of government]

Including conflict of interests of legislators.

328.37   **Enactment of legislation**

For bills, hearings, reports, see 342–347: s.s. 0262.

328.375   Passage [of legislation]

Class here the voting behavior of legislators and the legislative response to vetos.

Class veto messages from executive branches at 351.00372 and cognate numbers in 353–354.

Class the analysis of voting records of legislators in 328.XX09, e.g., analysis of the voting record of a U.S. senator 328.7309.

328.38   Lobbying

Lobbying as part of the legislative process only. Lobbyists as interest or pressure groups in the entire political process are classed at 322.43, in practical politics at 324.4.

330 Economics

SUMMARY

331   **Labor economics**
332   **Financial economics**
333   **Land economics**
334   **Cooperatives**
335   **Socialism and related systems**
336   **Public finance**
337   **International economics**
338   **Production**
339   **Macroeconomics and related topics**

Economics encompasses the production, distribution, and consumption of wealth. Classic Western thought holds that all wealth grows from human resources (Labor economics 331), capital resources (Financial economics 332), and natural resources (Land economics 333). The production of wealth (goods and services) is dealt with in 338. Most of the distribution of wealth (commerce, transportation, marketing, and so on) and certain aspects of the consumption of wealth are classed in 380. Sometimes the production and distribution of the goods and services are done through cooperatives (that is, no individual, state, or other kind of corporation owns the means to produce or to distribute the goods and services). Works treating this situation are classed in 334 Cooperatives. If the cooperation is promoted or enforced by the government, the economic and the political have merged, and thus socialistic economic systems are engendered. These are classed in 335 Socialism and related systems.

In order to produce and distribute goods and services, and often to consume them, capital resources must be marshaled and applied. Works dealing with the use of capital resources in the private sector are classed in 332 Financial economics, with the use of capital resources in the public sector in 336 Public finance. (Note, however, that tax law is classed in 343.04, tax administration in 351.724.)

The levels of economy to which economic analysis is applied are three: (1) international (337 International economics); (2) national (339 Macroeconomics); and (3) firm (338.5 Microeconomics).

As the reader can see, economics in the Dewey Decimal Classification is a congeries of elements divided between 330 and 380. Where once 330 was blessed with a logical structure, it now has lost it for at least three reasons: (1) Economics has become greater than itself; its content extends without effort. (2) The meanings of the divisions of the class have broadened as more and more topics have been gathered to them. (3) The meanings of the divisions have altered to meet the literary warrant; for example, 339 Pauperism in early editions has become Macroeconomics; the two subjects, as the reader can see, are not intimately related.

The divisions of Economics 330 are not facets: some are standard elements of economics (331, 332, 333); others are levels (international 337, national 339); one is a polity (socialism 335); one is a function (production 338); one is a means (public finance 336); most are interwoven. Almost all are substantial classes in their own right. The consequence to the DDC classifier is that successful classing in economics requires great care.

Use the following table of precedence when two or more divisions are treated with respect to the topic of a work:

Cooperatives	334
Public finance	336
Economic factors	331–333
Production, Commerce (381–382), Transportation (385–388)	338
Macroeconomics and related topics	339
International economics	337
Socialism and related systems	335

330.0151 [Mathematical principles of economics]

Class econometrics applied to economics as a whole in 330.028, mathematical economics as a school of thought at 330.1543.

330.153 Classical economics

Including the school of Mill, and the Scarcity School.

330.9 **Economic situation and conditions**

Class here a work describing the situation and conditions of an area at all levels, both the macroeconomic and the microeconomic levels.

331–333 **[Factors of production]**

Class comprehensive works at 338.01.

331 **Labor economics**

Class here comprehensive works on labor.

Class sociology of labor at 306.36, comprehensive works on personnel management in 658.3, on personnel management in government in 350.1.

Class full employment policies in 339.5.

Unless other instructions are given here or in Edition 19, use the following table of precedence for works with aspects in two or more subdivisions of 331:

Labor force by personal characteristics	331.3–.6
Labor force and market	331.1
Wages, hours, other conditions of employment	331.2
Labor unions (Trade unions) and labor-management (collective) bargaining	331.8
Labor by industry and occupation	331.7

See also 658.3 vs. 331.

331.11 **Labor force**

This is a very broad number. The note in Edition 19 states that it covers "all who are employed *or* available for employment." This means, of course, a good share of the adult population, which is here described with reference to the world's work, and the population's various aptitudes and fitnesses for work. 331.11 also includes such topics as Systems of labor 331.117 and Labor productivity 331.118.

Class comprehensive works on labor force and market in 331.12. If in doubt, prefer 331.12.

331.119 vs. **[Labor force in] Specific occupations and groups of occupations vs.**
331.7 **Labor by industry and occupation**

Do not confuse 331.119 Labor force in specific occupations and groups of occupations with 331.7 Labor by industry and occupation. To be classed in 331.7 a work should include a fairly substantial number of all topics in the entire 331 schedule discussed with respect to that specific occupation. 331.7 is, in effect, the comprehensive works number for specific occupations. Thus, a work on the teaching profession from the labor standpoint (331.7613711) would have to include not only descriptive material on the teaching force both actual and potential, but on such topics as teachers' wages and working conditions; women, men, veterans, homosexuals as teachers; unions and collective bargaining in the teaching profession. A specific topic with respect to specific occupations or industries is classed with the topic. Thus, descriptive material on the teaching force, both actual and potential, would be classed in 331.11913711.

331.12 **Labor market**

This is a narrower topic than 331.11 Labor force. 331.12 covers the activity of workers in finding, keeping, and changing jobs and the opportunities provided by the general economy or through special assistance for them to do so. Undoubtedly 331.12 (and 331.14, which is part of this topic) will be more heavily used than 331.11. In 331.12 and its subdivisions are classed such matters as the demand for labor (331.123), e.g., how many workers (over and above workers already employed) are likely to be needed over a given period. Actual job openings are classed in 331.124. 331.125 Labor actively employed is devoted (as its name states) to surveying those workers actually employed at a given time. The relation of this factor to the number of unemployed is, of course, relevant to the state of the labor market. Maladjustments in labor market 331.13 is part of the total labor market picture.

331.12791   International [mobility of labor]

Including brain drain.

331.133   Discrimination in employment

Class in 331.3–331.6 discrimination against groups having specific personal characteristics, e.g., against women 331.4133.

331.137804   General classes of unemployed

Be cautious in the use of this number; 331.3–331.6 takes precedence for specific classes of unemployed persons, e.g., unemployed women 331.4.

331.23   Guaranteed-wage plans

Including minimum wage.

331.25   Hours and other conditions of employment

Including economic aspects of physical working conditions, e.g., ventilation, space, working facilities.

331.252   Pensions

Class government pension plans for the population at large at 368.43.

See also 331.255.

331.255 Fringe benefits

Pensions and other fringe benefits to workers are analogous to certain forms of insurance and investment. See the following table:

The Benefits	Pensions	Other Fringe Benefits
Comprehensive works and the benefits for employees in general	331.252	331.255
For government employees except military	331.2529	331.255
For veterans of military service and their survivors	355.1151	355.115
Pensions (annuities), other benefits provided through insurance	368.37	368.3
Annuities resulting from retirement and estate planning	332.02401	
Benefits provided through social insurance	368.43	368.4

Note that the actual benefits provided to government and private employees are classed as shown above, not in public administration (350) or management (658).

331.287 [Wages in manufacturing industries]

Class here average factory wages.

331.29 **Historical and geographical treatment of wages**

Class here wage-price policies of specific jurisdictions; but if the policies are discussed in relation to stabilizing the economy, class in 339.5.

331.6209 [Historical and geographical treatment of immigrant and alien workers]

Class here immigrants to a specific jurisdiction without regard to place of origin, e.g., immigrants to Canada 331.620971.

Class immigrants from a specific jurisdiction to another specific jurisdiction in 331.621–331.629.

331.7 **Labor by industry and occupation**

See 331.119 vs. 331.7.

331.702   **Choice of vocation**

Class here choice of vocation for persons with specific personal characteristics, e.g., veterans. Note that this is an exception to the general citation order which directs that persons with specific characteristics are classed in 331.3–331.6 regardless of occupation. *See 331.3–331.6 in Edition 19.*

331.79   **Specific groups of occupations**

Class groups with two or more characteristics with the number coming last in 331.792–331.798, e.g., white-collar public service occupations 331.795, not 331.792.

331.88091   **International unions, and treatment by areas, regions, places in general**

Class specific international unions dealing with a specific occupation or group of occupations in 331.881.

331.88097   [International unions of the United States and Canada]

Including the American Federation of Labor-Congress of Industrial Organizations (AFL-CIO).

331.8832   Craft unions

Unions of workers practicing a specific trade or occupation regardless of the industry in which they are employed.

Example: American Federation of Labor (AFL).

331.8833   Industrial unions

Unions of workers in a specific industry regardless of craft or occupation practiced.

Examples: Congress of Industrial Organizations (CIO), Knights of Labor.

331.8834   Company unions

Unaffiliated labor unions of the employees of a single firm.

331.886   Revolutionary unions

Example: International Workers of the World (IWW).

332.024   Personal finance

Standard subdivisions may be added to this number, e.g., personal finance in Great Britain 332.02400941. Note that two zeros must be used when adding standard subdivisions here.

332.02401   Increasing income, net worth, financial security

"Planning for retirement" should be interpreted to include Keogh plans and Individual Retirement Accounts (IRAs).

332.0415   **Capital formation**

General economic studies of the ways, means, and problems of raising money for industry.

Class financing of specific kinds of industries in 338.1–338.4, financing of firms at 338.6041, managerial techniques for capital formation in 658.15.

332.042   International finance

Class exchange of currencies in 332.45.

332.1028   [Techniques, procedures, apparatus, equipment, materials of banking]

Including electronic funds transfer systems.

332.11   **Central banks**

Example: the U.S. Federal Reserve System 332.110973.

332.2   Specialized banking institutions

Including development banks serving one country. Class international development banks in 332.15.

332.3   Credit and loan institutions

Including credit and loan functions of travel agencies, e.g., American Express Company.

Class comprehensive works on travel agencies at 338.76191.

332.45   **Foreign exchange**

Exchange of currencies.

Including special drawing rights, Eurodollar market.

Class here international monetary systems.

Class comprehensive works on international finance at 332.042, Eurobonds at 336.3435.

332.67   **Specific fields of investment**

Investment as a whole in specific fields of investment.

Class specific types of security in 332.63, e.g., investment in bonds 332.6323.

332.6732   **Government policy [with respect to international investment]**

Class here works describing advantages and disadvantages of establishing businesses in various specific areas. *See also 338.09.*

333   Land economics

Land economics is a broad term covering all of the contents of 333 including (1) land as space (which has an economic value of its own), (2) land as property with its attendant problems of transfer and right to use, (3) land as a natural resource, a source of economic goods (chiefly agricultural and mineral). The first two of these concepts are classed in 333.1–333.5; land as a natural resource is classed in 333.73.

333.009   [Historical and geographical treatment of land economics]

Class here land surveys.

Class surveying techniques in 526.9.

333.1–.5 vs.   Ownership and control of land and natural resources vs. [Law of]
346.043   Real property

Class economic aspects of the various forms of ownership, use and transfer of land in 333.1–333.5. Class legal aspects in 346.043. If in doubt, prefer 346.043.

333.31   Land reform

Class here land redistribution, settlement and resettlement of people on the land.

333.3234   Qualified ownership

Including time sharing.

333.7   Natural resources

Class economic geology in 553.

See also 363.6 vs. 333.7; 363.7.

333.7313   [Consumption (Use, Utilization) of land]

Including desertification.

333.7316   [Conservation and protection of land]

Class here comprehensive works on soil and water conservation.

Class soil and water conservation in rural lands at 333.7616, water conservation at 333.9116.

333.79   Energy and energy resources

Class here power resources.

If only electric power is discussed, class the work in 333.7932.

333.8 **Subsurface resources**

Note that there is no development of subsurface resources comparable to that possible with other types of resources. New coal mines cannot be grown. What is often referred to as development here is almost always some form of extraction which is classed in 338.2. Therefore, subdivision 15 of the table under 333.7 is not applicable here and should not be used.

333.9162 Rivers and streams

Class river basins in 333.73.

333.917 **Shorelands and related areas**

Class here continental shelves.

Class river basins in 333.73.

334.683 [Cooperatives in agriculture]

Class kibbutzim and moshavim at 335.95694; Soviet agricultural communes at 338.763. If these are studied as communities, class in 307.77.

335 **Socialism and related systems**

The section of the schedules devoted to socialism has been built on historical lines. Socialism is basically of two kinds: Marxian and non-Marxian. Non-Marxian varieties developed mostly before Marxism and are now largely of historical interest, since no actual economies are built on them. These varieties are classed in 335.1–335.3. Marxian socialism is classed in 335.4 and 335.5, with Fabian socialism (a quasi-Marxist system) at 335.14. Early forms of Marxism appear in 335.42. Present-day Marxism is again of two kinds: communism and forms of democratic socialism. Communism and its various sects are classed in 335.43, democratic socialism at 335.5. The regime in the Soviet Union is an example of communism, the Socialist Party in the United States advocates democratic socialism. Many works, it should be noted, use the word socialism to denote one of these narrower concepts.

335.02 Utopian systems and schools [of socialism]

Utopian systems usually have political aspects. If a work is predominantly a description of an ideal state, class it at 321.07; if it is a description of an ideal society, class it at 301.7.

335.4112 Dialectical materialism

Class here only works on dialectical materialism as the philosophical foundation of Marxism. Studies on dialectial materialism as a philosophical viewpoint are classed at 146.32.

335.434   **National variants [of communism]**

National variants of communism are treated as if they were schools of thought and are classed here. The actual economic systems existing in such countries, their practical effects and development, are classed in 335.43, using the appropriate area notation. For example, Cuban communism as a theory of communism is classed at 335.4347. The functioning of this theory in the day-to-day life of Cuba is classed at 335.43097291.

It should be noted that Soviet communism is taken as the standard form of communism and is therefore classed at 335.43. If stress is laid on the system as peculiarly Soviet in contrast to other national variants, the work is classed at 335.434. Communism as it functions on a practical basis in the Soviet Union is classed at 335.430947.

335.9   Voluntary socialist and anarchist communities

Such communities are in sharp contrast with communes and similar organizations when these are organs of totalitarian or authoritarian states. Be wary of propaganda about involuntary organizations claiming that they are voluntary. Such involuntary organizations are classed at 338.763 if they are treated as organizations for production, at 307.77 if treated as communities.

Class kibbutzim in Israel at 335.95694.

336.2   **Taxes and taxation**

Class here comprehensive works on, and economic aspects of, taxes and taxation. Note that most works on taxes will be classed in tax law (343.04–343.06), since they in fact are telling the user what the law is and what has to be done to comply with it. This is particularly true of popular works. Assessment and collection of taxes are classed in tax administration 351.724, and cognate and related numbers in 352–354.

336.201   **Taxes by governmental level**

Class here works discussing the level as a whole or various jurisdictions at the same level. Individual jurisdictions regardless of level are classed in 336.2009.

336.242   Personal (Individual) [income taxes]

Class negative income tax at 362.582.

336.24316   Reductions [in corporate income taxes]

Class here any measure that reduces the tax paid, e.g., oil depletion allowance.

336.3435   International [public borrowing and debt]

Including Eurobonds.

337   **International economics**

Class here comprehensive works on international economic relations and economic cooperation.

Class a specific aspect of international economics not provided for here with the subject, e.g., foreign trade 382.

337.1   **Spheres of economic cooperation**

Class here works on the listed international economic organizations only if they relate to general economic cooperation.

Class works dealing only with trade and trade agreements in 382, dealing only with the general organization of these groups, including membership, in 341.2, comprehensive works on these organizations in 341.2.

338   **Production**

Class here comprehensive works on both the economic and technical aspects of industry and production, e.g., the economy and technology of the sponge industry 338.37234.

Class production technology in 620–690.

338.06   Production efficiency

Including technical innovations.

338.09   **Historical and geographical treatment of production**

Class here works showing where industry is in fact located.

Class how to locate a business at 658.11, how to locate a specific type of enterprise with the subject, using s.s. 068, e.g., how to locate a drycleaning business 667.12068.

Class laws and regulations governing investment in and initiation of businesses in 346.07.

See also 332.6732, 338.6042.

338.1–.4   **Specific kinds of industries**

Class here lists of products by manufacturer, but not items for sale. *See 380 in Edition 19 where full instructions appear.*

Class biographies of people chiefly known as entrepreneurs in specific kinds of industries in 338.6–338.9, e.g., collective biographies of big-business men 338.6440922, a biography of an entrepreneur in aeronautics 338.76291300924; biographies of people known for their contribution to technology in 600, e.g., a biography of a railroad engineer 625.100924.

338.1–.4 vs. Specific kinds of industries vs. Business organizations
338.7–.8

Class in 338.1–338.4 general production economics of various specific industries. Class organizations in various specific industries in 338.7–338.8.

338.13   Financial aspects [of agriculture]   Prices [in agriculture]

Standard subdivisions may be added to the number for a work on a specific product even if only one financial aspect is covered.

338.14   Factors affecting production [in agriculture]

Do not confuse "factors" at this number with the traditional factors of production: land, labor, and capital. The latter are classed in 331–333.

338.17   Products and groups of products

Class here the seed industry as a whole.

Class a specific kind of seed with the kind, e.g., seed rice 338.17318.

338.2–.4   [Specific kinds of industries other than agriculture]

Government policies are classed with the specific industry being discussed, e.g., government policies with respect to extraction of minerals 338.2.

338.372   Products of fishing, whaling, hunting, trapping

It should be noted that the word "fishing" here includes the catching of such aquatic creatures as lobsters and oysters. Fishing for fish (pisces) alone is classed at 338.3727.

Class here comprehensive works on fishing (in the sense indicated above) and the culture of fish and other water animals.

Class the culture of fish and other water animals in 338.371.

Standard subdivisions may be added for works dealing only with fishing (in the sense indicated above). It should be noted that s.s. 09 is used to indicate the home base of the fishing industry in question, not the place where the fish and other water animals are being caught. Thus a fleet based at Los Angeles is classed at 338.3720979494, even though the fish are being caught off Lower California. It is not classed at either 338.37209722 Lower California, or at 338.372091641 Southeast Pacific Ocean.

338.43   Financial aspects [of secondary industries and services]
Prices [of products of secondary industries and services]

See 338.13. The same rule for adding standard subdivisions applies here.

338.47 **Goods and services**

Class economics of enterprises engaged in selling in 380–382.

338.5212 Theory of demand

Class here demand analysis of goods in general.

Demand analysis of a specific item is classed with the subject in 338.1–338.4, e.g., demand analysis of agricultural products in 338.1.

338.6042 Location [of business organizations]

Class here the rationale for and the process of locating business organizations.

Class in 338.09 surveys showing where businesses are actually located. A useful mnemonic device here is to consider location in 338.09 to be a condition, in 338.6042 to be an action. Class managerial techniques used in locating businesses at 658.11.

338.7–.8 **Business organizations**

See 338.1–.4 vs. 338.7–.8.

338.76 **Organizations in specific industries and groups of industries**

Class here directories of companies in an industry, using s.s. 025 when feasible, e.g., directories of law firms 338.761340025.

Class organizations engaged in trade in 380–382.

Class biographies of people associated with the development and operation of specific types of organizations but not confined to a specific industry or group of industries in 338.6–338.8, e.g., a person associated with trusts 338.850924. A company director on the boards of companies in several industries or groups of industries is classed at 338.70924.

See also 338.1–.4, 380.141–.145.

338.8 **Combinations**

Class here antitrust policies.

338.86 Holding companies

Class bank holding companies at 332.16.

338.9 **Economic development and growth**

Class here technology transfer. Note that such terms as technical assistance, research and development, and science policy may mean technology transfer.

339   **Macroeconomics and related topics**

Macroeconomics is the study of the economy as a whole, especially with reference to its general level of output and income and the interrelationships among sectors of the economy. It is one of the most difficult fields to understand and to classify correctly. As a rule of thumb, class in 339 works that say they are discussing macroeconomics, or that are discussing one or more of the topics listed in the various subdivisions. This does not, of course, solve all problems.

Topics appearing in 332 Financial economics and 336 Public finance are sometimes part of macroeconomics. These topics, however, will be classed in 339 only when they are quite clearly discussed in the context of their relation to the total economic picture of a country or region. If in doubt, prefer 332 and 336.

Other parts of the field of macroeconomics appear elsewhere in the schedules. These are indicated by the cross references under the various subdivisions of 339 and at 339 itself.

339.32   **Other measures [of national income]**

Personal income as a measure of national income is classed here.

Class personal income in the ordinary sense at 339.22.

339.47   Consumption (Spending)

Class here interdisciplinary works on consumption.

Class consumption in 381–382 only if the consumption is being discussed as a measure of the amount, volume, value, or kind of trade. Class the social aspects of consumption at 306.3, the relation of income to consumption at 339.41.

339.48   **Consumption of specific commodities and groups of commodities**

See 339.47.

339.5   **Macroeconomic policy**

Class here equilibrium.

340 Law

SUMMARY

Law, one of the chief instruments of social control, consists of the whole body of customs, practices, and rules recognized in a society as binding, and promulgated or enforced by a central authority.

Three general forms of literature may be distinguished in this field:

(1) the laws themselves as promulgated by a body officially authorized to do so;

(2) decisions of the courts or other adjudicative bodies on matters of dispute that arise under these laws;

(3) treatises written on various aspects of the laws.

The first two of these, laws and decisions, are considered to be original materials. Treatises are derivative in nature and are considered to be secondary. A special section (348) has been provided for original materials and guides to them when such materials are not confined to any specific branch or topic in law. Original materials that are confined to a specific branch or topic are to be classed with that branch or topic, using special law standard subdivision 026 and its subdivisions. (This standard subdivision is given in detail in Edition 19 under 342–347.)* Treatises have no special place or designation, but are classed in 349 if relating to the total law of a jurisdiction, or in the number for the specific branch or topic without further indication.

---

*Note that there is a similar development of s.s. 026 under 341 International law.

The facet order in law is branch of law plus jurisdiction plus specific topic plus standard subdivision if applicable. Thus, collected laws (law standard subdivision) relative to income taxes (topic) in Pennsylvania (jurisdiction) is built in the following manner: 34 (for law) + 3 (branch of law: miscellaneous public law) + 748 (jurisdiction: Pennsylvania) + 052 (topic: income tax) + 02632 (law standard subdivision: original materials: collected laws). The complete number is 343.74805202632.

For libraries using Option B, the facet order is as follows: jurisdiction plus branch of law plus topic plus standard subdivision if applicable. Thus, collected laws (law standard subdivision) relative to income taxes (topic) in the United Kingdom (jurisdiction) is built in the following manner: 34 (for law) + 41 (jurisdiction: United Kingdom) + 0 + 3 (branch of law: miscellaneous public law) + 52 (topic: income tax) + 02632 (law standard subdivision: original materials: collected laws). The complete number is 344.1035202632.

Terminology

Civil law: This term has two meanings that must be carefully distinguished. In one sense it is the name of a system of law (340.56) derived from Roman law and in use to a greater or lesser extent in most countries in the modern world, e.g., Germany, France, Japan, Brazil, and even in some subordinate jurisdictions of countries that otherwise use another system, e.g., the province of Québec in Canada and the state of Louisiana in the United States. It is frequently used in contrast to other great systems of law, e.g., the Common law (340.57), which is derived from the customs and laws of ancient and medieval England and is used in the United Kingdom, the United States, and most countries belonging to the British Commonwealth, e.g., Canada, Australia, New Zealand.

The commoner meaning of the term "civil law" is all law that is not criminal law (342–344, 346–347). It is used in stated or implied contrast to criminal law.

Municipal law: This is not the law of local jurisdictions, but the law of any specific jurisdiction (particularly law of a nation or a state) as opposed to international law. In the *Manual*, domestic law is occasionally used as a synonym for municipal law. Comprehensive works on law of local jurisdictions is classed at 342.09. Local law on specific topics is classed with the topic, e.g., traffic ordinances in New York City 343.74710946.

Law enforcement: This is not necessarily a police matter, although it may be. Any government agency may enforce the law. A department of education, for instance, is enforcing the law when it sees that the requirements of the law are being met by the schools. Enforcement of law in this sense is classed with the subject outside of law. A work about the law enforcement activities of the department of education mentioned above would be classed at 350.851 and cognate and related numbers in 352–354. Law enforcement by the police is classed in 363.23. It should be noted, however, that laws governing how such enforcement should be carried out are classed in law, e.g., law governing what measures police may use in enforcing the law 344.0523 (or 345.052 if it pertains to matters of criminal investigation).

Enforcement of the law through the courts is always classed in law, using law standard subdivision 0269 where appropriate, e.g., court enforcement of tax law 343.040269.

Law of countries with federal governments

In federally organized countries, e.g., the United States, Australia, Federal Republic of Germany, there are two sets of laws, those of the central jurisdiction (national laws) and those of subordinate jurisdictions (laws of the provinces or states). Laws of an individual state or province are classed using the area number for the jurisdiction in question, e.g., criminal law of Virginia 345.755, of New South Wales 345.944. However, the laws of the states or provinces taken as a whole are classed in the same numbers as the laws of the federal jurisdiction, e.g., criminal laws of the states of the United States 345.73, of the states of Australia 345.94.

Laws of local jurisdictions are treated in the same way. For the laws of a specific jurisdiction, use the area number for that jurisdiction; but for the laws of all the localities of a given area, use the area number for the jurisdiction that contains them: tax laws of Chapel Hill, North Carolina 343.75656504, rates laws of Leatherhead, Surrrey, England 343.42216504; but, tax laws of the cities of North Carolina 343.75604, of the cities of the United States 343.7304, rates laws of the cities of Great Britain 343.4104.

Jurisdiction in time

Laws of an area that was at some point not an independent jurisdiction are classed as follows:

(1) If still operative in the now-independent jurisdiction, class with the jurisdiction in question, e.g., the Limitation Act of 1908, which was enacted before Pakistan became independent but is still the currently operating law for Pakistan, is classed at 347.5491052.

(2) If the law is not still operative in the now-independent jurisdiction, class with the laws of the jurisdiction that was previously dominant, e.g., a law of 1908 no longer operative in Pakistan is classed with the law of India, using area 54.

Law and aboriginal groups

Certain groups, such as the aborigines of Australia and the native races of the United States, had legal systems of their own prior to their incorporation into the national systems of other groups. Such laws are classed in 340.52 Primitive law, e.g., laws of North American native tribes before becoming a part of the United States 340.5273. Class laws of such groups on a specific subject with the subject in law, using standard subdivision 089, e.g., family law of North American native races 346.01508997.

Class relations between aboriginal groups and a nation established in their territory before their incorporation into the nation, in international law, e.g., treaties between the United States and native American groups on territorial matters 341.42026.

Relations between an aboriginal group and a nation established in its territory, after its incorporation into the nation, are classed in the regular numbers for law of the jurisdiction, e.g., law regulating nursing services for Australian aborigines 344.940414.

Policy

Policy is not necessarily law and ordinarily is classed with the subject outside of law, e.g., conservation policy 333.72. Only policy embodied in specific laws and court interpretations is classed in law, e.g., a law passed to enforce conservation policy 346.044.

Use of jurisdiction in number building

It is redundant to repeat the number for the jurisdiction if the same jurisdiction has been represented earlier in the number. For example, the number for legal aspects of extra compensation for United States military personnel who have the additional duty of serving as judge advocates or law specialists (344.73012813430143) is made up of the following elements: 344.7301 (labor law of the United States) + 281 from 331.281 (wages for a specific service or occupation) + 3430143 (the law number for military legal procedure, used here to indicate the profession occupied in this activity, added from the whole classification as instructed at 331.281). The number for the jurisdiction (the United States) is not inserted following 343 since it has already been used once in building this number.

The principle of approximating the whole does not apply to jurisdictions for which there is no specific area number, i.e., subdivisions may be added for a jurisdiction not having its own number, e.g., Flint, Michigan's ordinance governing mental health services to the addicted 344.774370446. Flint is in an including note, which normally means subdivisions may not be added for it.

Use of area number for capital districts

Use area 753 for laws of Washington, D.C., even though some of these laws are passed by the United States Congress. These are, in effect, local laws even though passed by the national legislature. The same situation occurs in Australia, where all laws of the Capital Territory are passed by the national legislative body. Use area 947. The same situation may occur in other jurisdictions.

Legal writing

Class works on the composition of legal briefs, law reports, and other documents at 808.06634; however, if the work emphasizes how to make the document comply with the law, class it with the subject in law, e.g., how to draw a legal contract 346.022.

Terminology employed in law section of the *Manual*

To avoid cumbersome repetition the phrase "the law of" is frequently omitted. Unless otherwise stated, law is understood. If, for example, the phrase "taxes are classed in 343.04" is used, it means that the law of taxes is classed in 343.04.

Notation used

When referring to law of specific topics in 342–348 the number is given as it physically appears in Edition 19, e.g., law of taxes 343.04. It is to be understood that in most instances, to use the above example, the number will actually be 343 plus area notation plus 04.

340.023   [**Law as a profession, occupation, hobby**]

Distinguish 340.023 carefully from legal practice (347.0504) which deals with the technicalities of conducting a lawsuit. Class in 340.023 such topics as what it is like to be a lawyer, professional relationships, specialities available in the profession, career opportunities, and the like.

Including legal assistants.

340.024   [**Law for specific types of users**]

Example: law for secretaries 340.024651. To be classed here the work must so present the law as to enable the secretary to have a deeper knowledge of the subject with which he is working. Class works discussing only clerical and management procedures for a law office at 651.934.

The same principles apply to the use of s.s. 024 throughout the law schedule, e.g., English law for English secretaries 349.42024651.

Use of s.s. 024 to designate works written for lawyers is, of course, redundant and it should not be added for this purpose.

340.092   [**Persons associated with law**]

Class the biography of a lawyer in a specific jurisdiction in 349, e.g., a biography of a lawyer in the German Democratic Republic 349.4310924. If the lawyer is associated with a specific branch of law, class him with the branch, e.g., biography of a criminal lawyer in Texas 345.76400924.

340.1   **Philosophy and theory** [**of law**]

The regular divisions of standard subdivision 01 may be used here, e.g., legal language and communication 340.14.

340.112   Law and ethics

Class here ethics of law (ethics applied to the legal system as a whole).

Class the ethics of the legal profession in 174.3.

340.115   Law and society

Class here ethnological jurisprudence, sociological jurisprudence.

340.5 Systems of law

Class a specific subject in a specific system of law with the subject in law, e.g., juristic persons in ancient Roman law 346.37013, juristic persons in Byzantine law 346.495013, in civil law 346.013.

340.52 **Primitive law**

See 340 Law and aboriginal groups.

340.59 Islamic law (Fiqh)

Islamic law in a specific country may be designated by the addition of s.s. 093–099, e.g., Islamic law (Fiqh) in Indonesia 340.5909598. Note that law of Indonesia in general (which is based in part on Civil law) is classed at 349.598.

340.9 **Conflict of laws**

This topic is often called private international law, which is something of a misnomer, since it is not law governing the interrelationships of nations, but conflicts and disputes between private citizens of different nations. It is analogous to 346 Private law. The chief point at issue is usually which jurisdiction's laws are to govern the case, hence the term conflict of laws. For example, whose laws will govern in the case of a Canadian citizen married in France to a citizen of Germany and later divorced in Mexico when a dispute arises as to disposition of jointly owned personal property?

Domestic conflicts of law can also arise in federally organized countries. Works on such conflicts are classed in 342.042, e.g., disposition of jointly owned property in the case of a resident of New York, married in Missouri, divorced in Kansas (the other party being now a resident of California) 342.73042.

341 **International law**

International law may be defined as that body of rules, principles, and standards to which independent states (nations) are bound by common consent. It lacks two of the features that commonly characterize law: genuine enforceability and promulgation by a central authority. The validity of international law depends on the good faith of nations, their national self-interest, the pressure of world opinion on them, their fear of reprisal, and sanctions imposed by international bodies. This law is embodied in treaties, protocols, conventions, and other international agreements (analogous to statutes); decisions of international courts; and writings (treatises) by recognized publicists.

It should be noted that comprehensive works on international organizations and works dealing with the structure and overall functions of such organizations are classed in 341.2, even when no substantial discussion of the organic law establishing such organizations appears in the work under consideration. A specific aspect of one of these organizations is classed with the subject outside of law, e.g., economic aspects of the European Economic Community 337.142.

Class comprehensive works on international and municipal law at 340, private international law in 340.9, a combination of private international law and municipal law in 342–347.

341 vs. 327   International law vs. International relations

Distinguishing between International law and International relations is difficult and tricky. To some extent it might be considered as the difference between what actually is (327) and what ought to be (341). Works on international relations will discuss what is actually, concretely going on (including theory as to why things happen as they do), and the effects of what has happened. Works on international law will discuss those standards and principles which it is commonly felt should govern international relations, and will also discuss concrete events from the standpoint of the problems that they pose to this system of order. Included in international law, of course, will also be works on treaties and cases of international courts. If in doubt, prefer 341.

341.026   Treaties and cases

Use this extended standard subdivision for texts of treaties and judicial decisions, not for discussions, commentaries, or popular works.

Class comprehensive works on treaties at 341.37, treaties as a source of international law at 341.1.

Class approval of a treaty by the legislative body of a nation in international law. However, legislation passed by such a body to enforce the provisions of a treaty within national boundaries is municipal, or domestic, law and is classed accordingly. Thus, a work on a treaty between the United States and Canada with respect to fish and wildlife conservation is classed at 341.762, but a work on a fish and game law passed by the United States Congress to enforce the provisions of such a treaty on the citizens of the United States would be classed at 346.73046954.

341.0265 Multilateral treaties

An agreement between a United Nations organization and a specific country or countries is not a multilateral treaty and should be classed at 341.026, not 341.0265. If the treaty is on a specific subject, class with the subject in international law, e.g., a treaty between the World Health Organization and Spain on pollution control 341.7623026.

341.0268 **Cases [in international law]**

Class here general collections of cases on international matters tried in any court system (most frequently in international courts). Class cases on a specific subject with the subject in international law, using law standard subdivision 0268 where applicable.

341.04 Relation of international and domestic law

This deals with the question of whether domestic or international law prevails in a certain situation. Class domestic law that carries out the provisions of an international agreement in 342–347.

341.1 Sources of international law

Class here treaties when discussed as sources of international law. *See also 341.026, 341.37.*

341.2 **The world community**

Class here privileges and immunities for international organizations.

Class administration of international organizations in 354.1.

341.242 European [organizations and associations]

Including legal aspects and organization of Concert of Europe, Council of Europe, European Parliament.

Class general legal questions relating to socioeconomic and sociopolitical regions in 340.09, e.g., Commonwealth of Nations 340.09171241.

341.2422 European Economic Community (European Common Market)

Class here comprehensive works on this organization.

Class international laws promulgated by the European Economic Community with the subject in international law, e.g., economic enactments 341.750614; nonlegal aspects with the subject outside of law, e.g., general economic activities 337.142.

341.26   States

Class liability of states with respect to a specific subject with the subject in international law, e.g., liability for safety of diplomatic personnel 341.33, liability for damages caused by testing nuclear weapons 341.734.

341.27   Semisovereign and dependent states

Treat semisovereign and dependent as a unitary term.

341.28   Nonself-governing territories

Including colonies.

341.33   Diplomacy

See 351.2.

341.37   Treaties

Including the making of treaties.

Class here comprehensive works on treaties. (*See note in Edition 19.*)

Class treaties on a specific subject with the subject in international law, adding extended standard subdivision 026 if appropriate, e.g., a disarmament treaty between the Soviet Union and the United States 341.733026647073. *See also 341.026.*

341.448   [Jurisdiction over] Territorial waters

Class access to the sea at 341.45.

341.55   Adjudication [of disputes and conflicts between states]

Including interpretation of general international law in courts, adjustment of nonwar claims.

Class interpretation of a specific subject with the subject in international law, e.g., interpretation of basic human rights 341.481.

341.58   Coercive methods of settlement [of disputes] short of war

Including ultimatums.

341.63   Conduct of war

Including abolition of privateering, prize law.

341.65   Treatment of sick, wounded, prisoners

Class international welfare services to veterans at 341.766.

341.66 Termination of war

Class here military government of occupied countries.

Class war claims by private individuals of one country against another country in 340.9, adding as directed at this number in Edition 19 as appropriate, e.g., claims for damage to property 340.94.

341.67 [Law of war relative to] Individuals

Including law or agreements relative to war victims.

341.68 International law and civil war

Including responsibility of the state for acts of unsuccessful insurgent governments.

Class general liability of states at 341.26.

341.69 War crimes

Including trials of war criminals, e.g., Nuremberg war criminal trials.

341.72 Defense and mutual security

Class here legal aspects of the North Atlantic Treaty Organization (NATO) and other international mutual security pacts.

Class specific aspects and activities of such organizations with the subject in 000–999, e.g., military aspects 355.031.

341.75 International economic law

Class here taxation.

Class double taxation (the taxation of the same individual by two separate jurisdictions) at 341.484.

341.751 Money and banking

Including international fiscal law, international loan agreement.

341.752 Investments

Class international licensing at 341.753; laws of a specific jurisdiction governing business investment by foreign nationals in 346.07, e.g., laws of Brazil governing investment by foreign nationals 346.8107.

341.753 Organization and conduct of business

Including international licensing.

341.754   Trade and commerce

Including the right of preemption (in international law, the right of a nation to detain foreign merchandise passing through its territories or territorial waters in order to afford its subjects or citizens priority of purchase).

341.7566   Water transportation (Maritime law)

Class prize law at 341.63.

341.759   Economic and social development

Including World Food Conference.

Class specific aspects and activities of this organization with the subject in 000–999.

341.76   Social law and cultural relations

Including social security; United Nations Children's Fund (UNICEF).

Class specific aspects and activities of this organization with the subject in 000–999.

341.7632   [Labor] Conditions in specific industries

Class wages in specific industries at 341.7636.

341.766   Welfare services

Including welfare services to veterans.

341.77   International criminal law

Class here International Criminal Court (proposed); legal aspects of the services of the international police, of INTERPOL.

342–347   **Law of individual states and nations (Municipal law): standard subdivisions**

s.s. 026   Laws, regulations, cases, procedure, courts

Note that other standard subdivisions may be added to s.s. 026 and its subdivisions.

s.s. 0262–   Preliminary materials [and] Laws and regulations
s.s. 0263

Do not class here commentaries or critical works. Class these in the number for the specific topic in 342–347 without further designation.

s.s. 0262   Preliminary materials

Preliminary materials are documents relating to proposed legislation. Even after passage of the legislation these documents continue to be relevant in law as showing the mind and intention of the legislators responsible for the bill.

The main forms are:

Bills (the proposed laws themselves).

Hearings on the bills.

Statements of witnesses.

Executive messages with respect to bills.

Reports on the hearings.

Class in 342–347:

Bills.

Including authorizations and appropriation bills that establish government agencies; both of these are classed in law with the subject with which the agency deals, e.g., a bill to establish an education department 344.070262.

Hearings, reports, and resolutions relating to bills.

Hearings on proposed appointments of judges.

These are classed in 345 or 347, e.g., a hearing on the proposed appointment of a justice to the United States Supreme Court 347.732634.

Class in 350–354:

Appropriation and authorization bills and the hearings and reports pertaining to them.

Except for military appropriations and authorizations, and except as noted above, these are classed in 351.72236 and cognate numbers in 353–354.

Oversight hearings.

These are not hearings on a bill, but examinations into the effectiveness with which an agency is doing its job. Class them with the subject with which the agency deals, e.g., an oversight hearing on the U.S. Bureau of Indian Affairs 353.0081497.

Hearings on proposed executive branch appointments.

For example: a hearing on the proposed appointment of a U.S. Secretary of Agriculture 353.81.

Class in 355–359:

Military appropriation and authorization bills and the hearings and reports pertaining to them.

Including appropriations and authorizations for departments of defense, which are classed in 355.622.

Class in other places throughout the classification:

General hearings and reports on them.

Reports on legislative investigations not related to proposed legislation, e.g., an investigation of organized crime 364.106.

Note that reports are classed with the hearings to which they pertain. Materials containing statements such as "under authority of," "pursuant to," are not usually classed in law.

s.s. 02632   Collected laws

Including model codes.

s.s. 0264   Cases

Do not use this standard subdivision for casebooks, since these are, in effect, textbooks.

s.s. 02643   Court decisions

Use for official court decisions, not for treatises on such decisions or for popular treatment of cases.

s.s. 07   [Study and teaching of law]

Watch the use of this standard subdivision in law. Added to a number in the law schedule it means the study and teaching of that particular subject in law, e.g., 344.04607 the study and teaching of the law of environmental control. It does not mean the law applied to the study and teaching of the subject with which the law deals. Hence a law providing aid to a college to promote the teaching of environmental topics is not classed in 344.04607, but in 344.0769 finance for specific educational programs.

342.02   Constitutions and other basic instruments of government

Class here county charters.

342.023   Texts of constitutions

Including texts of proposed constitutions.

See also 340 Law and aboriginal groups for the principles involved in classing the laws of such groups; the same principles apply to constitutions.

342.03   Revision and amendment of constitutions and other basic instruments

Class amendments dealing with a specific subject with the subject in constitutional law, if there is provision for that subject under 342, e.g., amendments dealing with election law, 342.07. If the subject is not provided for in 342, class with the subject elsewhere in law, e.g., the United States prohibition amendment (dealing with alcoholic beverages) 344.730541.

342.035 Proposed and pending amendments

Class texts of proposed constitutions at 342.023.

342.042 Levels of government

Including home rule (*see also 342.09*), interstate compacts.

Class interstate compacts on a specific subject with the subject in law, e.g., compacts on seaports and their facilities 343.0967.

342.05 Legislative branch of government

Including lobbying.

Since the Library of Congress is part of the legislative branch of the U.S. government, class legal matters relative to the Librarian of Congress as a government official of the United States at 342.7305.

342.06 **Executive branch of government**

·Administrative law involves the exercise by the executive branch of certain judicial functions, e.g., settling disputes, imposing fines, specifying certain remedies. When a work deals with such functions, it is classed here. Class administrative law on a specific subject with the subject in law, e.g., the role of the U.S. Federal Aviation Administration in settling a dispute with air traffic controllers 343.730976. Standards set by an agency in connection with a specific subject are classed with the subject outside of law, e.g., standards for safety in health care facilities 363.1562.

Class here executive advisory bodies.

342.062 Chief and deputy chief executives

Including provisional courts (usually existing under martial law); war powers.

342.064 Executive departments and ministries

Including reorganization.

342.066 Administrative procedure

Including government records management.

Class maintenance of privacy at 342.0858.

342.0664 Regulatory agencies and administrative courts

Including Conseil d'État of France (342.440664); hearing examiners.

Class general works on the executive function of administering and enforcing the law in 350–354.

342.068   Officials and employees

Including personal liability of public officials.

Class legal matters relating to the Librarian of Congress as a government official of the United States at 342.7305.

342.07   Election law

See 324.6 vs. 342.07.

342.08   Jurisdiction of governmental units over persons

Including census law.

342.085   [Jurisdiction of governmental units over] Individual activities

Including individual rights of servicemen.

Class here comprehensive works on individual rights (342.085), citizenship (342.083), and capacity and status of persons (346.013).

Class claims of denial of constitutional rights to specific social groups or aggregates in 342.087, to aliens at 342.083; specific claims with the subject in law, e.g., land claims of native races of United States 343.73025.

342.0858   Maintenance of privacy

Including privacy of individual records.

342.087   [Jurisdiction of governmental units over] Groups and social aggregates

Class occupational groups in 344.01.

342.088   Government liability

See 341.66.

342.09   Local government

Including laws relating to municipal corporations (municipal in this case pertaining to local jurisdictions).

Class general corporation law in 346.066, home rule at 342.042.

343.01   Veterans' law, and military and defense law

Class military appropriations at 355.622.

For war claims, see 341.66.

343.011   Veterans' law

Class veterans' insurance claims at 346.086364.

343.012   [Military] Manpower procurement

Class individual rights of servicemen in 342.085; reserve officers' training corps and military academies at 344.0769.

343.013   Military services

Including rank, promotion, demotion.

Class school finance for specific military educational programs at 344.0769.

343.0143   Military legal procedure and courts

Class international war trials at 341.69.

343.01997   [Coast guard]

Including coast guards when part of the armed forces.

Class peacetime functions of coast guards, e.g., safety and protection, in 344.05286.

343.025   Real property

Class here preemption of land.

See 341.754 for international preemption.

343.03   Law of public finance

Class the Finance Act (United Kingdom) in 343.4103.

343.032   Monetary law

Including commemorative medals and coins that are legal tender, limitations on the amount of gold, silver, other metals used in coinage.

Class comprehensive works on commemorative medals at 344.091.

343.034   Budgeting and expenditure

Including budgetary law.

Class the budget and its preparation in 351.722 and cognate numbers in 353–354.

343.04   **Tax law**

Class here internal revenue code, even though it contains a substantial discussion of income tax laws; legal matters relative to tax auditing.

Class Finance Act (United Kingdom) in 343.4103.

Class double taxation at 341.484, tax privacy at 342.0858, fiscal policy at 343.034, tax accounting at 343.042, taxation by levels at 343.043, tax planning applied to a specific kind of tax in 343.05–343.06, tax shelters and investment credit at 343.0523; economic aspects of and comprehensive works on taxes in 336.2.

343.042   Assessment and collection [of taxes]

Including tax accounting.

343.043   Taxes by level

Class here only comprehensive works and comparisons, e.g., national taxes in North America 343.7043, state taxes in the United States 343.73043, local taxes of jurisdictions in Pennsylvania 343.748043.

Taxes of a specific jurisdiction are classed in 343.04 or with the specific kind of tax, e.g., tax laws of the United States 343.7304, income taxes of United Kingdom 343.41052.

343.05   Kinds of taxes by base

Class internal revenue code at 343.04, social security taxes (United States) at 344.73023.

343.052   Income tax

Class internal revenue code at 343.04.

343.0523   Reductions in tax

Including income tax shelters, investment credit.

343.053   **Estate, inheritance, gift taxes**

See 346.052 for discussion of estate planning.

343.056   Customs taxes (Tariff)

Class courts dealing with this subject at 343.0560269. Note that since it deals with more than one subject, the U.S. Court of Customs and Patent Appeals is classed at 347.7328.

Class works on customs that include shipping and commerce in 343.087.

343.064   [Taxes] On fiduciary trusts

Including taxes on pension trusts.

343.066   [Taxes] **On organizations**

Class here status of tax-exempt organizations.

343.07   **Regulation of economic activity**

Including daylight-saving time.

Class here comprehensive works on licensing, on industry and trade.

Class international licensing at 341.753; licensing in connection with a specific subject with the subject in law, e.g., licenses for motor vehicles 343.0944, for operators of motor vehicles 343.0946, for specific occupations 344.0176 (however, class legal aspects of certification of teachers at 344.078, educational aspects at 379.157); administrative aspects of licensing in 351.7–351.8.

343.072   **Unfair [business] practices**

Class antitrust policies in 338.8.

343.075   Production controls

Including standardization.

343.078   **[Regulation of] Secondary industries and services**

Note that social insurance, social welfare, and regulation of industry with respect to public health are classed in 344 Social law.

343.07869   [Regulation of construction of buildings]

Class here comprehensive works on legal aspects of the construction of buildings.

Class construction law relating to regional or city planning or land use at 346.045.

343.08   Regulation of trade

Including warranties and guarantees.

Class comprehensive works on the regulation of trade and industry in 343.07.

343.082   [Regulation of] Advertising and labeling

Class restrictions on posting of advertisements at 346.045, legal aspects of advertising industry in 343.0786591, interdisciplinary works on advertising in 659.1.

343.083   [Regulation of] Prices

Class price support for agricultural products in 343.076.

343.0851   [Regulation of trade in products of agriculture]

See 343.083.

343.087   **[Regulation of] Foreign (International) trade**

Class here works combining treatment of trade, customs taxes (343.056), and general shipping (343.0932).

343.088   [Regulation of] Domestic trade

Including domestic trade on days of religious observance, e.g., Sunday.

343.093   **[Control of] Transportation**

Class here comprehensive works on the law of carriers.

Class transportation safety in connection with a specific mode of transportation with the mode, e.g., rail transportation safety 343.095; transportation insurance at 346.0862.

343.094–.097 [Control of] Nonlocal transportation

Class local transportation in 343.098.

343.0944   **[Control of] Vehicles**

Including warranty and product recall.

Class vehicle product liability at 346.0382, vehicle insurance at 346.086092.

343.0948   **[Control of] Commercial [vehicular] services**

Class local bus and truck services, taxicabs at 343.0982.

343.096   [Control of] Water transportation

Including municipal (domestic) prize law.

343.0981   [Control of] Pedestrian traffic

Including footpaths and trails.

343.099   **[Control of] Communications**

Class here mass media.

343.0992   [Control of] Postal service

Class postal offenses at 345.0236.

343.0998   Press law

Class here a national publications act.

344.01   **Labor**

Class here fees, wages, licensing for specific occupations and professions.

Class factory law in 344.01767, U.S. National Labor Relations Board in 344.730189.

344.0176134 [Labor law with respect to legal profession]

> Including admission to the bar.

344.0189041 [Labor-management (Collective) bargaining and disputes in industries and occupations other than extractive, manufacturing, construction]

> Do not add 331795 to 344.0189041 for collective bargaining in the public service; instead add 3511 and cognate numbers in 353–354, and related numbers in 352.

344.023 Old age and survivors' insurance

> Class "social security" in the United States at 344.73023.

344.031–.032 Welfare work and services

> Class welfare services to the addicted in 344.0446; legal aid in criminal cases at 345.01, in civil cases at 347.017.

344.035643 [Discipline of prisoners]

> Including legal rights of prisoners under the rules of the institution.

> Class constitutional rights in 342.085.

344.04 Public health

> Note that "public health" in law includes topics that are not in 614.

> Class forensic medicine at 614.1.

344.0419 Specific problems in medical practice

> Including acupuncture; legal aspects of medically approved abortions.

> Class legal aspects of abortion control at 344.0546, legal use of abortion for birth control at 344.048, criminal abortion at 345.0285.

344.044 Mental health services

> Class the capacity and status of persons of unsound mind at 346.0138.

344.048 Birth control

> Including population law.

> *See also 344.0419.*

344.049 Veterinary public health

> Class business aspects of pet shops at 343.07660887.

344.0546 [Abortion]

> *See 344.0419.*

344.063635   [**Housing**]

Including private housing.

344.079   Students

Including authority of law over students.

Class general rights of students in 342.085.

344.0794   Student services

Including school transportation.

Class busing used to achieve school integration at 344.0798.

344.0798   Segregation and discrimination

Including busing.

344.09   Culture and religion

Including language code (the official language or languages of a specific jurisdiction), flag code; medals.

Class commemorative medals at 344.091.

344.091   Historic commemoration and patriotic events

Including commemorative medals.

Class commemorative medals and coins that are legal tender at 343.032.

344.094   Historic preservation and monuments

Including historical parks.

344.097   Arts and humanities

Including laws concerning the cultural and social aspects of the performing arts.

Class regulation of economic aspects of the performing arts in 343.078791.

344.099   Amusements

Including professional and amateur athletics.

Class performing arts at 344.097, fish and game laws at 346.046954.

345 **Criminal law**

Criminal law deals with actions of so damaging a nature that the interests of society are considered to be directly at stake. For this reason cases in criminal law are always between the state in its capacity as the body politic and the individual charged with a crime. A dispute between two private persons (natural or corporate) becomes a civil law case (compare meaning of "civil law" in 340 Terminology: Civil law). Penal action is the possible result of a criminal case. In a civil case damages are awarded or some other remedy is found. It should be noted that the state can also bring a suit at civil law, acting in this case as a juristic person rather than as the body politic.

Care must be taken in determining the jurisdiction involved in procedure and courts. *See 347 for a fuller discussion of this.*

Class comprehensive works on civil and criminal courts and procedures in 347.

345.01 Criminal courts

Class legal aid in civil cases at 347.017, military legal procedure and courts at 343.0143.

Special developments for criminal procedure and courts in Scotland and England follow 345.3–345.9 in Edition 19.

345.02 **Criminal offenses**

Class here specific trials and trials of specific offenses and classes of offenses, e.g., trials of offenses against persons 345.0250269, a trial of a specific case of murder 345.025230269.

It should be noted that certain acts listed as criminal offenses here are also to be found in 346.03 as torts (a part of civil law). Works on these acts should be classed according to the point of view taken in the work or the type of legal action being brought. Thus libel and slander considered from the standpoint of criminal law are classed at 345.0256, considered as a tort at 346.034. *See 345 for distinction between civil and criminal law.*

Observe that the area used is that for the court where the trial took place, not the place where the crime took place. (*See 347.*).

345.04 Liability, responsibility, guilt

Including defenses for a specific offense (e.g., self-defense); double jeopardy.

345.05   General criminal procedure

Class interdisciplinary works on criminal justice, i.e., those that discuss also criminology and police services, in 364.

345.052   Criminal investigation and law enforcement

Class here police manuals: in most instances these manuals address themselves to questions of what police officers may or may not legally do in the course of carrying out their duties. If broader in scope, the manuals are classed in 363.2.

Note that "interception of communication" in the first note in Edition 19 includes wiretapping.

345.072   Pretrial procedure

Including plea bargaining, summons.

Note that one form of pretrial release is release on bail.

346.013   Capacity and status of persons

Including capacity and status of physically handicapped persons.

Class rehabilitation of criminals (reinstatement, after service of sentence, of a criminal's personal rights lost by judicial sentence) at 345.077.

346.0163   Husband and wife

Including legal status of homemakers.

346.0166   Divorce, separation, annulment

Class child support at 346.0172.

346.017   Parent and child

Including custody.

346.02   Contracts and agency

A contract is an agreement, implicit or explicit, between two or more parties. The contract itself is not law, but is enforceable at law. The following aspects of contracts are classed in law: their legality and enforceability, disputes concerning them, breach of contract, how to draft contracts so that they will be legal.

Class law of contracts on a specific subject not provided for here with the subject in law, e.g., a partnership contract 346.0682. The contract itself is classed with the subject outside of law: if governmental in 351–354, e.g., civil defense contracts 351.755; if nongovernmental with the specific subject using standard subdivision 0687 if applicable, e.g., roofing contracts 695.0687.

346.024   Contracts of service

         Including mechanics' liens.

346.03   Torts (Delicts)

         Physical and personal damages are inherent in all torts.

         See discussion at 345.02 for distinction between torts and crimes.

346.032   Negligence

         Class malpractice at 346.033, medical malpractice at 346.0332.

346.038   Strict liability

         Including liability for damages caused by pollution as a result of a hazardous activity or occupation.

346.0382   Product liability

         Including product liability for specific products.

346.043   **Real property**

         See 331.1–.5 vs. 346.043.

346.043   Real property

         Including swimming pools; mobile homes.

346.0432   Ownership [of real property] (Land tenure)

         Including squatters' rights.

346.0435   Easements and servitudes [on real property]

         Including rights of way, e.g., for pipelines.

346.0436   Transfer [of real property]

         Including vendors and purchasers of real property; escrows.

346.04362   Acquisition and purchase [of real property]

         Class preemption in international law at 341.754.

346.0437   Real-estate business

         Including real-estate investment trusts.

346.045   Regional and city planning

         Including building codes that relate to regional or city planning or land use.

         Class laws governing construction of buildings in 343.07869.

346.046954   **[Government control and regulation of animal resources]**

         Class here fish and game laws.

346.047   Personal property

Personal property is normally movable property, e.g., automobiles, books, animals. However, despite the fact that it is movable, a mobile home is considered to be real property and should be classed in 346.043.

Including leasing of computers.

346.048   Intangible property

Including public lending rights (a scheme allowing authors and publishers to receive fees when their books are lent out by libraries).

Add law s.s. 0269 as usual to subdivisions of this number marked by * to designate courts and court procedures, e.g., a court dealing exclusively with copyrights 346.04820269. *But see note at 346.0486.*

346.0486   Patents

Class U.S. Court of Customs and Patent Appeals at 347.7328.

346.052   Succession

Class here comprehensive works on how to plan the disposition of an estate. Note that many works called estate planning are primarily about avoidance of taxes on the estate. These should be classed in 343.053.

346.056   Administration of estates

Including bankruptcy related to estates.

346.065   Business enterprises

Including sale of businesses, record requirements for businesses.

Class record requirements for a specific kind of organization with the kind, e.g., record requirements for a government corporation 346.067; record requirements for a specific subject with the subject in law, e.g., workmen's compensation insurance records 344.021.

346.0652   Small business

Class small corporations in 346.066.

346.066   Corporations

Class comprehensive works on corporation and commercial law in 346.07.

346.0666 Securities and security holders

Including what a corporation must do to make certain that its securities are valid, shareholders' rights, shareholders' meetings.

Class a tender offer with the subject in law to which it applies, e.g., tender offers for settlement of debts 346.077, a tender offer for treasury bills 346.0922.

346.0668 Kinds of corporations

Including credit unions.

346.068 Unincorporated business enterprises

Including land trusts.

346.0682 Partnerships

Including joint ventures.

346.07 Commercial law

Class here comprehensive works on how to plan the disposition of an estate. Note that many works called estate planning are primarily about avoidance of taxes on the estate. These should be classed in 343.053.

Class a specific aspect of business law with the subject in law, e.g., law concerning securities 346.092.

346.072 Sale

Class conditional sales at 346.074.

346.073 Loan

Including usury, truth in lending.

346.074 Secured transactions

Including securities for bankers' advances, liens.

Class mortgage insurance as a form of economic assistance at 343.0742, mechanics' liens at 346.024.

346.077 Debtor and creditor relationships

Including assignment.

346.078 Bankruptcy

Class a specific aspect of bankruptcy with the subject, e.g., bankruptcy in relation to the administration of estates 346.056.

346.086 Insurance

Class mortgage insurance as a form of economic assistance at 343.0742.

346.092   **Securities**

Examples: stocks, bonds.

Class what a corporation must do to make certain a security is valid at 346.0666, the security a borrower must provide to assure that he will repay a debt at 346.074.

346.0926   Marketing agents and arrangements [for securities]

Including par value modification.

347   **Civil procedure and courts**

Care must be taken in determining the jurisdiction involved in procedure and courts. The location of the court does not necessarily determine this. For example, procedure in a court in Boston, Massachusetts, would be classed at 347.744 if a state court, at 347.73 if a United States district court; only a local Boston court, established under and interpreting Boston ordinances, would be classed at 347.74461. Except for local courts, this problem does not usually arise in countries with unitary rather than federal governments, e.g., France.

347.01   Courts

Class juvenile procedure and courts in 345.08; courts dealing with a single specific subject with the subject in law, using law s.s. 0269, e.g., tax courts 343.040269; provisional courts at 342.062, e.g., U.S. Provisional Court for the state of Louisiana 342.73062.

Special developments for civil procedure and courts in Scotland, England, and the United States follow 347.3–347.9 in Edition 19.

347.012   General considerations [of courts]

Including judicial review, power to use contempt of court prerogative.

Class contempt of court as an offense in 345.0234.

347.013   Judicial administration (Court management)

Including judicial statistics, cost of running a court in the cost-benefit sense.

Class the economics of a court system at 338.4734701.

347.014   Judges

Class a judge or judges associated with a specific court with the court, e.g., judges of the High Court of Justice in England 347.4202534, judges of a juvenile court 345.081.

347.016   Other court officials

Including manuals for specific types of officials.

See also 347.014; the same reasoning applies to other officials.

347.017   Legal aid

Class here comprehensive works on legal aid.

Class legal aid in criminal cases at 345.01, legal aid as a welfare service at 362.58.

347.02   Courts with general original jurisdiction

For many countries and U.S. states, courts with such names as Circuit, District, County, Municipal, Superior Court are classed here. Note that in Massachusetts and New Hampshire the General Court is the legislative body.

347.04   Courts with specialized jurisdiction

Including claims courts.

347.05   Generalities of procedure

Class court procedure with respect to a single specific subject with the subject in law, using law s.s. 0269, e.g., court procedure in tax matters 343.040269.

347.0504   Practice

As defined in Edition 19 this is the art and science of conducting a . court case. *For a discussion of the difference between this and law as a profession, see 340.023.*

347.064   Kinds [of evidence]

Including methods of analyzing, understanding, utilizing hospital records for trial practice.

347.067   Expert testimony

Class medical jurisprudence (the science that applies the principles and practice of the different branches of medicine to the elucidation of doubtful questions in a court of justice) at 614.1. (*See examples under 614.1 in the text of Edition 19.*) Forensic psychiatry and forensic toxicology are also classed at 614.1. Class presentation of medical evidence in court in 345.06 or 347.06 depending on the kind of case, medical science as a means of detecting crime in 363.25, other branches of science with the subject, e.g., forensic chemistry 543–545.

347.07   Trials

Class a trial dealing with a specific subject with the subject in law, using law s.s. 0269, e.g., a bankruptcy trial 346.0780269.

347.08   Appellate procedure

See 340 Legal writing.

348   **Laws (Statutes), regulations, cases**

The forms listed here are comprehensive in nature, i.e., they cover the whole of the law of a specific jurisdiction or a major portion thereof. Class these forms confined to a specific branch or topic with the branch or topic, using law s.s. 026 and its subdivisions, e.g., a digest of tax laws 343.0402638. Class treatises covering the whole of the law of a jurisdiction in 349.

A special development for the United States follows 348.3–348.9 in Edition 19.

348.01   Preliminary materials

Including statistical reports of bills passed or vetoed, reports on the status of bills.

See discussion under 342–347: s.s. 0262.

348.02   Laws (Statutes) and regulations

Including statutes arranged in alphabetical order.

348.022–.023 Statutes [and] Codes

For statutes and codes of localities use the most specific area number that will contain the jurisdiction in question, e.g., local ordinances of Rocky Mount, North Carolina 348.75646022, in which the area part of the notation is for the broader concept of Edgecombe County, North Carolina.

348.026–.028 Guides [to laws (statutes) and regulations]

Class guides to a specific collection of laws with the collection, e.g., a citator to the United States Code 348.7323.

348.028   Checklist, tables, indexes [to laws (statutes) and regulations]

Class union lists of general legal materials in 016.34, of legal materials on a specific subject with the subject, e.g., of criminal materials 016.345.

348.041–.043 [National, regional, state and provincial] Reports

Reports of cases should contain a relatively full treatment of each case as well as the ultimate decision. *See also 348.044.*

348.044 Court decisions

Contains chiefly the decisions themselves. May or may not have brief background information on each case. *See also 348.041–.043.*

348.046–.048 Guides [to cases and combined guides to laws (statutes), regulations, cases]

Class guides to a specific set of court reports with the reports, e.g., a citator to the United States Supreme Court reports 348.73413.

348.3–.9 **[Laws (Statutes), regulations, cases of] Specific jurisdictions and areas**

Class here general collections of repealed laws. Class repealed laws on a specific subject with the subject in law; legislative procedure involved in repealing a law in 328.37.

349 **Law of individual states and nations (Municipal law)**

Class here comprehensive works on the law of specific jurisdictions, e.g., the law of Australia 349.94, of Mexico City 349.7253.

Class original materials on the law of a specific jurisdiction in 348.

350 Public administration Executive branch of government Military art and science

SUMMARY

The division falls into two major parts: 350–354 for public administration and the executive branch of government; 355–359 for military art and science. Military art and science, which include naval, marine, air, coast guard, and any other defensive or offensive arms of central governments, are also found at the general number 351, but only when accompanied by a treatment of the administration of government by the executive branch.

351 Central governments does *not* deal with specific central governments. It is primarily a table for the synthesis of numbers for the individual central governments found in 353 (U.S. federal and state governments) and 354 (all other central governments at analogous levels). That is, 351 provides numbers for the administrative activities of the governments in 353 and 354. The numbers in 351 in their pure state will be assigned to works only when they deal with the subject in general or when several central governments not falling within the same larger jurisdiction are treated together, e.g., a treatise comparing the executive branches of the United States, France, Republic of South Africa, and China is classed at 351. (Standard subdivision 09 plus area may be added to 351 for several governments in the same area, e.g., executive branches of several South American governments 351.00098.)

Note that 350 and 351 contain duplicate sets of subdivisions. Those in 350 are expressed only in an add note at 350.0001–350.996, while those in 351 are spelled out in full. In previous editions the subdivisions were spelled out at 350, and the add note appeared at 351. The change was made for Edition 19 because the presence of the extra 0 in 350 caused numerous errors in number building. The presence of an elaborate set of subdivisions at 351 must not be taken to imply that 351 is more comprehensive. Such is not the case.

Branches of government

An examination of 320 Political science discloses that the legislative branch of government is the only one of the three major branches of government dealt with separately there. The judicial branch of government is classed in 347, the executive branch in 350–354. The executive and judicial branches belong to the field of political science, but political works on them are classed in the appropriate number for the branch. *Administration* of a specific branch of government is classed with the branch. Hence, administration of the legislative branch of government is classed at 328.306, of the offices of individual members at 328.331. Administration of the judicial branch of government is classed in 347.0068, of courts at 347.013.

Class in 350–354 political works on the executive branch, administration of the executive branch, and comprehensive works on the administration of all three branches. However, comprehensive works dealing with all aspects of all branches are classed in 320.

Levels of government

In addition to branches of government consideration must be given to levels of government: national, state or provincial, and various types of local jurisdiction. In the Dewey Decimal Classification the term "central governments" includes both national and state or provincial governments. Regardless of level, the specific branch of government is classed with the branch. Thus, city councils (in the United States) are classed in 328, local courts in 347.01. Consequently, 352 is used only for the executive branch at the local level (politics and administration) or for administration of all three branches at the local level.

350   Class here works dealing with all three levels of government comprehensively, or with both central and local governments, whether these be national and local or state/provincial and local.

351   Class here works dealing with central governments only, whether national, state or provincial, or both. Do not use this number if local government is included, *but see 351.093.*

352   Class here works dealing with local governments only.

Jurisdictions

In addition to branch and level the jurisdiction must be considered. Specific branches of specific jurisdictions are classed with the branch, e.g., United States Congress 328.73, United States courts 347.731.

351   This section will be used most frequently as the basis for synthesis in other sections allotted to specific jurisdictions. 351 numbers are used directly only for general and theoretical works referring to no specific jurisdiction, and for works treating of several jurisdictions. *See paragraph 2 of introduction to 350.*

353–354   These are the numbers allotted to specific central jurisdictions. The same combination of levels applies here as at 351. *See 351 Levels of government.*

353   Class here comprehensive works on the executive branch, on the administration of all three branches of the United States government.

353.9   Class here comprehensive works on the executive branches, on the administration of all three branches of the state governments of the United States treated comparatively or comprehensively.

353.97–.99 Class here comprehensive works on the executive branches, on the administration of all three branches of the governments of specific states, e.g., the executive branch of the government of South Dakota 353.9783.

354   Class here comprehensive works on the executive branch, on the administration of all three branches of central governments of jurisdictions other than those of the United States and the states that comprise it. The area number for the jurisdiction is added directly to 354, e.g., the executive branch of the government of Canada 354.71. The numbers for the states or provinces of those nations that are so divided are built in the same way as the numbers for the national government, e.g., the executive branch of the government of Prince Edward Island 354.717. In 354 comprehensive works on the governments of states or provinces of a specific jurisdiction are classed in the same number as the national government, e.g., the executive branches of the various provinces of Canada 354.71.

Citation Order

The basic citation order for 353–354 is level + jurisdiction + specific topic (agency, activity, etc.) + standard subdivision. For example:

(1) A discussion of leaves of absence for employees of the government of Spain:

Level	Jurisdiction	Specific topic	S.s.
national	Spain	leaves of absence	none
354 +	46	+ 00164 =	354.4600164

(2) Duties of the lieutenant governor of California:

Level	Jurisdiction	Specific topic	S.s.
state	California	executive branch (lieut. gov.)	none
353.9 +	794	+ 0318 =	353.97940318

(3) A dictionary of the terms used in administering the mining operations of South Africa:

Level	Jurisdiction	Specific topic	S.s.
national	South Africa	mining	dictionary
354 +	68 +	0082382	+ 03 =

354.68008238203

Local government

Class in 352 comprehensive works on executive branches of local governments, comprehensive works on the administration of all three branches of local governments. In this section the basic citation order differs from that in 353–354: level + specific topic + jurisdiction. For instance:

(1) A directory of the local government organizations dealing with the fisheries of Los Angeles County:

Level	Specific topic	Jurisdiction
county	primary industries (fish)	Los Angeles County
352 +	942362 +	0979493 = 352.9423620979493

(Directories cannot be attached as a standard subdivision, since s.s. 09 [jurisdiction] has already been attached.)

(2) Property tax assessment in Budapest, Hungary:

Level	Specific topic	Jurisdiction
city	prop. tax asses.	Budapest
352 +	13521 +	094391 = 352.13521094391

Public administration

In several respects public administration is a difficult concept to deal with. It includes the usual components of administration: planning, organizing, staffing (personnel administration), financing, housing (plant administration), and equipping a unit to do a job or perform a function. These activities, which might be called "internal management," are the specific province of 350–354.

The performance of the function for which an agency or other unit exists is classed with the subject. Take, for instance, an agency regulating railroads. If the work in question is about the history of the agency, or about its internal administration it is classed in 351.875 and cognate and related numbers in 352–354. However, what the agency does with respect to railroads is classed in 385. A grant of money to a railroad by the agency, for instance, is classed at 385.1, fares approved by it are classed at 385.12, not in the public administration number.

Some government agencies (internal administration and all) are classed entirely outside 350–354. A railroad owned and operated by a government corporation is classed in 385, not in 351.875. Prisons and their administration are classed in 365, not in 351.8495, the latter number being reserved for agencies that supervise and regulate prisons. Public schools and their administration are classed in 370–379, not in 351.851, the latter number being reserved for departments and boards of education. This principle applies with special force to socialist countries where most enterprises are run by the government.

The type of agency classed in the 350s, then, is the type that enforces the law, grants charters and licenses, and registers and certifies. Those agencies that perform a direct service to members of the public, e.g., transporting them, educating them, incarcerating the delinquent among them, are classed with their respective subjects outside public administration.

Regrettably, there is a class of agencies that can turn up both in the 350s and with the subject: the class of agencies doing research or procuring and disseminating information. For example, an agency taking the census is classed at 351.819, but a state library or federal library is classed at 027.5 and a public library at 027.4. Careful use of the notes of instruction in the text of Edition 19 will help in such cases.

Citation order of specific topics

In general, 351 follows an order of precedence in which topics bearing a notation with no zeros are preferred to those with one zero, those with one zero to those with two, and so on. Standard subdivisions (which have three zeros in 351) are fourth, or last, in the order of choice. A consideration of bureaucracy (351.001) in a police department (351.74) is classed at 351.74. A consideration of bureaucracy (351.001) in a justice department at the cabinet level (351.05) is classed at 351.05. Intergovernmental cooperation (351.09) in police work (351.74) is classed at 351.74. This is the normal order for any schedule unless there are explicit instructions to the contrary.

Such instructions appear at 353. Here an order of precedence prevails which corresponds to that of 351 rather than one governed by the number of zeros in the numbers of 353. For instance, 353.001–353.009 corresponds to 351.1–351.9. Therefore, the numbers in 353.001–353.009 take precedence over all others. 353.1–353.8 corresponds to 351.01–351.08, although the development is not strictly parallel. These subsections are second in the order of precedence. 353.01–353.09 corresponds to 351.001–351.009 and comes third in the order of precedence. Standard subdivisions come last, as they always do. Thus a study of bureaucracy (353.01) in the Federal Bureau of Investigation (353.0074) is classed at 353.0074. A work on bureaucracy (353.01) in the Department of Justice (353.5) is classed at 353.5. There is no parallel to the third example of the first paragraph of this section. Intergovernmental administrative relations between the federal government and other governments at the same level (other national governments) are international in scope and are classed in 353.0089 (corresponding to 351.89). Relations of the federal government with state governments are classed in the appropriate numbers in 353.9 that deal with state governments. Relations of the federal government directly with local governments must be classed in 353 without subdivision. *But see 351.093.*

Citation order varies also in 353.91–353.93, where state governments of the United States are considered comprehensively or comparatively. Again, the citation order follows that of 351. First in choice of order are the subdivisions corresponding to 351.1–351.9. In this case, that means 353.931–353.939. Second in order are the subdivisions corresponding to 351.01–353.09, in this case 353.921–353.929. Third are the subdivisions corresponding to 351.001–351.009, or 353.911–353.919. Fourth, and last, are standard subdivisions, in triple-zero position in 351, but appearing here at 353.901–353.909. A consideration of bureaucracy (353.911) in state police departments (353.9374) is classed at 353.9374. A consideration of bureaucracy (353.911) in state justice departments (353.925) is classed at 353.925. Intergovernmental cooperation (353.929) between the Federal Bureau of Investigation and the various state police departments (353.9374) is classed at 353.9374.

The same kind of variations appear again in 353.97–353.99 governments of specific states of the United States. The citation order for the specific states is again that which prevails in 351. (*See the table at 353.97–353.99 in Edition 19; applicable subdivisions are shown at this point.*) Citing the various subdivisions in their 351 order, we get the following:

351.1–.9	001–009	
351.01–.09	1–9	From the table of subdivisions
351.001–.009	01–09	under 353.97–353.99 in Edition 19
351.0001–.0009	0001–0009	

Therefore, a work on bureaucracy (353.978301) in the South Dakota state police department (353.97830074) is classed at 353.97830074. A work on bureaucracy (353.978301) in the justice department of South Dakota (353.97835) is classed at 353.97835. Intergovernmental cooperation (353.97839) between the state police of South Dakota (353.97830074) and the Federal Bureau of Investigation is classed at 353.97830074.

Again, in 354 the citation order for central governments other than those of the United States corresponds to that of 351. (*See table at 354.3–354.9 in Edition 19.*) In order of choice and with their equivalents:

351.1–.9	001–009	
351.01–.08	061–068	
351.09	08	From the table of subdivisions
351.001–.004	01–04	under 354.3–354.9 in Edition 19
351.007	07	
351.009	09	
351.0001–.0009	0001–0009	

Thus, bureaucracy (354.4501) in the national police of Italy (354.450074) is classed at 354.450074. Bureaucracy (354.4501) in the justice department of Italy (354.45065) is classed at 354.45065. Intergovernmental cooperation (354.4508) between the national (354.450074) and local police in Italy is classed at 354.450074.

350   **Public administration   Executive branch of government**

Class annual reports, nominations, and other administrative reports for a specific agency with the appropriate number for the agency in the 350s.

Class proposed legislation with the specific subject in 340 Law. Class a specific service of government with the subject, e.g., education 370.

See also note at 350 under Levels of government.

350.0005   Serial publications

> Class serial administrative reports at 351.0006.

351   **Central governments**

> For all comments below on 351 and its subdivisions, numbers in 351 are used directly only for works dealing with no one jurisdiction.

351.0006   Reports

> Standard subdivision 06 throughout the 350–354 complex is to be used for administrative reports, i.e., those covering primarily internal administration. Reports covering the actual dealings with and effects on the clientele of the agency are classed with the subject. For example, a report on the internal administration of a bureau of mines is classed at 351.8238206; but a report by the bureau on the number of mines (of all sorts) inspected and its findings is classed in 338.2 if the thrust of the report is economic, in 622 if technical. If in doubt, class in 351.0006 and cognate and related numbers in 352–354.

351.003   **General considerations of executive branch**

> Works classed here are usually, but not always, largely political in nature.

351.0036   Termination of tenure of chief executive before expiration of term

> Class the power of the legislature to impeach at 328.3453 (for a specific legislature in 328 + area number + 07453 from the table under 328.4–328.9 in Edition 19, e.g., the United States Congress 328.7307453).

> Class impeachment of other public officials at 351.993.

351.004   Cabinets and councils of state

> Class here works dealing with the cabinet as such, its role and place in government. Broader works, describing the whole government, its structure and services, are classed in 351 without subdivision or the comprehensive number for the specific jurisdiction. Confusion is possible, because this second type of work does, of necessity, name and discuss the major (cabinet level) departments. If in doubt, prefer 351 without subdivision.

351.0076   Evaluation and reporting

> *See 351.0006 for the reports themselves.*

351.009   **Special commissions, corporations, agencies, quasi-administrative bodies**

Class here only general works dealing with the nature of such bodies, their role and function in government. A specific commission, etc., is classed with its function in public administration, e.g., one dealing with labor problems 351.83.

351.0092   Government corporations (Public enterprises)

Class public corporations dealing with education at 351.851.

Public corporations that are in fact businesses are treated in the same manner as business corporations. For instance, the history of such a body is classed in 338.76, e.g., a government corporation operating a mine 338.7622.

351.01–.08   **Specific executive departments and ministries of cabinet rank**

It should be observed that government agencies are divided into two classes: (1) those of cabinet or council of state (the "cabinet" of a state or province) level and (2) all the others whether subordinate to one of the cabinet level departments or independent. Agencies of the second class are provided for in 351.74–351.89.

Class here specific departments only.

Class comprehensive works at 351.004 subject to the limitations noted there.

351.093   Relations of local governments with higher levels

This is the only exception to the rule stated under 350 Levels of government 351 that works including local government are not classed in 351. When the relations between two levels are discussed, the work is classed with the central government level; but the work must stress the factor of relationship. If in doubt, prefer 350.

351.1–351.72 **Specific aspects of administration of public agencies**

Class specific aspects of administration of specific kinds of agencies in 351.74–351.89.

351.1 **Personnel management**

Class in this number and its subdivisions the government's relations with its own employees. Administration of similar measures with respect to the work force at large (outside of government employment) is not classed here. For example, equal employment opportunity in the government's own hiring practices is classed at 351.104, the administration of equal employment opportunity programs for the work force at large is classed at 351.833, but the actual measures employed and their effect are classed at 331.128. Employee benefits for the government work force are classed at 351.1234, but administration of government insurance for the work force at large at 351.8256. Labor relations with respect to the government work force are classed in 351.17, but general regulation of labor-management relations in 351.83.

351.2 **Lists of officials and employees**

Although registers of civil service personnel are classed here, registers of diplomatic personnel are classed elsewhere in 350–354.

Registers of diplomatic personnel of a specific country are classed with the appropriate country in 353–354, e.g., diplomatic personnel of the United States 353.00892, of France 354.4400892.

Lists of personnel accredited by various countries to one specific country are classed in 351.892 plus 09 plus the appropriate area notation for the country *to which* they are assigned. For example, a list of diplomatic personnel assigned *to* the United States by various countries is classed at 351.8920973. NOTE THAT THIS IS THE ONLY INSTANCE IN WHICH AREA NOTATIONS FOR JURISDICTION ARE ADDED TO 351 NUMBERS. Ordinarily, specific topics considered with respect to a specific country are classed in 353–354.

351.3   Civil service examinations

Class here discussion of civil service examinations in general, their role and function in the process of selecting government personnel, their construction and evaluation. Class here works on how to prepare for civil service exams, unless they are restricted to examinations for a particular type of job. Class examinations for a particular type of job and works about such examinations with the subject, using s.s. 076, e.g., a civil service examination in accounting 657.076.

351.4   Government work force

Be cautious in the use of this quite general number. Follow the definition note in Edition 19 closely. Almost all the particulars are classed elsewhere, e.g., compensation 351.12, lists 351.2.

351.5   Pensions

Class economic aspects and interdisciplinary works on pensions at 331.252, general works on administration of pensions at 658.3253.

351.6   Merit system (Civil service)

This is confined largely to the history of the civil service and the merit system, and to works about its role and function in government, in personnel selection, and its relation to the political structure.

351.7   Other administrative activities; administration of agencies maintaining social order

This miscellaneous subsection includes (in 351.71–351.72) certain aspects of internal administration of agencies (with the rest of the aspects in 351.007 and 351.1–351.6), and (in 351.74–351.78) the administration of certain specific governmental functions as well.

351.7122–   Purchase and rental of land for government buildings |and| Purchase
.7123   and rental of buildings for government use

Class here the acquisition of real estate by the government for its own use in performing its functions, e.g., a new building for the U.S. Library of Congress 353.007122. Government ownership of land (including its acquisition) in general and for use of the general public is classed in 333.1.

351.722   **Budgets and budgeting**

Class here the total government budget, e.g., U.S. budget 353.00722. Class appropriations for a specific cabinet-level agency with the agency, e.g., appropriations for the U.S. Department of Justice 353.5; for a subordinate agency with the function, e.g., the budget for a bureau of forestry 351.82338.

Bills to authorize appropriations are classed with the specific subject in law. *See discussion under 342–347: s.s. 0262.*

351.7232   Auditing and audits

Audits are often management surveys that deal with the whole operation of an organization and occasionally also with parts of it. Such an audit does not deal with policy, but does concern itself with whether the policy that has been established is being implemented properly; often it recommends revised procedures. Class such an audit of a government agency or activity with the subject, e.g., of the U.S. Department of Defense 353.6, of public works by the Department of Defense 353.0086, of the U.S. Patent Office 353.00824, of U.S. regulation and control of museums 353.00853, of a court in 347.01, of a legislature in 328 plus area plus 076. Regular financial audits are classed at 351.7232.

Government audits of private enterprises occur when the private firm performs work for the government and it becomes desirable to determine whether the firm is carrying out its end of the bargain; class such audits with the subject plus s.s. 0681, e.g., an audit of a company making desks for the government 684.140681.

351.724   Tax administration

Despite the elaborate array of subdivisions (which are inherited from earlier editions) these numbers include only the agencies administering taxes of all kinds and the problems and procedures used by the government in handling tax matters. This is not the place for interdisciplinary works on taxes. These are classed in 336.2. Note that most works on taxes deal with the law and are classed in 343.04–343.06. *See discussion at 336.2.*

351.74–.8   Administration of agencies maintaining social order [and] Administration of agencies controlling specific fields of activity

These subsection constitute a series covering government agencies and projects grouped by function: their history, general description, general internal administration. (*See also 351.01–.08.*) Several examples follow:

351.74   Police agencies

Class here the administration of general intelligence organizations. The organization of the FBI is classed at 353.0074, similar organizations in other countries are classed in 354 plus the number for the country plus 0074. Methods used by such organizations in crime detection are classed in 363.25.

Class functional activities of police agencies (what police do) in 363.2.

351.7782   [Agencies dealing with] Adulteration and contamination of food

Class functional activities of such agencies (what they do) in 363.192.

351.83   [Agencies dealing with] Labor

Class functional activities of such agencies in 331.

351.761–
.765   [Agencies regulating] Alcoholic beverages [and] Drugs

Here are classed the regulation and control (or prohibition) of the traffic in alcohol and drugs. Administration of services to persons addicted to these substances is classed at 351.8429.

351.8   Administration of agencies controlling specific fields of activity

See 351.74–.8.

351.819   Information and research services

Information programs of a specific agency are classed with the agency, e.g., the information program of a highway department 351.864. The specific documents produced are classed with the subject with which they deal, e.g., a government bulletin issued by an agriculture department on crop rotation 631.582. Class methods of census taking in 001.433, results of a census with the subject, e.g., population 312.

351.824   [Administration of agencies controlling] Secondary industries

Class here administrative aspects of solid waste management.

351.829   Rationing

Class here comprehensive works on administration of rationing.

Class the administration of rationing of a specific commodity with the subject, e.g., rationing of natural gas 351.8723043.

351.852   [Administration of agencies controlling] Libraries

Including governmental regulation of library finance.

Class government support of libraries at 021.83.

351.892   Embassies and legations

Class here lists of diplomatic personnel accredited by various countries to one specific country. *See also 351.2.*

351.99   **Specific aspects of malfunctioning [of government]**

Class here conflict of interest, corruption, abuse of powers in general and as they affect government and its functions. Malfunctioning of a specific agency is classed with the agency, e.g., corruption in agencies supervising railroads 351.875.

Particular omissions and malfeasances can also be considered as crimes. In this case they are classed in 364.13. If in doubt, prefer 364.13.

352   **Local governments**

Observe the following parallels between 351 and 352:

351.0006	352.0006
351.0076	352.00476
351.009	352.009
351.1	352.0051
351.2	352.0052
351.3	352.0053
351.4	352.0054
351.5	352.0055
351.6	352.0056
351.71–.72 (*See 351.7*)	352.1
351.71	352.16
351.7122–.7123	352.1622–.1623
351.72	352.12–.13, 352.17
351.722	352.12
351.7232	352.172
351.724	352.13
351.74	352.2
351.761–.765	352.9361–.9365
351.7782	352.4
351.8	352.5–.9
351.819	352.9419
351.824	352.9424
351.852	352.9452
351.99	352.002

Notes in the manual at 351 apply to the corresponding points in 352.

See also 350 Local government.

352.009   **Intergovernmental cooperation and special districts and authorities**

Class here cooperation between local governments only.

352.03–.09   **Treatment [of local governments] by specific continents, countries, localities**

Class the following topics in 352.03–352.09:

(1) The topics found in 352.002–352.009 when applied to a specific local government, e.g., regulatory agencies in New York City 352.07471.

(2) Comprehensive works on the government of a specific local jurisdiction, e.g., the government of New York City 352.07471.

(3) Comprehensive works on the local governments in a larger area, e.g., local governments in New York (state) 352.0747.

Class the topics found in 352.002–352.009 when applied to the jurisdictions in a larger area in 352.002–352.009, e.g., regulatory agencies in the local governments in New York (state) 352.009209747.

In all instances, the topics found in 352.1–352.9 are classed in 352.1–352.9, not 352.03–352.09, e.g., the budget in New York City 352.12097471, budgets in the local governments in New York (state) 352.1209747.

353–354   **Specific central governments**

Except for 353.1–353.8 (cabinet level departments of the United States federal government) and 354.1 (international administration), the subdivisions of these two sections are based on add notes using the provisions of 351, or, if spelled out, are strictly parallel to and cognate with the provisions of 351. Notes and instructions at 351 in the *Manual* and in Edition 19 are applicable in 353–354.

See also 350.

355   **Military art and science**

Military institutions as social institutions are closely related to and often interact with other social institutions. When treated in a context that is broader than military art and science, they are classed with the broader subject, e.g., military sociology 306.27, military involvement in politics and the political control of the army 322.5.

Military hardware appears both in military art and science and in military engineering (623). Physical description, design, manufacture, operation, and repair are classed in 623; procurement, deployment, and control of the units and services necessary to use them are classed in 355–359. If in doubt, prefer 355–359.

When topics in 355 are considered within the limits of a specific branch of the services, they are classed with the branch, e.g., naval tactics 359.42, not 355.42.

355.0023   [Military science as a profession]

Career guides for a specific military service are classed with the appropriate service, e.g., careers in the navy 359.0023. Area number may be added even if the guide is directed to a specific class of persons, e.g., careers for women in U.S. Navy 359.002373.

355.00711   **[Military colleges]**

Class specific military colleges as follows:

If the college in question is the official academy for the jurisdiction, class it in 355 plus s.s. 00711 plus the notation for the area it serves, e.g., the Royal Military Academy at Sandhurst, England 355.0071141, the U.S. Military Academy at West Point, New York 355.0071173.

Military schools that are not official training schools, most of whose students (except in wartime) enter civilian occupations, are treated like other higher educational institutions and classed in 378 plus the number for the area where they are located, e.g., the Virginia Military Institute (Lexington, Virginia) 378.755853, The Citadel (Charleston, South Carolina) 378.757915.

See also 355.55.

355.009   **Historical and geographical treatment [of military art and science]**

Class here only works covering or representing a number of the specific topics in 355.02–355.88.

Class the history of specific military establishments in 355.309, e.g., the Red Army 355.30947, military situation and policy in specific areas 355.03301–355.03309, militarism in specific countries 355.021309.

355.009 vs.   **Historical and geographical treatment [of military art and science] vs.**
900   **General history**

Class in 355–359 works emphasizing military art or science without consideration of the course of the war, e.g., changes in tank tactics during the course of World War 2 358.18.

Class in 900 works on military history of a war that deal with the outcome of significant events, e.g., the use of tanks on the eastern front in World War 2 and how this affected the various battles 940.5421.

If in doubt, prefer 900.

See also 930–990 Wars.

355.0092　　　**[Persons associated with military art and science]**

Class here biographies of persons associated with the whole field of military science and warfare, e.g., a biography of Karl von Clausewitz 355.00924. Class here also biographies of military officers that deal with their whole military career, e.g., Douglas MacArthur.

However, if an officer is closely associated with the history of a specific war, class his biography with the history of the war, e.g., a biography of William Tecumseh Sherman 973.730924. Class the biography of a person closely associated with a specific branch of service with the branch, e.g., of an intelligence officer 355.34320924.

355.021 vs.　**Overall concepts [of war and warfare] vs. Strategy**
355.43

"Overall" in 355.021 covers strategy in the nonoperational sense, in its broadest application. If in doubt, class strategic studies in 355.021 rather than 355.43, in which the term is used in its operational sense. (*See 355.43.*)

355.0213　　　Militarism and antimilitarism

Class here works against the military establishment, e.g., anti-Pentagon material, critiques of war and munitions.

Class critiques of the "military-industrial complex" and its profiteering in 338.47355, controversy over civil supremacy at 322.5.

355.0217　　　Nuclear and conventional warfare

Including nuclear deterrence formulas and problems, e.g., SALT.

See also 327.174.

355.028　　　Aftermath [of war]

Class here occupation in general terms only, e.g., a description of occupation forces in a country. Class government of occupied territories in 355.49.

The history of a country during a period of occupation is classed with the history of the country. Class the legal aspects of military occupation at 341.66. Government of a country by its own military establishment is classed as ordinary government in 320, its administration in 351–354.

355.031　　　Mutual security pacts

Class pacts on a specific subject with the subject, e.g., a pact on staff and high command problems 355.331. Add s.s. 09 plus area notation, if applicable, for specific pacts, e.g., NATO 355.031091821.

355.032 **Military missions and assistance**

Add area notations as instructed for the area *receiving* assistance. Use 355.03209 for the country *giving* assistance, e.g., United States assistance to South Korea 355.0325195, but United States assistance throughout the world 355.0320973.

355.0332– Military situation [and] Military policy
.0335

Situation and policy are concepts difficult to separate; therefore, use the numbers with caution. Prefer 355.03301–355.03309. Note that at 358.403 and 359.03 no distinction is made between works on situation and policy, and s.s. 09 is added whenever a specific period or place is brought out.

355.115 **Veterans' rights and benefits**

The benefits referred to here are only those provided immediately at the end of service, or discussed in the context of promises made to promote efficiency of service. In any other context, the benefits are considered social services and are classed in 362.86 or other 362 subdivisions. Class services to persons connected only indirectly with the military in 362, unless the service is provided by the military establishment, e.g., services to dependents of military personnel offered by the civil government 362, but services provided to dependents on a military post 355.34.

See also 331.255. .

355.1154 Employment and reemployment

Class planning of second careers for military retirees in 331.702 or numbers referred to from there.

355.1334 Offenses against military discipline

Including mutinies.

355.134092 **[Persons associated with awards]**

Class here biographies of persons to whom awards have been made, e.g., persons to whom the Croix de Guerre has been awarded 355.1340922. Do not, however, class a comprehensive biography of an award winner here if the person's life embraces other significant activities. Class with the subject for which the person is otherwise noted, e.g., Audie Murphy 791.430280924, not 355.1340924.

355.1342 Decorations, medals, badges, other honorary insignia

Class comprehensive works on decorations and uniforms in 355.14.

355.14 vs.   Uniforms vs. Clothing, equipment, food
355.81

> Class works on uniforms at 355.14 if the emphasis is on cut, style, color of uniforms; on insignia, identification of units or branches of service, or history of uniforms.
>
> Class works on military clothing at 355.81 if the emphasis is on function of various articles of clothing or on supply administration (from development through issue).
>
> If in doubt, prefer 355.81.

355.1409   [Historical and geographical treatment of military uniforms]

> Class uniforms of several participants in a particular war with the area number used for the war, e.g., uniforms of the Peninsular War 355.14094, not 355.140946.
>
> Class military uniforms of a specific branch with the branch, e.g., uniforms for the Royal Air Force 358.41140941. But note that it is not possible to specify area when uniforms do not approximate the whole of the number, e.g., uniforms for British paratroopers 356.166, where, since paratroop uniforms are only a small part of the scope of 356.166, s.s. 0941 is not added.

355.2232   Preservice and postservice training

> This number covers all general training of reserves.

355.224   Conscientious objectors

> Class here draft resistance.
>
> Class ethical aspects of draft resistance at 172.1, techniques for beating the draft at 355.22363.

355.26   [Military] Industrial resources

> Class manufacturing of war matériel by military forces at 358.3.

355.33   **[Military] Personnel and their hierarchy**

> *See 355.0092.*

355.332   Commissioned and warrant officers

> Officers' manuals usually cover the whole of the military service of a given country and therefore are classed in 355.009.

355.338   Enlisted personnel

> Class military unions in 331.8811355.

355.34 **Noncombat services**

Including services for military dependents, e.g., schools; social and financial services for soldiers.

Class here interdisciplinary works on civic and civilian activities of armies; but class a specific activity with the subject outside military science, e.g., public works of the U.S. Corps of Engineers 363.0973.

Class military police at 355.13323, military postal services at 355.69.

355.341 Administrative and supply services

Including the "unit level" treatment dealing directly with the persons and goods involved.

Class overall administration and supply problems in 355.6. If in doubt, prefer 355.6.

355.345 Health services

Including hospital dietary services, therapy services, services to the addicted. Consider for sanitation services if the emphasis is on promoting health of units.

355.346 Recreational services

Including NCO clubs and officers' clubs.

355.347 Religious and counseling services

Standard subdivision 09 plus area notation may be added regardless of religion, e.g., Roman Catholic chaplain services in the British army 355.3470941.

355.35 Combat units according to field of service

Including auxiliaries.

355.351 Home guards and frontier troops

Note that some home guards are actually reserve units and are classed at 355.37.

355.352 Colonial and expeditionary forces

The term "colonial" may mean either of two things: the colonies' troops in the mother country or its wars; the mother country's troops in the colonies. Class such forces with the place of service, e.g., troops raised in the French colonies serving in regular French forces 355.3520944; French units in permanent service in French African colonies 355.35209600971244. Class the services of "colonial" forces in a specific war with the history of the war.

Class the French Foreign Legion at 355.350944.

355.37   Reserves

Including military departments of the states of the United States, and military national guards and their administration. Add the area number for the individual state regardless of type of reserve.

Class training of reserves at 355.2232, reserve units of a specific kind of military force with the force, e.g., engineering reserves 358.28.

355.413   Reconnaissance

Class here comprehensive works on antisubmarine patrols.

Class aerial antisubmarine patrols at 358.45, naval antisubmarine patrols at 359.413.

355.425   [Tactics] In guerrilla warfare

Class role of guerrilla warfare in war at 355.02184.

355.43   **Strategy**

"Strategy" here is used in the context of military operations, involving only the armed forces. Class a work covering the philosophy, national policies, influence and effectiveness of civilian populations and leaders in 355.021. If in doubt, class in 355.021. *See also 355.021 vs. 355.43.*

355.45   Defense of home territory

Class a specific defensive fort or installation in 355.709.

355.48   Technical analysis of military events

Including war gaming for purposes of training and development of military understanding. Class recreational war gaming at 793.9.

355.5   **Training**

Including training of individuals.

Class training of reserves at 355.2232; training in a specific service with the service, e.g., training of air forces 358.415.

Standard subdivision 07 Study and teaching is inherent here, so prefer s.s. 09, e.g., military training schools in the Soviet Union 355.50947, not 355.507047.

355.547– .548   **Small arms and bayonet practices [and] Self-defense**

While these are essentially infantry arts, they have broader application. Class them at 356.184 if in a specifically infantry context.

355.55 Training of officers

Class the collegiate type of service academies in 355.007. However, schools for on-the-job and mid-career training of officers are classed at 355.55 or cognate numbers, even if given academic-sounding names, e.g., the Air University (United States) 358.41550976147.

See 355.48 for war gaming.

355.6 Military administration

This number is intended for top-level military planning and administration.

Class here military consultants.

·Class cabinet-level military departments at 351.06 and cognate numbers in 353–354. Administration of a specific function is classed with the function, e.g., administration of maneuvers 355.52.

355.621 Supply administration

Class administration of housing supply at 355.67.

355.622 Financial administration

Including planning for the cost of a volunteer army.

355.69 Other [military] administrative services

This number may be used for administrative services not spelled out, e.g., military postal services.

355.7 Military installations and land reservations

Installation is used here in the sense of a military camp, fort, or base.

Add s.s. 09 for the general treatment of a specific fort or system of forts, ancient or modern, used for the defense of an area, e.g., the Maginot Line 355.7094438; for installations having two or more purposes, e.g., Fort Sam Houston (training center, military headquarters, and medical center) 355.709764351.

Class installations of a specific force with the force, e.g., Fort Benning (primarily an infantry center) 356.18709758473, Fort Belvoir (primarily an engineering center) 358.209755291.

Use the area number for the location of the installation, not for the country maintaining it, e.g., the U.S. naval base on Diego Garcia 359.709697.

355.71–.75   **[Military installations]**

Note that the services provided by many of the installations listed here are classed elsewhere, e.g., post exchanges 355.341, medical services 355.345, engineering forces 358.2. Class comprehensive works on military installations and their services in the number for the service, e.g., a medical installation and its services 355.345.

355.8   **Military equipment and supplies (Matériel)**

The word "description" has been deleted from the first note in Edition 19. Class physical and technical descriptions of military equipment in 623 or other 600 numbers. (*See also 355.*)

Class comprehensive works on the research and development connected with military equipment and supplies at 355.07. Class research and development connected with specific equipment and supplies in 355.81–355.88. The word "development" at 355.8 in Edition 19 refers to procurement history rather than to the development of technology.

355.81   Clothing, equipment, food

See 355.14 vs. 355.81.

355.82–.83   **Ordnance [and] Transportation equipment and supplies**

Class here and in cognate and related numbers in 356–359 problems of arms limitation and the verification of arms control treaty provisions.

Class negotiations for arms control limitation at 327.174, arms control treaties at 341.733.

355.82   **Ordnance**

Class here only ordnance common to two or more kinds of combat forces. For example, use 355.821 for a work on both coast and naval artillery ordnance, but use 358.16, not 355.8217, for coast artillery; 359.821, not 355.8218 or 359.8218, for naval artillery.

357   **Mounted forces and warfare**

Class here without further addition the comprehensive history of specific units that started as horse cavalry but developed into mechanized or armored cavalry, e.g., the U.S. Third Cavalry Division 357. Class a history of such a unit covering only its existence as either horse or mechanized cavalry with the appropriate kind, e.g., U.S. Third Cavalry Division during the period when it was a horse unit 357.1.

357.1 **Horse cavalry**

Class here dragoons, lancers.

Class horse artillery with artillery at 358.1.

358.39 Nuclear [forces and warfare]

Class here field use of nuclear weapons, field defense against nuclear and radiological warfare, verification problems connected with nuclear test bans.

Class comprehensive works on nuclear warfare at 355.0217.

358.4 **Air forces and warfare**

Class here works on the air arms of other military branches, e.g., the British Fleet Air Arm 358.400941.

358.403 Situation and policy

Add s.s. 09 plus area number for the situation or policy of a specific country.

358.4142 [Air warfare] Tactics

Including close air support of combat.

358.4183 [Air force transportation equipment and supplies]

Class here comprehensive works on military aircraft; however, class a specific type of aircraft with the type of operation in which it is used, e.g., bombers 358.42, fighters 358.43.

358.44 Transportation forces and operations

Example: U.S. Military Air Transport Service (MATS) 358.440973.

358.45 Reconnaissance forces and operations

Including antisubmarine patrols and operations, patrolling with lighter-than-air airships.

359.03 Situation and policy

Add s.s. 09 plus area number for the situation or policy of a specific country.

359.32 **Types of ships**

Note that ships here are treated as units of naval organization and personnel. Ships treated as equipment are classed in 359.83. For example, the USS Nimitz as a unit of naval organization is classed at 359.32550973, but the development of carriers for the Japanese navy in 359.83.

359.97   Coast guard

Note that the U.S. Coast Guard is not a part of the military establishment except during time of war.

Class comprehensive works on the U.S. Coast Guard at 363.2860973, public administration aspects in 353.0074.

359.982   [Naval] Engineering [forces]

Example: U.S. Military Sealift Command 359.9820973.

360   Social problems and services; association

SUMMARY

361   **Social problems and social welfare**
362   **Social welfare problems and services**
363   **Other social problems and services**
364   **Criminology**
365   **Penal and related institutions**
366   **Association**
367   **General clubs**
368   **Insurance**
369   **Miscellaneous kinds of associations**

360 standing alone will seldom be used except for the rare work giving substantial emphasis to association (366, 367, 369) and insurance (368) as well as to social problems and services. In case of doubt, prefer 361.

361–365   Social problems and services

Problems and services in this section of the schedules are often linked terms, and, where one is spelled out, the other is implied. Thus, addictions at 362.29 implies services to the addicted, while services of extended care facilities at 362.16 implies the problems that require such services.

See also 300 vs. 600, and 301–306 vs. 361–365.

Government reports

A large proportion of the material classed by the Decimal Classification Division in 361–365 consists of reports of government agencies on their official activities. *See 351.0006 for guidance in distinguishing reports that are classed in public administration from those describing social problems and services, which are classed here.*

Political, economic, and legal considerations

Many publications give considerable emphasis to the political, financial, and legal considerations related to social services. So long as the focus is on the problem or the service, class such publications here. Thus, a discussion of political obstacles to effective poverty programs is classed in 362.5, of the expense and costs of needed hospital expansion at 362.11, of the political maneuvering behind the adoption of an act of the United States Congress spelling out a new housing program at 363.580973. *See also notes on cost control and control of costs under the add table at 362–363: Add table: 8.*

361   **Social problems and social welfare**

Class here comprehensive works on socioeconomic planning and development, on programs and services encompassing several branches of the social sciences. Class community planning and development in 307. Be alert for works on planning and development that are predominantly economic in character, and class such works in 338.9. If in doubt about the predominance of economic emphasis, prefer 338.9.

Class works dealing with social problems considered purely as social phenomena in 301–307. Works describing the present or past social conditions and phenomena in a given area are to be classed in 930–990. *See also 301–307.*

361 vs. 362   **Social problems and social welfare vs. Social welfare problems and services**

Both sections are concerned with social welfare, but in different ways. 361 deals with methods and means of carrying out social welfare programs. It does not address itself to specific problems. These are to be found in 362. Application of the 361 principles to 362 problems is accomplished through the use of subdivision 5 in the table under 362–363. Subdivision 5 is developed like 361. 362 will almost certainly be more heavily used than 361.

If the table of contents reads like a summary of the subdivisions of 362, class the work in this number. If it looks like a summary of the subdivisions of 361, class the work there. A combination of the two should be classed in 361.

If this rule of thumb does not prove helpful, the focus of the book should be taken into consideration. If the emphasis is on services designed to remedy various specific social problems, class in 362; if the emphasis is on methods, ways and means, organizations, class in 361. The same considerations apply, of course, to the use of standard subdivisions and historical and geographical treatment under each number.

361.02–.06   [Types of assistance]

This span of numbers is for general discussions covering various problems and client groups, and both public and private assistance. If the work deals only with public assistance, as will probably be the case a good share of the time, class it in 361.6. Most works on welfare are in fact about public assistance even though it is not stressed. If the work deals with private assistance, class it in 361.7. Class assistance with respect to a specific problem with the subject in 362, e.g., free assistance to the elderly 362.6.

361.1   Social problems

This number comprises social problems as a background to social action, and should be used sparingly. In most cases prefer 301–307, especially if the problem is discussed purely as a social phenomenon. Class specific problems in 362.

361.1 vs.   Social problems vs. **Social problems**
362.042

Social problems at 362.042 should be thought of as social welfare problems, a narrower concept than 361.1. 361.1 encompasses any and all kinds of social problems from child care to water supply. Class at 362.042 social problems that apply to individuals as such and the remedial measures for these problems.

361.25   Action within established social framework

Class here comprehensive works on public and private action. If material on protest, dissent, or reform is included, class the work in 361.9 (or in 361 if not limited by place or time). Class public action in 361.6, private action in 361.7.

361.323   Counseling

Including telephone counseling, e.g., hot lines.

361.38   Casework for specific types of counselors

The legal and ministerial counseling mentioned in the example note must be about social problems. Legal counseling about law is classed in 340, ministerial counseling on religious subjects in 200.

361.6   **Public action**

Note that the word "public" is defined at 361.6 in Edition 19 as governmental. Use this number for general treatment of government-sponsored socioeconomic planning and development and government-sponsored social action comprising several branches of the social sciences. Class public action in general in specific areas in 361.91–361.99.

361.615   Relations of public and private sectors [in social action]

Including citizen participation.

361.7   Private action

Class the relation of public and private sectors in 361.615.

361.74   [Private action] By individual philanthropists

If the philanthropist has donated money to an organization that controls the use of the money, class the work with the controlling organization. For example, the Rockefeller Foundation (though founded by an individual philanthropist) is classed at 361.7632, not 361.74.

361.75–.77 **[Private action by organizations]**

Do not add standard subdivisions for individual organizations.

See also 361.76.

361.76   [Private action] By other private organizations

The word "other" refers only to kinds of organizations listed in the subdivisions of 361.76. Class organizations not listed in 361.75–361.76 at 361.7.

361.763   [Private action] By nonprofit organizations

Class comprehensive works on the Red Cross at 361.77.

361.77   [Private action] By private international organizations

International refers to the scope of the membership, which must include two or more nations. It does not refer to the scope of the service provided. The Rockefeller Foundation, an American organization providing service throughout the world, is classed in 361.7632 not 361.77.

Class here comprehensive works on the Red Cross and affiliates such as the Red Crescent. Class Red Cross societies of a specific nation at 361.7634.

361.8   Community action

Including such activities as united givers funds and community chests, which, though the funds gathered are for the benefit of private welfare organizations, are often sponsored by the community government and have the cooperation of various public agencies.

Class planning for the community as a whole in 307.

361.9   **Historical and geographical treatment of social problems and social welfare**

Class here only the most comprehensive works. To be classed here a work should include both public and private action, together with some treatment of protest, dissent, and reform.

Class action of local communities in 361.8.

362–363   **Specific social problems and services**

For a discussion of criminal offenses vs. specific social problems and services, see 364.1 vs. 362–363, of incidence, distribution, control of specific diseases vs. specific social problems and services, see 614.3 vs. 362–363.

Add table

These digits are to be added to numbers bearing an asterisk (*) in 362–363. Topics are not usually marked with an asterisk when the concepts in this table have already been provided for in another manner. In such cases Edition 19 inserts the concepts missing in the earlier editions wherever a convenient place can be found for them. In some cases these concepts have been provided for in another location altogether. 362.1 is a good example of all these contingencies. In general, causes of disease are medical in nature and are classed in 616–618 using notation 071 from the table under 616.1–616.9 in Edition 19. Strictly social causes are classed at 362.1042, e.g., changes in social attitudes leading to an increase in various diseases. Boundaries of disease are ordinarily classed in 614.42, social effects at 362.10422. Control of disease is classed in 614.43 and 614.5, prevention in 614.44–614.48 and 614.5.

The chief remedial measures, of course, are medical treatment, classed in 616–618, and hospital and related services, classed in 362.11–362.19. 81 Rescue operations is not applicable with respect to diseases. Its closest relative, emergency services, is classed at 362.18. Financial assistance to the sick is classed at 362.104252. (However, class medical insurance in 368.38 and 368.42.) Subdivisions 83–85 are not applicable here. Counseling and guidance are provided for at 362.104256.

When certain subdivisions are not applicable under numbers marked with an asterisk, they will often be listed with an instruction that they are not to be used. Subdivisions with altered meanings are also listed. For example, at 362.82 Families in Edition 19, subdivision 8 Remedial measures has been spelled out with a slightly altered meaning: Services and forms of assistance. Various subdivisions of 8 are also spelled out to carry additional information not found in the table. At 362.292 Alcoholism in Edition 19 the following subdivisions are spelled out: 6 and 7 with "do not use" instructions, 8 with one of its subdivisions 86. In the absence of contrary instructions this does not mean that other subdivisions of 8 may not be used. Thus residential care for alcoholics is classed at 362.29285.

Do not use s.s. 0218 Standards with numbers in 362–363. Be cautious in adding s.s. 088 since many of the groups listed there are already provided for in regular subdivisions of these numbers. Class standards for the control of a specific hazard with the hazard using 62 from the table under 362–363, e.g., standards for hazardous machinery 363.1862.

5 Social action

This is the number for comprehensive works covering a substantial proportion of the topics provided for in subdivisions 6–8. It is also a general number that has been subdivided like 361, so that numbers may be constructed for the following types of topics: private services to alcoholics 362.29257, social work with the mentally retarded 362.353.

6–8 Specific forms of action

In applying these subdivisions the "first of two" rule does not operate. Works containing topics from any two of these subdivisions are to be classed at 5.

6 vs. 7   Control vs. Prevention

Subdivision 6 is called control, subdivision 7 is called prevention. They are intended to distinguish two quite different situations. The works classed will almost certainly not confine themselves to using the terms in these ways.

Subdivision 6 is intended to designate social effort to eliminate a hazard altogether, to see to it that there is in fact *no* hazard. Standards (62) are imposed so that buildings will be constructed and products made in such a manner that they present no hazard. Monitoring (63) is undertaken to be sure that certain factors are kept below a level where they become a hazard. Inspection (64) is undertaken for the same reason. Untoward incidents are investigated (65) in order to determine what must be done so that the situation will not recur.

Subdivision 7 on the other hand is intended to designate measures aimed at precluding the operation of hazards that do exist and have to be taken into account, e.g., safe methods of operating hazardous machinery. Prevention also includes means of warning people so that they may escape from a hazardous situation.

8   Remedial measures, services, forms of assistance

These are measures applicable primarily to individuals, even though there may be thousands of them to be fed, given or lent money, employed, or sheltered in institutions.

Remedial measures directed toward altering some social function, on the other hand, are classed in 5, not in 8. For instance, cost control is not to be considered a remedial measure in the sense of subdivision 8. All social services (including the ones listed in 8) cost money and the need to keep costs within reasonable limits is a perennial topic of concern. Class managerial measures to control costs with subject in 362–363 plus s.s. 0681, e.g., managing a hospital in a cost-efficient manner 362.110681. Larger social programs to hold down costs are classed with the subject using 5 from the table under 362–363, e.g., rent control 363.55. If this is public action (which is usually the case), the number would be 363.556. The administration of such measures is classed with the appropriate number in 351–354, e.g., administration of rent control 351.865044.

362 **Social welfare problems and services**

Note that according to the table of precedence (except for families and poverty) specific problems are preferred to the kind of person they affect, e.g., emotionally disturbed children 362.2088054, not 362.7. *See note at 362.82 for instructions on classing social problems of families.*

To indicate the relation of a specific kind of problem to a specific kind of person, add s.s. 08 Treatment of the subject with respect to specific kinds of persons to the number for the problem, e.g., drug addiction among young adults 362.293088055. This number is created by adding s.s. 088 plus persons notation 055 Treatment of the subject with respect to young adults to 362.293 Drug addiction.

362.042 **Social problems**

See 361.1 vs. 362.042.

362.0425 Social action

Do not use for methods of social action; class these in 361.2.

362.1–.4 **Illness and disability**

362.1–362.4 is the span for public health as that term is generally used, i.e., for health problems that lend themselves to public action. Note that "public health" as used in 614 is largely limited to traditional measures to control the spread of contagious diseases. 614 also covers reports of incidence and distribution of physical diseases. However, raw statistics of diseases are classed in 312.3.

Use care in distinguishing between illness and disability as social problems and as medical problems. Setting a broken bone is medicine. Making sure someone is there to set it is social welfare.

Biographies

Class in 362.1–362.4, using s.s. 0924, biographies and memoirs of the sick, the handicapped, and the dying that lack any other disciplinary focus. The rationale behind this rule is that these biographies illustrate the way society addresses itself to fundamental health problems and their solution. Be alert, however, for significant disciplinary emphasis, e.g., a work offering guidance in the Christian life with respect to health misfortunes is classed at 248.86, Christian meditations at 242.4. Use s.s. 0926 for studies of individual cases designed for the use of researchers, practitioners, and students in the field.

Class in 616–618, using either subdivision 09 from the table under 616.1–616.9, or s.s. 0926 from the table under 617, studies of patients describing their illnesses in medical terms rather than their lives in social terms, e.g., case studies of heart disease 616.1209. In case of doubt between a medical case study and a social one, prefer the 362 number except for psychiatric disorders. For the latter prefer 616.8909 and related numbers since the consideration of external circumstances is generally subordinated to the discussion of the state of mind of the patient.

While most personal and biographical treatment of medical personnel is classed in 610, class in 362 works on public health doctors or nurses emphasizing their influences on public health services and awareness, e.g., a biography of a doctor noted chiefly for promoting nursing homes 362.160924.

362.1   **Physical illness**

Use s.s. 068 here and in subdivisions of this number to indicate the process of peer evaluation and review, but do not use this standard subdivision for the results of a peer review. For example, the results of an evaluation of hospitals in New York City is classed at 362.11097471. Class the public administration of a peer review system at 351.841043; the discussion of peer relationships in the medical profession at 610.696.

See also 610 vs. 362.1, and 613–614 vs. 362.1.

362.1023   [Services to people with physical illnesses as a profession, occupation, or hobby]

This number does not mean illness as a profession, occupation, or hobby.

Class here comprehensive works on the health occupations peripheral to the medical and paramedical professions classed in 610. Specific peripheral professions are classed with the subject, e.g., medical social workers 362.10425023, hospital clerks 651.374.

Class works covering both the medical and peripheral occupations in 610.

362.1042   **Social aspects [of physical illness]**

See 362–363.

362.10425   Forms of assistance [with respect to physical illness]

Class health and accident insurance in 368.38 and 368.42.

362.108 |History and description of services to the physically ill with respect to groups of persons|

> Services rendered to persons belonging to various groups. Do not use for history and description of physical illness among groups of persons. Class this topic in 616–618.

> Class services rendered by groups of persons to the physically ill in 362.1 without further subdivision.

362.12   Services of clinics and related institutions

> Consider the different names of clinic-like institutions to be more or less interchangeable and add standard subdivisions if appropriate for a specific "kind," e.g., health centers in Tanzania 362.1209678.

> Community health services and ambulatory services are usually equivalent to the services of clinics. If so, standard subdivisions may be added, e.g., a journal of community health services 362.1205.

362.16   Services of extended care facilities

> Make no distinction between extended care facilities for the general public and those devoted to the elderly. However, for other groups of people, use s.s. 08, e.g., extended care facilities for children 362.16088054. Use 362.61 for residential care of the reasonably healthy aged, but 362.16 for facilities for the elderly who are no longer able to dress and feed themselves.

362.17   **Various specific services to the physically ill**

> Class here the social arrangements for providing the services but not the technical aspects of the services, e.g., provision of blood banks 362.1784, but techniques of storing blood in the banks 615.39; interdisciplinary works on provision of nursing services, 362.173, but technical aspects of the work of nurses 610.73.

> Class here medical screening programs.

> Class terminal care at 362.175, group practice at 610.65, medical services of doctors and nurses in 610.

362.19   **Services to patients with specific conditions**

Class here services relating to specific physical diseases, except for the public health measures spelled out in 614.43–614.48. Class these measures in 614.5 when applied to a specific disease. Note that raw tabular statistics on the incidence of specific diseases are classed in 312.3, while the nontabular analysis of their incidence and distribution is classed in 614.5.

362.2   **Mental and emotional illnesses and disturbances**

The provisions here are basically similar to those at 362.1. (*See discussion under 362–363: Add table.*) Note, however, that prevention is classed in 362.20425, not 614.58 as formerly. Control is not applicable here.

362.22   Services of psychiatric clinics

This number should be considered as though it were defined as at 362.12, i.e., "services of psychiatric clinics and related institutions," adding standard subdivisions freely as suggested at 362.12, e.g., community mental health services in Brazil 362.220981.

362.292   Alcoholism

Class here interdisciplinary works on alcoholism.

Class a specific aspect with the subject, e.g., medical aspects 616.861.

362.293   Drug addiction

Drug addiction is used here in its ordinary sense as addiction to the "hard" or heroin-like drugs. Use subdivisions freely for specific drugs. Addictions to tobacco, barbiturates, marijuana, and purely hallucinogenic drugs are classed at 362.29 without subdivision. If no distinction is made between the hard and soft drugs, class in 362.293.

Class here interdisciplinary works on drug abuse.

Class the subculture of drug users at 306.1, drug use as a custom at 394.1, medical aspects in 616.863.

362.3   Mental retardation

In some instances, the term mentally handicapped includes the concept of mental illness as well as that of mental retardation. Class works on the combined concept in 362.2. *See also 362.4.*

362.36   [Control of mental retardation]

Class here proposed eugenic measures to reduce mental retardation, since the intent of such measures is to eliminate entirely the conditions that produce mental retardation, insofar as these are genetically determined.

362.4   **Problems of and services to people with physical handicaps and disablements regardless of cause**

Class here comprehensive works on the handicapped.

Class comprehensive medical works in 617, the developmentally handicapped (a term usually referring to neurological diseases as well as mental retardation and sometimes also mental illness) at 362.1968. Developmentally handicapped and mentally handicapped are ambiguous, equivocal, and sometimes overlapping terms. *See also 362.3.*

362.42   Deaf and partially deaf people.

Class comprehensive works on linguistically and communication handicapped people at 362.196855; teaching of the deaf in 371.912.

362.43   **Crippled people**

Subdivisions may be added to works on any single condition, e.g., residential care for paraplegics 362.4385.

362.57   [Prevention of poverty]

Class economic measures to prevent poverty in 339, eugenic and genetic measures at 363.98.

362.58   Remedial measures, services, forms of assistance [to poor]

Except for special programs for which only the poor are eligible, class assistance to the poor under social security programs in 368.4, e.g., social security pensions 368.43; however, class supplementary social security for low income people at 362.582.

Class food stamp programs at 363.882, birth control as a remedy for poverty at 363.96.

362.61   Residential (Institutional) care [for older adults]

Class here institutions providing complete care for older adults, including such things as shelter, food, medical care, and recreation. Housing for older adults is classed at 363.59.

See also 362.16.

362.7044   Various specific problems [of young people]

Class here general and comprehensive works on the problems of young people in general, on specific problems afflicting them, on services to them generally, on services to them with respect to specific problems.

Class specific services to young people, either general or with respect to specific problems, in 362.71–362.73, e.g., aid to dependent children 362.713, residential care for orphaned children 362.732, protection in the home setting for abused children 362.71.

Class child abuse as a crime at 364.1555.

362.71–.73   Specific kinds of services to young people

Class comprehensive works on services to young people having specific kinds of problems at 362.7044, to specific kinds of young people in 362.74–362.79.

362.734   Adoption

Including the issue of confidentiality of adoption records.

Class comprehensive works on the activities of people seeking their natural parents at 362.8.

362.74   Maladjusted young people

Class here halfway homes insofar as these provide services to young people who have not committed a crime. The same term is used for penal institutions that offer a transition experience between the reform school and return to society. This type of institution is classed at 365.42.

362.8   Problems of and services to other groups

Including interdisciplinary works on people seeking their natural parents. Class a specific aspect of this problem with the aspect, e.g., confidentiality of adoption records 362.734, genealogical searching 929.1.

362.82 **[Problems of and services to] Families**

Note that Families heads the table of precedence at 362 and that services to families with specific problems are classed here. This is an exception to the general rule that the problem is classed with the problem, not with the client group. The reason is that when specific problems loom so large that they must be treated as family problems they involve a host of normally unrelated services to individuals not directly affected: baby sitting, homemaker services, job counseling. The work must emphasize the "family complications" in order to be classed here. The problem as it affects only the single member of the family with the problem (even the breadwinner) is classed with the problem, e.g., the problems of an alcoholic husband 362.292, not 362.82; child abuse 362.7044, not 362.82.

However, "family welfare" is often loosely used to cover welfare to everybody (362) on the presumption, evidently, that everybody is a family member.

362.83 [Problems of and services to] Women

Class wife beating as a crime at 364.1555.

362.86 **[Problems of and services to] Veterans**

Class veterans' benefits provided immediately at the end of military service, or discussed in the context of a benefit designed to promote efficiency of service, in 355.115.

362.88 [Problems of and services to] Victims of crime

Including victimology, the study of why people are crime victims, and what the individual can do to prevent crime from happening to himself.

363   **Other social problems and services**

Class here the work of agencies by which the government carries out the detailed intent of the law in matters of population, safety, the environment, and provision of basic necessities. Class the internal administration of agencies concerned with these fields, including their administrative annual reports, in 350–354. The law itself, draft laws, and enforcement of the law in courts is classed in 341–346. But most of the discussions of policy and most of the detailed procedures for enforcing law, policy, or regulation are classed here.

Choice of discipline

Several subdivisions involve control of technology, particularly under safety (363.1) and environment (363.7). Class in 363 works addressing themselves to what must be done, regulating how it is to be done, inspecting to see whether or not it has been done, and investigating to find out why it was not done. Only works dealing with the technical procedures for carrying out a given operation are classed in technology. Finding out what broke is 600; finding out who let it break is 363. Machinery breakdown is 600; system breakdown is 363.

A useful clue in choosing the appropriate discipline is the perspective of the author or publishing agency. If the author is interested in social service and social need, the work is classed in 363; if the interest is in the economics of what we have to live on, 333.7 should be chosen; if in how the environment works, 304.2; in how to make things, 620–690; in how organisms survive, 570–590; in how crops survive, 632–638; in physical techniques for controlling pollution, 628.5. In general, commercial publishers and environmental or safety advocacy groups tend to produce works that are classed in the social sciences, e.g., 304.2, 333.7, or 363.

To summarize: class comprehensive works and works oriented toward problems and their solution in 363, resource-oriented material in 333.7, works giving significant consideration to the social dynamics of the problem in 302–307, those emphasizing technology in 600.

See also 300 vs. 600, and 301–306 vs. 361–365.

363 Other social problems and services

Add standard subdivisions freely to 363 for comprehensive treatment of the way society copes with both its environmental and safety problems, e.g., assuring a safe and secure environment for Japan 363.0952. Also add standard subdivisions freely to 363 for comprehensive treatment of public works, e.g., a journal of public works 363.05.

363.1 **Public safety programs**

Note that all the headings in this section, however worded, include the conditions or potential conditions that pose a threat to safety, the measures of prevention and control contemplated or adopted, disasters resulting from the failure or lack of such measures, and the measures of relief and rehabilitation resulting therefrom.

Note also that the word "safety" is used loosely and equivocally in many instances. It may be so broad as to cover most of the social services. In this case the work is classed at 363, or even at 361 if sufficient 362 material is included. On the other hand, it may be so narrow as to comprise only the work of the police and fire departments, in which case the work is classed at 363.2.

Safety management

Class the managerial response to safety requirements in 658, e.g., management to insure employee safety 658.382, management to insure product safety 658.56. Safety management in a specific industry is classed with the industry, using s.s. 068 where feasible, e.g., safety management in mines 622.8068.

See also s.s. 0289.

Safety regulations

Class safety regulations that spell out operating and construction techniques in explicit detail with the technology involved even if they are in the form of an officially promulgated regulation by a safety authority. In some cases such regulations may not even warrant the addition of s.s. 0289 for safety measures because they cover more or less the whole construction picture. On the other hand, manuals written by or for safety agencies may discuss, among other things, various technical details useful as background for regulation and inspection of various operations while still focusing primarily on safety services. These are classed in 363.1 and its subdivisions as appropriate, often with numbers using subdivision 6 from the add table at 362–363.

Priority of safety

Class the safety aspects of any subject in the social sciences in 363.1 or 363.3 rather than with the subject in the rest of the social sciences, e.g., railroad safety 363.122, not 385.0289. However, the public administration of safety is classed as instructed at 351.783 and 352.3 in Edition 19.

Accident statistics

Class tabular statistics of accidents in 312.4. However, an analysis of the statistics including a substantial amount of text as well as tables is classed with the subject in 363.1 or 363.3.

363.1065   [Investigation of specific safety incidents]

Class here comprehensive works on accident investigation. Prefer this and cognate numbers in 363.1 over 600 numbers for accident investigations, unless the emphasis is on technical or engineering aspects. This is particularly true when the investigation implicates large, impersonal agencies (companies or governments) that should have prevented the accident by proper supervision, inspection, or regulation. For example, class a technical description of what went wrong at Three Mile Island at 621.48350974818, but an investigation of why it took so long to find out what went wrong at 363.179.

Be alert for accounts of specific accidents (usually of the disaster type), which, if they affect general social life and history, are classed at 904.7 or in the history of the area where the accidents took place. *See also 363.34.*

363.119   **Occupational and industrial hazards in specific industries and occupations**

The "Class generalities . . ." note in Edition 19 has been deleted (see *DC&,* Vol. 4, No. 1, p. 15).

Class here generalities applied to specific industries and occupations.

363.12   **Transportation hazards**

Class transportation fires, e.g., fires caused by defective electrical wiring in a railroad car, at 363.379. However, class fires resulting from an accident with the accident in 363.12.

363.12465   [Investigation of specific air and space accidents]

Prefer this number to the wreckage study number at 629.13255 for general investigations of aircraft accidents.

363.1249   **Specific types of accidents and accidents in specific types of services**

The "Class generalities . . ." note in Edition 19 has been deleted (see *DC&,* Vol. 4, No. 1, p. 15).

Class here generalities of specific types of accidents, of accidents in specific types of services.

363.12565   [Investigation of specific vehicular and highway accidents]

Prefer this number to the wreckage study number 629.2826 for general investigations of automobile accidents.

363.1259   **Hazards in use of specific types of vehicles**

The "Class generalities . . ." note in Edition 19 has been deleted (see *DC&,* Vol. 4, No. 1, p. 15). Class here generalities of accidents in use of specific types of vehicles.

363.17   **Hazardous materials**

Class here interdisciplinary works on hazardous materials. Class here works on the control of such materials in their ordinary commercial setting: manufacture, sale, commercial and industrial use, disposal. While 363.17 stands at the head of the table of precedence at 363.1 in Edition 19, note that hazardous materials as components of articles that thereby become hazardous products are classed in 363.19, e.g., contaminants in food 363.192; as hazardous wastes in 363.728, as environmental pollutants in 363.738, as impurities in the water supply in 363.61.

Be alert for works on hazardous materials that are not classed in 363 at all. The material as an environmental factor affecting the natural ecology is classed at 574.5222, as a cause of disease or injury in an organism at 574.24, and as a cause of injury to persons in 615.9 (for chemicals) and 616.9897 (for radiation hazards).

363.176 vs. 604.7   [Control of hazardous materials] vs. Hazardous materials technology

While the technology of handling hazardous materials is classed at 604.7, be alert for works on "handling" that are addressed to those responsible for monitoring or inspecting the handling, and that may be devoid of technical considerations. Class such works in 363.176. If in doubt, prefer 363.176.

363.1763   [Monitoring, surveillance, reporting in control of hazardous materials]

Class here and in cognate numbers in 363.1–363.9 studies on the applicability of the findings of environmental chemistry and additive toxicology to the monitoring of hazardous materials even though the technology is 615.907; for example, class the use of an indicator organism to see if a river is being polluted at 363.739463.

363.179 Specific hazardous materials

The "Class generalities . . ." note in Edition 19 has been deleted (see *DC&,* Vol. 4, No. 1, p. 15). Class here generalities of specific hazardous materials.

Class here general safety considerations with respect to especially flammable materials. However, class in 363.377 control and investigation of materials that are just normally combustible but promote the spread of fires when carelessly accumulated.

See also 363.33 vs. 363.179.

363.189 Specific kinds of hazardous machinery

The "Class generalities. . ." note in Edition 19 has been deleted (see *DC&,* Vol. 4, No. 1, p. 15). Class here generalities of specific kinds of hazardous machinery.

363.19 Product hazards

It is understood that the emphasis here is on domestic products, or on products in general use. Observe carefully the table of precedence at 363.1 in Edition 19.

Class here hazards due not only to the product alone, but also to accompanying containers and applicators, e.g., hazards connected with disposable hypodermic syringes 363.194.

363.1929 [Hazards occasioned by] Specific foods

The "Class generalities . . ." note in Edition 19 has been deleted (see *DC&,* Vol. 4, No. 1, p. 15). Class here generalities of specific foods.

363.2 Police services

Class here and in 363.22–363.25 public and private police treated together. Class private detective services treated separately at 363.289.

363.23 Police functions

Class police services in control of problems and controversies related to public morals in 363.4; the social service functions of police in 362, e.g., counseling of rape victims 362.88.

363.232 Patrol and surveillance

Including undercover work.

Class here tracking people in order to apprehend them. Class tracking people in order to rescue them at 363.348.

363.2332   Traffic control

Class comprehensive works on traffic accident investigation at 363.12565, investigation of traffic offenses in 363.25, wreckage studies to determine mechanical failure at 629.2826.

363.24   Auxiliary police services

Class the use of police files in criminal investigation in 363.256–363.258.

363.25   Detection of crime (Criminal investigation)

Although the investigation of specific types of crime is classed here, the investigation of a specific crime is classed in 364.1.

363.256–.258 Analysis of evidence [and] Identification of criminals

Class the files resulting from criminal investigation, e.g., fingerprint files, at 363.24.

363.258   Identification of criminals

In the second note at 363.258 in Edition 19 the word "other" means only those kinds of evidence listed in 363.252–363.256.

Class here the kind of evidence that is not listed either here or at 363.252–363.256, e.g., voice prints.

363.28   **Services of special kinds of security and law enforcement agencies**

Including park police.

Class agencies to carry out specific police functions in 363.23, e.g., highway patrol 363.2332; to investigate a specific kind of crime 363.25, e.g., homicide squads. If in doubt, class at 363.2 without subdivision.

363.3   **Other aspects of public safety**

Class here only those aspects of public safety listed in the subdivisions. Class a topic not listed here or in 363.1 at 363.

See also 363.1.

363.31   Censorship and control of information

This number is used for censorship and control of information as more or less routine political functions. Class controversies over civil rights aspects at 323.445, over legal aspects at 344.0531. Class censorship as an illicit governmental activity at 351.996.

363.33   Control of explosives and firearms

In the controversies over gun control, the *pro* arguments tend to be in terms of a desirable public safety issue, and are classed here. However, the *con* arguments often emphasize fundamental civil rights and are classed at 323.43.

363.33 vs.   Control of explosives and firearms vs. Specific hazardous materials
   363.179
Control at 363.33 refers to control of the ultimate use of explosives and firearms by potentially reckless or sinister users. Control of explosives as ordinary hazardous materials is classed at 363.179.

363.34   Disasters

Disaster here means a sudden, calamitous event producing great material damage, loss and distress, such as the eruptions of Mount Saint Helens. Beware of equivocal uses of this word; it is sometimes used to mean simply widespread social problems.

Be cautious in adding numbers from the table under 362–363 in Edition 19 to numbers in this section. Numbers should be used only for forms of assistance applied immediately at the time and site of the disaster, e.g., emergency food and shelter 83. Rescue of flood victims is classed at 363.349381, but hospital services for the victims rescued is classed at 362.11. Immediate shelter for flood victims is classed at 363.349383, but a long-range program to restore housing in the damage area is classed at 363.58.

Raising funds for mounting and carrying out the disaster relief (again using floods as the example) is classed in 363.34935. *See discussion under 362–363: Add table: 8.*

Be alert for disasters treated as history, which are classed in 904 or in the specific area where the disaster took place. Class here treatments that focus on the cause, effects, control, prevention, remedial measures, and controversies over blame or responsibility. Consider as history a disaster treated as a famous event, as a biographical reminiscence, as a factor influencing famous people, or as an incident that brought out a display of human character (bravery, panic, resiliency, leadership). If in doubt, prefer 363.34.

363.348   Rescue and salvage operations

This number comprises rescue and salvage operations for disasters in general. Rescue and salvage operations for a specific type of disaster are classed with the specific type of disaster using subdivision 81 from the table under 362–363 in Edition 19 where called for.

Comprehensive works on disaster relief are classed in 363.348 or with the specific type of disaster using subdivision 8 from the table under 362–363 in Edition 19 where called for.

363.349   **Specific kinds of disasters**

Class specific kinds of disasters resulting from one of the hazards listed in 363.1 with the subject in the appropriate subdivision of 363.1, e.g., shipwrecks 363.123, nuclear accidents 363.179. Class disastrous fires in 363.37.

363.34936   [Control of] Floods

Class the technology of flood control in 627.4.

363.3493809   **[Historical and geographical treatment of flood relief]**

Here s.s. 09 plus an area number indicates the area receiving the assistance, not the area providing the assistance. Flood relief to Florence provided by the United States is classed at 363.34938094551, not 363.349380973. Flood relief provided by the United States (to many countries) is classed at 363.34938, not 363.349380973.

363.34988   **[War relief]**

Class the problems of war refugees when not treated directly in the context of the war at 362.87, e.g., the problems of Vietnamese refugees adjusting to life in California 362.8709794.

363.3498809   **[Historical and geographical treatment of war relief]**

Follow the same principles given at 363.3493809, except class war relief during a specific war with the history of the war, e.g., relief work of the United States during World War 2 940.5477873.

363.35   Civil defense

Many works use the phrase "civil defense" in a broader sense than used here where it means measures to defend the civilian population against war. Class measures against disasters in general in 363.347, against social emergencies in general at 361.25 and cognate numbers.

363.37   Fire hazards

Class technology of fire fighting and fire safety in 628.92, e.g., flammability studies 628.922.

363.377   [Fire prevention]

Class here measures to control accumulation of ordinary combustible materials, but class control of especially flammable materials at 363.179.

Class safety of products that might constitute unsuspected fire hazards (e.g., sweaters and mattresses) in 363.19.

363.37809   [**Historical and geographical treatment of fire extinction services**]

Class here the nonadministative history of fire companies and departments. Class administrative histories at 351.782 and cognate numbers (usually 352.3). For example: an administrative history of the Vienna fire department 352.30943613; a history of the fires fought, the heroes, the fire inspection work of the same department 363.3780943613.

For treatment of fires as history, see the discussion under 363.34.

363.379   Fire hazards in specific situations

Including forest fires.

The "Class generalities . . ." note in Edition 19 has been deleted (see *DC&*, Vol. 4, No. 1, p. 15). Class generalities of fire hazards in specific situations in 363.379.

363.4   Problems and controversies related to public morals and customs

Class here the topics listed in the subdivisions of 363.4 only when treated as social problems. Class other aspects of each topic in the appropriate discipline. For example, class gambling treated as a social problem at 363.42, but class gambling as an everyday aspect of society at 306.482, gambling as a crime at 364.172, the ethics of gambling at 174.6, and gambling systems at 795.01.

363.5, 363.6,   **Housing, Public utilities and related services, [and] Food supply**
    and 363.8
These three sections deal with the problems of providing the basic necessities of life. Each of them necessarily has economic implications, so a careful distinction must be made between these numbers and the economics of industries under 338. If the work deals with the effect of these topics on the economic aspects of society, or the impact of economic conditions on the availability of housing, water, fuel, or food, it is classed in 338. If it deals with broader social factors affecting these commodities, or with social measures to insure an adequate supply, class it in whichever of these numbers is appropriate. For example, a study of the effect of a drop in farm prices on the food supply is classed at 338.19; a study of the mismatch between the expected growth of the food supply and population growth is classed at 363.81.

Control of prices and costs

See discussion of cost control at 362–363: Add table: 8.

Rationing and allocation

Use subdivision 56 from the table under 362–363 where permitted for the social aspects of rationing, e.g., food rationing 363.856. Public administration of rationing programs is classed at 351.829 and related numbers, e.g., rationing natural gas 351.8723043. Class the rationing of natural resources still in their natural state at 333.717 and cognate numbers in 333.7–333.9, but of final products in 363, e.g., wellhead allocation of natural gas for companies or jurisdictions 333.823317, but rationing of natural gas among consumers or classes of consumers at the other end of the line 363.63.

363.5 **Housing**

Although housing is often considered to be a welfare problem, this number is not so limited. It includes housing as a broad social problem as well as "welfare" housing.

363.508 [Housing of specific classes of persons]

Do not use; class at 363.59.

363.51 Housing conditions

Class housing allocations to relieve discrimination at 363.55.

363.55 [Social action with respect to housing]

Including housing allocations to relieve discrimination. (Do not class this topic in 363.51.)

363.58 Programs and services [with respect to housing]

Do not use the subdivisions of 8 appearing in the table under 362–363 in Edition 19.

363.59 Housing of specific classes of people

The "Class generalities . . ." note in Edition 19 has been deleted (see *DC&,* Vol. 4, No. 1, p. 15). Class here generalities of housing of specific classes of people.

Do not treat "the poor" or "low income families" as a specific class in this connection, since their needs are dominant and pervasive in most discussions of housing problems.

Do not use s.s. 08.

Class institutional care for healthy older adults at 362.61, extended medical care at 362.16.

363.6   **Public utilities and related services**

Class here problems of allocation among ultimate users, as well as measures to assure the abundance of immediately available supplies and services.

See also discussion at 363.5, 363.6, and 363.8.

363.6 vs.   **Public utilities and related services vs. Natural resources**
333.7

Use care in distinguishing between the resources in 333.7–333.9 and the utilities delivering the resources to the public for use (363.6). For instance, class in 333.7 comprehensive works on resources, projection of needs and supplies, development, conservation, protection of resources. Class in 363.6 problems and services related to supplying and distributing the resources to users. A useful device in distinguishing the two is to consider that "supply" as a noun is classed in 333.7, while "supply" as a verb is classed in 363.6.

363.61   Water supply

Class here comprehensive works on water supply, on water-related public works, e.g., a study covering waterworks, treatment plants, canals, flood control, hydroelectric generation. Class a specific topic with the subject, e.g., flood control 363.34936.

Water reports

Water supply reports concentrating on the supply of water on hand are classed in 553.7; on water used, or needed in the future, in 333.91; on the problem of treating and delivering water to consumers at 363.61; on assuring that waste waters are properly treated at 363.728; on protection of natural waters at 363.739472.

Water quality monitoring reports may serve several purposes. As tools for assuring compliance with water supply standards they are classed at 363.61, for assuring compliance with waste water pollution standards at 363.739463, for determining plant loads and technical difficulties in water treatment in 628.16 (e.g., pollution surveys in specific areas 628.1686), and for checking the effectiveness of sewage treatment works in 628.3. Those reporting the present chemical and biological status of available water, but not focusing on a specific objective, are classed as economic geology in 553.7, using area numbers where appropriate, e.g., a base-line study of the quality of Uruguay surface waters 553.7809895. The most general works on monitoring "to protect water quality" are classed at 333.9116, e.g., an environmentalist's alert "we must monitor our water supply."

363.62 **Power supply**

"Power supply" here means delivery of energy to the consumer. 363.62 serves as standing room for the problems and services of supplying forms of energy not listed here, e.g., allocation of heating oil, rationing of gasoline at the consumer end.

363.68 **Park and recreation services**

Including services maintained or proposed after land has been designated for parks, works on the establishment and operation of recreation centers primarily serving the general population.

Class a discussion of park policy and park development at 333.783, traditional cultural institutions with the subject, e.g., theaters 792, museums 069.

363.69 **Historic preservation**

Including identification and designation of historic buildings and areas, and public policies to protect, restore, and enhance appreciation of them. Class the technology of building restoration and preservation at 721.0288.

363.7 **Environmental problems and services**

"Environmental" is an equivocal word with many shades of meaning. At 363.7 it is intended to indicate social living space. The type of thing meant is well illustrated by the subdivisions of this number: sanitation, pollution, noise, disposal of the dead, pest control.

Use caution in classing "environmental problems." The phrase is often used as the equivalent of social ecology, which is classed in 304.2, or as the equivalent of natural resources and their protection, which is classed in 333.7. To a certain extent the environmental movement is a rechristening of the old conservation movement and its main thrust is resource conservation 333.72. If the natural environment or the natural ecology and its protection is referred to, the choice is between 333.95 for social measures and 639.9 for technical ones.

Impacts

Class in 363.7 a general work on the impact of wastes, pollutions, or actions to control them. However, class impacts on specific environments or resources with the type of impact (e.g., economic, social, ecological) and, within that discipline, with the subject being impacted. For example, the social implications of the impact of man-induced eutrophication of Lake Erie on its watershed are classed at 304.282; the economic impact on Rome of a major new waste treatment facility 330.945632, the impact of the same treatment plant on the waters of the Tiber River 333.91621094562, the impact of the same treatment plant on the fish in the waters of the Tiber 597.0526323094562.

The foregoing is applicable to the studies of actual, existing impacts. However, projected impacts are part of the planning, design, and policy formulation process and should be classed with the program or development that is being studied, e.g., the projected impact of proposed standards for water pollution 363.739462.

363.72   **Sanitation problems and services**

Do not use subdivisions 1–7 from the table at 362–363 in Edition 19 for specific wastes.

363.728   Waste disposal

Class dangerous wastes still in the hands of a processor or user as a hazardous material in 363.17, a dangerous waste that has escaped both safety and sanitary controls as a pollutant in 363.738.

363.729   **Sanitation in specific social environments**

The "Class generalities . . ." note in Edition 19 has been deleted (see *DC&*, Vol. 4, No. 1, p. 15). Class generalities of sanitation in specific social environments in 363.7291–363.7299.

363.73   Pollution

Class at this number a work on pollution that covers noise pollution (363.74) as well as topics referred to in subdivisions of 363.73, but if the work covers solid wastes and sanitation problems as well, class it at 363.7.

363.737   [Pollution prevention]

Class pollution prevention that consists of efficient waste disposal at 363.728.

363.738   **Various specific pollutants**

Class remedial measures for pollution in 363.735.

363.739   **Pollution of specific environments**

Note that subdivisions may not be used for specific pollutants in specific environments, e.g., automobile exhaust pollution in Australia 363.7392. No area number has been added.

363.7394   Water pollution

Class here comprehensive works on water pollution.

Class assurance of clean water supply at 363.61.

See also 628.168 vs. 363.7394.

363.78 Pest control

Including dog pounds; rat and mosquito abatement programs.

Class technology of pest control in 628.96. However, class the control of specific medical pests in 614.43, of agricultural pests in 632, even when not limited to technology.

363.8 Food supply

Problems and practices involved in assuring an adequate food supply.

Class economic aspects of food supply at 338.19, food stamp programs at 363.882.

Subdivisions may be added for hunger and for famine.

See also discussion at 363.5, 363.6, and 363.8.

363.856 [Public action on food supply]

Class here food rationing.

363.9 Population problems

Class here comprehensive works on population problems.

Class works on specific manifestations of a population problem with the manifestation, e.g., pressure on food supply leading to famine 363.8; the defeat of economic development programs by escalated population growth 338.9; demographic changes undermining military strength 355.22; population growth as a cause of poverty 362.51 (however, class birth control as a remedy for poverty at 363.96).

See also discussion at 301–306 vs. 361–365.

363.91 [Population] Quantity

Class remedial measures for overpopulation at 363.96.

363.92 [Population] Quality

Class remedial measures for population quality problems at 363.98.

363.98 Genetic and eugenic control of population

Class application of eugenics to a specific social problem with the problem using subdivision 6 from the table under 362–363 in Edition 19 where permitted, e.g., eugenic measures to reduce mental retardation 362.36. However, civil rights controversies over such measures are classed in 323.4.

364 **Criminology**

Class here comprehensive works on criminal justice that include criminology, police services, and criminal law; however, class works in which law predominates at 345.05.

Class social services to victims of crimes, and self-protection from crime at 362.88.

364.1 **Criminal offenses**

Class here investigations of specific crimes, the concept of crimes without victims, terrorism as a crime.

Class a crime as an event in history in 900. For example, the assassination of John F. Kennedy in its historical setting is classed at 973.9220924; however, the same event treated as a crime is classed at 364.1524. Class the sociology of terrorism at 303.625.

Biography

Standard subdivision 092 can be added to indicate either criminals or victims.

Class the biography of an individual criminal with the crime for which the individual is most noted, e.g., the robber Jesse James 364.15520924; however, class the same individual with relation to a specific crime with the specific crime, e.g., Jesse James in relation to a murder 364.15230924.

See also 364.106.

364.1 vs. **Criminal offenses vs. Specific social problems and services**
362–363

Some human activities can be considered either as social problems or as crimes. Such activities treated as crimes are, of course, classed in 364.1. The same activities treated as social problems are classed with the problem in 362–363. Thus, illegal use of drugs as a crime is classed at 364.177, but drug addiction as a social problem is classed in 362.293. Suicide treated as a crime is classed at 364.1522, but suicide as a social problem is classed in 362.2. If in doubt, prefer 362–363.

364.106 **Organized crime**

Class the biography of a person connected with organized crime who is also associated with a specific offense with the offense, e.g., a biography of a drug peddler connected with organized crime 364.1770924; of a person connected with organized crime, but not with a specific offense at 364.10924.

Class the biography of an individual offender not associated with a specific type of crime and not associated with organized crime in 364.3.

To indicate area, add as instructed under s.s. 06 in Edition 19, e.g., organized criminal groups in the United States 364.106073.

364.1066 Gangsterism

Class comprehensive works on and the sociology of gangs at 302.34.

364.1323 Corruption

Including police corruption.

364.138 War crimes

Class a specific kind of war crime with the crime, e.g., genocide 364.151.

364.154 Kidnaping, abduction, taking and holding of hostages

Taking and holding of hostages has been added officially to the Edition 19 heading.

364.1552 Robbery

To be classed here, a theft must include either a threat of violence or bodily harm, or an actual occurrence of violence. If neither occurs, e.g., a bank divested of its money through tunneling into the vault, the crime is classed at 364.162, even though the word "robbery" is used.

Class here comprehensive works on hijacking. Class a specific kind or aspect of hijacking with the subject in criminology, e.g., taking of hostages 364.154.

364.1555 Assault and battery

Class child abuse as a social problem at 362.7044, wife beating as a social problem at 362.83.

364.18 Miscellaneous offenses

    Class at this number without further addition crimes not otherwise provided for, e.g., illegal adoption, body snatching. However, before classing here make certain that the crime does not logically belong in another number even though it is not listed there. For example, in Edition 18 the crime of wife beating is not listed. This crime would not have been classed at 364.18 because it is logically a type of assault and battery, as Edition 19 indicates at 364.1555.

364.2 Causes of crime and delinquency

    Class victimology, the study of why certain people are victims of crimes, at 362.88.

364.36 Juvenile delinquents

    Including status offenders (juveniles who have broken laws pertaining only to their own age group, e.g., curfew laws, drinking below legal age).

364.4 **Prevention of crime and delinquency**

    Class here what society does to prevent crime.

    Class with the subject what a potential victim can do to prevent crime, e.g., an individual's actions to prevent crime from happening to himself 362.88, household security 643.16, business intelligence and security 658.47.

364.62 Parole and indeterminate sentence

    Class services to prisoners to prepare them for parole at 365.66.

    Standard subdivisions may be added for parole alone.

364.63 Probation and suspended sentence

    Standard subdivisions may be added for probation only, for probation and parole, for probation and suspended sentence.

364.68 Noninstitutional penalties

    The note in Edition 19 consists of examples of noninstitutional penalties and is not meant to exclude other types, e.g., community service.

365 **Penal and related institutions**

    For 365 and its subdivisions penitentiaries and prisons are to be treated as synonymous terms.

    Class prison reform at 365.7. The first note at 365 in Edition 19 has been revised.

365.3 **Kinds of penal institutions**

Class specific institutions in 365.93–365.99.

365.34 [Penal institutions] By purpose or type of program

Class here halfway homes as a type of penal institution. Class halfway homes for juvenile delinquents at 365.42, for maladjusted young people at 362.74.

Class the history of a penal colony as an aspect of the history of a place with the history of the place, e.g., the penal colony at Botany Bay as the founding settlement of New South Wales 994.402.

365.44 [Penal institutions] For adult men

Works about penal institutions usually treat those for adult men as synonymous with institutions in general. Do not use 365.44 unless the book emphasizes that the inmates are adult men. However, class the biography of adult male inmates in 365.44092.

365.45 [Penal institutions] For political prisoners and related persons

Class concentration camps considered to be prisoner-of-war camps at 355.1296 and 355.71

365.48 Military prisons and prison camps

Military prisons and prison camps are penal institutions whose inmates are military personnel. Do not confuse with prisoner-of-war camps, which are classed in 355.1296 and 355.71.

365.6 **Prison economy**

Class here community-based corrections, social aspects of prison life, e.g., conjugal rights, drug abuse.

365.643 Discipline

Class work furloughs at 365.65.

365.647 Release and discharge

Class work release at 365.65, services to prisoners to prepare them for release at 365.66.

365.7 Reform of penal institutions

Class reform designed to eliminate prisons as a form of punishment for certain types of crime at 364.6.

366 Association

Class religious associations in 200, e.g., Young Men's Christian Associations 267.3; fraternal insurance at 368.363.

367   **General clubs**

Class here social clubs for specific types of people, e.g., The Lambs, a social club in New York City composed chiefly of actors, musicians, and playwrights 367.97471.

Class clubs dealing with a specific subject with the subject, using s.s. 06, e.g., pinochle clubs 795.41606.

368   **Insurance**

The following table shows some of the ramifications involved in classing works in insurance:

Insurance and related arrangements

	Provision for retirement and old age	Health and accident insurance
Government sponsored		
For its own employees	351.5	351.1234
Administration	351.5	351.1234
For general public	368.43	368.42
Administration	351.835	351.835
For veterans	355.1151	Not applicable
Administration	355.1151	Not applicable
Privately sponsored		
By management	658.3253	658.3254
On an individual basis	368.37	368.38
IRAs (Independent Retirement Accounts) and Keogh plans	332.02401	Not applicable

Economic aspects of most of the above are classed at 331.252 and 331.255.

See also chart at 331.255.

368.012   Underwriting

Class Lloyds of London at 368.012094212.

368.096   Real property insurance

Standard subdivisions may be added for either land alone or buildings (improvements) alone.

368.1 Insurance against damage to and loss of property

Including crop insurance.

Class a combination of property and liability insurance in 368.09.

368.3 **Insurance against death, old age, illness, injury**

See 331.255.

368.37 Annuities

Annuities purchased and sold as a form of insurance.

See also chart at 368 for related arrangements.

368.382 **Prepaid health care**

Including Blue Cross, Blue Shield, health maintenance organizations (HMOs).

Class here comprehensive works on health insurance.

To be classed in 368.382 a work on health insurance plans must relate to their insurance features, e.g., a work on the need to raise Blue Cross rates in California 368.38201109794, but a work on the adequacy of health services under Blue Cross in California 362.109794.

See also chart at 368.

368.4 **Government-sponsored insurance**

Class here contributory plans even if not fully self-sustaining. The note on social security in Edition 19 refers to it in its broadest aspects. A work limited to social security as an old-age and survivors' insurance plan is classed in 368.43.

See also 331.255, chart at 368.

368.42 Accident and health insurance

Class financial benefits provided under United States Medicaid at 362.1042520973, medical services provided under it in 362.10973.

369 Miscellaneous kinds of associations

Including clubs based on nationality or ethnic ties, e.g., Sons of Italy.

369.4 **Young people's societies**

Class a specific aspect of a young people's society with the aspect, e.g., Boy Scout camps 796.5422.

370 Education

SUMMARY

371 **Generalities of education**
372 **Elementary education**
373 **Secondary education**
374 **Adult education**
375 **Curriculums**
376 **Education of women**
377 **Schools and religion**
378 **Higher education**
379 **Education and the state**

Education might be considered as a social technology rather than a social science. Here are the methods and processes involved in one of the chief means of socializing the young.

One of the ways in which the field of education is divided is according to the kind of student taught. A number of the sections of 370 are devoted to the education of students at various levels: 372 Elementary education, 373 Secondary education, 378 Higher education. One section (376) is devoted to education of students of a specific sex; one section to students at a certain age (374). The education of students who are set apart from the mass of students by one or another characteristic is found in 371.9.

Certain subdivisions represent the agencies doing the educating, e.g., 371.01 Public schools and school systems, 371.02 Private schools and school systems, and (a branch of private schools) 377 education by religious groups.

Another set of subdivisions deals with the processes and techniques of education, e.g., 371.3 Methods of instruction and (occupying most of the rest of the subdivisions of 371 and 379) administration of the educational process. Section 375 Curriculums deals with what is to be taught.

Order of precedence

In general it may be said that the order of precedence for classing combinations of these various facets is:

(1) education of exceptional students (371.9),
(2) education of various kinds of nonexceptional students (372–374, 376, and 378),
(3) processes and techniques (371 and 379),
(4) curriculums (375),
(5) agencies (371.01–371.02 and 377).

However, except for 371.9 Special education, this order is by no means invariable. The exceptions are numerous; there are other topics that do not fit into this order at all (e.g., 371.8 The student), and great care must be taken to follow exactly the directions given in Edition 19. Examples follow:

Secondary education of blind students 371.911, not 373.

Methods of teaching secondary school students 373.13, not 371.3.

Methods of teaching blind secondary school students 371.9113, not 373.13 or 371.3.

Curriculums for secondary school students 373.19, not 375. Curriculums for blind secondary school students 371.911, not 373.19 or 375.

Private secondary schools 373.222, not 371.02. Private secondary schools for the blind 371.911, not 373.222 or 371.02.

Note that study and teaching of a specific subject above the elementary level is classed with the subject plus s.s. 07, e.g., teaching of mathematics at the secondary level 510.712.

370.1 **Philosophy, theory, generalities [of education]**

In accordance with the new practice of the Decimal Classification Division, standard subdivisions may be added to other standard subdivisions that have an extended meaning (see *DC&*, Vol. 4, No. 2, p. 41). Accordingly, standard subdivisions may be added to the subsections of 370.1, e.g., a dictionary of educational psychology 370.1503.

370.113   Vocational education

Since this number is part of the theory of education, class here only works discussing vocational effectiveness as an educational objective.

Class work-study programs at 371.38, vocational schools in 373.246, apprenticeship training undertaken by industry at 331.25922, schools teaching a specific subject with the subject, using s.s. 07, e.g., medical schools 610.711. Class choice of vocation in 331.702, vocational counseling in schools at 371.425.

370.114   Moral, ethical, character education

Class moral, ethical, and character training of children in the home at 649.7.

370.15   Educational psychology

Class here learning, perception, memory, other psychological topics applied to education. Class psychology applied to a kind or level of education with the kind or level using s.s. 019, e.g., psychology of adult education 374.0019.

Class behavior modification for classroom discipline in 371.1024.

370.19   Social aspects of education

Class here educational anthropology (the application of anthropological concepts and methods to the study of educational institutions and processes); educational policy (the overall strategy for achieving social goals for education); sociology applied to the solution of large-scale social problems in education.

Class the functional planning carried out by superintendents, principals, and others in connection with the operations of a given school system at 371.207.

370.1934   Sociocultural factors affecting education

Class here comprehensive works on equal educational opportunity, on general sociology of the student.

Class students in the school in 371.8, students' attitudes and behavior at 371.81.

370.19342   Racial and ethnic factors [affecting education]

Class here general discussions of affirmative action in education. Class affirmative action with respect to teachers at 331.133.

370.195 vs. 370.9	Comparative education vs. [**Historical and geographical treatment of education**]

To be classed in 370.195, a work must actually compare and contrast two or more educational systems. A mere discussion of the educational systems of several jurisdictions without specific attention to comparison is classed in 370.9 with the appropriate area notation, e.g., a comparison of European systems of education 370.195094, but the educational systems in various European countries 370.94. If in doubt, prefer 370.9.

In either case, select the area to be used according to the following criteria:

Use the area notation coming first in the schedules if only two systems are involved, e.g., a comparison of education in the United Kingdom and the United States 370.1950941. If more than two systems are involved, use the most specific area notation that will contain them all, e.g., schools in Germany, France, and Italy 370.94. If one area is heavily predominant, the notation for that area is used even if some systems outside the area are included, e.g., a comparison of schools in France, Germany, Spain, Italy, Russia, and the United States 370.195094.

370.196	Intercultural education

Class the legal aspects of international educational exchanges in 341.767, the legal aspects of domestic educational and cultural exchanges at 344.08; administration of exchange programs at 351.851.

370.1965	Educational aid

Add s.s. 09 plus area notation only for recipients of the aid.

370.71	**Professional education of teachers**

Class here the study of how to teach, the teaching of teachers. Class works on how to teach a specific subject with the subject using s.s. 07, e.g., methods of teaching mathematics 510.7.

Standard subdivisions may be added to this number and its subdivisions.

370.711	[Institutions of higher education]

Do not use; class in 370.73.

370.72	Teachers' conferences, institutes, workshops

Including teacher centers.

370.73 **Institutions of higher education**

Class here normal schools, teachers' colleges, education departments of universities.

370.732 Courses and programs

Including competency-based instruction.

Standard subdivision 09 plus area notation may be added to this number.

370.733 Practice teaching

Including microteaching.

Class here comprehensive works on practice teaching regardless of level.

Class practice teaching in a specific subject at the elementary level with the subject in 372.3–372.8, using special subdivision 044 from the table at 372.3–372.8 in Edition 19, e.g., practice teaching in mathematics 372.7044. Class practice teaching in a specific subject at secondary and higher levels with the subject, using s.s. 07, e.g., practice teaching in U.S. history at the secondary level 973.07.

370.9 **[Historical and geographical treatment of education]**

See 370.195 vs. 370.9, and 379.4–.9 vs. 370.9.

371 **Generalities of education**

Class here school policy.

See also 370.19.

371.01 Public schools and school systems

Class here comprehensive works on public schools. Class public education by specific continents, countries, localities in modern world in 379.4–379.9; a specific kind or level of public schools with the subject, e.g., public elementary schools 372.10421.

Class public education and the state in 379.2.

371.02 Private schools and school systems

Class here comprehensive works on private schools.

Class a specific kind or level of private school with the subject, e.g., private secondary schools 373.222.

Class private education and the state in 379.3.

371.04 Experimental schools

Schools that feature an unstructured curriculum and an informal relationship between faculty and students.

371.1-.8 **Organization and administration [of education]**

Each specific level contains a section or sections built on these general principles, e.g., teaching 371.102, elementary school teaching 372.1102.

371.1 Teaching and teaching personnel

Class economic aspects in 331, e.g., supply of and demand for teachers 331.12313711, teachers' unions 331.88113711, bargaining by teachers 331.890413711.

Class affirmative action, equal employment opportunity programs for teachers at 331.133.

371.12 **Professional qualifications of teachers**

Class here the training and education required of teachers. Class the training itself in 370.71. Note that the requirements for teachers of specific subjects are classed here, but the techniques and methods of teaching a specific subject are classed with the subject at the secondary and higher levels and in 372.3–372.8 at the elementary level. *See also 370.71, and 370.733.*

371.14 Organization of teaching force in the school

Class economic aspects of tenure at 331.2596.

371.206 Financial administration [of schools]

See 658 and s.s. 068: (1) Financial management.

371.207 Generalities of [school] administration

Class here planning as a part of educational function, planning carried out by superintendents, principals, and others in connection with the operations of a given school system.

Class broad social planning in education in 370.19, planning with respect to a particular function with the subject, e.g., planning for school health and safety 371.7.

Class student participation in the maintenance of discipline at 371.59.

371.218 Articulation

Class here comprehensive works on credits. Class credits in relation to promotion and failure at 371.28.

371.26   **Educational tests and measurements**

Testing in a specific subject or discipline at the secondary or higher level is classed with the subject plus s.s. 076, e.g., testing in chemistry 540.76. In elementary education, testing is inherent in subdivision 044 in the table at 372.3–372.8 in Edition 19.

Class use of educational tests and measurements in guidance in 371.42.

371.26 vs.   **Educational tests and measurements** vs. Tests and examinations
   371.271

As indicated by the cross reference in the text of Edition 19 at 371.26 leading to 371.27, the latter number is part of Educational tests and measurements. Class in 371.26 works on school-wide standardized tests and tests set by authorities outside the classroom or the school that gives the instruction, e.g., entrance examinations for admission to a higher level education 371.264. Class in 371.26 also comprehensive works on tests and the testing process. Class at 371.271 only works on the classroom use of tests and examinations.

371.264   Academic prognosis and placement

Class comprehensive works on and psychological aspects of aptitude tests in 153.94.

371.271   Tests and examinations

See 371.26 vs. 371.271.

371.295   Truancy

Class truancy treated as a discipline problem at 371.58.

371.3078   Teaching aids, materials, devices

Including educational technology, instructional materials centers, and school resource centers. Class school libraries in 027.8.

When an instructional materials center or school resource center is combined with a collection of library materials for students, class in 027.8.

371.32   Textbooks and other printed media

Class here works about textbooks and other printed media in general, not the textbooks themselves. These are classed with the subject they treat.

371.332   Teaching methods

Class drama as a subject of study at elementary levels at 372.66, at higher levels in 792.07. Class teaching of plays as literature at 372.64 at the elementary level, in 800 at higher levels.

371.392 Montessori system

The Montessori method is usually confined to the elementary level; therefore, most works dealing with it are classed at 372.1392. Discussions of advancing the method to higher grades are classed with the appropriate level.

371.42 Educational and vocational guidance

Including the use for guidance purposes of aptitude and interest tests, and compilation of cumulative school records.

371.422 Intellectual and educational [guidance]

Including counseling with respect to advanced education, assistance in choosing appropriate educational institutions.

371.425 Vocational [guidance]

Including counseling with respect to vocational training and job placement.

371.7 **School health and safety**

General measures to promote safety in the school environment, health and food services to students.

Class instruction in health and safety given to elementary school students in 372.37, to students at higher levels in 613.07.

371.77 **Safety programs [for students]**

Class outside of 370 a work dealing with safety of teachers and other school personnel, e.g., work injuries in California public schools 363.1193710109794.

371.805 Student periodicals

Class here student periodicals dealing with the school and its activities. Class student periodicals on another subject with the subject, e.g., a student periodical devoted to sports 796.05. Class general student periodicals in 051-059.

371.9   **Special education**

Special education is a subdiscipline in its own right. Every aspect of special education is classed at the appropriate subdivision in this array and not at the specific level or kind, e.g., teaching slow learners in secondary schools 371.926, not 373.1102.

Class mainstreaming (the integration with the normal school population of children who have special educational needs) at 371.9046.

Specific schools for a specific kind of exceptional student are classed with the appropriate exception in 371.9, e.g., Gallaudet College, Washington, D.C. (a college for the hearing-impaired) 371.91209753.

Observe the following table of precedence for 371.9:

Gifted students	371.95
Retarded students and slow learners	371.92
Emotionally disturbed students	371.94
Students with physical handicaps	371.91
Students with linguistic handicaps	371.914
Crippled students	371.916
Blind and partially-sighted students	371.911
Deaf and hard-of-hearing students	371.912
Socially and culturally deprived students	371.967
Delinquents and problem students	371.93
Students belonging to the upper classes	371.962
Students exceptional because of racial, ethnic, national origin	371.97

371.928   **Mentally retarded [students]**

Class autistic students at 371.94.

371.94   Emotionally disturbed [students]

Including maladjusted students.

371.967   **Socially and culturally deprived [students]**

Class here teacher corps.

371.97   **Students exceptional because of racial, ethnic, national origin**

Class here works on the education of students who need special consideration because of language problems, e.g., North and South American Indians 371.9797.

Class bilingualism as a linguistic phenomenon at 404.2.

372.1392   [Montessori system]

See 371.392.

372.21   **Preschool institutions**

Class here Headstart. Class equal educational opportunity in 370.1934.

372.3–.8   **Specific elementary school subjects**

Class textbooks with the subject with which they deal regardless of the level of treatment, e.g., an elementary textbook on United States history 973.

Class testing in a specific subject at the elementary level with the subject being taught, using subdivision 044 from the table 372.3–372.8 in Edition 19, where instructed to do so, e.g., testing in arithmetic 372.72044.

372.35   Science [in elementary education]

Including teaching of the metric system.

Class technology in elementary education at 372.8.

372.66   Drama [in elementary education]

Class here drama as a subject of study in elementary education.

Class comprehensive works on use of drama as a method of instruction at 371.332, on its use at the elementary level at 372.1332. Class plays taught as literature in elementary education at 372.64.

372.7   Mathematics

Class the teaching of the metric system at 372.35.

372.73   **Modern mathematics**

The term "modern mathematics" is often used loosely in the titles of books. Many works using this expression are merely about the teaching of arithmetic and should be classed at 372.72.

372.8   Other elementary studies

Including religion, which is taught in many private schools in the United States and in the elementary schools of the United Kingdom.

373.222   Private schools

Class here endowed schools (private schools and the "public schools" of the United Kingdom).

373.236   Lower level [secondary schools]

Class here middle schools (United States).

373.246   Vocational schools

Vocational schools here are those that offer both a general education and a vocational program. If the school in question concentrates wholly or almost wholly on teaching a specific subject, class with the subject, using s.s. 07, e.g., a business school concentrating solely on commercial courses 650.07.

Class vocational training for adults in 374.013, subject to the principles outlined in the previous paragraph. Class the theory of vocational education at 370.113.

374   **Adult education**

Class here vocational education, further education, continuing education.

Whenever the granting of a degree is involved, class the work with higher education in 378. Class university extension work at 378.1554.

See also 373.246.

374.29   Institutions and agencies [of adult education]

Including day-release courses (United Kingdom).

Class study-release courses (United States) at 365.66.

374.8   **Schools**

Further examples: proprietary vocational schools, folk high schools.

375   **Curriculums**

Class here curriculums in demonstration schools with no specific level.

375.88   [Curriculums and courses of study in literatures of Hellenic languages]

Class here classical literature in the curriculum; however, class at 370.112 the much broader topic of "classical education."

377   **Schools and religion**

Curriculums for comprehensive schools supported by religious bodies are classed in 375; individual schools supported by religious groups are classed with the appropriate level, e.g., a specific secondary school in New York City 373.7471, not 377.82. *See also 207.*

378.1553   Graduate departments and schools

Class here postdoctoral work.

378.1554   Extension departments

Class here university studies for adults, whether for a degree or not.

378.198	[The student in higher education]

Including choice of college.

378.3 **Student finances**

Finances of students in a specific field are classed with the subject using s.s. 071, e.g., medical education 610.711.

378.4–.9 **Higher education and institutions by specific continents, countries, localities in modern world**

Class a school, institute, or college of a university with the subject taught by the school, institute, or college, using s.s. 0711, e.g., Harvard Law School 349.7307117444.

Class alumni of a specific university with the university. Faculty of the university are classed in 378.12, college administrators at 378.111.

379 **Education and the state**

Class here citizens' advisory councils.

Regulations of a duly constituted public body have the force of law and are classed in 344.07.

379.11 **Financial administration in public education**

Class financial administration of schools in a specific field with the subject, using s.s. 071, e.g., costs for medical schools 610.711.

379.13 Revenue sources [for education]

Including education voucher system.

379.15 Supervision and control [of education by the state]

Class reports on accountability with the subject or school.

379.157 Supervision of teachers, administrators, their activities

State certification, aid, and control are classed here. Selection of teachers in general is classed in 371.1.

379.158 School standards and accreditation

Class here governmental commissions on higher education that operate in a supervisory capacity and play an important role in accreditation and the development of school standards. Class accreditation of schools teaching a specific subject with the subject, using s.s. 07, e.g., accreditation of library schools 020.711.

379.4–.9 vs.   Education and the state, public education by specific continents, countries,
370.9   localities in modern world vs. [Historical and geographical treatment of
**   education]**

> Class in 379.4–379.9 public education by area, public and private education (considered together) by area. Class comprehensive treatment of education by area in 370.9. If in doubt, prefer 370.9.

380 Commerce, communications, transportation

SUMMARY

381	Internal commerce (Domestic trade)
382	International commerce (Foreign trade)
383	Postal communication
384	Other systems of communication
	Telecommunication
385	Railroad transportation
386	Inland waterway and ferry transportation
387	Water, air, space transportation
388	Ground transportation
389	Metrology and standardization

Commerce deals with the distribution of goods and services, and is a part of the discipline of economics. So too is transportation, an activity that adds to the value of the goods moved. Both communication and transportation developed primarily in response to commercial needs and practices, i.e., to trade, banking, accounting, and so on; therefore, they have been placed in 380 with commerce. The technical aspects of commerce, transportation, and communication are classed in 600.

In order of precedence of subjects under 330 in the *Manual*, commerce and transportation take the same position as production. Therefore, a work on the labor force in transportation would be classed at 331.12513805, but transportation in socialist countries 380.5.

Comprehensive numbers in 380

The organization of the 380s is reflected in the organization of 380.1–380.5. 380.1 provides comprehensive treatment of 381 and 382, 380.3 the same for 383 and 384, 380.5 for 385–388. Each of the numbers under 380.1 is comprehensive for the appropriate subdivisions of 381–382, those under 380.3 for 383–384, and those under 380.5 for 385–388, e.g., a comprehensive work on the facilities of Spanish organizations engaged in radio, television, and telephone 380.350946.

380.1 **Commerce (Trade)**

Class here warehousing.

Class warehousing of a specific commodity with the commodity in 380–382, e.g., warehousing of grain moving in domestic commerce 381.14131.

380.1 vs. 658.8 **Commerce (Trade) vs. Management of distribution (Marketing)**

Class in 380.1 the economic aspects of trading and selling goods, what is, in fact, traded and in what amounts. Class managerial techniques for disposing successfully of the products and services of enterprises in 658. If in doubt, prefer 380.1.

380.106 **[Organizations connected with commerce]**

Class here chambers of commerce.

Class organizations engaged in commerce in 380.141–380.145, 381–382.

380.141– .145 **[Trade in products of primary and secondary industries]**

Class here and in cognate numbers in 381–382 organizations engaged in trade.

Class here and in cognate numbers in 381–382 lists of products offered for sale, using s.s. 0294 as instructed at 380 in Edition 19, e.g., a general mail-order catalog 381.45000294.

380.3 **Communications**

Many books containing the term "communications" in the title are actually limited to telecommunication and are classed at 384. Class here only those works that cover postal communication as well as telecommunication.

380.5 Transportation

See 385–388 for a general discussion on transportation.

380.51 Comparative studies of kinds of transportation

Class a comparative study of a specific kind of transportation with the subject, e.g., comparative study of ground transportation 388, of local transportation 388.4.

381–382 **General internal and international commerce (Trade)**

Class here organizations engaged in trade, lists of products offered for sale.

See also 384–388.

381.4   **[Internal commerce (Domestic t. ade) in] Specific commodities and services and specific groups of commodities and services**

See 380.141–.145.

382.3   Commercial policy

Public policies to control or encourage foreign trade.

382.4   **[International commerce (Foreign trade) in] Specific commodities and services and specific groups of commodities and services**

See 380.141–.145.

382.5   **Import trade**

Class the combined import and export trade of a country (or the trade between two countries) in 382.09. The first of two rule does not apply to combined import and export trade since this is the whole of foreign trade.

382.6   **Export trade**

See 382.5.

382.9   **Trade agreements and their implementation**

Class here works dealing only with trade agreements.

Class works dealing with international trade as a whole in 382.1, with the totality of international economic relations in 337.

383   Postal communication

Class philately in 769.56.

383.06   [Organizations and management of postal communication]

Class postal organization and management in 383.4.

383.12   **Classes of mail**

Class a specific service connected with a specific class of mail with the service in 383.14–383.18, e.g., special delivery of letters 383.183.

383.145   Collection and delivery [of mail]

Class special delivery at 383.183, delivery of mail within the military services at 355.69.

383.4   **Postal organization**

Class purely internal administration of postal communication at 351.873, e.g., financing, staffing; but use 351.873 with caution. If in doubt, class in 383.4.

384–388   [Telecommunication and transportation]

Offers for sale vs. Economic aspects

The second note under 380 in Edition 19 directs the addition of s.s. 0294 to certain numbers in 380–388 that are designated by an asterisk (*). This standard subdivision is intended to designate offers for sale made by organizations producing various kinds of goods and services.

Throughout 384–388 telecommunication and transportation (usually in .1 under a given topic, but sometimes in standing room in the general number) there are also provisions for "economic aspects" of the various services listed.

In distinguishing between these two concepts the following may be helpful:

(1) Class in the "economic aspects" number schedules of rates and fares published by a government agency, since these are in no sense offers to sell. A listing of railroad fares put out by a regulatory agency is an example of this and is classed at 385.12.

(2) Class a list of rates and fares published by the agency offering the service in the "economic aspects" number when such a list is no more than a list of charges for various services, even though this is, in some sense, an offer to sell. For example, class at 387.51 a list emanating from a shipping company that gives only the following kind of information:

To London	$500
Hamburg	600
Singapore	1000

(3) Class in the number for the appropriate activity or service (a number bearing an *), using s.s. 0294 as directed in the note under 380 in Edition 19, a publication containing a more or less full description of the services being offered as well as the information about rates and fares. Thus, if the shipping company were running a passenger liner and put out a brochure describing the various classes of accommodations offered, the kinds of staterooms, the dining facilities, the garage accommodations, and the medical facilities aboard, such a publication would be classed at 387.5420294, not 387.51, even though fares are given.

384   **Other systems of communication   Telecommunication**

Class a comprehensive work on the activities, services, and facilities of a system in the number for the system, e.g., radio broadcasting activities, services, and facilities 384.54, not 384.544.

Standard subdivisions

Use s.s. 06 when the work discusses the corporate history of the organization, e.g., the corporate history of the Western Union Telegraph Company 384.106573. Use s.s. 09 when the book discusses the system (facilities, activities, services) maintained by the organization in a specific area, e.g., telegraphic communication provided by Western Union 384.10973. If in doubt, prefer s.s. 09.

384.5443   Presentation of |radio| programs

Class the techniques of producing radio programs in 791.44.

384.55443 |Presentation of television programs|

Class the techniques of producing television programs in 791.45.

385–388   **Specific kinds of transportation**

Class comprehensive works on the activities, services, and facilities of a system in the number for the system, e.g., seaport activities, services, and facilities 387.1, not 387.15 or 387.16.

Class services designed to facilitate the use of transportation services by the elderly at 362.63, by the handicapped at 362.40483 and related numbers, e.g., use of city buses with wheelchair lifts 362.4383, not 388.41322.

Class government departments operating transportation services according to the principles discussed at 350–354, the section on public administration.

Order of precedence

The order of precedence for transportation is as follows:

    (1) Economic aspects
    (2) Activities and services
    (3) Facilities.

If a precise provision for economic aspects is not made, class a work on them in the base number for the form of transportation, e.g., economic aspects of handling freight in ports 387.1, not 387.153 or 387.164.

Standard subdivision

Use s.s. 06 when the work discusses the corporate history of the organization, e.g., the corporate history of the Union Pacific Railroad 385.06578. For international companies use the area number for the country which is its home base, e.g., Pan American World Airways 387.706573.

Use s.s. 09 when the work discusses the system (facilities, activities, services) maintained by the company in a specific area, e.g., railroad transportation provided by the Union Pacific Railroad 385.0978, air transportation provided by Pan American World Airways 387.7.

If in doubt between s.s. 06 and s.s. 09, prefer s.s. 09.

385–388 vs. 629.046   **[Vehicles in] Specific kinds of transportation vs. Vehicles**

See 629.046 vs. 385–388.

385   **Railroad transportation**

Class a work combining railroad and other forms of ground transportation at 388.

386.8   Ports

Inland ports are ports on nontidal waters, e.g., port of Chicago 386.80977311.

387.506   Organizations and management [of ocean transportation]

Including shipping conferences.

388.314   Highway use

See 388.41314; the same principles apply to classing highway traffic surveys.

388.4   **Local transportation**

Class here suburban transportation.

388.41314   [Use of local streets and highways]

Use s.s. 0723 for works on the techniques of conducting traffic surveys, e.g., how to survey Detroit's highway uses 388.413140723. Use s.s. 09 to indicate the results of a traffic survey, e.g., a survey of Detroit's highway use 388.413140977434.

389.1   **Metrology and standardization**

This number formerly included the actual units of measurement and their use. Since these units measure physical quantities, however, they belong in physics (530.8), not commerce, even though they are heavily used in the latter field. 389.1 is now used only for the social aspects of measurement, e.g., the problems of the United States in international trade because of its failure to adopt the metric system (389.160973), or the problems involved in converting from one system to another (389.16).

390 Customs, etiquette, folklore

SUMMARY

391   **Costume and personal appearance**
392   **Customs of life cycle and domestic life**
393   **Death customs**
394   **General customs**
395   **Etiquette (Manners)**
398   **Folklore**
399   **Customs of war and diplomacy**

Customs, etiquette, and folklore are among the raw material of the social sciences, particularly of anthropology and sociology—the descriptive and analytical aspects of the study of the behavior of mankind in general social groups. Melvil Dewey considered customs to be the culmination of social activity and classed them in 390, just before language, the last of the social sciences and a main class requiring a whole digit (4) to itself.

390.4355   [Customs of military personnel]

Class works on the customs of military life in 355.1.

391.001–.007 Standard subdivisions [of costume and personal appearance]

Standard subdivisions may be used for costume alone.

391.04355   [Costumes of military personnel]

Class works on military costumes at 355.14.

391.43   Headgear [as costume]

Including masks.

394   General customs

Class here kissing.

394.12   **[Customs of] Eating and drinking**

Class eating and drinking customs connected with a specific meal at 394.15, food taboos at 394.16.

394.26   **Holidays**

Class here not only the day of the holiday but also the season connected with it, e.g., class at 394.268282 the twelve days of Christmas as well as Christmas day itself.

394.4   Official ceremonies and observances

Class military ceremonies at 355.17.

394.5   Pageants, processions, parades

Class pageants, processions, and parades connected with holidays in 394.26, with official ceremonies and observances at 394.4.

395   **Etiquette (Manners)**

Etiquette includes prescriptive works on rules of conduct designed to make life pleasanter and more seemly and to eliminate causes of friction in the numerous inevitable minor opportunities for conflict or offense in daily life. Weightier matters of conduct are classed in 170 Ethics.

398   **Folklore**

Folklore is divided into the theory of the origins of folklore (398.1), folklore as literature (398.2), the sociology of folklore (398.042), and the sociology of specific themes in folklore in 398.3–398.4. The minor forms of folk literature found in 398.5–398.9 (chapbooks, riddles, rhymes, games, proverbs) belong logically to 398.2. Works combining sociology of and literary treatment of folklore are classed at 398.042.

398.2   **Folk literature**

Folklore as literature.

Literary form cannot be indicated for works of folk literature, and there is no notation for criticism or collections; both are classed in 398.2 and its subdivisions without further addition.

Standard subdivisions may be added to subdivisions of this number even if the subject of the work does not approximate the whole, e.g., a collection of Russian folk tales about witches 398.220947.

398.2 vs.   **Folk literature** vs. Mythology and mythological foundations [of religions]
   291.13
Class in 398.2 mythology having a real, legendary, or other non-religious basis. Myths populated by gods, goddesses, or quasi-gods and -goddesses are classed in religious mythology. In classical and Teutonic mythology it is unusual to find a myth without such personages; consequently, most works in this field are classed in 292.13 (classical mythology) or 293.13 (Teutonic mythology).

Class religious myths and legends on a specific subject with the subject, e.g., legends of Jesus' coming to Britain 232.9.

398.2 vs. 800 **Folk literature vs. Literature**

Anonymous literary classics are not considered to be folklore and are classed in 800. *See 800: Special problems: Folk literature.*

Some legendary or historical events or themes, such as the search for the Holy Grail or the battle of Roland with the Saracens, appear as the basis for works in many literatures, periods, and forms, the medieval works involving them often being anonymous. Although the theme rather than the literature is the binding thread, what is read is a literary work. Consequently, class each retelling of the event or theme with the literature, form, and period in which it was written. Class works about the theme treated in several literatures in 809.933.

398.204   [Folk literature] By language

Class here collections of folk literature that bring together material from various countries or geographic areas having a common language, e.g., a collection of folk literature from French-speaking areas of the world 398.20441. However, a collection of French folk tales, all tales coming specifically from France regardless of language, is classed at 398.20944.

398.22   Tales and lore of historical and quasi-historical persons and events

Class accounts of witches that are clearly not 398.22 folklore or 800 Literature at 133.43.

398.25   Ghost stories

Class accounts of ghosts that are clearly not 398.25 folklore or 800 Literature in 133.1.

398.353   Human body, mind, personality, qualities, activities [as subjects of folklore]

See 615.882.

398.6 Riddles

Class here interdisciplinary works on riddles. However, if the riddles are not truly a compilation of folk riddles but are presented as being original with their author or authors, class the collections in belles-lettres.

Riddles as parlor games are classed at 793.735.

398.9 Proverbs

Class here folk aphorisms.

400 Language

This schedule is used with and is inseparable from Table 4, Subdivisions of Individual Languages; the entries of Table 4 are referred to as lang. sub.

The 400s and Table 4 are limited to language based on human vocal capabilities. Booing and hissing are parts of vocal language; clapping, gnashing one's teeth, punching, and slouching are not. Body language is classed in 153.6. *See 001.56 in Edition 19 for other forms of nonlinguistic communication.*

The major components of a language are the word and the sentence, each of which has two aspects, the purely vocal and the semantic. The sounding of words is phonology, that of sentences is intonation. The semantic aspect, how words and sentences convey meaning, is grammar. The forms of words and changes therein (morphology) and the way words are marshaled to convey meaning (syntax) together comprise the study of this subject. However, in practice, many grammatical works contain elements of phonology and intonation as well. Usage deals with the acceptable rendering of a language and is consequently the broadest concept in dealing with a language.

Class here general works on language, e.g., Mario Pei's *Voices of Man.* Be sure that the work in hand does not have a particular focus that can be accommodated elsewhere in the schedules, e.g., an historical approach 409.

Class here studies that emphasize language and literature, even though some material on culture and history is included; but class in 900 studies in history and culture that include but do not emphasize language and literature.

Class examples and collections of "text" whose purpose is to display and study a language with the language, even if limited to a particular subject, e.g., Kok Cheong Lee's *Syntax of Scientific English* 425. Works on the language of a specific subject are classed in the number for the subject followed by s.s. 014, e.g., Lancelot Hogben's *The Vocabulary of Science* 501.4. Language analysis of a specific work is criticism and is classed with the work, e.g., George Caird's *The Language and Imagery of the Bible* 220.014.

Citation order

The citation order of the 400s is straightforward and without exception: Language + language subdivision + standard subdivision.

(1) Grammar of the Hungarian language
494.511 + 5 = 494.5115

(2) History of the Korean language
495.7 + 09 = 495.709

(3) Administrative reports of the Association for the Advancement of the Intonation of the Italian Language
45 + 16 + 06 = 451.606

401.41   [Communication through language]

Including semiotics and content analysis in a linguistic context. *See 001.51 for general discussion of semiotics, s.s. 0141 for general discussion of content analysis.*

401.51   [Mathematical aspects of language]

Including mathematical linguistics.

401.9   Psycholinguistics and sociolinguistics

It is difficult to distinguish among linguistics, psycholinguistics, and psychology of speech. Some topics that usually fall within the area of psycholinguistics are the problem of how language is acquired by children, speech perception, and neurolinguistics.

See 153.6 for discussion of the psychology of communication.

404.2   Bilingualism

Class specific instances of bilingualism with the language dominant in the country in which the linguistic interaction occurs, e.g., a discussion of Spanish-English bilingualism in the United States 420.4261. If neither language is dominant, class with the language coming later in Table 6.

408.9   [Treatment of language among specific racial, ethnic, national groups]

Class here ethnolinguistics.

410 Linguistics

SUMMARY

411 Notations (Alphabets and ideographs)
412 Etymology
413 Polyglot dictionaries
414 Phonology
415 Structural systems (Grammar)
417 Dialectology and paleography
418 Usage (Applied linguistics)
419 Structured verbal language other than spoken or written

Class a comparison of two languages with the language requiring local emphasis (usually the language that is less common in the particular setting). For example, a work comparing English and Japanese is classed at 495.6 in English-speaking countries, but at 420 in Japan. If no emphasis is required, class the work with the language coming later in Table 6.

Class a comparison of three or more languages in the most specific number that will contain them all, e.g., a comparison of Dutch, German, and English is classed at 430 since all are Germanic languages.

If there is no number that will contain them all (e.g., a comparison of French, Hebrew, and Japanese), class the work at 410.

The same considerations, of course, apply to comparisons of just one feature of various languages, e.g., a comparison of Dutch, German, and English grammar is classed in 435.

411–418 [Specific elements of linguistics]

Note that most of these topics correspond to those listed in Table 4, although, of course, there cannot be a complete correspondence in the extent to which the notations are developed or applied. For example, a general bibliographic guide to foreign-language courses and texts is classed at 016.418, but a bibliographic guide to English courses and texts for non-English-speaking students is classed at 016.42824.

411   Notations (Alphabets and ideographs)

Class at this number the history of letters and other symbols that are used to express sound and that form or combine to form words, e.g., alphabets, syllabaries, ideographs.

Class in 652 works on the practical methods of recording these symbols by hand or machine, e.g., penmanship 652.1.

General works on transliteration, and on braille as a system of notation, are also classed at 411.

415   Structural systems (Grammar)

Including transformational grammar and generative grammar.

418   Usage (Applied linguistics)

Including multilingual phrase books.

418.02   Translation and interpretation

Note that this is a unitary term; standard subdivisions may be added for either element, e.g., a dictionary for the analysis of translation 418.0203.

420-490 Specific languages

427.1–.8   Regional variations [of English] in England

Note that regional variations in Scotland, Wales, and Ireland are classed in 427.9 plus the appropriate area notation.

429   Anglo-Saxon (Old English)

Note that the Old English is treated as a separate language; Middle English 427.02 is not.

470 Italic languages   Latin

Old Latin is defined in part by the terminal date of 80 B.C. The dates
of the Classical Age of Latin are 80 B.C. to 130 A.D. (the Ciceronian
Age 80 B.C. to 43 B.C., the Golden Age of Augustan literature 43
B.C. to 18 A.D., the Silver Age 18 A.D. to 130 A.D.). The formal or
literary Latin of the Classical Age, or Latin written at any time
thereafter that conforms to the standards of that age, is classed in
471–476 and 478. However, works on Vulgar Latin, on Old Latin (80
B.C. or earlier), or on Postclassical Latin are classed in 477. The
phrase "Postclassical Latin" refers to the nonclassical or vulgarized
Latin used from the death of Juvenal (A.D. 140) until the period of
renewed interest in the "pure" Latin of the Classical Age in the
eleventh and twelfth centuries, and from the fourteenth century
onward. Classical Latin did not die out during the interim, however;
and a linguistic study written on, say, Latin manuscripts of the monks
of Iona is properly classed with Classical Latin.

480 Hellenic languages   Classical Greek

A work on both Greek and Latin is classed here unless Latin is
preponderant.

500 Pure sciences

In the DDC the pure sciences are divided into the physical sciences (astronomy [520], physics [530], chemistry [540], and geology [550]), the study of inorganic, lifeless objects; and the life sciences (paleontology [560], life sciences [570], botany [580], and zoology [590]), the study of organic objects that live or once lived. Part of zoology—human anatomy and physiology—is classed in 611 and 612. The "tool" science Mathematics precedes the pure sciences at 510.

The DDC retains a comprehensive number for the physical sciences at 500.2; however, Edition 19 dropped the former comprehensive number for the natural sciences at 500.1, which are now classed at 500. Natural history (formerly 500.9) is now classed in *508 (see DC&,* Vol. 4, No. 2, p. 30). *See 508.*

Relation to other disciplines

Science is both descriptive and analytical. It tells what exists in the world, and explains (or attempts to explain) how and why the natural world is as it is. When we begin to apply what we have learned about the world, a new class is born: Technology 600, the manipulation of the natural world or the use of data from it for the benefit of mankind. Description of a material in order to explain its place in nature is classed in 500; description of a material to explain those characteristics that are of practical interest to man is classed in 600, e.g., chlorine as an element 546.732, as a bleaching agent 667.14.

Be alert, however, for certain DDC classes that do not observe this distinction, notably surveying and cartography in 526, and celestial navigation in 527 (both of which would fit better in Engineering 620), and human anatomy and physiology in 611–612, which clearly are part of 599.9 Hominidae.

Be very careful about equating the word "science" with the pure sciences in 500. Quite often the term science includes the social sciences and the analytical aspects of other disciplines. Class a work on science pertinent to disciplines outside 500 at Scholarship and learning 001.2, or related numbers. Works on scientific method and scientific research are particularly apt to belong in 001.4 Research rather than 501.8 or 507.2. According to current practice, however, history of science more often relates to the pure sciences, and so is classed at 509.

"Science policy" generally refers to consideration of what society should do to promote the utilization of science and the growth of industries and activities based on science. Thus, it generally should be regarded as a policy or program to promote economic development and growth (338.9). Class works on public administration of science policy at 351.855 and cognate numbers in 353–354, unless there is heavy emphasis on economic development or on specific industries, in which case prefer 351.82 and cognate numbers. However, in the absence of a focus on the social sciences, use 509 for science policy of an area.

Dominant subdivisions

One complication in classing in 570, 580, and 590 is that in each discipline the usual DDC principle of hierarchy has been badly skewed by the concentration of topics in a single dominant subdivision. This single subdivision so dominates the field that the third summary "section" number winds up being used more often for general works than the slightly more comprehensive second summary "division" number. In the life sciences this skew is formally recognized: 574 is clearly defined as biology, while 570, Life sciences, is to be used only for works including physical anthropology (572–573) and paleontology (560), as well as biology. Similarly, 581 Botany is used much more often than 580 Botanical sciences (which differs only by the inclusion of paleobotany) and 591 Zoology is used more often than 590 Zoological sciences.

This dominance in Astronomy 520, and Earth sciences 550, is not formalized in the schedule, but use 520 only when the work in hand goes significantly beyond Descriptive astronomy 523, and use 550 only when the work goes significantly beyond subdivisions of 551. Only in paleontology, where 560 is used jointly for the subject as a whole and for paleozoology, is the normal hierarchy observed.

Applications

Class with science interdisciplinary works on any science and its applications in technology. For example, a combination of space science (500.5), engineering in space and extraterrestrial worlds (620.419), and astronautics (629.4) is classed at 500.5.

500.2 Physical sciences

See first and second paragraphs under 500.

500.5 Space sciences

Space sciences consist of Astronomy 520; sciences of other worlds (559.9 and other numbers in 550, using s.s. 09 plus area 99, e.g., 551.21099923 volcanoes on Mars); and biology (natural and experimental) in space, e.g., monitoring monkeys on space flights 599.82. It may also include other scientific topics that are studied in anticipation of space travel.

501.8 [Methodology of pure sciences]

See third paragraph of "Relation to other disciplines" under 500.

502.82 Microscopy

Class the application of microscopy to a specific discipline with the discipline, e.g., microscopy in biology 578.

507.2 [Research in the pure sciences]

See third paragraph of "Relation to other disciplines" under 500.

507.23 [Descriptive research in the pure sciences]

Class results of surveys in 508.

508 Description and surveys of natural phenomena

Class here natural history.

If the emphasis of the work is on living things and their settings, prefer 574 Biology and its area subdivisions in 574.9. If the emphasis is on the relations of human institutions to the natural environment, class the work in 304.2.

Class general descriptions of areas that include human settlement as well as scientific phenomena in 910 General geography.

Note that the heading at this number has been changed from that appearing in Edition 19 (see *DC&*, Vol. 4, No. 2, p. 50).

509   Historical and geographical treatment [of the pure sciences]

Class here only history of the disciplines of the pure sciences, of natural sciences, of pure and applied sciences treated together.

Class historical and geographical treatment of natural phenomena in 508. Class natural history of the seasons in 574.543 Seasonal changes, using s.s. 09 for area, if appropriate.

See also 500.

510 Mathematics

SUMMARY

511   Generalities
512   Algebra
513   Arithmetic
514   Topology
515   Analysis
516   Geometry
519   Probabilities and applied mathematics

Mathematics is traditionally counted as the first of the pure sciences, though perhaps in the Dewey Decimal Classification (DDC) schedules it might be more logically located as the first discipline in 001, since it is a universal tool. In itself mathematics is only a tool. Numerical phenomena do not exist in nature, and can only stand in for the world, describe it, and help predict its behavior. It is a valuable tool, and may be used in the behavioral sciences, technology, the professions, or any other field where counting and measuring can be put to use.

Because this schedule is designed to organize an abstract discipline having many complex subjects, the type of math taught in elementary and secondary schools does not usually have three-digit numbers. The following table lists these "school" subjects and their numbers:

Algebra	512.9
Arithmetic	513
Geometry	516.2
Trigonometry (as a branch of Euclidean geometry)	516.24

Use of index

When looking up a term in the index composed of an adjective and a noun, check the complete term first; if no entry is found under the adjective, look for the noun. For example, when looking up Boolean algebra, the adjective "Boolean" leads to 511.324, the correct number; but the noun "algebra" leads to 512, an incorrect number. However, this does not mean necessarily that the adjectival form of a branch of math is never classed with the branch. For example, algebraic number theory is classed with algebra at 512.74. However, algebraic topology is not classed with algebra but with topology in 514.2.

Do not class precalculus here. *See 512.1 and the first paragraph at 515 for further discussion of this topic.*

Combinations of topics

Unlike other schedules 510 provides numbers for the combination of one branch of the subject with other branches, e.g., algebra with Euclidean geometry. Use the following instructions when classing in 512.1, 512.5, 513.1, and 515.1:

(1) These sections are designed for works that deal basically with one subject but have some information on another subject either added at the end or interspersed throughout the work. For example, class a textbook with ten chapters on algebra and two chapters on Euclidean geometry at 512.12.

(2) The work must be classed with the branch that predominates. For example, to be classed at 512.13 Algebra and trigonometry, the work must be about algebra with some trigonometry added. If it is about trigonometry with some algebra added, it is classed at 516.24 Trigonometry.

511.5 Theory and construction of graphs

Including works that describe in general terms how to construct graphs, or telling why and how graphs work, or both. Interdisciplinary works on how to collect data for graphs, and how to interpret the graphs, are classed in 001.422; however, class construction and use of graphs in a specific subject with the subject, using s.s. 072.

512 Algebra

Class school algebra in 512.9.

512.02 Abstract algebra

Class specific aspects of abstract algebra in 512.2–512.5.

512.1   Pedagogical algebra combined with other branches of mathematics

Here, "precalculus" means those math subjects one studies in a basic school math course: set theory, arithmetic, school algebra, Euclidean geometry, and trigonometry; and sometimes also number theory, analytic geometry, probabilities, and statistics. Be careful not to class in 510 books entitled *Mathematics* that contain only this kind of precalculus information. *See first note at 515 for the other type of "precalculus."*

See also 510: Combinations of topics.

512.2   Groups

The groups of topological algebras are classed at 512.55. For example, class Lie groups with Lie algebras at 512.55, not 512.2.

512.22   Group theory

Group theory applied to a specific. group or type of group is classed with the group or type of group, e.g., group theory of cyclic groups 512.2.

512.5   Linear, multilinear, multidimensional algebras

Standard subdivisions may be added for linear algebra alone.

See also 510: Combinations of topics.

512.9   Pedagogical algebra

Pedagogical algebra is school algebra. Most textbooks with the title *Algebra* are classed at 512.9.

512.904   Elementary, intermediate, advanced algebra

This number and its subdivisions have been discontinued.

513.0212   [Tables, formulas, specifications, statistics in arithmetic]

See 513.92.

513.1   Arithmetic combined with other branches of mathematics

In the subdivisions of this number the term "separate treatment" means that the nonarithmetic branch is found in a unit entirely apart from the arithmetic, usually in the last chapter or two of the work. "Combined treatment" means that the nonarithmetic branch is interspersed throughout the work.

See also 510: Combinations of topics.

513.2–.4   Arithmetic operations [and] Arithmetic and geometric progressions

Because arithmetic is a part of algebra, class works dealing with both in 512.92–512.93 rather than in 513.2–513.4.

513.92   Rapid calculations and short cuts [in arithmetic]

This number should not be confused with the idea of arithmetic formulas 513.0212. Class here useful hints on quick methods of solving basic arithmetic problems, e.g., when adding nines, add ten and subtract one for each nine added.

513.93   Business arithmetic

Business arithmetic means the basic math used in business operations, e.g., price markups.

514   Topology

Because topology is a part of geometry, class works dealing with both topics equally in 516 rather than 514.

515   **Analysis**

Here, "precalculus" means the mathematical information needed to study calculus. A work on precalculus of this type contains information on what a function is and usually concentrates on algebraic and trigonometric functions; it does not contain information on functional analysis, functions of real variables, or functions of complex variables. *See 512.1 for the other type of "precalculus," basic school math.*

Class "elementary functions" when this term refers to a specific type of real variable functions at 515.83.

Standard subdivisions may be added for calculus alone.

515.1   **Analysis and calculus combined with other branches of mathematics**

See also 510: Combinations of topics.

515.3–.4   Differential calculus and equations [and] Integral calculus and equations

These two subdivisions approximate the whole of calculus, which is classed at 515. Do not class with the first of two.

515.35   **Differential equations**

Class boundary-value problems with one or both of their limits set by a definite numerical value in 515.62.

515.62   **Calculus of finite differences**

Class boundary-value problems with both limits unknown, and of no definite numerical value, in 515.35.

515.7   **Functional analysis**

A valued function is a function in which the result of the operation on the variables is known, e.g., $x + y = 10$.

515.8 **Functions of real variables**

Because functions of real variables are a special type of the functions of complex variables, a work discussing both is classed at 515.9 unless it deals predominantly with functions of real variables.

516 Geometry

The geometry usually taught in elementary and secondary schools is Euclidean geometry 516.2.

516.02–.04 Classical geometry [and] Modern geometry

Class works in these numbers only when the author makes a distinct difference between "classical" and "modern" geometries.

516.204 Famous problems

The famous problems are trisecting an angle, squaring the circle, and doubling the cube.

516.6 Abstract descriptive geometry

Class descriptive geometry, the geometrical aspect of technical drawing, at 604.201516.

519.2 **Probabilities**

Class a work that gives equal treatment to probabilities and statistics at 519.2, but class one that treats probabilities as an introduction to statistics at 519.5.

519.24 Descriptive probabilities

Descriptive probabilities are methods of describing probabilistic data and are similar to the methods of describing statistical data given under 519.53.

519.4 Applied numerical analysis

Class the finding of a numerical solution to a mathematical problem with the problem, e.g., determining the square root of a number 513.23.

519.5 **Statistical mathematics**

See 519.2.

519.5 vs. **Statistical mathematics vs. Statistical method**
001.422
The subject of statistics can be divided into three parts:

(a) how to obtain and arrange the data of the problem;

(b) how to manipulate the data by mathematical means to produce statistics;

(c) how to interpret and present the statistical information to answer the problem.

When a work gives equal treatment to a, b, and c, or contains information only about a or c or both a and c, class it in 001.422 Statistical method. When it contains only b or b with a or c or both as incidental information, class it in 519.5 Statistical mathematics.

520 Astronomy and allied sciences

SUMMARY

521 **Theoretical astronomy and celestial mechanics**
522 **Practical and spherical astronomy**
523 **Descriptive astronomy**
525 **Earth (Astronomical geography)**
526 **Mathematical geography**
527 **Celestial navigation**
528 **Ephemerides (Nautical almanacs)**
529 **Chronology (Time)**

Class works on astronomy at 520 only if they include and give separate treatment to topics of theoretical or practical astronomy (521–522) or both in addition to Descriptive astronomy 523. In effect, Descriptive astronomy 523 includes the whole of astronomy (520) except for two standard subdivision concepts (theory s.s. 01, which is classed in 521, and techniques, procedures, apparatus, equipment, materials s.s. 028, which is classed in 522). Thus 523 is the number of choice when these secondary aspects are not emphasized.

See also 523.

521.5 vs. **Theoretical astronomy vs. Descriptive astronomy**
523
Theoretical astronomy covers aspects of various astronomical bodies and phenomena that are being theorized about; actual data and interpretations of data are classed in the appropriate 523 number. Thus, the theory of sunspots is classed at 521.57, but spectroscopic observations of sunspots are classed at 523.74. However, class theories concerning the origin and development of the universe (cosmology) in 523.101 or 523.12–523.19.

523 **Descriptive astronomy**

Including black holes.

Class "earth sciences" of other worlds in 550, e.g., volcanic activity on Io, a moon of Jupiter 551.2109925, not 523.985. *See also 559.9.*

See also 521.5 vs. 523.

523.1 **Universe (Cosmology)**

Unlike the rest of 523, 523.1 includes theory, specifically at 523.101 for theory of the universe in general, and 523.12–523.19 for specific cosmological theories. However, theories of galaxies are classed in 521.582, not 523.112.

See also 523.8.

523.8 **Stars**

Class here comprehensive works on stars and galaxies.

Class a treatment of the universe or galaxies without significant reference to individual stars or classes of stars in 523.1.

525.6 **Tides**

Class here interdisciplinary works on tides.

Class tides as an aspect of oceanography at 551.4708.

526–529 |**Sciences allied to astronomy**|

The majority of material classed in these numbers will be technological applications of the various sciences, specifically cartography (526); surveying (526.9 or 526.3), Celestial navigation 527, and Ephemerides 528. Only Geodesy 526.1 and certain related numbers, and Chronology 529 are pure sciences.

529.78 vs. Instruments for measuring time vs. |**Manufacture of**| **Instruments for**
681.11 **measuring time**

Note that 529.78 is a much narrower concept than the same topic under manufacturing. Class in 529.78 only works explaining how instruments measure time, a subject most works on clocks in 681.11 take for granted. If in doubt, prefer 681.11.

530 Physics

SUMMARY

Physics deals with the ultimate nature and behavior of matter and energy. As originally formulated in what is now called classical physics (exemplified in most of the span 531–538), it dealt largely with matter and energy on a visible or palpable scale. Thus, it was logically located between astronomy (520), which deals with matter and energy on an extremely large scale, and chemistry (540), which deals with matter and energy an extremely small scale. In this classical view the atoms of chemistry were the smallest particles of matter. The three disciplines together constituted the physical sciences, and coopted mathematics, which had not yet been recognized as a universal tool valid far beyond the domain of the pure sciences.

Over time, chemistry has continued its focus on atoms, and their interactions and combinations with each other to form the molecules of familiar and not-so-familiar solids, liquids, and gases. However, modern physics has outflanked chemistry by developing physical theories about the even smaller components of atoms. Chemistry has borrowed just enough of this new physics to explain the behavior of atoms and molecules in set types of chemical reactions. Preoccupied with the fascinating way these chemical reactions explained so much of both the inorganic world and the phenomena of life, chemists for the most part left all other physical relationships and reactions to the physicists. Thus physics has grown to a point where it can be fairly said that chemistry is but a part of physics.

However, the expansion of physics has created anomalies in the Dewey Decimal Classification schedule. Not only does physics in 530 conceptually outflank chemistry at both the macro and micro levels, but also modern physics, dealing with the smallest of components, is developed at the two ends of the 530s, 530.1–530.4 and 539, leaving the classical physics of large-scale phenomena in the middle. The classical and modern approaches to sound, light, heat, and electromagnetic phenomena are combined in 534–538.

The upshot is that 530 and its standard subdivisions are used for comprehensive works on classical physics, on classical and modern physics, and on physics and chemistry. If mathematics *per se* or astronomy, or both, are added to the mix, the result is classed in Physical sciences 500.2.

Class works on specific topics common to both physics and chemistry with chemistry when they relate to composition, and to reactions affecting the combination of atoms in chemical processes. Class other works with physics. (*See also 539.12 vs. 541.22.*) Clues more useful here than in most DDC disciplines are the occupations of the authors or the fields of the sponsoring organizations, the presumption being that chemists are writing about chemistry and physicists about physics. In cases where this is no indicator, class the topic in physics.

See also 621 vs. 530.

530.1   **Theories [of physics] and mathematical physics**

This number is used interchangeably for theories of classical physics, of modern physics, or of both. Most of the subdivisions, however, except Mathematical physics 530.15 and Measurement theory 530.16, are devoted to theories of modern physics.

Note that only theories and mathematics are classed here. All other topics of s.s. 01 as spelled out in Table 1 are classed in 530.01 or 539.01, e.g., indexes of modern physics 539.016.

530.12   **Quantum mechanics (Quantum theory)**

Quantum mechanics is the concept that energy exists in small separate units (quanta), and is not continuous. It is contrasted with continuum mechanics (classical mechanics [531]), which operates with the large-scale phenomena of the solids, liquids, and gases of everyday observation. Since the two mechanics have practically nothing in common, and are fundamental to modern (sometimes called quantum) and classical physics respectively, class works covering both at 530.

Class the theory of continuum physics in 530.14.

530.124   Wave mechanics (Schrödinger representation)

Class attempts to explain matter in terms of electromagnetic waves in 530.141.

530.124 vs.   Wave mechanics (Schrödinger representation) vs. Waves
531.1133

Wave mechanics considers waves as a fundamental property of matter, and should not be confused with the kinetics of waves under classical mechanics at 531.1133. Wave mechanics at 530.124 attempts to explain all behavior of matter and energy, while 531.1133 assumes the existence of the matter of classical physics, and studies only the waves observable in such matter.

530.13   **Statistical physics (Statistical mechanics)**

Statistical physics is a somewhat misleading term, since it refers only to the mechanics of matter as derived from the statistical study of its component particles, e.g., protons, electrons.

Class the wider applications of statistics to physics in 530.1595.

530.14   Field and wave theories

Including the theory of continuum physics, the problem of few bodies. However, note that the problem of many bodies is classed at 530.144.

530.141   Electromagnetic theory

Note that this subject considers electromagnetic waves and fields in terms of fundamental theories of the structure of matter. These same waves and fields studied as phenomena in their own right, and not offered as explanations of what constitutes matter or energy, are classed in 537.

530.143   Quantum field theory

Including gauge fields.

530.15   **Mathematical physics**

Class mathematical description of physical phenomena according to a specific theory with the theory in 530.11–530.14, e.g., statistical mechanics 530.13, not 530.1595. *See also 530.13.*

530.4   **States of matter**

Class here properties of solids, liquids, gases, or plasmas only when emphasis is on matter in one or more states. If emphasis is on the phenomenon itself, class with the subject, e.g., sound vibrations in the solid state 530.41, but transmission of sound in solids 534.22.

531	Mechanics

Including the mechanics of points.

See also 530.12.

531.11	Dynamics

Including pressure.

531.112	Kinematics (Pure motion, Abstract motion)

Including search for a moving target.

531.1133	Waves

See 530.124 vs. 531.1133.

531.14	Mass and gravity

Class gravity surveys of the earth at 526.7.

531.5	**Mass and gravity of solids; projectiles**

Class here only works specifically limited to solids. If any fluid or fluid body like the sun is significantly considered, or if no reference is made to state, class works on mass and gravity at 531.14.

533.27	**Velocity [of gases]**

Transonic refers to velocities approximately the speed of sound. plus a margin on either side; supersonic to speeds one to five times that of sound; hypersonic to speeds over five times that of sound.

534.5	**Vibrations related to sound**

Class here sound that cannot be heard by the human ear.

537	Electricity and electronics

See 530.141.

539	Modern physics

Relatively few works are classed at 539; modern physics is much more written about in parts than as a whole.

See also 530.

539.01	**Philosophy and theory [of modern physics]**

Note that all the subdivisions of s.s. 01 as spelled out in Table 1 in Edition 19 remain valid here, except s.s. 0151 Mathematics. Mathematics is so central to physical theories that comprehensive works on the mathematics of modern physics must be classed in 530.15 or with the specific theory in 530.1 to which it applies.

539.12 vs. **541.22**   Molecular structure [physics] vs. **Molecular structure [chemistry]**

Instructions in the last paragraph under 530 do not apply at 539.12. Molecular structure is so central to chemistry that it is safe to assume that a work belongs with molecular structure in chemistry (541.22) unless it specifically emphasizes the nonchemical implications of structure.

539.6   Molecular physics

Including molecular spectra, vibrational spectra.

539.6028   **Techniques, procedures, apparatus, equipment, materials [of molecular physics]**

Class here comprehensive works on mass spectrometry.

Class spectrometry of nonmolecular masses with the subject, e.g., atomic spectrometry 539.7028.

539.7   **Atomic and nuclear physics**

Class here atomic spectra, using 539.7028 for atomic spectrometry.

539.723   Nuclei

Class here only works treating nuclei essentially as particles. Works on nuclear physics taken as a whole are classed at 539.7.

539.754   Interactions

When interest seems to be more in the behavior of a particular kind of particle in a given reaction than in the interaction as a whole, class with the kind of particle, e.g., interactions of electrons with other particles studied to determine characteristics of electrons 539.72112, not 539.754.

540 Chemistry and allied sciences

SUMMARY

See 530.

540	Chemistry and allied sciences

Note that many surveys of chemistry give little or no coverage to organic chemistry. Class such surveys at 546.

541	**Physical and theoretical chemistry**

Class any topic of physical or theoretical chemistry pertaining to crystals in 548.

See also 530, and 546 vs. 541.

541.22	**Molecular structure [chemistry]**

See 539.12 vs. 541.22.

541.363	Change of state (Phase changes)

Including Gibbs' phase rule equation.

541.37	Electro- and magnetochemistry

Including electrophoresis.

541.372	Electrolytic solutions

Including electrodialysis.

543 vs. **544–545**	**Analytic chemistry vs. [Qualitative and quantitative chemistry]**

The distinction between qualitative and quantitative chemistry has been rendered obsolete by the growing sophistication of new techniques. In case of doubt, prefer numbers in 543.08 over those in 544–545 unless the qualitative or quantitative use of the technique is emphasized.

544	**Qualitative chemistry**

See 543 vs. 544–545.

544.1	Systematic separations

Including decomposition analysis.

545	**Quantitative chemistry**

See 543 vs. 544–545.

546 **Inorganic chemistry**

Except as stipulated for acids at 546.24 in Edition 19, class an inorganic compound with the first element named. Note that a different rule is provided for organic compounds at 547.01–547.08 in Edition 19.

In using the add table at 546, consider the following:

2 Compounds

Names of compounds usually end with -ide or one of the suffixes shown in 22–24 below.

22 Acids and bases

Names of acids usually end with -ic or -ous.

24 Salts

Names frequently end with -ate or -ite.

3 Molecular and colloidal mixtures

Class here alloys.

546 vs. 541 **Inorganic chemistry vs. Physical and theoretical chemistry**

The second note at 546 in Edition 19 does not apply when one or two elements or compounds, or examples drawn from one of the large groupings like metals (546.3) or nonmetals (546.7), are used primarily to study or explain a specific topic in physical or theoretical chemistry (541). In such cases use the number in 541, e.g., hydrogen-ion concentration 541.3728, not 546.2.

546 vs. 549 **Inorganic chemistry vs. Mineralogy**

In the DDC, Chemistry 541–547 and Mineralogy 549 are treated as coordinate, which implies that elements and compounds treated as minerals are classed in 549. This means that works on many topics of physical and theoretical chemistry pertaining to the structure and physical behavior of homogeneous crystalline solids will not be classed in 546. Use 546 numbers for comprehensive works on the chemistry and mineralogy of such minerals, but if in doubt between 546 and 549, prefer 549.

See also 549.13–.18.

546.3 vs. **Metals, their compounds and mixtures vs. Physical and chemical metal-**
669.9 **lurgy**

Much of what might be regarded as the physical and theoretical chemistry of metals and their alloys has been incorporated in Physical and chemical metallurgy 669.9. If in doubt, prefer 669.9.

546.6812   [Carbon compounds]

Class carbon compounds in 547 with the following exceptions, which remain in 546.6812:

(1) carbon dioxide and the various carbonates;

(2) other carbon oxides, metal carbonyls, and carbon halides when treated as inorganic chemicals by the author.

547   **Organic chemistry**

Class works on biochemicals in 547 only if they are not considered in their biological context. If so considered, class in 574.192 and cognate numbers in 576 and 580–590.

547.7   **Macromolecular and related compounds**

See 547 and 547.84.

547.84   **High polymers**

Class here only works mainly about topics listed in subdivisions, e.g., elastomers, plastics, gums, and resins.

Class works using "high polymers" as a synonym for macromolecules at 547.7.

548   **Crystallography**

Unlike chemistry (541–547), crystallography has incorporated all the advances of modern physics (*see 530*), and is now usually regarded as part of Solid-state physics 530.41. Note the reference in Edition 19 from 530.41 to 548.

548 vs. 549 **Crystallography vs. Mineralogy**

The relation between crystallography (548) and mineralogy (549) is approximately the same as that between physical and theoretical chemistry (541) and inorganic chemistry (546): the crystallography of specific minerals and mineral groups is classed in 549 unless used to study or explain a topic in 548, e.g., barium titanate 549.7, but the study of ferroelectric effect in barium titanate crystals 548.85.

549   **Mineralogy**

Mineralogy is simultaneously a branch of the physical and a branch of the natural sciences, being concerned with both the physicochemical characteristics of minerals considered in the abstract, and with their description in nature.

See also 546 vs. 549, and 548 vs. 549.

549.13–.18   [Chemical and crystallographic mineralogy]

Interpret these topics narrowly, within the context of Determinative mineralogy 549.1. The purpose of the chemistry and crystallography here is to identify and characterize minerals. If in doubt between 549.1 and either 541–545 or 548, use either 541–545 or 548.

549.23   Metals

Note that metals are considered here only as native elements, i.e., as found in nature. The chemistry of manufactured metals is classed in Physical and chemical metallurgy 669.9.

550 Sciences of the earth and other worlds

SUMMARY

551   **Geology, meteorology, general hydrology**
552   **Petrology**
553   **Economic geology**
554   **Treatment in Europe**
555   **Treatment in Asia**
556   **Treatment in Africa**
557   **Treatment in North America**
558   **Treatment in South America**
559   **Treatment in other parts of world and in extraterrestrial worlds**

550   Sciences of the earth and other worlds

Use 550 (either alone or with standard subdivisions) only for works covering significantly more than the topics in 551, i.e., covering significant material on Economic geology 553 or Paleontology 560 or both.

551   **Geology, meteorology, general hydrology**

551 is so much the dominant subdivision of 550 that few works on the earth sciences are broad enough to be classed at 550. 551 includes all descriptive and analytic topics on the lithosphere, hydrosphere, and atmosphere that are not predominantly concerned with the economic importance of geologic materials (553), with embedded life forms (Paleontology 560), or with both.

Class here geology both in its broad sense, as the science of the earth's solids, liquids, and gases, and in the narrow sense, as the science of the solid earth.

Class geology of the lithosphere, general geology in specific areas in 554–559.

551 vs. 910.02	**Geology, meteorology, general hydrology vs. The earth (Physical geography)**

The difference between geophysics (551) and physical geography (910.02) is primarily one between the analysis of the structure of the earth and the forces shaping it (geophysics) and the description (location, appearance) of the resulting landscape taken as a whole (physical geography). Descriptions of the results of various specific forces and processes remain with the subject in 551; the operation of all the forces and processes taken as a whole to create topographical land forms is classed in 551.4; the operation of all the forces and processes taken as a whole in a specific area, especially if emphasizing solid geology, is classed in 554–559. For example, physical description of Burma 915.9102; geophysical processes operating in Burma or the geology of Burma 555.91; earthquakes in Burma 551.2209591; beaches of Burma 551.457. However, topographical features described for travelers are classed in 910–919 using "travel" notation 04 from the tables in Edition 19 at 913.1–913.9 or 914–919 as appropriate, e.g., contemporary tourist beaches in Burma 915.91045.

551.0222 [Pictures, charts, designs in geology, meteorology, general hydrology]

Class geological maps in 912.155. Class maps and charts giving cross-sectional detail of structural geology in 551.80222.

551.09162 [Geology, meteorology, general hydrology of oceans and seas]

Class submarine geology in 551.4608.

551.093– .099 [**Historical and geographical treatment of geology, meteorology, general hydrology by specific continents, countries, localities; extraterrestrial worlds**]

Class here only history of the disciplines named in the heading. Class description and analysis of the actual phenomena described by earth sciences with the specific subject in 551–559, e.g., glaciers in Switzerland 551.31209494, geology of Switzerland 554.94.

See also 551, and 551 vs. 910.02.

551.136 Plate tectonics (Continental drift)

See 551.41 vs. 551.136.

551.2 **Plutonic phenomena**

Class volcanic eruptions and earthquakes as disasters at 363.3495; as events of larger historic importance at 904.5 if collected, or in 930–990 if individual.

551.3   **Surface and exogenous processes and their agents**

Including gravity, temperature, and vegetation as geological agents; creep, subsidence, planation, compaction. Landslides are considered to be the work of water and so are classed at 551.353.

Class here sedimentation.

Class specific land forms created by specific surface and exogenous processes in 551.4, e.g., beaches created by action of marine waves and currents 551.457, not 551.36.

551.4   **Geomorphology and general hydrology**

Class here specific topographic land forms created by surface and exogenous processes. However, class land forms considered as manifestations of plutonic activity in 551.2, of plate tectonics in 551.136, of other tectonic activity in 551.8.

Class the explanation of geomorphological processes that shaped the topography of an area in 551.4, using s.s. 09 if appropriate; the description of the overall results of the processes in a specific area in 910–919. *See also 551 vs. 910.02.*

Class submarine geomorphology in 551.46084, except for continental shelves, slopes, and terraces, which are classed at 551.41 Continents.

551.4   Geomorphology and general hydrology

Use standard subdivisions of 551.4 interchangeably for geomorphology, for general hydrology, or for both.

551.41   Continents

Including continental slopes, continental terraces.

551.41 vs.   Continents vs. Plate tectonics (Continental drift)
551.136
If in doubt whether to regard a continent as a topographic land form (551.41) or as a feature of the earth's crust and its plate tectonics (551.136), prefer 551.136.

551.46–.49   **General hydrology**

Hydrology in the broad sense covers all waters of the earth (whether or not ice or atmospheric moisture is included), but hydrology in the narrow sense is limited to fresh waters. Class hydrology in the broad sense at 551.4 and its standard subdivisions, in the narrow sense at 551.48.

Class all hydrological aspects of ice in 551.31 and related numbers, even if unrelated to surface and exogenous processes, and class hydrometeorology at 551.57.

551.46 **Oceanography**

While 551.46 is the comprehensive number for physical oceanography and marine biology, note that Marine biology 574.92 may include significant consideration of ocean waters as part of the ecology of marine organisms. If in doubt between 551.46 and 574.92, prefer 574.92. *See also 574.526.*

Class here marine science.

Class oceanographic engineering in 620.4162.

551.46084 Topography of ocean floor

Class geomorphology of continental shelves, slopes, terraces at 551.41.

551.4609 Special salt-water forms

Class specific salt-water lagoons, coastal pools, and estuaries with the ocean to which they belong in 551.461–551.469.

551.4708 Tides and tidal currents

Class comprehensive works on tides in 525.6, their geological work at 551.36.

551.48 **Hydrology**

See 551.46–.49.

551.49 **Ground waters (Subsurface waters)**

Class here aquifers.

551.5 vs. **Meteorology vs. Climatology and weather**
551.6

Meteorology 551.5 analyzes and describes the properties and phenomena of the atmosphere, and thus explains weather and climate (551.6). Meteorology is also the larger subject, encompassing both climatology and weather. Unfortunately, however, many works on the larger subject (meteorology) may be called "climatology" or "weather," but must be classed in 551.5 regardless of the words in the titles. These two words as used in 551.6 are confined to three senses:

(1) the description of the phenomena of the atmosphere taken as a whole, weather usually being the short-range description, and climate the long-range description;

(2) the prediction of weather, climate, or specific meteorological phenomena, i.e., weather forecasting 551.63–551.64; and

(3) the attempt to modify weather or any specific meteorological phenomena (551.68), which is actually a technology.

All other elements, including description (weather reports) of specific phenomena, remain in 551.5, regardless of the terms used in the work in hand. For example, reports of rainfall are classed in 551.577, forecasts of rainfall in 551.6477, a forecast of a rainy day in Singapore at 551.655957, a description of rain belts of Asia at 551.62, a discussion of how the weather works at 551.5.

551.513–.514 Regions [of the atmosphere]

The approximate range of the regions is as follows:

Troposphere: surface to 8 km. (5 miles) at the poles, to 15 km. (10 miles) at the equator.

Stratosphere: from 8 to 15 up to 50 km. (from 5 to 10 up to 30 miles).

Mesosphere: from 50 up to 80 km. (30 to 50 miles).

Ionosphere (thermosphere):   from 80 up to 480 km. (50 to 300 miles).

Magnetosphere (exosphere):   above 480 km.

The mesosphere and magnetosphere have no separate numbers, and are classed at 551.514.

551.52509   [Air temperatures of specific continents, countries, localities]

Note that most geographical treatment of air temperatures is limited to reports at the earth's surface (551.5252).

551.5252   Distribution [of air temperatures] at earth's surface

Including urban heat islands.

551.5409   [Atmospheric pressure in specific continents, countries, localities]

Note that most geographical treatment is limited to reports at the earth's surface (551.542).

551.543   Variations [of atmospheric pressure] at earth's surface

"Variations" refers to differences in pressure over time.

Class chronological variations in a specific area at 551.542.

551.5773   Variations [of precipitation]

"Variations" refers to differences in precipitation over time.

Class chronological variations in a specific area in 551.5772, floods at 551.489.

551.6   **Climatology and weather**

See 551.5 vs. 551.6.

551.64   Forecasting specific elements and phenomena

Class forecasting of floods at 551.489.

551.69   Climate of various specific areas

Class here synoptic meteorology. However, if the work encompasses a whole weather belt or worldwide climate zone, class it at 551.62.

551.7   Historical geology

Class the history of specific features of the geological record with the subject, e.g., formation of volcanic strata during the Jurassic period in the Pacific Northwest 551.2109795, not 551.76609795.

It is not anticipated that the periods and epochs presently provided for in subdivisions of 551.7 will be further subdivided, so standard subdivisions may be added for specific epochs, stages, or formations, e.g., Albian stage (of Lower Cretaceous) in France 551.770944.

551.7 vs. 560   Historical geology vs. Paleontology

Paleontology 560 is the study of life in former geologic ages through the interpretation of fossils. It utilizes the same material as Historical geology 551.7 (i.e., the geological record), but is interested in it only as a record of life and the environment in which it evolved. Historical geology emphasizes inanimate rocks, using paleontological facts to help date and interpret their deposition, movement, and erosion. If in doubt, prefer 551.7.

551.7009   [Historical geology of specific continents, countries, localities]

Class here only the history of the discipline. Class the phenomena of historical geology of a specific place in 554–559, even if the strata of only a few periods remain; the historic geology of a specific period in a specific place in 551.71–551.79.

551.81   Stratifications

Class here only comprehensive works on stratifications.

Class stratifications of specific periods in 551.7, in specific areas in 554–559, in specific periods in specific areas in 551.7.

551.9   Geochemistry

Geochemistry largely duplicates petrology. (*See Petrogenesis 552.03 and Properties, composition, analysis, structure of rocks 552.06 in Edition 19.*) Class in 551.9 only the rare work including chemistry of the atmosphere and hydrosphere as well as that of the solid earth.

552   **Petrology**

Rocks can be defined as aggregates of minerals, the minerals being the homogeneous, usually crystalline grains (large and small) that give rocks their texture. Petrology encompasses the study of rocks and minerals, or of rocks alone. The homogeneous minerals studied by themselves are classed in 549.

See also 553.5 vs. 552.

552.03   Petrogenesis (Origin of rocks)

Class in 553 the petrogenesis of all materials named in subdivisions of 553; however, make an exception to this rule for stony materials (553.5), which are fundamental to petrology even though they are incidentally useful. Class these in 552, e.g., petrogenesis of granites 552.3.

552.09   **Geographical distribution of rocks**

Class in 552.09 works concentrating on rocks (or rocks and minerals) when studied without regard to their geological setting or economic utility. Consideration of geological setting points to the use of 554–559, of economic utility to the use of 553.09.

553   **Economic geology**

Economic geology is a mixture of scientific analysis and economic evaluation of certain useful natural resources. The works range from the very technical to the very superficial, and exhibit considerable emphasis on quality analysis. Deposits may be defined in terms of volume, monetary worth, years' supply, or simply as good, rich, promising, or some other designation.

While 553 is the number for interdisciplinary works on specific nonmetallic materials, be alert for works in fact emphasizing economics as a whole, not just reserves, stocks, supply, e.g., a work on the importance of water, not giving much consideration to scientific or other aspects, 333.91, not 553.7.

Be alert for works having a heavy but unstated emphasis on metallic deposits: these are classed at 553.4.

553.28   **Petroleum and natural gas**

Be particularly wary of the word "petroleum," which is often loosely used for oil *and* gas. Such usage is standardized in the phrase petroleum geology, as defined in Webster's *Third New International Dictionary.* Therefore, class petroleum geology at 553.28, not 553.282, unless specifically limited to oil geology.

See also 622.3382.

553.5   **Stony materials**

Class comprehensive works on stony and earthy materials at 553.6.

553.5 vs. 552   **Stony materials vs. Petrology**

Class in 553.5 only rocks useful as structural components in more or less their natural state. Since such rocks are basic components of the rocky earth, class works on their distribution and petrogenesis here only when the rocks are being emphasized as particularly accessible or especially desirable. Otherwise, class in 552. *See 552.03.*

553.6   **Earthy materials**

"Earthy" is used very loosely here. Class here minerals that are neither fossil fuels (553.2), metal ores (553.3–553.4), stony structural materials (553.5), nor gems (553.8). For example, fluorspar is classed here.

Class here comprehensive works on stony and earthy materials.

Class stony materials in 553.5.

553.7   **Water and aqueous deposits**

This number is used, for lack of a better one, for water quality studies not having reference to any other specific discipline. However, prefer 363.73942 for works emphasizing man-made pollutants as parameters of quality.

553.78–.79   [Surface and ground waters]

Class works covering both Surface 553.78 and Ground 553.79 waters at 553.7 rather than with the first of two.

553.9   Other economic materials

Including air and air quality. The note at 553.7 on water quality applies to air quality, with 363.73922 being the preferred number for air pollutants as parameters of quality.

554–559   **Treatment [of earth sciences] by continent, country, locality in modern world; extraterrestrial worlds**

Until Edition 19 this span was called regional geology. Most of the works classed here will probably continue to be limited to geology of the lithosphere.

Class here, with caution, geological survey reports. Make sure the reports do not emphasize useful materials (553.09) or metalliferous deposits (553.409).

Use modern area numbers for whatever material there may be on geological phenomena in the areas of the ancient world.

559.9   [Treatment of earth-like sciences in extraterrestrial worlds]

This subject refers to sciences of other worlds analogous to earth sciences, i.e., observation and analysis based on close exploration, in contrast to observations made by astronomical techniques. The analogy holds only if there is a distinct lithosphere, otherwise the hydrology and meteorology are moot concepts. For example, class atmosphere of Mars, which has a lithosphere, at 551.5099923, but atmospheres of stars, which do not, in 523.8, the red spot of Jupiter (a planet without a distinct lithosphere) at 523.45.

560 Paleontology Paleozoology

Class the analysis of paleontological evidence to determine geological time and age in 551.701 or with the specific age in 551.71–551.79.

See also 551.7 vs. 560.

560   Paleontology   Paleozoology

Class at 560 any organism of uncertain biological relationships, e.g., acritarchs, or animals of uncertain taxonomic position. However, class conodonts in 562.2.

560 vs. 575   **Paleontology vs. Organic evolution and genetics**

Paleontology provides a major part of the evidence for evolution, and many works are about the substance of both fields. Class at 575 works that cite paleontological evidence primarily to show how various factors may have influenced evolution. Prefer 560 for works emphasizing the description of organisms and environment as the history of life. Class works adding significant nonpaleontological evidence to the picture at 575, works on the evolution of extinct taxons in 560. If in doubt, prefer 575.

561   **Paleobotany**

Class here plantlike fossils of uncertain taxonomic position; however, class fernlike fossils at 561.597.

Note that stratigraphic study of plants as a whole is classed in 560.17, but that statigraphic study of particular groups of plants is classed in the subdivisions of 561.

569.9   Hominidae (Humankind and forebears)

Class at 573.3 any remains assigned to the genus *Homo* by any reputable authority. Remains clearly of a different genus are classed at 569.9.

570–590 [Biological sciences]

Because of the human interest in living things, give the benefit of the doubt to life science numbers over general science or inanimate science numbers, unless substantial separate treatment is given to sciences other than biology, e.g., prefer 574.9 Geographical treatment of organisms for natural history of specific areas over 508 Description and surveys of natural phenomena.

Similarly, because of human medical and agricultural interests, give the benefit of the doubt to medical (610) and agricultural (630) numbers over life science ones, especially for diseases and pathological phenomena. *See also second and third notes at 574.*

570–590 vs.   **[Biological sciences] vs. Technology (Applied sciences)**
600

While 574–599 numbers are used for interdisciplinary works on plants and animals significant in technology, note that many works that are basically technology will provide a biological background to the growing, harvesting, or utilization of organisms. Class these works in 600, e.g., a handbook of drugs from forest and meadow 615.321, not 581.634; wild flowers for your garden 635.9676, not 582.13; where your trout hide out 799.1755, not 597.55.

Note that 641.3 is the interdisciplinary number for food, so works that cover the preparation and utilization of food as well as the biology and agriculture of edible plants and animals are classed in 641.3, not 574.599.

570 Life sciences

SUMMARY

572 **Human races**
573 **Physical anthropology**
574 **Biology**
575 **Organic evolution and genetics**
576 **Microbes**
577 **General nature of life**
578 **Microscopy in biology**
579 **Collection and preservation of**
     biological specimens

570   Life sciences

By itself 570 is little used, except for works including substantial separate treatment of paleontology. Class general biology at 574.

572.3   Causes of physical differences [among races]

Note that 572.3 refers only to physical differences *among races*. Class works on nonracial physical differences, or on racial and nonracial physical differences, in 573.

573.2   Organic evolution and genetics of humankind

Class here works concentrating on human genetics, on human evolution.

Note that the subdivisions of this number apply only to genetics, and that, therefore, human evolution must be classed in standing room at 573.2 unless there is substantial discussion of the role of genetics in the evolutionary process.

Class comprehensive works on evolution at 575, on genetics at 575.1.

Beware of misleading and equivocal titles. Some works entitled "evolution of man" may actually cover the whole field of evolution and are thus classed at 575. In the same way, such a work may be a review of paleontology and be classed at 560, or may concentrate on paleontological evidence of the immediate forebears of humankind and be classed at 573.3 or 569.9. *See 569.9.*

See also 575.

573.3   Prehistoric man

Class prehistoric men and women considered as progenitors of contemporary races at 572.2.

See also 569.9.

573.6   Anthropometry

Class the raw statistics of physical measurements at 312.6.

573.6 vs. 611 Anthropometry vs. Human anatomy

Anthropometry is concerned with measuring human beings to determine variation and presumed evolutionary development. The emphasis is generally on external variation and bone structure, in contrast to anatomy (611) which is more concerned with norms of structure, internal as well as external. Prefer 573.6 for external features and shapes, and gross bone structure (e.g., the comparison of heavy- and thin-boned people, indexes of length and breadth of skeletal features); 611 for all other features.

573.8   Abnormal dimensions

Class pathological aspects of abnormal dimensions in 616–618, e.g., gigantism a manifestation of pituitary gland function at 616.47, not 573.8.

574   **Biology**

Class the biological processes and systems of a specific organism or group of organisms with the organism or group, even if the object of the work is to study the particular process or system, e.g., circulation in mammals 599.011. *See also 591.*

Class medically oriented physiological research on plants and animals in 574–599, but pharmacological research regarding them in 615, experimental research on diseases and pathological processes found in humankind in 616–619, in agricultural plants and animals in 630.

Class the physiology and anatomy of agricultural plants in 580, of agricultural animals in 636.0891–636.0892 and cognate numbers under specific animals.

574.028   **Techniques, procedures, apparatus, equipment, materials [in biology]**

The notes in Edition 19 referring to microscopy in 578 and preservation of biological specimens in 579 override the usual citation order, which gives precedence to type of organism. Class microscopy and preservation in 578–579 irrespective of organism or group or organisms.

574.072   **Research [in biology]**

Class here biometrics and biostatistics.

574.1   **Physiology**

See 574, 591.1.

574.133   Metabolism

Class metabolism of specific chemicals in 574.192, e.g., metabolism of hormones 574.1927; of a specific system or process with the system or process under the specific organism or group of organisms, e.g., metabolism of mammalian blood 599.0113.

574.166 Sexual reproduction

When adding subdivisions of 574 according to instructions under subdivision 04 General principles from the tables under 582–589 and 592–599 in Edition 19, or according to analogous instructions regarding general principles at certain other taxonomic numbers, note that for taxa whose reproduction is always sexual, this subdivision is redundant. In such cases add to base number only the segment 16 representing physiology of reproduction, e.g., reproduction in mammals (which do not reproduce asexually) 599.016, not 599.0166.

574.191 Biophysics

Including effects of magnetism.

574.192 **Biochemistry**

See 547.

574.24 Diseases and injuries caused by physical and chemical factors

Class here pathological conditions caused by environmental factors, e.g., by pollution. However, class general observations on the deleterious effects of various aspects of the environment on organisms at 574.5222 or cognate numbers in 576 and 580–590. *See also 574.5222.*

574.29 **Immunity**

See 591.29.

574.4 Anatomy and morphology

Note that comprehensive works on anatomy, morphology, and physiology of biological structures are classed in 574.1.

574.5222 Effects of specific aspects of environment on organisms

Including the effects of pollution.

Class pathological conditions caused by environmental factors at 574.24.

Class observation of the ecological effects of pollution as a means of surveying social environmental problems in 363.73, e.g., monitoring water pollution by counting the instances of survival among indicator organisms 363.739463, not 574.5222; counting organisms as indicators of water quality (when considered apart from pollution problems) in 553.7; technology of treating pollution in 628.5.

574.526   [Ecology of] **Specific kinds of environments**

Ecology emphasizes interrelationships among various elements of the environment, and is thus usually easy to distinguish from descriptive accounts of organisms in a kind of region (574.909–574.929). If the distinction is not clear, prefer 574.526.

See also 582.1605, and 584.9045.

574.6   **Economic biology**

Class the physiology of beneficial and deleterious organisms in 574.1 and cognate numbers in 580–590, or in 630; the pathology of beneficial organisms in 630, of agricultural pests in 630, of the few remaining economic organisms that do not usually appear in agricultural contexts (such as poison ivy or pit vipers) in 574.2 and cognate numbers in 580–590.

See also 574.

574.61   Beneficial organisms

See 570–590 vs. 600.

574.8   **Tissue, cellular, molecular biology**

Class here the study at the *tissue* or *cellular* level of any process or structure defined in 574–574.5 (except for gametogenesis, which is classed at 574.32, not 574.8762). In contrast, class *molecular* biology of a specific process or structure with the process or structure, e.g., molecular biology of hormones 574.1927, not 574.88.

574.87322   Chromosomes

Including meiosis. Class meiosis in gametogenesis in 574.32.

574.88   Molecular biology

The emphasis in molecular biology is on the structure of the biochemicals which are found in 574.192. If in doubt between 574.192 and 574.88, prefer 574.192.

See also 574.8.

574.9   **Geographical treatment of organisms**

See 508, and 574.526.

575   **Organic evolution and genetics**

Class evolution of a specific process or structure with the process or structure, e.g., evolution of birdsong 598.259.

See also 560 vs. 575, and 573.2.

575.2 **Variation**

If in doubt between 575.2 Variation and 575.1 heredity and variation, prefer 575.1.

575.28 Variations

Class variations caused by a particular factor with the factor, e.g., mutations caused by radiation 575.131.

575.29 Abrupt deviations

Including crossing over.

576 Microbes

See 589.

576.64 Viruses

Do not class interferons here, but rather in 591.295. (This change was announced in *DC&*, Vol. 4, No. 1, p. 18.)

578 **Microscopy in biology**

See 574.028.

579 **Collection and preservation of biological specimens**

See 574.028.

580–590 [Botanical and zoological sciences]

The sequence of taxonomic groups of plants and animals can be described as following the course of the letter U. The sequence begins at one tip of the U with the most highly developed and complex plants (the flowering plants) and moves down to the base of the U for algae and organisms that may be considered either plant or animal, or neither one. Tradition classes most of these as plants. The sequence then moves up the other arm of the U, beginning with protozoa, continuing up to man, the most highly developed and complex animal.

580 Botanical sciences

SUMMARY

581 **Botany**
582 **Spermatophyta (Seed-bearing plants)**
583 **Dicotyledones (Dicotyledons)**
584 **Monocotyledones (Monocotyledons)**
585 **Gymnospermae (Naked-seed plants)**
586 **Cryptogamia (Seedless plants)**
587 **Pteridophyta (Vascular cryptogams)**
588 **Bryophyta**
589 **Thallophyta**

580   Botanical sciences

By itself 580 is little used, except for works including substantial separate treatment of paleobotany. Class general botany at 581.

580.74   **Museums, collections, exhibits [of botanical sciences]**

Class here general herbariums and botanical gardens, and those limited to vascular plants, spermatophytes, angiosperms, or dicotyledons.

Class herbariums and botanical gardens limited to groups of plants other than those listed above with the specific group, e.g., non-ornamental gardens of gymnosperms in Asia 585.074095.

580.742   Herbariums

Herbariums are collections of dried plants. Class collections of living plants at 580.744.

581   **Botany**

Use 581 with caution, since many works on "plants" are in fact limited to spermatophytes (582), angiosperms (comprehensive works 582.13), or dicotyledons (583). Substantial treatment of nonspermatophytic plants must be present to justify the use of 581.

Keeping the caveat described in the preceding paragraph in mind, class here the physiology and anatomy of agricultural plants.

Class processes and systems of a specific plant or group of plants with the plant or group, even if the object of the work is to study the particular process or system, e.g., genetics of peas 584.322, not 581.15.

All notes at subdivision of 574 apply to cognate numbers here also.

581.074   Museums, collections, exhibits [of botany]

See 580.74.

581.133	Metabolism [of plants]
	Class nitrogen fixation at 589.9504133.
581.29	**[Immunity in plants]**
	See 591.29.
581.4	Anatomy and morphology of plants
	Be especially mindful of cautions at 581 and 574.4.
581.6	Economic botany
	Note carefully instructions at 570–590 vs. 600 and at 574.6.
582–589	**Specific plants and groups of plants**
	Do not add provisions as instructed under 04 at 582–589 in Edition 19 where redundant. *See 574.166 for example.*
	See also 580–590, and all notes under 581 and 574.
582.033	[Embryology of Spermatophyta]
	Including formation of seeds and the seedling stage up to the development of regular leaves.
582.0332	[Embryological anatomy of Spermatophyta]
	Class anatomy of seeds at 582.0467.
582.1 vs. 635.9	**Special groupings [of plants] vs. Flowers and ornamental plants**
	Note that the groupings at 582.1 are similar to those often found in gardening books in 635.9. Class works in 635.9 (often 635.97 gardening of other groupings) if the emphasis is on plants to be cultivated or appreciated in man-made settings, in 582.1 if the emphasis is on the plants in nature, or on their biology. If in doubt, class in 635.9.
	See also 570–590 vs. 600.
582.1605	[Ecology of trees]
	Class ecology of forests, jungles, and woodlands at 574.52642.
584.9045	[Ecology of Graminales]
	Class ecology of grasslands, meadows, and prairies at 574.52643.
589	Thallophyta
	Class comprehensive works on microorganisms (protists) in 576, even when there is heavy emphasis on those regarded as plants.

589.9   **Schizomycetes**

Class here comprehensive works on procaryotic organisms.

Class cyanophytes at 589.46.

589.9504133 [**Metabolism of Eubacteriales**]

Class here comprehensive works on nitrogen fixation. Class fixation by other organisms with the organisms, e.g., by certain blue-green algae 589.46.

590 Zoological sciences

SUMMARY

  591   **Zoology**
  592   **Invertebrates**
  593   **Protozoa and other simple animals**
  594   **Mollusca and molluscoidea**
  595   **Other invertebrates**
  596   **Chordata   Vertebrata (Craniata, Vertebrates)**
  597   **Cold-blooded vertebrates   Pisces (Fishes)**
  598   **Aves (Birds)**
  599   **Mammalia (Mammals)**

590   Zoological sciences

590 by itself is little used, except for works including substantial treatment of Paleozoology 560. Class general zoology at 591.

590.744   **Zoological gardens**

Class here general zoos, zoos limited to vertebrates, to land vertebrates, and to mammals.

Class zoos limited to groups of animals other than those listed above with the specific group, e.g., insect zoos 595.70074, aquariums for marine vertebrates in Spain 596.09207406.

591 **Zoology**

In zoology it is often difficult to apply the rule spelled out at 574, that a biological process or system is classed with the type of organism in which it is studied. Often the type of animal is not stated, or each of a compilation of studies uses a different species. When the interest appears to be medical, and in the absence of obvious contrary clues, give the benefit of doubt to 599 and its zero subdivisions, the comprehensive numbers for warm-blooded vertebrates. 599 can be used when warm-blooded animals predominate, even if there is a sprinkling of material on other animals. However, note that works on diseases of humankind are classed in 616–618; diseases of useful animals in 636–639 even if studied experimentally in laboratory animals, not in 599.02 and cognate numbers.

Class in 800 stories, anecdotes, and reminiscences about animals that are not intended to illustrate their zoological characteristics. *See also notes about animals at 800: Special problems: Works about animals.*

Class the physiology and anatomy of agricultural animals in 636.0891–636.0892 and cognate numbers under specific organisms.

All notes at subdivisions of 574 apply to cognate numbers here also.

591.074 Museums, collections, exhibits [in zoology]

See 590.74.

591.1 **Physiology of animals**

Consult 612.1–612.8 in Edition 19 for guidance in locating processes and structures not provided for under parallel subdivisions in 591.11–591.18. However, use 591.3 for development and maturation concepts that are expressed in 612 in the span 612.63–612.68.

See also 612.1–.8.

591.113 [Circulatory fluids in animals]

Class the role of circulating chemicals and cells in immunity in 591.29.

591.29 **Immunity [in animals]**

Including cellular immunity (the engulfing or destroying of foreign bodies by leukocytes and similar cells), T cells, interferons.

Class here internal defense mechanisms.

591.29 vs.   **Immunity [in animals] vs. [Medical immunity]**
616–618

Class in 616.079 and cognate numbers works emphasizing immunity in relation to diseases and problems in human beings, such as hay fever, organ grafts, and cancer. If in doubt between a 590 number and a 616–618 number, prefer 616–618.

591.292   [Antigens in animals]

Use 591.292 only for works limited to antigens. Class their role in producing antibodies at 591.293.

591.293   [Antibodies in animals]

Class here humoral immunity, or what might be called the antibody system, including B cells, plasma cells, memory cells.

591.295   [Immune reactions in animals]

Since the concept "immune reactions" largely overlaps "immunity" at 591.29, 591.295 will seldom be used.

Class antigen-antibody reactions at 591.293.

591.3   **Development and maturation of animals**

See 591.1.

591.4   Anatomy and morphology of animals

Class comprehensive works on anatomy, morphology, and physiology in 591.1.

591.51   Habits and behavior patterns [of animals]

See 156.

591.564   Habitations [of animals]

Examples: nests and nesting.

591.6   Economic zoology

Note carefully instructions at 570–590 vs. 600 and at 574.6.

592–599   **Specific animals and groups of animals**

Do not add provisions as instructed at 592–599 in Edition 19 where redundant. *See 574.166 for example.*

See also 580–590, and all notes under 591 and 574.

594   **Mollusca and molluscoidea**

Class here malacology.

Class shells at 594.0471 skeletal organs.

599   **Mammalia (Mammals)**

See 591.

599.03   [Development and maturation of mammals]

Including pregnancy, lactation, placentas, other concepts brought out in 612.63–612.68 (subdivisions of human development and maturation) not provided for at 574.3.

599.5   **Cetacea and Sirenia**

Class here comprehensive works on marine mammals; however, class marine carnivores at 599.745.

600 Technology (Applied sciences)

SUMMARY

610 **Medical sciences**   **Medicine**
620 **Engineering and allied operations**
630 **Agriculture and related technologies**
640 **Home economics and family living**
650 **Management and auxiliary services**
660 **Chemical and related technologies**
670 **Manufactures**
680 **Manufacture of products for specific uses**
690 **Buildings**

Class technology as a cause of cultural change at 303.483; works on industrial and technological enterprise that emphasize economics in 338 (338.1–338.4 if a specific enterprise is being discussed). *See 338.9 for a discussion of technology transfer and technical assistance, and 300 vs. 600.*

602.75   [Trademarks and service marks in technology]

Class here comprehensive works on engineering (technical) trademarks. Class interdisciplinary works on trademarks at 929.9.

604.7   Hazardous materials technology.

See 363.176 vs. 604.7.

607.34   **[Technological] Museums, collections, exhibits, fairs, expositions**

Fairs and expositions are limited here to "trade" and similar types of fairs and expositions that emphasize the technology of the exhibits. Class a fair or exposition whose exhibits emphasize any other subject with the subject, e.g., New York World's Fair of 1964–65 909.8260740147243.

608   **Inventions and patents**

Class here description of inventions and patents. The overall history of inventions approximates the history of technology and is classed at 609.

609   Historical and geographical treatment

Class works on industrial technology that emphasize the history or civilization of the area where the industry is located in 900.

610 Medical sciences   Medicine

SUMMARY

611	Human anatomy, cytology, tissue biology
612	Human physiology
613	General and personal hygiene
614	Public health and related topics
615	Pharmacology and therapeutics
616	Diseases
617	Surgery and related topics
618	Other branches of medicine Gynecology and obstetrics
619	Experimental medicine

610 deals with the technology of achieving and maintaining the health of human beings. Only home care of the sick and infirm by family members is classed elsewhere (649.8).

What the individual can do to gain and keep his health is found in General and personal hygiene 613. What medical science can do on a general scale to gain and keep the health of the public is found in Public health and related topics 614. The means to gain, regain, and maintain health through external agents (materia medica) and specific therapies are found in Pharmacology and therapeutics 615.

Medicine proper begins with 616 Diseases, where the first of the four classical branches of this discipline is found, i.e., internal medicine, which through the use of its preferred therapy and materia medica seeks to regain the health of a patient. When health cannot be gained or regained through internal medicine, the practitioner may employ the second classical branch of medicine, i.e., surgery (617.1–617.5). The other classical branches of medicine, obstetrics and pediatrics, occupy most of the numbers under 618. (Note that any of the subdivisions of 616–618 are available and are to be used for systems of medicine other than that practiced by "medical doctors," e.g., the disease and surgery numbers are to be used for osteopathy or chiropractic or both.)

611 Human anatomy, cytology, tissue biology and 612 Human physiology are sometimes considered to be medical sciences and sometimes pure sciences. They are not really technological in nature even though they are found in the 600s. 619 Experimental medicine might be considered a topic which should be classed at 610.724. It supports the medical sciences through its study of diseases and their treatment in animals.

Class here comprehensive works on human and veterinary medicine. Class veterinary medicine in 636.089.

Class the results of anatomical and physiological research with animal models in zoology 591–599, but class the results of pharmacological, therapeutic, and pathological research with animals and plants in 615–619 if medical relevance is stated or implied.

610 vs. 362.1   Medical sciences vs. [Social aspects of] Physical illness

Health services from the social point of view are classed in 360, e.g., social measures for the provision of dental care through clinics 362.1976, but how the dentist actually uses his skill 617.6. Class works treating both the medical sciences and the medical social services in 362.1. If in doubt, prefer 362.1.

610.69   Medical personnel

Be careful not to confuse the nature of the duties performed by the personnel with the technology of the operations used to discharge the duties, e.g., the technology of the services of medical technicians 610.737, not 610.6953; of surgeons 617, not 617.0232.

610.73   Nursing and other activities ancillary to medical profession

As the nursing profession continues to expand its responsibilities and gain recognition for those it already performs, more and more works by and for nurses are about the subjects of medical science in a larger context than intended here. Class such works in other medical numbers, adding s.s. 024613 (the subject for nurses), e.g., the medical sciences for nurses 610.24613; a work treating the problems and techniques of surgery written to help nurses understand the context of their duties 617.0024613, not 610.73677, even if called surgical nursing.

610.730692   Professional nurses and nursing

Including the role of nurse practitioners.

610.736   Specialized nursing

Use numbers in 610.736 only for general works emphasizing what the nurse does, not for works (often written by nurses) on a subject in 616–618 to explain to nurses the background and context of specialized nursing. *See also 610.73.*

610.9   [History of the medical sciences]

The history of a particular medical science is classed with the science, e.g., the history of nursing 610.7309, of surgery 617.09, of internal medicine 616.009; of three or more medical sciences at 610.9.

Be alert for histories of major diseases and their distribution (614.42) and histories of medical service and the resulting medical welfare of people (362.109). If in doubt where a work is to be classed among the three numbers, or between 362.109 and one of the others, prefer 362.109.

Note that works on former medical practices emphasizing therapy are classed at 615.88, or in the numbers for folk medicine (615.882) and primitive, ancient, medieval remedies (615.899).

611   Human anatomy, cytology, tissue biology

See 573.6 vs. 611.

611 vs. 612   Human anatomy, cytology, tissue biology vs. Human physiology

Anatomy or morphology concerns the shape and structure of organs in contrast to their physiology, which deals with how they work. Be on the watch for works bearing the names of organs, but emphasizing their physiology or covering physiology as well as anatomy. Class these in 612 unless the physiology is limited to the cytological or histological level, in which case use 611.018.

611.1–.9   Gross anatomy

See 612.1–.8.

611.41   [Anatomy of the] Spleen

Class here comprehensive works on the anatomy of the blood-forming (hematopoietic or hemopoietec) system. Class the anatomy of bone marrow at 611.0184.

611.84   [Anatomy of the] Eyes

Class here the orbit.

612   Human physiology

Class here comprehensive works on structure and function (anatomy and physiology). However, class treatment of anatomy, physiology, and pathology at the cytological and histological level in 611.018.

See also 611 vs. 612.

612 vs. 616   Human physiology vs. Diseases

Class in 612 comprehensive works on physiology and pathological physiology (612 plus 616.07), but not the more comprehensive works on diseases that discuss enough normal physiology to help the reader understand what has gone wrong and then move on to a more general consideration of causes of disease, complications, prevention, and therapy, e.g., the normal and pathological conditions of the circulatory system 612.1, but the physiology, pathology, and therapeutics of the circulatory system 616.1.

612.0142   Physical phenomena in humans

Including human aura when scientifically considered. Class the aura as a manifestation of psychic power at 133.8.

612.0144   Effects of terrestrial agents [on human physiology]

Including aerospace physiology.

Class space physiology in 612.0145.

612.014415   [Effects of pressures on human physiology]

Including submarine physiology.

612.1–.8   [Physiology of] Specific functions, systems, organs

Here is found the basic division of the human body into physiological systems. Parallel subdivisions 1–8 are used in cut-back or slightly altered form under human anatomy in 611.1–611.8; under pharmacodynamics in 615.71–615.78; under diseases in 616.1–616.8; under surgery by system in 617.41–617.48; and in comparable physiology, anatomy, and disease numbers in biology 574–599.

If in doubt where to class an organ or function not provided for in one of the parallel arrays, use 612.1–612.8 as a guide. For example, use 615.74 Drugs affecting glandular system for pharmacodynamics of the pituitary gland. This is comparable to 612.4 Secretion, excretion, related functions, where this gland is named at 612.492. In the same manner use 615.73 Drugs affecting digestive system for pharmacodynamics of the pancreas. This is comparable to 612.3 Nutrition, where the pancreas is named at 612.34. However, class pharmacodynamics of the kidneys in 615.761, where the urinary system is provided for, even though kidney physiology is at 612.463 under secretions.

612.1181   Biophysics [of the blood]

Including hemorrheology (study of blood flow).

612.39   **Metabolism**

Class metabolism within a specific function, system, or organ with the function, system, or organ, e.g., the metabolism of plasma 612.116.

612.3923   Metabolism of water

Only water may be considered here. Class fluid metabolism in the sense of the sum total of biochemical and metabolic processes taking place in cellular and interstitial fluids at 612.01522. Class also at 612.01522 fluid balance and electrolytic balance.

612.41   [Physiology of the] Spleen

Class here comprehensive works on the blood-forming (hematopoietic or hemopoietic) system. Class physiology of bone marrow at 612.491.

612.63   [Physiology of] Pregnancy and childbirth

Class comprehensive works on pregnancy and childbirth at 618.2.

612.67   Aging

Class death at 616.078.

612.75   [Physiology of] Bones, joints, connective tissues

Class bone marrow at 612.491.

612.76   [Physiology of] Locomotion, exercise, rest

Including body mechanics.

Note that this subject is in the context of the neuromuscular system. The total physiology of physical movements, i.e., muscle contractions, breathing, blood flow, digestion during exercise, is classed in 612.04.

612.8   [Physiology of] Nervous and sensory functions

Class here psychophysiology. *See also 152 vs. 612.8.*

612.82   **[Physiology of the] Brain**

Class here the physiology of memory, of thinking.

612.821   [Physiology of] Sleep phenomena

See 154.6 vs. 612.821.

**613–614 vs.   General and personal hygiene [and] Public health and related topics vs.
362.1   [Social aspects of] Physical illness**

Neither 613 nor 614 includes social provision of services to the physically ill. These are classed in 362.1. Works on 362.1 topics are frequently also (confusing enough) called public health. Use 613 and 614 and their subdivisions as long as the interest is scientific or technical. Once the emphasis shifts to social problems and services in connection with health problems, 362.1 is the number of choice. For example, industrial and occupational hygiene is classed in 613.62 as long as emphasis is on the technical measures to be taken, but becomes 363.11 Occupational and industrial hazards when the emphasis shifts to social and institutional arrangements. Studies of disease incidence and epidemics are classed in 614 when treated solely from the medical standpoint. Any emphasis on diseases as social problems points to 362.

613 vs. 614   General and personal hygiene vs. Public health and related topics

In 613 the emphasis is on the individual and his diseases, their prevention and control by him and his medical advisers. Some prevention and control is effective only when done collectively, which is the idea informing 614. In 614 public health is used in a narrow sense, covering only the incidence of disease and the technology of public preventive medicine. 613 is the place for comprehensive works on the two concepts.

613 vs. 615.8 General and personal hygiene vs. Physical and other therapies

Note that many of the topics in 613 appear also in 615.8, e.g., breathing 613.192 and 615.836, diet 613.2 and 615.854, exercise 613.71 and 615.824. In each case the 613 number refers to the preventive or "staying healthy" aspects, while the 615.8 number refers to the therapeutic or "regaining health" aspects.

Class works treating both aspects equally in 613. If in doubt, prefer 615.8.

613.04   Hygiene of specific sex and age groups

See third paragraph at s.s. 08.

613.2   Dietetics

Class here health aspects of nutrition, comprehensive works on nutrition. Class physiological aspects in 612.3, therapeutic aspects at 615.854, disease aspects in 616.39, and home economics aspects in 641.1.

If in doubt whether to class a work in 613.2 Dietetics or 641.1 Applied nutrition, prefer 613.2.

613.62	Industrial and occupational hygiene

See 613–614 vs. 362.1.

613.7   Physical fitness

Class comprehensive works on diet and physical fitness at 613.2.

613.7042– **[Physical fitness of] Specific age and sex groups**
.7045

See third paragraph at s.s. 08.

613.71   Exercise and sports activities

Class parental supervision of children's exercise and sports activities at 649.57.

613.8   Addictions

Class here addiction as a personal problem.

Class addiction as a medical problem in 616.86, works combining social with medical aspects of addiction in 362.29, works emphasizing pharmacology of addictive drugs in 615.78.

613.94   Birth control (Contraception)

Including measures to increase the likelihood of having a child of the desired sex.

Class social aspects of and interdisciplinary works on birth control and family planning at 363.96.

613.942   Surgical methods of birth control

Class here only the personal health aspects of surgery. Class surgery for males in 617.463, for females in 618.1.

614   **Public health and related topics**

See 613 vs. 614, and 613–614 vs. 362.1.

614.4   **Incidence, distribution, control of disease**

Class here epidemiology. However, note that the term occasionally refers to a research technique with increasing application outside 614, e.g., in determining etiologies such as smoking as a cause of cancer 616.994071; in determining the dimensions of social service requirements such as the boundaries of the mental retardation problem 362.32; in exploring the possible effectiveness of proposed preventive measures, for example, in reducing traffic accidents 363.1257.

614.40212   [Tables, formulas, specifications, statistics of incidence, distribution, control of disease]

> Class the statistics of incidence and control of disease in 312.3, of deaths caused by disease in 312.26. The interpretation of these statistics in terms of social problems and services is classed in 362.1 and related numbers.

614.5   **Incidence, distribution, control of specific diseases**

> Note the use of standard subdivisions at the add notes scattered in 614.526–614.598 directing the addition of certain digits from 616. Most diseases listed under 616 have an asterisk and require two zeros for standard subdivisions; diseases and groups of diseases not marked by an asterisk require only one zero.
>
> *See also 614.40212.*

614.5 vs.   **Incidence, distribution, control of specific diseases vs. Specific social prob-**
362–363   **lems and services**

> Class control concepts in 614.5 with caution. Avoid using them for programs that provide services for persons suffering from disease. For example, class fluoridation and programs advising people how to avoid cavities at 614.5996, but class programs to identify and treat people with cavities at 362.19767. Also, class control of hazardous materials causing cancer at 363.179, control of carcinogenic foods at 363.192, not 614.5999 in either case. If in doubt, prefer 362–363.

615   Pharmacology and therapeutics

> Note that 615 will seldom be used by itself because pharmacology (615.1) and therapeutics (615.5) are usually treated separately or with a notable preponderance of one or the other.
>
> Class a work treating both drugs 615.1 and drug therapy 615.58 at 615.1.

615.1 vs.   **Drugs (Materia medica) vs. Pharmacodynamics**
   615.7

> "Pharmacology" is often used in the titles of works mainly limited to Pharmacodynamics 615.7. If the table of contents is arranged by physiological system (as 615.7 is), the chances are good that the work emphasizes the physiological and therapeutic action of drugs, making 615.7 the appropriate number. If in doubt, prefer 615.1.

615.2–.3 **Specific drugs and groups of drugs**

Note that most drugs are organic (615.3). Class comprehensive works in 615.1 even if there is a strong predominance of organic drugs so long as coverage of inorganic drugs is in proportion to their importance. However, class comprehensive works on crude drugs and simples (products that serve as drugs with minimal processing, e.g., medicinal teas, baking soda, royal jelly) at 615.321.

The reference in Edition 19 from 615.2–615.3 to 615.7 means that 615.2–615.3 will not be used for drugs known primarily for their effect on a single system, e.g., digitalis will be classed at 615.711 Heart stimulants (or 616.129061 drug therapy for heart failure), not at 615.3231 drugs derived from the Personales order; alcohol at 615.7828, not at 615.32.

615.2   Inorganic drugs

Class radiopharmacy (the use of radioactive medicines) in 615.842.

615.3 **Organic drugs**

See 615.2–615.3 on question of predominance.

615.321   Pharmacognosy

Class here comprehensive works on crude drugs and simples, i.e., products that serve as drugs with minimal processing, e.g., medicinal teas, baking soda, royal jelly.

615.4   Practical pharmacy

This number covers only a limited aspect of pharmacy: putting drugs into forms that can be used by human beings. Class works on the larger meaning of pharmacy in 615.1, e.g., managing a pharmacy 615.1068. Follow the same procedure when adding 615 numbers in other disciplines, e.g., economics of the pharmacy industry 338.476151.

615.5 **Therapeutics**

Class here comprehensive works on iatrogenic diseases, patient compliance, patient education (if not considered as an aspect of nursing), and placebo effect. Class specific occurrences of each of these with the subject, e.g., drug interactions not anticipated by a doctor 615.7045, patient education by nurses 610.73, surgical complications and sequelae 617.01.

615.53   **General therapeutic systems**

Use this number and its subdivisions only when the discussion is historical or theoretical, e.g., a discussion of the theory of naturopathy 615.535. When these systems are discussed in their application to therapy, class them in a therapy number, e.g., the application of chiropractic 615.82. When the therapies are applied to specific conditions, class in 616–618, e.g., chiropractic in musculoskeletal diseases 616.7062.

Be careful of biography. Founders of systems may usually be safely classed with the respective systems, e.g., a biography of Andrew Taylor Still 615.5330924. Practitioners of a specific system are usually classed in 610.924.

Subject to the cautions given above, use 615.53 for Ayurveda ("Hindu medicine"), psionic medicine, and siddha.

615.531   Allopathy

Do not use for allopathy as a synonym for orthodox or standard medical practice. Allopathy as used here is a system based on the theory that the best cure is a treatment having effects that are opposite to the effects of the disease.

615.533   Osteopathy

Use only for a consideration of osteopathy as a therapeutic system. Treat osteopathy as a medical science exactly as you would "orthodox" medicine, using 610 and its subdivisions other than 615.533.

615.534   Chiropractic

Note that some chiropractors limit their practice to therapeutic manipulation (615.82) or to manipulation for diseases of the musculoskeletal system (616.7062). If the chiropractor does not limit his practice, use 610 and its subdivisions rather than 615.534. However, in the absence of specific other emphases, class works on chiropractic as a therapeutic system at 615.534, e.g., a biography of a chiropractor 615.5340924.

615.537   Eclectic and botanic medicine

This number will be little used as the schools have largely been abandoned. Note that botanic remedies are classed in 615.32, usually 615.321 Pharmacognosy.

615.6   **Methods of medication**

Note that this number is limited to general methods. Methods applied to specific therapies are all classed elsewhere, e.g., therapeutics of blood transfusions 615.39, not 615.65; ointments in external medication 615.58, not 615.67.

615.7 **Pharmacodynamics**

See 615.1 vs. 615.7.

615.7 vs. **Pharmacodynamics vs. Toxicology**
615.9
The reference at 615.7 in Edition 19 to 615.9 for toxicology does not carry with it the concept of toxic adverse effects and interactions of drugs primarily of pharmacodynamic interest; class these in 615.704 or with the system affected. However, a drug primarily of pharmacodynamic interest may be considered to be a poison if it is so toxic that a single inadvertent ingestion would cause serious complications or death, e.g., the pharmacodynamics of atropine (belladonna) 615.7 (not in any specific subdivison because it affects several systems), but the toxicology of belladonna 615.952379. If in doubt between 615.7 and 615.9, prefer 615.7.

615.7 vs. **Pharmacodynamics vs. [Diseases, surgery, other branches of medicine]**
616–618
Class here only general works on the pharmacodynamic action of drugs, its modus operandi and general effects on the human body. Class use of the drug in treatment in 616–618 using subdivision 061 from the various tables under these numbers. If in doubt, prefer 616–618.

615.704 **Special effects and actions of drugs**

Class here adverse reactions, toxic reactions.

Class drug allergies at 616.975.

615.71–.78 **[Drugs affecting specific systems]**

See 612.1–.8.

615.78 **Drugs affecting nervous system**

Class here comprehensive works on addictive and disorienting drugs. Class works emphasizing the personal implications for the users of such drugs in 613.8, comprehensive medical works on addictions in 616.86, works combining social and medical aspects of addictions in 362.29.

615.8 **Physical and other therapies**

Several therapies listed in 615.8 are usually applied only to certain specific types of disorders, and works on them take such application for granted without highlighting them in the title. Note the unstated emphasis and class accordingly, e.g., radiotherapy emphasizing cancer treatment 616.9940642, not 615.842; music therapy emphasizing psychiatric uses 616.891654, not 615.85154.

See also 613 vs. 615.8.

615.82   **Physical therapies**

Class here physiotherapy.

615.845   Electrotherapy

Class radiesthesia, radionics at 615.8.

615.854   Dietotherapy and vitamin therapy

Use with caution; when a single food element is heavily emphasized, it may amount to a drug therapy, e.g., megavitamin diets
(using heavy doses of vitamins) 615.328; a diet distinctive largely
by its use of enzymes 615.35, by its use of royal jelly 615.36.

615.856   Controversial and spurious therapies

Do not evaluate the effectiveness of the therapy, but class it with
the subject if anyone takes it seriously, e.g., primitive remedies
615.899.

Class here once accepted remedies, e.g., bloodletting.

If in doubt regarding a specific remedy, class with therapy outside
615.856.

615.8809   **[Historical and geographical treatment of] Empirical and historical remedies**

Note that we are concerned here with therapy. If pathological or
etiological beliefs are also emphasized, e.g., the theory of the four
humors, or the influence of bad airs, the work must be classed in
610.9.

Class here discussions of old remedies of a specific geographic
area that are not limited by the terms of Folk medicine 615.882 or
primitive, ancient, or medieval remedies 615.899. If in doubt
whether to class treatment in a place in 615.8809 or either 615.88209
or 615.89909, prefer 615.8809.

615.882   Folk medicine

Class a work of medical folk literature at 398.27 if the emphasis is
on the story told; a work on the sociology of medical folklore at
398.353 if the emphasis is on the tales as cultural and social
phenomena. Class at 615.882 only if the emphasis is on the medical
practice.

Note that 615.882 is under therapy. If a work gives more than a
token consideration to folk theories on the causes of disease, it
must be classed in 610, e.g., folk etiologies and therapies of India
610.954 (or 616.00954 when the material is arranged by class of
disease as in 616.1–616.9).

See also 615.8809.

615.899	Primitive, ancient, medieval remedies
	See 615.8809.
615.9	**Toxicology**
	See 615.7 vs. 615.9.
615.900287	[Testing and measurement in toxicology]
	Do not use; class at 615.907.
615.902	Industrial toxicology

Including environmental toxicology, toxicology of pollution.

Class toxicology of food additives at 615.954, toxic reactions and interactions of drugs in 615.704.

615.907	Tests, analysis, detection of poisons and poisoning

The topics in Edition 19 under 616.075 Diagnoses and prognoses are all implied here.

615.92	Inorganic poisons

Class radiation poisoning in 616.9897.

615.954	Food poisons and poisoning

Including toxicology of food additives.

616–618	**[Diseases, surgery, other branches of medicine]**
	See 615.7 vs. 616–618.
616	**Diseases**

Class here comprehensive works on the diseases listed in 616–618. However, if a work contains separate treatment of health, pharmacology, and therapeutics, as well as of diseases, class it at 610.

When the whole of medicine is brought to bear on the concept of diseases in a single treatise discussing group after group of diseases, class the work at 616. The table of contents will usually offer guidance. If it reads like a summary of topics in 610.73–619.98, class the work in 610; if like a summary of topics in 616.01–616.99 or in 616–618, class the work in 616.

Be alert for two meanings of the term "clinical medicine." In one sense it approximates 616, i.e., the application of all branches of medicine to treatment of various diseases. However, just as often it is shorthand for the work of a clinical diagnostic laboratory, and is properly classed at 616.075.

See also 612 vs. 616, and 617 vs. 616.

616.001–
.009

Standard subdivisions [of diseases]

Use standard subdivisions under 616 with caution except for internal medicine or works clearly limited to the concept of diseases, e.g., prefer 610.3 for medical dictionaries, 610.711 for medical schools, 610.92 for doctors not having a distinct specialty.

616.00212

[Tables, formulas, specifications, statistics of diseases]

Class statistics of diseases in 312.3.

616.0023

[Work with diseases as a profession]

Do not use; class in 610.69.

616.00287

[Testing and measurement of diseases]

Do not use; class in 616.075.

616.01

Medical microbiology

Do not confuse medical microbiology with the classes of communicable disease in 616.91–616.96 caused by various types of microorganisms. The emphasis in 616.01 is on the organism, usually as the cause of disease, while in 616.9 it is on the whole disease and its course, cure, and prevention. Each is comprehensive in its own way, 616.01 as the interdisciplinary number for pathogenic organisms affecting man and his domestic animals, and 616.9 for the resulting diseases. If in doubt, prefer 616.9.

Also, do not confuse 616.01 with 576.165 Deleterious microorganisms and cognate numbers for the biology of microorganisms in 575, 589, and 593.1. If in doubt between a biology number and numbers in 610 for microorganisms, prefer the biology number.

Medical microbiology includes the study of drug resistance in microorganisms.

616.024

Domestic medicine

Including advice on when to go to a doctor.

616.043

Congenital diseases

See 618.92.

616.047

Manifestations of disease

Think of this as a number for works that do not fit anywhere else. Manifestations of a specific disease are classed with the disease, but class here manifestations of unknown origin, or manifestations that become problems in their own right, e.g., excruciating pain caused by a disease that is not otherwise serious 616.0472.

616.0472   Pain

Including headaches and other pains as manifestations of disease in general. Class headaches and other pains as manifestations of neurological disease in 616.849. In case of doubt, prefer 616.849 over 616.0472.

616.07   Pathology

Pathology refers to the detailed description of the diseased conditions, of precise mechanisms of cause and manifestations, and of diagnostic techniques. For a work lacking detail, prefer 616 over 616.07.

Class forensic pathology at 614.1.

616.072   Symptomatology (Semiology)

Symptomatology is almost invariably applied to diagnosis 616.075, so that 616.072 as a comprehensive number is seldom used. The cognates of semiology in other languages, e.g., *semiologia* in Italian, are sometimes used in titles of works on diagnostics, so use this number with caution.

Any symptom that becomes a problem in its own right is classed in 616.047.

616.075   Diagnoses and prognoses

Consider 616.075 for clinical medicine. *See 2nd paragraph under 616.*

616.0756   Chemical diagnosis

Including immunodiagnosis.

Class here clinical chemistry.

616.0757   Radiological diagnosis

Note that many diagnosticians use the word radiology and its derivatives to refer to x-ray examinations. Class a work using the term in this sense at 616.07572.

616.07572   Roentgenology (X-ray examination)

Roentgenology is often called simply radiology.

616.07575   Radioisotope scanning

Radioisotope scanning is often called nuclear medicine.

616.078   Death

Class interdisciplinary works on human death at 306.9.

616.079   **Immunity (Immunology)**

Including failures of immunity (immunological disorders).

Class autoimmune diseases at 616.978.

See also 591.29.

616.08   Psychosomatic medicine

This number is largely limited to the psychosomatic aspects of the diseases defined in 616.1–616.7, i.e., such disorders when resulting from emotional stress or mental conflict. Class comprehensive works on psychological and psychosomatic aspects of diseases in 616.0019 Psychological principles of diseases or 616.89 Psychiatric disorders and their somatic manifestations. Class psychosomatic symptoms considered as problems in their own right in 616.047 Manifestations of diseases, e.g., pain 616.0472.

616.1–.9   **Specific diseases**

When a disease of one system affects another system so strongly that it is the second system that must be the focus of concern and treatment, class the work with the affected system, e.g., retinal complications of diabetes 617.73 Diseases of optic nerves and retinas, not 616.462 Diabetes mellitus.

See also 612.1–.8.

Add table

All notes under 616.01–616.08 are applicable here. The notes at 616.00212 and at 616.00287 are also applicable here.

01   **Microbiology**

When the etiological agent of a disease or class of diseases is known to be a single type of microorganism, class a work about it in 01 without further subdivision, since any added digits would be redundant, e.g., etiology of viral diseases 616.92501.

023   **Personnel**

Do not use for the technology of the operations that the personnel perform, e.g., techniques used by a cardiological paramedic 616.12, not 616.120233.

042   Genetic diseases

When a specific type of genetic disease has an indirect etiology, class with the system showing the most visible manifestations, e.g., mental retardation caused by inborn errors of metabolism 616.8588042, not 616.39042.

06   **Therapy**

Class comprehensive works on therapy and pathology (07) in the base number, e.g., cause, course, and cure of heart disease 616.12, not 616.1206.

071   [Etiology]

When the etiological agent is known to be a single type of microorganism use 01 for the work without further subdivision, unless predisposing and contributing factors are emphasized, e.g., microorganisms causing venereal disease 616.95101, predisposing factors leading to severity of venereal disease 616.951071. Class social factors contributing to the spread of a disease in 362.19, e.g., social factors contributing to the spread of venereal disease 362.196951.

072   **Symptomatology**

Class symptoms of a specific disease which have become so serious as to be problems in their own right in 616.047, e.g., excruciating pain from a chronic but nonthreatening muscular disorder 616.0472, not 616.74072.

616.123028   [Intensive care in] Coronary diseases

Use caution with the phrase "coronary care." It often extends to intensive care for any serious heart disease and in this case is classed in 616.12028.

616.12806   [Therapy for] Arrhythmia

Class implantation of heart pacers at 617.412059, their functioning at 617.4120645.

616.3   **Diseases of digestive system**

Class allergies of the digestive system in 616.975.

616.31   **[Diseases] of mouth and throat**

Class diseases of the teeth and gums in 617.63.

See also 617.522 vs. 616.31.

616.396   Other deficiency diseases and states

Class anorexia nervosa at 616.852.

616.39808   [Psychosomatic aspects of obesity]

Including food addiction.

616.5   **Diseases of integument, hair, nails**

Class comprehensive works on allergies of the skin at 616.973, dermatological manifestations of food and drug allergies at 616.975.

616.61   [Diseases] Of kidneys and ureters

Class kidney dialysis at 617.461059.

Numbers from the table at 616.1–616.9 in Edition 19 may be added for diseases of the kidneys. Do not add for diseases of ureters.

616.63   Urinary manifestations

Class psychosomatic enuresis and stress incontinence at 616.849.

616.8048   [Psychosomatic aspects of neurological diseases]

Class psychosomatic manifestations of neurological diseases that require treatment in their own right in 616.84, e.g., enuresis 616.849.

616.837   **Paraplegia**

Class here medical treatment only.

Class comprehensive treatment in 617.58.

616.84   Symptoms of neurological diseases

Notes at 616.047 and 616.0472 are applicable here. Class here psychosomatic manifestations of neurological diseases that require treatment in their own right.

616.852   **Neuroses**

Including anorexia nervosa.

Class neurotic aspects of a specific disease with the disease, e.g., of impotence 616.692.

See also 616.892–.898.

616.858   Disorders of personality, character, intellect

See 616.892–.898.

616.86   Addictions and intoxications

Class food addiction at 616.39808.

See also 616.892–.898.

616.8605   [Preventive measures for addictions]

Do not use subdivision 05 (Preventive measures) from the table at 616.1–616.9 in Edition 19 here or in subdivisions of this number; class in 613.8.

616.89   **Psychiatric disorders**

Class physical manifestations of psychiatric disorders involving a specific system with the system, using 08 from the add table at 616.1–616.9 in Edition 19 if appropriate, e.g., psychosomatic ulcers 616.34308. However, class psychosomatic enuresis, pain, and sleep disturbances at 616.849 when they are considered as symptoms so serious that they become diseases in their own right. Class fatigue of psychiatric origin, since it is a more routine symptom, in 616.89072 and related numbers.

See also 150 vs. 616.89.

616.890019   [Psychological principles of psychiatric disorders]

Including psychoanalytic principles applied to psychiatric disorders. Note that 157 Abnormal and clinical psychologies is not used except for works having no application to medicine.

616.8917019 [Psychological principles of psychoanalysis]

Do not use; class in 150.195 unless applied to therapy, in which case, class at 616.8917.

616.8917092 **[Persons associated with psychoanalysis]**

Use with caution. Prefer 616.890092 for psychoanalysts who are doctors, not just therapists. Class founders of systems in 150.195. Class patients undergoing analysis at 616.8909 unless the cases are cited strictly to illustrate therapy.

616.892–   **Psychoses**
.898

Note that 06 Therapy in the table under 616.1–616.9 in Edition 19 is added to like 615.8 and therefore contains no provision to bring out psychotherapies (except mental and activity therapies in 0651) under specific psychiatric disorders. Use 06 for psychoanalysis and group therapy, e.g., in treating schizophrenia 616.898206, not 616.89820651.

616.91–.96 **Communicable diseases**

See 616.01, 616.1–.9: Add table: 01.

616.97   **Allergies and autoimmune diseases**

Except for dermatological and digestive allergies, which are classed in 616.973–616.975, allergies of a specific system or region are classed with the system, e.g., respiratory allergies 616.202.

616.973   **Contact allergies**

Class here dermatological allergies.

616.975   **Food and drug allergies**

Class here allergies of the digestive system.

616.992 vs.   **Neoplasms and neoplastic diseases (Tumors) vs. Malignant neoplasms**
616.994   **(Cancers)**

Because of the negative emotions associated with cancer (616.994), writers tend to use euphemisms in describing it, specifically "neoplasms," "tumors," and "oncology." Therefore, before using 616.994, check the table of contents and other front matter to see whether benign tumors are also included. If still in doubt as to whether or not benign tumors are significantly represented, prefer 616.994.

616.994   **Malignant neoplasms (Cancers)**

See 616.992 vs. 616.994.

616.995   **Tuberculosis**

Many authors concentrating entirely on pulmonary tuberculosis (616.99524) do not mention the fact because the other forms are so much less common. Check the front matter carefully for signs of an implicit interest in the disease in the lungs. If no such indication is found, class the work at 616.995.

617   **Surgery and related topics**

Add table

All notes between 616.01 and 616.08 and at 616.1–616.9: Add table are applicable here.

059   **Surgical therapy**

It is important not to use 059 redundantly with 617 numbers whose meaning is limited to surgery. With such numbers use 059 only for surgery by specific instrument or technique, e.g., cryosurgery, dialysis, and bypass surgery; and 0592 for plastic surgery.

Note that 059 is limited to operative surgery. Class other physical procedures (included in the broader concept of surgery) in 06.

06   **Therapy**

Do not use 06 by itself redundantly under surgery numbers, since surgery is a therapy. Subdivisions of 06 may be added to surgery numbers for specific physical therapies used in preparation for or rehabilitation from operative surgery, or for branches of surgery in which operation is not a choice, e.g., whirlpool baths for sprains 617.170653. Otherwise, add the subdivisions of 06 only to "medicine" numbers in 617.5–617.8.

617 vs. 616   **Surgery and related topics vs. Diseases**

617 contains a mixed set of medical and surgical specialties. Note that if there is a provision in both 616 and 617 for an organ that defines a specialty, use the 617 number only for surgery. *See also 617.5.*

Class comprehensive works on medical treatment of the handicapped in 617 unless the term is clearly used to cover all disabling diseases, in which case, class in 616. If in doubt whether to class a work on the handicapped in 616 or 617, prefer 617.

617.023   **Personnel**

Do not use for the technology of the operations that the personnel perform, e.g., physical diagnosis by a surgeon 617.0754, not 617.0232.

617.3   **Orthopedics**

If in doubt whether to class a work on orthopedics in 617.3 correction of deformities or in 616.7 Diseases of musculoskeletal system, prefer 616.7. If in doubt between 617.3 and 617.5 regional medicine, prefer 617.5.

617.307 vs.   Orthopedic appliances vs. **Surgical techniques, procedures, apparatus,**
617.9   **equipment, materials, specialties**

If in doubt whether to class a work on appliances in 617.307 or with prosthetic equipment or surgical appliances, both in 617.9, prefer 617.9.

617.4   **Surgery by systems**

Note that this number is primarily limited to operative surgery of systems, and that nonoperative therapies are usually classed in 616, e.g., therapeutic manipulations of muscles 616.74062, not 617.473062. Nonoperative therapies are classed here only if they have some connection with operative surgery, e.g., electrotherapy by heart pacer 617.4120645, since the pacer must be surgically implanted (617.412059).

See also 612.1–.8.

617.461   [Surgery of] Kidneys, adrenal glands, ureters

Numbers from the table at 617 in Edition 19 may be added for surgery of kidneys. Do not add for surgery of adrenal glands or ureters.

617.461059   Operative surgery of kidneys

Including kidney dialysis.

617.5   **Regional surgery [and regional medicine]**

Two quite different concepts are spliced together here: regions, which incorporate parts of several physiological systems, and organs, which are parts of single systems. Since the numbers for regions are used for regional medicine as well as regional surgery, subdivision 059 from the add table at 617 in Edition 19 must be used with such numbers. However, since the medical treatment of specific organs is provided for with the system in 616.1–616.8, the numbers for specific organs in 617.5 are used only for surgery, and subdivision 059 is not used except for surgery utilizing specific instruments or techniques. Subdivision 0592 remains valid here for plastic surgery. In the case of regions, resolve doubts in favor of 617.5 numbers. In the case of organs, resolve doubts in favor of 616 numbers or numbers in 617.6–617.8 for teeth, eyes, and ears.

617.522 vs.   **[Medicine of] Oral region vs. [Diseases] Of mouth and throat**
616.31
It should be observed that "oral region" is a broader term than mouth as a digestive organ (616.31). If in doubt, prefer 617.522.

617.522 vs.   **[Surgery of] Oral region vs. Dentistry**
617.6
Note that oral surgery is a term much used in the dental profession. Do not class a work so identified in 617.522 unless it covers substantially more than procedures for which one would go to a dentist (617.6).

617.6   **Dentistry**

See 617.522 vs. 617.6.

617.9   **Surgical techniques, procedures, apparatus, equipment, materials, specialties**

Class here comprehensive works on prosthetic equipment, on surgical appliances. Class a specific appliance or piece of equipment with its specific use, e.g., dentures 617.692. *See also 617.307 vs. 617.9.*

618.1–618.8   Gynecology and obstetrics

Add table

All notes between 616.01 and 616.08 and at 616.1–616.9: Add table and 617: Add table are applicable here.

618.1   Gynecology

Including endocrine gynecology.

618.178059   [Surgical treatment of sterility]

Including embryo transplant ("test-tube baby").

618.2052   [Preventive health measures in obstetrics]

Do not use; class at 618.24.

618.8   Obstetrical surgery

Class embryo transplant at 618.178059.

618.92   Pediatrics

Use caution in classing here certain diseases that are most often treated in children, but which remain lifetime problems or threats, e.g., congenital diseases, mumps. Class these in 616 numbers unless actually limited to their occurrence in children.

Class adolescent medicine in 616.

618.920043   [Congenital diseases in children]

See 618.92 before using this number.

618.92097   Regional medicine, ophthalmology, otology, audiology [in pediatrics]

Note that the word "surgery" is carefully avoided under this number in Edition 19. The logic described at 618.977 geriatric diseases related to surgery also applies here.

Class medical as well as surgical aspects of pediatric dentistry in 617.645.

618.977   [Geriatric diseases related to surgery]

Class here medical specialties provided for in 617 when applied to persons in late adulthood. Class surgical specialties applied to persons in late adulthood in 617. For example, class medicine of the back for those in late adulthood in 618.97756, but surgery of the back in 617.56; class diseases of the teeth and gums in 618.97763, but dental surgery in 617.6059.

619   Experimental medicine

Class experimental study of pharmacology and therapeutics in 615, of anatomy and physiology in 591–599, not 611–612.

620 Engineering and allied operations

SUMMARY

621 **Applied physics**
622 **Mining engineering and related operations**
623 **Military and nautical engineering**
624 **Civil engineering**
625 **Engineering of railroads, roads, highways**
627 **Hydraulic engineering**
628 **Sanitary and municipal engineering**
629 **Other branches of engineering**

620 treats the nature and manipulation of materials and energy, *how* to manipulate material and energy. The natural laws that describe matter and energy, the *why* of their nature and behavior, are classed in 500.

Some manufacturing is classed here, e.g., the manufacture of radio receiving sets 621.38418; however, class comprehensive works on manufactures at 670.

620.0092 **[Persons associated with engineering and allied operations]**

Class biographies of engineers who are known primarily as entrepreneurs in 338.76, e.g., Henry Ford 338.7629220924, not 629.220924.

620.1 Engineering mechanics (Applied mechanics) and materials

The corresponding physics number for engineering mechanics is 531. *See 621 vs. 530 for discussion of corresponding numbers.*

Standard subdivisions may be added for engineering mechanics alone.

620.112 Various specific properties and tests of materials

Class comprehensive works on properties of materials at 620.11.

620.1121– .1126 **Specific strength properties of materials**

Class the failure of a particular strength property with the property, e.g., melting 620.11217, fractures 620.1126.

620.1121 **Resistance of materials to thermal forces**

The note at 620.1121 in Edition 19, "Class thermal radiation in 620.11228," refers only to the resistance of materials to thermal radiation. Class thermal properties of materials not related to strength and resistance at 620.11296.

620.17 Ferrous metals (Iron and steel) and their alloys

Subdivisions may be added as instructed at 620.17 in Edition 19 for either iron or steel alone.

620.18   **Nonferrous metals and their alloys**

For each subdivision in Edition 19 identified by an asterisk (*), subdivisions may be added as instructed under 620.12–620.19 in Edition 19 for works dealing only with the alloy, e.g., thermal properties of brass or of bronze as well as of copper 620.18296.

620.2   Sound and related vibrations

The corresponding physics number is 534. *See 621 vs. 530 for discussion of corresponding numbers.*

620.4162   [Engineering for oceans and seas]

Class engineering of ocean craft in 623.82; civil engineering for oceans in 627; any other aspect with the subject, e.g., laying underwater electric cables 621.31934, underwater mining 622.29.

620.7   Systems engineering

Class interdisciplinary works on systems at 003.

620.85   Environmental health engineering

Class pollution engineering in 628.5.

621 vs. 530   **Applied physics vs. Physics**

Many subdivisions of 621 Applied physics have corresponding physics numbers, each of which will be given at the appropriate place. Use the following criteria in deciding whether to use 621 or 530:

Class a work in 621 when the focus is on technology, even though much of the work is scientific background.

Class in 530 a work treating equally the science and technology aspects of physics.

If in doubt, prefer 530.

621.042   Energy engineering

Class the nontechnological aspects of energy resources in 333.79, e.g., social utilization of electrical energy 333.793213.

621.3   Electromagnetic and related branches of engineering

The corresponding physics number is 537. *See 621 vs. 530 for discussion of corresponding numbers.*

621.31042   Electrical machinery and other equipment

Class electric motors at 621.462.

621.31242   **Applied electrochemistry**

Class electrochemistry applied to chemical technology in 660.297.

621.34   Magnetic engineering

The corresponding physics number is 538. *See 621 vs. 530 for discussion of corresponding numbers.*

621.36   Applied optics (Engineering optics) and paraphotic engineering

The corresponding physics number is 535. *See 621 vs. 530 for discussion of corresponding numbers.*

621.367   **Technological photography and photooptics**

Class here optical data processing.

See also 778.3 vs. 621.367.

621.3678   Remote sensing technology

Class a specific application with the subject, using s.s. 028, e.g., remote sensing technology in archaeology 930.1028.

621.381   Electronic engineering

The corresponding physics number is 537.5. *See 621 vs. 530 for discussion of corresponding numbers.*

621.3815   **Short- and long-wave electronics**

Class here digital electronics.

621.388   Television

Class television photography in 778.59.

621.402   **Heat (Thermal) engineering**

The corresponding physics number is 536. *See 621 vs. 530 for discussion of corresponding numbers.*

Class heating of buildings in 697.

621.4023   Fuels and combustion

Class air pollution by unspecified or general combustion or by industrial plant combustion at 628.532.

621.48   Nuclear engineering

The corresponding physics number is 539.7. *See 621 vs. 530 for discussion of corresponding numbers.*

621.55   Vacuum technology

The corresponding physics number is 533.5. *See 621 vs. 530 for discussion of corresponding numbers.*

621.56–.59   Low-temperature technology

The corresponding physics number is 536.56. *See 621 vs. 530 for discussion of corresponding numbers.*

621.59   Cryogenic technology

Cryogenic temperatures are temperatures below $-100°C$ or $-148°F$.

621.8672   Pipes and pipelines

Including pipelaying.

Class pipelines for transporting coal at 662.624, petroleum at 665.544, industrial gases at 665.744; the manufacture of pipes made from a specific material with the material, e.g., metal pipes 671.832.

621.994   Measuring tools

Class here only simple tools, e.g., folding rulers.

Class measuring instruments, e.g., flowmeters, at 681.2.

622.12–.17   Generalities [of prospecting and exploratory operations in mining engineering]

Class general principles applied to exploring for treasure at 622.19.

622.18   Prospecting for specific minerals

Standard subdivisions may be added to 622.18 and its subdivisions even if only one type of prospecting technique is used, e.g., vibrational exploration for petroleum in Texas 622.1828209764.

622.18282   [Prospecting for petroleum]

Class works purporting to discuss prospecting for "petroleum" but actually discussing prospecting for both oil and natural gas at 622.1828.

622.187   [Prospecting for water]

Do not use; class at 628.114.

622.19   Prospecting and exploring for treasure

Class archaeological methods and equipment in 930.1028.

622.2   Subsurface mining

Class subsurface mine environment technology in 622.4, subsurface mine transport systems in 622.6.

622.29   Underwater mining

Class drilling platforms at 627.98.

622.31–.32   Surface mining

Class surface mine environment technology in 622.4, surface mine transport systems in 622.6.

622.31	Open pit and strip mining

Class surface mine reclamation at 631.64.

622.33–.39 **Mining specific minerals and their ores**

Class here the waste technology of mining a specific mineral and its ore, e.g., engineering of coal mine tailings 622.334.

Class drilling platforms at 627.98.

622.3382 [Petroleum mining]

Class works purporting to discuss "petroleum" mining but actually discussing mining of both oil and natural gas at 622.338.

622.37 [Water extraction]

Do not use; class at 628.114.

623 Military and nautical engineering

See 355 for a discussion of the relations between these numbers.

623.38 Protective [military] construction

Including construction designed to protect civilians against the effects of war.

623.44 **Small arms and other weapons**

Class artistic aspects of arms in 739.7.

623.441 Weaponry of pre-firearm origin

Class here armor.

623.451 Delivery devices

Class small arms ammunition, e.g., bullets, at 623.455.

623.459 **Nonexplosive [ordnance] agents**

Class here detection of the use of nonexplosive agents.

623.74 **[Military] Vehicles**

See 629.046 vs. 385–388.

623.812 **Design of [nautical] craft**

Unless parts of the ship other than the hull are discussed, e.g., propellers and steering gear, class the hydrodynamics of the ship with the design of hulls at 623.8144.

623.82 **Nautical craft**

Class here comprehensive works on modern ships; however, many works purporting to discuss "modern ships" are limited to the discussion of power-driven ships and are classed at 623.8204.

See also 629.046 vs. 385–388.

623.8201   Models and miniatures [of nautical craft]

Class ships in bottles at 745.5928.

623.8207   [Nautical] Craft of specific materials

To be classed here, the work must discuss parts of the ship other than the hull, e.g., decks, cabins. If the work is basically limited to the hull, it is classed in 623.84.

623.824   Power-driven merchant and factory ships

Class trawlers at 623.828.

623.8243   Passenger [ships]

Class ferryboats at 623.8234.

623.828   Other power-driven vessels

Class lightships at 627.923.

623.86   **Equipment and outfit of nautical craft**

Class the use of the equipment in 623.88.

623.8920222   [Geonavigational pictures, charts, designs]

Class here nautical charts and maps.

623.8922 vs.   **Piloting and pilot guides vs. Approach and harbor pilot guides**
623.8929
623.8922 has been subdivided (*DC&,* Vol. 4, No. 2, p. 45) to allow direct subdivision by specific body of water. Thus, the primary emphasis in 623.8922 is upon the sea or other body of water whose shores are being described, while the emphasis in 623.8929 is upon the land whose harbors are being approached.

The distinction between a general pilot guide and an approach and harbor guide is not always clear cut. If in doubt between the two, prefer 623.8929 when a land area or a stretch along the coast of a single country is emphasized, but 623.8922 when a body of water or a stretch of coast including several countries is emphasized. For example, a guide to the North Sea is classed at 623.8922336 even if there is little emphasis on the coasts between harbors; but a guide to the east coast of the United States is classed in 623.892974 even if little of the material is on harbors.

623.8929   **Approach and harbor pilot guides**

See 623.8922 vs. 623.8929.

624   **Civil engineering**

See 690 vs. 624.

624.176 **Stresses and strains (Deformation) [of structures]**

Class here wreckage studies.

625.2 **Railroad rolling stock**

See 629.046 vs. 385–388.

625.7 Roads and highways

Class grade crossings of railroads at 625.163.

627 Hydraulic engineering

Class comprehensive works on ocean engineering at 620.4162.

627.4 **Flood control**

Class flood control for and flood wreckage studies of a specific type of structure with the structure, e.g., flood wreckage studies of bridges 624.2.

627.98 Artificial islands

Class underwater mining at 622.29.

628 **Sanitary and municipal engineering**

Do not confuse the engineering aspects of this subject with its social aspects, which are classed in numbers like 363.7 Environmental problems and services, 363.61 Water supply, 363.37 Fire hazards, 333.7–333.9 natural and waste resources. Engineering terminology in a discussion does not call for an engineering number if public policies, regulations, or appropriations are at issue. *See notes on the distinction between social science and technology at 300 vs. 600, and 363: Choice of discipline.*

628.1 Water supply

Class here works discussing the engineering both of water supply and of sewerage and sewage (628.1–628.3). If solid wastes are also considered (and the work covers 628.1–628.3 plus 628.44, with or without 628.54 industrial wastes and 628.7 water supply, sewage, and waste in rural areas), the work is classed at 628.4. If any other significant topic within 628 is added to the above mix, e.g., pollution, fire fighting, or pest control, the work is classed at 628.

628.10287 [Testing and measurement of water supply]

Class qualitative testing and measurement in 628.161.

See also 628.161.

628.11   Sources [of water]

Class here the protection and treatment of sources, the engineering evaluation of resource alternatives.

If the water discussed is underground or in natural streams, lakes, and oceans, class the work in 553.7. Only when people control it, or plan to control it, does it become engineering.

Class economic and social evaluation of requirements, use projections, development, and conservation in 333.91; hydraulic engineering of sources in 627.

628.114   Wells

Including the digging of wells.

The section of the note on artificial recharge at 628.114 in Edition 19 has been deleted; class artificial recharge at 627.56 (*see DC&*, Vol. 4, No. 2, p. 18).

628.119   Waste water

This number will seldom be used. Use 628.16 for testing, treatment, and evaluation.

The note on artificial recharge in Edition 19 has been changed to refer to 627.56 (*see DC&*, Vol. 4, No. 2, p. 18).

628.161   Analysis [of water supply]

Class here comprehensive works on qualitative testing and measurement of water.

Class a specific application with the subject, using s.s. 0287, if appropriate, e.g., testing and measurement of water resources 553.70287.

628.162   **Treatment [of water]**

Class here comprehensive works on the treatment of water supply and sewage.

Class sewage treatment in 628.3.

See also 628.168 vs. 628.162.

628.164   Mechanical treatment [of water]

Including membrane (osmotic) processes.

628.168   **[Water] Pollution and countermeasures**

Class here comprehensive works on liquid wastes.

Class sewage in 628.2, industrial liquid wastes (liquid wastes generated by industry alone) in 628.54.

628.168 vs. [Water] **Pollution and countermeasures** vs. Water pollution
363.7394
Class the engineering aspects of water pollution in 628.168, the social aspects in 363.7394. If in doubt, prefer 363.7394.

628.168 vs. [Water] **Pollution and countermeasures vs. Treatment [of water]**
628.162
Note that "pollution and countermeasures" is a term often used to describe routine sewage and water supply treatment (628.162). If in doubt as to whether to use 628.168 or 628.162 for such works, prefer 628.162.

628.1683 [Water] **Pollution from industrial waste**

Class here remedial measures by public authorities alone.

Class remedial measures either by industry alone or by industry and public authorities in 628.54; countermeasures by originating industry with the industry, e.g., engineering control of acid mine drainage by a coal mining company 622.334.

628.1686 [Water] Pollution in specific areas

Use with caution. Prefer 363.7394209 Boundaries (extent, distribution, severity, incidence) of water pollution in specific areas.

628.1688 [Water pollution] Abatement programs

Use with caution. Prefer 363.73945 social measures for the alleviation of water pollution or 628.162 the engineering number for pollution treatment.

628.17 Water requirements and use

This number has been deleted. Class water requirements at 333.9112, water use at 333.9113, technical aspects of measurement of consumption at 628.144.

628.34–.35 **Primary treatment [and] Secondary and tertiary treatment**

Class comprehensive works on procedures that can be used in more than one level of treatment with the secondary treatment in 628.351–628.354, e.g., primary and secondary aeration 628.351, not 628.3 or 628.34.

628.358 Demineralization

Demineralization is the removal of all soluble minerals.

Class the removal of a specific mineral or group of minerals, e.g., nutrients, at 628.357.

628.362 Sewage effluent disposal

The note on artificial recharge of ground water in Edition 19 has been changed to refer to 627.56.

628.4   Public sanitation

See 628.1.

628.44   Refuse (Solid waste)

Class here comprehensive works on solid wastes; collection, treatment, and disposal solely by public authorities of industrial solid wastes.

Class industrial solid wastes (solid wastes generated by industry alone), remedial measures to deal with industrial solid wastes either by industry alone or by both industry and public authorities in 628.54.

628.53   **Air pollution and countermeasures**

Class here the immediate dispersal from the source of pollution, e.g., the study of plumes from chimneys.

Class pollution studies and reengineering of a specific technology that causes air pollution with the technology, e.g., air pollution by automobiles 629.253; however, class pollution by unspecified or general combustion and by industrial plant combustion at 628.532, not 621.4023.

Class air quality studies, i.e., measurement of pollution that has escaped into the atmosphere, at 363.73922.

628.532 [Air pollution] By smoke, fumes, gases

Note that this subject encompasses almost the whole of air pollution. Therefore, class here specific pollutants and manifestations, e.g., combustion products, fluorocarbons, gaseous paper mill wastes. However, class comprehensive works, regardless of predominance, at 628.53.

628.54   **Industrial waste treatment and disposal by type of industry**

The "by type of industry" in the heading refers to the fact that this number includes works considering wastes according to the industry generating them.

Class here comprehensive works on waste and its control by type of industry, industrial solid wastes (solid wastes generated by industry alone), industrial liquid wastes (liquid wastes generated by industry alone), remedial measures to deal with industrial solid wastes or industrial liquid wastes either by industry alone or by both industry and public authorities.

Standard subdivisions may be added to 628.54 and its subdivisions for industrial solid wastes alone.

Class remedial measures solely by public authorities to deal with industrial liquid wastes in 628.1683, with industrial solid wastes in 628.44; air pollution by industry in 628.53, soil pollution by industry at 628.55. *See also 628.1683, and 628.44.*

Class waste and its control solely by the originating industry with the industry, e.g., treatment of mining waste by mining companies 622, not 628.542.

628.746   **Treatment and disposal of agricultural waste**

Class water pollution from agricultural waste in 628.1684, treatment of water so polluted in 628.162.

628.922   Fire safety technology

Including flammability studies for specific materials to determine how likely they are to increase fire hazards.

Class measures to develop fire resistance in a specific product with the product, e.g., in textiles 677.689, in buildings 693.82.

628.96   Pest control

See 363.78.

629.04   **Transportation engineering**

Class technical problems peculiar to transportation of a specific commodity with the commodity, e.g., slurry transportation of coal 662.624.

629.046 vs.   **Vehicles vs. [Vehicles in] Specific kinds of transportation**

385–388

These instructions for the use of the 380s vs. the 600s apply to 385–388, 623.74, 623.82, 625.2, 688.6, and the subdivisions of 629.

Class in 385–388:

(1) Services provided by the vehicle, e.g., transportation of passengers by trains 385.22;

(2) Operation (general) of the vehicle, e.g., duties of the ship's captain 387.54044; and

(3) With caution, the economic and social aspects of the vehicle, e.g., a register of the airplanes owned by a company 387.73340216.

Class in 629.046 and related numbers in the 600s:

(1) General description of the vehicle, e.g., steam locomotives of the 1930s 625.26109043;

(2) Technology of the vehicle, e.g., design tests for ships 623.819;

(3) Operation (technical) of the vehicle, e.g., piloting of spacecraft 629.4582; and

(4) Maintenance and repair of the vehicle, e.g., repair of motorcycles 629.28775.

If in doubt, prefer 629.046 and related numbers in the 600s.

629.049   Land transportation engineering

Class pipes and pipelines at 621.8672.

629.132523   Operation of gliders

Class hang gliding at 629.14.

629.13333   Gliders

Class hang gliders at 629.14.

629.14   Portable flight vehicles

Including hang gliders and gliding.

629.2272   Bicycles and motor bicycles

Including mopeds.

629.2275   Motorcycles and motorscooters

Including minibikes.

Class mopeds at 629.2272.

629.287	Maintenance and repair [of motor land vehicles and cycles]

Most works on car tune-ups are limited to maintenance and repair of the engine and are classed in 629.25.

629.4092	[Persons associated with astronautics]

Class astronauts in 629.450092.

629.442	Space stations

Class here space colonies.

629.892	Automatons

Many works use the word automata in a broader sense than that in which it is used here. Class simple automatic machines dealt with comprehensively in 629.891; a specific machine with the machine, e.g., vending machines 629.82, alarm clocks 681.113.

630 Agriculture and related technologies

SUMMARY

631 **Crops and their production   Plant crops**
632 **Plant injuries, diseases, pests**
633 **Field crops**
634 **Orchards, fruits, forestry**
635 **Garden crops (Horticulture)   Vegetables**
636 **Animal husbandry**
637 **Dairy and related technologies**
638 **Insect culture**
639 **Nondomesticated animals and plants**

Agriculture 630 deals with the technology of agriculture, the "how to" of food production, extraction, and nurturing. Works on the sociology of country life are classed at 307.72, on rural conditions and civilization in 900. The economics of production is classed in 338.1, of land use and conservation in 333.71–333.78.

631   **Crops and their production   Plant crops**

This number comprises various agricultural techniques, structures, implements, systems, and their use in agriculture in general, and in the production of plant crops in particular. Class the application of any or all of these generalities to a specific crop or type of agriculture with the specific crop or type of agriculture, e.g., organic farming in general 631.584, use of organic methods in truck gardening 635.0484, in raising asparagus 635.3184.

631.3   Agricultural tools, machinery, equipment

Application of 631.3 or any of its subdivisions to the other processes and techniques in 631 is classed with the other process or
technique. Where an implement or tool has only one use, only the
general description of the machine or tool can be classed in this
number; its use is classed elsewhere in 631. For example, class the
description of a reaper at 631.35, its use in harvesting in general at
631.55, its use in harvesting wheat at 633.115. If a topic in 631.3
can be applied to several processes, general use is classed in 631.3,
use in a specific process with the specific process. General use of
hand tools is classed at 631.315, use of hand tools in pruning at
631.542, use of hand tools in pruning apple trees at 634.1142.

Note that the manufacture of farm implements and machinery is
classed in 681.763.

631.4   Soil and soil conservation (Soil science)

Class here works dealing with soil considered in its relation to
agriculture. Soil in relation to the engineering of structures to be
built on it is classed in 624.15; interdisciplinary works on soils are
classed in 553.6.

631.47 vs.   Soil and land use surveys vs. Historical and geographical treatment [of
631.49   soil and soil conservation (soil science)]

Both numbers involve the use of the area table. Soil surveys
usually involve small areas (the size of a U.S. county or less), are
quite detailed, and are accompanied by numerous detailed maps.
Historical and geographical treatment usually covers much larger
areas and is not so detailed.

631.49   Historical and geographical treatment [of soil and soil conservation (soil
science)]

See 631.47 vs. 631.49.

631.57   Varieties of crops

This number is seldom used by itself. It has been inserted at this
point for use with the add notes under 633–635 in Edition 19, e.g.,
varieties of wheat 633.117.

According to standard citation order practice, kinds are preferred
to processes. Therefore 631.57 takes precedence over the other
subdivisions of 631.5, e.g., tillage of the soil for a specific variety of
wheat 633.117, not 633.111. This order should be reversed, however, if the work being classified makes it clear that the variety
being discussed is in fact serving only as a model to illustrate the
process. If in doubt, prefer 631.57.

631.587 vs.   Irrigation farming vs. Irrigation and water conservation
631.7

     Class irrigation of crops at 631.587. 631.7 is the general number for works oriented toward soil improvement rather than crop production. If in doubt, prefer 631.587.

631.6   Soil reclamation and drainage

     Including replanting, inland dune stabilization.

     Nonagricultural reclamation is classed in 627.5.

631.7   Irrigation and water conservation

     See 631.587 vs. 631.7.

631.8   **Fertilizers and soil conditioners**

     Class here the use of fertilizers and soil conditioners as well as description of them. Class manufacture of fertilizers in 668.62–668.63, of soil conditioners at 668.64.

632.4   **Fungus disease [of crops]**

     Each of the items mentioned in the first note in Edition 19 has its own specific number derived through the use of the add note; therefore, class at 632.4 only works on fungus diseases in general. The effect of a specific fungus on a specific plant is classed with the plant, e.g., corn smut 633.159427.

     Class bunts at 633.119427.

632.9   Pest control

     Class here only pest control in relation to agriculture.

     See also 363.78.

633–635 **Specific plant crops**

Possible confusion exists as to certain plants in 633.3–633.4 that are also named in the subdivisions of 635. In most instances the crops listed in 635 are being grown for direct human consumption. Carrots, for instance, are usually grown to be eaten raw, or after simple cooking. These are classed in 635.13, not 633.43. On the other hand, most of the crops in 633 are being grown for further processing before consumption (e.g., wheat), or for direct industrial use (e.g., cotton). Soybeans, normally processed into flour or other products before being eaten, are usually classed in 633.34 rather than 635.655.

There are several other instances in which certain plants appear in more than one number. The purpose for which the plant is being grown governs the place where the work is classed. Class in 633.1 a work on cereal grain plants grown for the grain. The same plants when grown for animal forage are classed in 633.25, which is developed like 633.1. At 633.5 Fiber crops are found certain plants that are grown also for other purposes. Class in 633.5 only production for the fibers, e.g., pineapples grown for fibers 633.576, not 634.774.

636.01 Ranches and farms [devoted to animal husbandry]

Class here general description of ranches and farms devoted to animal husbandry, and soil and water management on such farms. Class the production of forage crops in 633.2, range management emphasizing development of pasturage at 633.202, the grazing of livestock on forage crops at 636.084.

636.0887 [Production of animals] For pets

Class stories, anecdotes, and reminiscences about pets in 800, whether or not they are true. Class collections of reminiscences about domestic animals in 808.883; collections from literature in one language in lit. sub. 803. Class reminiscences by an individual author in the appropriate literature plus lit. sub. 8, e.g., reminiscences of a contemporary Italian about life with his cat 858.91403. *See also 800: Special problems: Works about animals.*

636.089 **Veterinary sciences   Veterinary medicine**

These sciences when applied to a specific animal or group of animals are classed with the specific animal or group, e.g., veterinary medicine of horses 636.1089. However, this does not apply to the kinds of animals listed by purpose at 636.088. Veterinary medicine of work animals is classed in 636.089.

636.10888 [Training horses for sports, stunts, exhibition]

Class here training of horses.

Class training of riders or drivers in 798. Also classed in 798 are comprehensive works on training both riders and horses, on training riders or drivers to train horses.

637.12 **Milking and inspection of cows' milk**

This subsection deals with the part of milk production that precedes processing, i.e., the extraction of milk from the cow and the initial testing and is, therefore, not applicable to 637.14 varieties of cows' milk. Note that except for milking, dairy farming is classed at 636.2142.

637.13 vs. **Processing of cows' milk vs. Varieties of cows' milk**
637.14

Processes applied to specific varieties of milk are classed in 637.14 because, in general classification practice, kinds take precedence over processes. A word of caution, however, about 637.141, which, on the face of it, seems to render the whole of 637.13 useless. Works about any of the other varieties of milk in 637.142–637.147 will usually say what kind of milk is being discussed, but works on fresh whole milk are likely just to call it milk. Processing of it may legitimately be classed in 637.13. If a special point is made that fresh whole milk is being talked about in contrast to other forms of milk, it should be classed at 637.141.

637.14 **Varieties of cows' milk**

See 637.13 vs. 637.14.

639.09162 [Nondomesticated animals and plants of the sea]

Including mariculture (the farming of the sea).

639.2 Commercial fishing, whaling, sealing

Class here works treating both fisheries and culture of cold-blooded animals. Comprehensive works on fisheries and the culture of invertebrates are classed in 639.4.

639.3 Culture of cold-blooded vertebrates

Class here comprehensive works treating only the culture of cold-blooded animals. Class culture of invertebrates (except insects) in 639.4–639.7, culture of insects in 638.

639.9 Conservation of biological resources

Note that only the technology (the "how to") of conservation is classed here. Assessments of the need for conservation and of the social and other costs and benefits are classed in 333.95.

640 Home economics and family living

SUMMARY

641   **Food and drink**
642   **Meals and table service**
643   **Housing and household equipment**
644   **Household utilities**
645   **Furnishing and decorating the home**
646   **Sewing, clothing, management of personal
      and family living**
647   **Management of public households
      (Institutional housekeeping)**
648   **Housekeeping**
649   **Child rearing and home care of sick
      and infirm**

640.202   [Synopses, outlines, manuals of home economics and family living]

Class here collections of helpful households hints, but only if they cover most of the subjects of the 640s, e.g., books of hints on cooking, cleaning, managing time, sewing, grooming 640.202. If the hints are confined to only one branch of home economics, class with the branch, e.g., helpful sewing hints 646.20202.

641.555   Time-saving cookery

Including works on the preparation and freezing of meals to save time later.

641.5784   Barbecue cookery

Note that this must be outdoor barbecuing, since the heading at 641.578 specifies outdoor cookery. Indoor barbecuing and comprehensive works on barbecuing are classed at 641.76.

641.6   **Cookery of and with specific materials**

Although cookery of vegetables is classed here, note that vegetarian cookery is classed at 641.5636.

641.76   Broiling, grilling, barbecuing

Including indoor barbecuing and comprehensive works on barbecuing. Class outdoor barbecuing at 641.5784.

641.874   Alcoholic [beverages]

Including home brewing.

642.1–.5   **Meals**

Note that only the planning, serving, and packaging of meals are classed here. Class cookery in 641.5–641.8.

642.4 vs.   Meals for social occasions vs. **Eating and drinking places**
647.95

Note that catering (in the first note at 642.4 in Edition 19) may have a broader meaning (particularly in Great Britain) that includes restaurant services. Works based on this meaning are classed in 647.95.

643.12   Selection and acquisition [of housing]

Information, procedures, standards, criteria for the home owner and dweller.

Economic aspects of home purchase and rental are classed at 333.338, legal aspects in 346.043. Housing construction is classed in 690.

643.3–.7   **Specific areas and their equipment [and] Applicances, and laborsaving installations [and] Renovation, improvement, remodeling.**

Like 643.12 these numbers are used for guides for the householder in his private capacity. The note "Class here repair by members of household" at various numbers in this span in Edition 19 indicates that manuals on how to repair various appliances and pieces of equipment are classed here if they deal with relatively simple repairs that may be performed by inexperienced people, e.g., maintenance in the home of a sewing machine 646.2044. A technical manual for professional repair personnel is classed with the number for the manufacturing of the object in question, e.g., professional repair of garbage disposal units 683.88.

644   **Household utilities**

See 643.3–.7.

645   **Furnishing and decorating the home**

Class here the choice, placing, and use of furnishings from the standpoint of suitability, convenience, economy. Class the decoration of interiors in 747, furniture and accessories from the standpoint of beauty and harmony in 749. If in doubt, prefer 747 and 749.

646.1   **Sewing materials**

"Use" in the first note in Edition 19 means general use only, methods of use. Use in a specific operation is classed with the operation, e.g., the use of pins in making dresses 646.432028.

646.21   Sewing for the home

Many of the articles listed here in Edition 19 also appear under 746.94–746.98. If the work in question strongly emphasizes elements of design and decoration, the 746 numbers are to be preferred. 646.2 involves strictly utilitarian operations. However, it should be noted that 746.92 Costume is design only. Construction of clothing is always classed in 646.4.

646.31–.36   [Clothing for specific groups]

See third paragraph at s.s. 08.

646.7   Management of personal and family living   Grooming

This number now includes much more than the subject of grooming, which occupied it in previous editions. Grooming is still here, of course, with other subjects added to form a complex of topics dealing with personal appearance, behavior, and relations. Since the 640s are a technology schedule, works classed here are strictly "how to" works: how to be charming, how to behave on a date, how to function within the family, how to cope with advancing age.

Note also that 646.7 relates solely to personal and family living. Business success is classed in 650.1.

Class the psychology of personal living in 158; social problems of old age in 362.6, of the family in 362.82.

646.704   Special topics of general applicability to grooming

See third paragraph at s.s. 08.

647.94   Multiple dwellings for transients

Class historical and geographical treatment of each of these kinds in 647.943–647.949. However, if the works are intended for travelers, class them in 910.

647.95   Eating and drinking places

See 642.4 vs. 647.95.

647.96–.99 [Institutional housekeeping in institutional households, religious institu-
vs. 658.2 tions, educational and research institutions] vs. Management of plants
and s.s. 0682 Numbers in 647.96–647.99 are developed like 725–727, which lists
buildings for most purposes. There is, therefore, a potential conflict with 658.2 and s.s. 0682 for plant management, which, of
course, includes maintenance.

Class in 647.96–647.99 such strictly housekeeping operations as
food service and cleaning. Class works broader in scope in 658.2 or
with the subject using s.s. 0682, e.g., maintenance of rest rooms
and food vending machines in gasoline-filling stations 647.9638,
but general maintenance of a filling-station plant (including maintenance of utilities and equipment) 381.45665538270682.

Be especially cautious with respect to hospitals. Cleaning, for
instance, in a hospital could be classed in 648.5 (*see note at 647.9*
in Edition 19), but if sanitation is involved this becomes a proper
and specific service of the hospital and is classed at 362.110682.

650 Management and auxiliary services

SUMMARY

651 Office services
652 Processes of written communication
653 Shorthand
657 Accounting
658 General management
659 Advertising and public relations

This division is concerned with the art and science of conducting
organized enterprises and the skills and operations auxiliary thereto.
These auxiliary skills and services consist chiefly of the communication and record keeping fundamental to management.

See also 158.7 vs. 650.

651 Office services

This number contains provisions for certain procedures, such as
data processing, mail handling, filing and storage of records. It
also contains provision for nontechnical activities, such as office
managmeent, which is the organization and direction of auxiliary
services.

Class here problems of security and confidentiality.

651.374 **Secretarial and related activities**

This subsection is for works describing the role of clerical personnel and their function and place in the work of the office. Stenographic techniques are classed in 652–653, accounting in 657.

651.7 **Communication   Creation and transmission of records**

Class here such topics as how to set up correspondence, techniques of dictation, use of the telephone, mail-handling techniques — in short, the mechanics of communication. Do not use for the composition of letters and other communications. Class composition of letters at 808.066651. Class communication in the sense of interpersonal relations at 153.6, its use in support of management objectives in 658.45. Communication theory is classed in 001.51, the social role of communication in 302.2.

651.8 **Data processing**

This subsection is for the office use only of data processing. General, interdisciplinary, and theoretical works are classed in 001.6.

657 vs. **Accounting** vs. Management accounting [and] Reports
658.1511–
.1512 The technology of accounting ("how to do it") is classed in 657. 658.1511 is for the use of accounting information by management. How to prepare a financial statement is classed at 657.32, use of a financial statement by management to improve business performance at 658.1512. Design of accounting systems in general is classed at 657.1. Works on design of accounting systems with specific emphasis on increasing the flow of information to management is classed at 658.1511. If in doubt, prefer 657.

657.48 Analytical (Financial) accounting

Including accounting for inflation.

658 and **Management [and] Management of enterprises engaged in specific fields**
s.s. 068 **of activity, of specific kinds of enterprises**

Class here energy management.

Class here management of safety. Note that a specific aspect of safety management is classed with the subject, e.g., personnel safety 658.382 and s.s. 0683, product safety 658.56 and s.s. 0685. *See also 363.1: Safety management.*

Management comprises the conduct of all types of enterprises except government agencies in the sense discussed under Public Administration.* (*See 350.*) It is not confined, as in Edition 16, to "business organizations."

Organizations to be managed can be divided in three ways. First is division by the size or scale of the enterprise. Management of organizations of specific sizes and scopes is classed in 658.02. Second is division by the legal form of the enterprise, e.g., corporations, partnerships, etc. Management of this type of organization is classed in 658.04. Third, and most important, is division by the kind of work the organization does. Does it sell books, manufacture light bulbs, carry freight, or care for sick people? Management of enterprises doing specific kinds of work is classed with the kind of work being done using Standard Subdivisions notation 068 in those cases (most of them) where other provision has not been made. 658 and its subdivisions are reserved for discussions of management applicable to any type of enterprise.

A word of caution is in order at this point. A work may be a general work on management, even though it proclaims itself to be related to a specific field. A work on airline management, for instance, if it deals with the generalities of organizing, staffing, planning, etc., is to be classed in 658 or one of its subdivisions as appropriate. In such a work it is frequently only the pictures and some of the examples that are actually connected with airline operations. If, however, the work deals with the intricacies of routing flights and scheduling equipment, the qualifications of airline crews specifically, and the problems of handling baggage, then the work is classed at 387.7068. Certain exceptions to this rule will be noted below.

Another word of caution is in order with respect to using s.s. 068 for very general subjects, such as technology 600, engineering 620, manufacturing 670, and factory operations engineering 670.42. These fields are so broad, and the applications are so general, that works on management applicable to all their branches would be useful to almost anyone interested in management and should be classed in 658. Class works in 606.8, 620.0068, and 670.42068 only in cases where there is an unusual degree of specificity that would seriously qualify the usefulness of works for managers in other types of enterprises.

---

*Government agencies so described are classed in 350–354 with the appropriate subject in public administration, not outside of public administration using s.s. 068.

What is the basis for deciding what field of work an organization is engaged in? In determining this, in general select the most obvious and straightforward number, the one that reflects the actual carrying out of the operation. Should the management of automobile manufacturing concerns be classed in 629.2068 or 338.76292068? Prefer 629.2068, because 338.76292 is for the economics of automobile manufacturing concerns. Class management of retail chain stores in 658.8702068 or 658.8703068, not 381.12068, since chain stores are a form of management organization. 381.12 is for the economic aspects of such an organization. However, class a retail store marketing a specific product in 381.4, e.g., management of a book store 381.45002068. For retail chain stores marketing a specific commodity, prefer the commodity, e.g., chain of retail book stores 381.45002068. The same holds true for any of the other subdivisions of 658.87.

There are six basic branches of management:*

---

*Under each branch of management examples will be given. The number assigned to each example is for comprehensive works on that topic. Subordinate topics pertaining to branches of management are often found in regular subdivisions of the number under consideration. This possibility should always be checked.

(1) *Financial management* (658.15 and s.s. 0681) deals, as its name implies, with money: how to raise funds to initiate or expand an organization, investment of capital in capital goods or in the securities of other organizations, allocation of funds to various operations (budgeting), and control of expenses and costs. These aspects of financial management do not vary greatly from enterprise to enterprise, except with respect to the source of funds. But in any context, financial management is easy to recognize. Examples follow:

Financial management of factories: 670.681.
Financial management of farms: 630.681.
Financial management of airlines: 387.71068.

> Note here that since this number already expresses financial considerations, the standard subdivision used is plain 068, the 1 being redundant.

Financial management of department stores: 658.8710681.
Financial management of book stores: 381.450020681.
Financial management of commercial banks: 332.120681.

> Be careful here. A bank's *work* is finance. Standard subdivision 0681 can apply only to its internal finance: raising money to start the bank; use of money in financing its internal operations, such as paying the employees and the light bills; keeping down costs of operation. The financial services that the bank renders to the public are part of production management, for which see below (4).

Financial management of hospitals: 362.110681.
Financial management of hotels: 647.940681.
Financial management of prisons: 365.0681.
Financial management of schools: 371.206.
Financial management of libraries: 025.11.

It should be noted that this number does not include bookkeeping or accounting for specific types of organizations. Class these in 657.8.

(2) *Plant management* (658.2 and s.s. 0682) deals with the physical environment and tools requisite to the performance of the organization's work. It includes land, buildings, utilities (e.g., light and heat), and the specific equipment (such as vehicles, machinery, furnishings) necessary to do the work. Acquisition of grounds, buildings, and major equipment is classed at 658.15242, since these are considered to be capital goods. Their maintenance is classed with plant management as is the use of land, buildings, and utilities. Use of production equipment is classed with production management. Equipment used in production will, of course, vary with the enterprise. As to the other elements, the common factors predominate. Examples follow:

Management of factory plants: 670.682.
Management of the plant of farms: 630.682.

> Note that specific subtopics of plant management are spelled out under 631.2 and 631.3. Note further that here soil management 631.4 (management of the land) is part of production management.

Management of plant for airlines: 387.73068.

> Note here that since this number already implies plant (as will be clear from an examination of the subdivisions) the standard subdivision used is plain 068, the 2 being redundant.

Management of department store plants: 658.8710682.
Management of book store plants: 381.450020682.
Management of plant for commercial banks: 332.120682.
Management of hospital plants: 362.110682.
Management of hotel plants: 647.940682.
Management of prison plants: 365.5068.

> *See comment on plant for airlines above.*

Management of school plants: 371.6068.

> *See comment on plant for airlines above.*

Management of library plants: 022.

See also 647.96–.99 vs. 658.2 and s.s. 0682.

(3) *Personnel management* (658.3 and s.s. 0683) deals with people, how to recruit, select, place, train, develop, and motivate them in performing the work of the organization. It also includes pay, hours, leave, retirement, and pensions, as well as subjects like discipline and discharge. Here, again, the elements are all much alike from organization to organization. The main differences are in job descriptions. Examples follow:

Personnel management in factories: 670.683.
Personnel management on farms: 630.683.
Personnel management in airlines: 387.70683.
Personnel management in department stores: 658.8710683.
Personnel management in book stores: 381.450020683.
Personnel management in commercial banks: 332.120683.
Personnel management in hospitals: 362.110683.
Personnel management in hotels: 647.2068.

Note that the 3 is redundant in this case, since the number already expresses employees.

Personnel management in prisons: 365.0683.

Note that this is management of prison employees. Management of prisoners is production management and is classed in 365.6.

Personnel management in schools: 371.201.

Management of teachers and other school employees and officials. Management of students is production management and is classed in 371.5 and other places throughout 371–378. Further directions concerning personnel management will be found at 371.201 in Edition 19.

Personnel management in libraries: 023.9.

(4) *Production management* (658.5 and s.s. 0685) is the management of the actual work that the organization exists to perform. It concerns itself with the organization of the work flow and the methods to be used in performing individual operations. It also deals with insuring the quality and accuracy of the operations and of their results. It is related to, but not the same as, the technology involved in the operations. It differs radically from one kind of organization to another. Examples follow:

Management of factory production: 658.5.

> This is the organization and direction of the process by which raw materials, parts, and subassemblies are combined and processed through the operation of people and machines to produce such concrete objects as automobiles, bottles, toys, bread, refrigerators, and light bulbs.

> Subsection 658.5 fits the nature of factory operations better than it fits production management of other kinds of enterprise. This is because of the historical development of this section, which in Edition 14 was plain "shop management." It reflects an earlier state of the management art when books on management were chiefly concerned with industrial management. It has been decided for the time being, therefore, to class production management in factories here rather than in 670.685. The same thing holds true for the management of production in the construction industries. However, class production management in a specific kind of manufacturing or construction with the subject, e.g., production management in an automobile factory 629.2220685.

Management of farm production: 630.685.

> Planning, scheduling, supervising the plowing, sowing, weeding, manuring, reaping, etc., that constitute farm production.

Production management for airlines: 387.70685.

> Note the presence of elements of production management in subsections of 387.7, e.g., planning airline routes 387.72, assigning airplanes to routes and scheduling them 387.74042; planning, organizing, and supervising meal services, baggage services, and reservation services 387.7420685.

> Production management here includes also the clerical activities involved in the above operations, e.g., making reservations. However, the clerical activities involved in other specific management activities are classed with the activity, e.g., clerical operations in payroll management 387.70683.

Production management for department stores: 658.8710685.

Selling goods is the basic activity for which the store exists. Therefore, the management of sales in this context is production management. Do not use s.s. 0688, which indicates marketing management. (In other contexts s.s. 0688 is used for the sale of goods in an organization whose primary purpose is, for instance, manufacturing or some activity other than selling as such. Standard subdivision 0688 may, however, be used for credit management in a department store. *See the section on marketing management below.*

Production management here includes the clerical activities involved in making sales. *See last note under production management for airlines above.*

Production management for book stores: 381.450020685.

See discussion under department stores above.

Production management for commercial banks: 332.120685.

Planning, organizing, and supervising customer services, maintenance of checking and savings accounts, vault services, loan services, trust services, etc.

Includes the clerical operations involved in these services, e.g., recording deposits. *See last note under production management for airlines above.*

Production management for hospitals: 362.110685.

Management of the processes involved in admitting, housing, feeding, diagnosing, treating, routinely caring for, and discharging patients.

Includes the clerical work involved in these operations, e.g., maintaining patients' records. *See last note under production management for airlines above.*

Production management for hotels: 647.940685.

Management of the operations directly involved in providing food, entertainment, and clean and attractive rooms and other facilities for guests.

Includes the clerical operations of making reservations, checking guests in and out. Billing, however, here as well as elsewhere, is part of credit management. *See last note under production management for airlines above.*

Production management for prisons: 365.60685.

Management of the activities involved in receiving, housing, feeding, supervising the activities of, rendering welfare services to, preventing the escape of, and discharging prisoners.

Includes the clerical work involved in maintaining prisoners' records. *See last note under production management for airlines above.*

Production management for schools: 371.0685.

Management of the activities involved in imparting knowledge and attitudes to students. Includes such things as scheduling classes, apportionment of teaching load, and grouping students for instruction.

Includes the clerical work of keeping student records. *See last note under production management for airlines above.*

Production management for libraries: 025.1.

Management of readers' services and technical processes. Includes the clerical work involved in these activities, e.g., filing into the catalog. *See last note under production management of airlines above.*

(5) *Management of materials* (658.7 and s.s. 0687) involves the raw materials, parts, and subassemblies used in creating the final product or service; the necessary supplies for conducting the business, e.g., ink, pens, paper; and other small pieces of equipment, e.g., typewriters, filing cabinets.

The activities dealing with these materials fall into three distinct categories: acquisition, internal management, and physical distribution.

Acquisition, or procurement, involves contracts and their negotiation, vendor selection, order work, receiving and unloading shipments, expediting and tracing when done by the purchaser, and the clerical work involved in all these activities.

Internal management involves storage and the maintenance of inventory, checking materials out of inventory for use in the work process, their movement from work station to work station, checking them into storage and storing them prior to sale, and maintaining the inventory at this point. In service organizations, where there is no sale of a final product, the process is complete when materials and supplies are issued for and used in the work process.

Physical distribution involves processing of orders received, matching these to items in inventory, checking the items out of inventory, packing them, loading them; selection of carrier and routing, expediting and tracing when done by the shipper, and the clerical work involved in all of these.

(Remember that major equipment is considered to be capital. Its acquisition is classed in s.s. 0681.)

It should be noted that physical distribution is not a factor in most service organizations.

Examples follow:

Materials management in factories: 670.687.
Materials management on farms: 630.687.
Materials management for airlines: 387.70687.
Materials management in department stores: 658.8710687.
Materials management in book stores: 381.450020687.
Materials management in commercial banks: 332.120687.
Materials management in hospitals: 362.110687.
Materials management in hotels: 647.940687.
Materials management in prisons: 365.0687.
Materials management in schools: 371.209.
Materials management in libraries: 025.1.

But class management of the acquisition of books and other information media at 025.2068, their internal management in 025.8, their circulation (analogous to physical distribution) in 025.6.

(6) *Marketing management* (658.8 and s.s. 0688) deals with the sale of the product created by the organization, or the service rendered by it. This concept also includes credit management. Examples follow:

Marketing management for manufacturing concerns: 670.688.
Marketing management for farms: 630.688.
Marketing management for airlines: 387.70688.

> Chiefly for sales promotion and credit management. Most sales effort for such an organization is concentrated in advertising, which is classed in 659.

Marketing management of department stores:

> Use s.s. 0688 only for credit management, i.e., 658.8710688. *See 658 and s.s. 068: (4) Production management.*

Marketing management for book stores:

> *See department stores immediately above.*

Marketing management for commercial banks:

> Chiefly advertising, which is classed in 659.

Marketing management for hospitals:

> Credit management only, i.e., 362.110688.

Marketing management for hotels: 647.940688.

> Credit management and other limited applications, e.g., sale of facilities for conventions.

Marketing management for prisons:

> Not applicable.

Marketing management for schools:

> Not applicable. Private schools do some advertising and public relations but these are classed in 659.2.

Marketing management for libraries:

> Class public relations of libraries at 021.7.

See also 380.1 vs. 658.8.

658 vs. 658.4 General management vs. Executive management*

> 658.4 is a murky area. It is concerned with the activities, duties, powers, and functions of top and middle management, which, of course, add up, simply, to management. It, therefore, to some extent duplicates 658 as a place for comprehensive works on management. Use 658 undivided only for the most general and theoretical works. Where emphasis is on the role of the manager, or, if in doubt, prefer 658.4.
>
> In addition to the criteria already mentioned, each of these numbers is the exclusive location for works on the topics listed as subdivisions of them. Do not attempt to distinguish between data processing 658.05 in a general sense as against data processing in an executive management sense (658.4) for instance, but simply class the work in 658.05 where the topic is mentioned.

658.05   **Data processing [in management]**

> Class here the use of data processing in management operations. Use of data processing in clerical operations is classed in 651.8.

658.11   Initiation of business enterprises

> The words "including location" in Edition 19 refer, of course, only to management techniques for locating businesses. Class purely economic considerations in 338.09.
>
> Note that this concept is not covered by s.s. 0681, which is for financial management only. Class initiation of a specific type of enterprise with the subject, using s.s. 068.

658.15   **Financial administration**

> *See 658 and s.s. 068: (1) Financial management.*

658.1511–   Management accounting [and] Reports
.1512
> *See 657 vs. 658.1511–.1512.*

658.153   [Management of] Taxes, insurance, charitable donations

> This number comprises the ways that management can deal with taxes, what insurance is needed for the organization. Class general works on and economic aspects of business taxes at 336.207, legal aspects at 343.068, general works on insurance in 368, general works on charitable donations at 361.765.

---

*Note that there is also a standard subdivision corresponding to this number, s.s. 0684.

658.159   **Financial administration in enterprises of specific types and scopes**

Class specific aspects of financial administration in these types of enterprises in 658.151–658.155, e.g., budgeting management for a small business at 658.154.

658.2   **Management of plants**

See 658 and s.s. 068: (2) Plant management.

658.21   Location [of plants]

Location here means how to locate individual plants as opposed to the location of a whole business. If in doubt, or if the location of the individual plant is synonymous with the location of the business, prefer 658.11.

658.3   **Personnel management**

See 658 and s.s. 068: (3) Personnel management.

658.3 vs. 331   **Personnel management vs. Labor economics**

Many of the topics in 658.3 are paralleled in 331 Labor economics. Class in 658.3 works written from the standpoint of management how management can cope with the various problems mentioned. If written from the standpoint of the employee (the worker), these should be classed in 331. They are also classed in 331 if written from a neutral standpoint, simply as a description of the phenomena.

658.322   **[Management of] Compensation plans**

Despite explicit mention at 658.3222 of wage and salary scales, the number and its subdivisions refer only to the management of compensation. Class the compensation itself in 331.21.

658.325   [Management of] Employee benefits

See 331.255.

658.4   **Executive management**

See 658 vs. 658.4.

658.402   Internal organization

Organization here means the functional (as opposed to the legal or ownership) organization of an enterprise. Functional organization is the division into units based on the work performed, e.g., into sales, finance, shipping departments. Class organization by legal form (corporations, partnerships) in 658.04 and 658.114.

658.4062   [Management of] Externally induced (Responsive) change

Including management measures for coping with conversion to metric system. Class general social problems involved in such conversion at 389.16.

658.408   Social responsibility of management

Including management responsibilities and measures with respect to protection and preservation of environment. Class general social measures for pollution prevention in 363.73, technology of pollution prevention in 628.5.

658.409   **Personal aspects of management**

Class here success as an executive. General success in business is classed in 650.1.

658.42   **Top management**

This somewhat overlaps 658.4. If in doubt, prefer 658.4. Class a work in this number only if it makes a real point of its being about top management as opposed to any other kind. Class specific activities of top management with the subject, e.g., decision-making by top management 658.403.

658.43   Middle management

Apply the same principles used in classing Top management 658.42.

658.45   [Management of] Communication

See 651.7.

658.455   [Management of] Informational programs

This number is for communication of information by management in order to achieve control of people and processes. Gathering of information by management and its use in decision-making is classed in 658.4038.

658.5   **Management of production**

See 658 and s.s. 068: (4) Production management.

658.7   **Management of materials**

See 658 and s.s. 068: (5) Management of materials.

658.8   **Management of distribution (Marketing)**

See 380.1 vs. 658.8, 658 and s.s. 068: (6) Marketing management.

658.809	[Management of] Marketing specific kinds of good and services

This provision has been dropped. With the introduction of s.s. 068 this topic is now classed with the specific subject, using s.s. 0688, e.g., management of the marketing of automobiles 629.2220688.

658.823	[Management of] Packaging

Class here management of packaging as a sales promotion device only. Comprehensive works on management of packaging are to be classed in 658.564 where further directions will be found in Edition 19.

658.83	Market research and analysis [in management]

Class here techniques of market study only. Results of market studies are classed in 380–382.

658.838	Market research on specific products

This provision has been dropped. With the introduction of s.s. 068 and its subdivisions, this topic is now classed with the specific subject, using s.s. 0688, e.g., market research on perfumes 668.540688.

658.89	Personal selling and retail marketing of specific kinds of good and services

This provision has been dropped. With the introduction of s.s. 068 this topic is now classed with the specific subject, using s.s. 0688, e.g., selling textiles 677.00688.

660 Chemical and related technologies

SUMMARY

661	Technology of industrial chemicals (heavy chemicals)
662	Technology of explosives, fuels, related products
663	Beverage technology
664	Food technology
665	Technology of industrial oils, fats, waxes, gases
666	Ceramic and allied technologies
667	Cleaning, color and related technologies
668	Technology of other organic products
669	Metallurgy

Chemical engineering (660.2), the materials used therein, and the methods of production used are classed in 660. However, not all aspects of chemical technology are found here, e.g., production of drugs is classed in 615.19, production of metals in 671–673, pulp and paper processes in 676, elastomer production in 678.

662.2   Explosives

Class nuclear explosives at 621.48.

662.8   Other fuels

Including comprehensive works on energy from wastes. Class a specific form of energy using wastes with the form, e.g., benzenes made from waste products 662.669.

663.2   Wines and wine making

Most works on wines are limited to grape wines and are classed in 663.22.

664.07   Tests, analyses, quality controls [in food technology]

Including grading.

664.6   Special-purpose foods and aids

Including snacks, foods for animals.

Class animal feeds made from grains and other seeds in 664.76.

664.64   Meatless high-protein foods

Including synthetic meat.

664.76   **Animal feeds**

Class comprehensive works on foods for animals at 664.6.

664.921– .929   **[Preservation and ancillary techniques for red meats]**

Subdivisions may be added as instructed in Edition 19 for specific red meats, e.g., canning beef 664.922.

664.931– .939   **[Preservation and ancillary techniques for poultry]**

Subdivisions may be added as instructed in Edition 19 for specific kinds of poultry, e.g., deep freezing turkeys 664.9353.

664.941– .949   **[Preservation and ancillary techniques for seafood]**

Do not add as instructed in Edition 19 for specific seafoods; class at 664.94.

665.5   Petroleum

Class synthetic petroleum in 662.662.

665.53	Refinery treatment [of petroleum] and [petroleum] products
	Class preliminary refining of oil sands and oil shale to obtain distillable fluids at 665.4.
665.538	Refinery products and by-products [of petroleum]
	Including waste products.
665.5388	Residues (Bottoms) [of petroleum refining]
	Class unusable residues at 665.538, asphalt concrete at 666.893.
666.893	Concrete
	Including asphalt concrete.
667.12	Dry cleaning
	Including manufacture of cleaning materials.
667.13	Laundering and finishing operations
	Class soaps in 668.12, detergents at 668.14.
667.14	Bleaching
	Class here manufacture of bleaching materials.
669	**Metallurgy**
	Class here process metallurgy.
669.1	[Metallurgy of] Ferrous metals
	Class here comprehensive works on production of iron and steel.
669.14	Reduction and refining of ferrous ores
	Class comprehensive works on production of iron and steel at 669.1.
669.1413	Blast furnace practice
	Class here casting as a part of the refining process.
	Class iron casting as a metal-working process in 672.25, cast iron products in 672.8.
669.2–.7	**Nonferrous metals**
	Class an alloy not listed here with the base metal if readily ascertainable, e.g., Monel®, a nickel alloy of 67% nickel and 30% copper 669.7332, not 669.3. If the base metal is not readily ascertainable, class with the metal coming first in the span 669.2–669.7. However, class all alloys of steel in 669.142.
	Standard subdivisions may be added for specific alloys, e.g., a dictionary of brass 669.303.

669.9   **Physical and chemical metallurgy**

See 546.3 vs. 669.9.

670 Manufactures

SUMMARY

671 **Metal manufactures**
672 **Ferrous metals manufactures**
673 **Nonferrous metals manufactures**
674 **Lumber, cork, wood-using technologies**
675 **Leather and fur technologies**
676 **Pulp and paper technology**
677 **Textiles**
678 **Elastomers and elastomer products**
679 **Other products of various specific materials**

The order of the subdivisions of 670 is based roughly on the hardness and strength of the material.

Unless separate provision is made, class comprehensive works on products made by a specific process with the process, e.g., seasoned wood 674.38; but coated papers 676.283, not 676.235.

671–679 vs. **Manufactures utilizing specific materials vs. Manufacture for specific uses**
680
The distinction between 670 and 680 cannot be drawn consistently because manufacture by material appears in 680 and products for specific uses in 670. If in doubt, prefer 670.

671.56   Soldering and brazing

Standard subdivisions may be added for soldering alone and for brazing alone.

676.2845   Vulcanized and parchment papers

Class parchment prepared from the skin of an animal for writing purposes at 685.

677.62   **Woven felts**

Class comprehensive works on felts in 677.63.

677.63   **Nonwoven felts**

Class here comprehensive works on felts.

Class woven felts in 677.62.

679.7   **[Products] Of tobacco**

Class tobacco substitutes at 688.4.

680 Manufacture of products for specific uses

The order of the subdivisions of 680 is drawn from that of 670; the products or processes are in some way related to the general materials:

672	Ferrous metals	682	Small forge work
673	Nonferrous metals	683	Hardware and household appliances
674	Lumber, cork, wood	684	Furnishings and home workshops
675	Leather and fur	685	Leather and fur goods
676	Pulp and paper	686	Printing
677	Textiles	687	Clothing

See also 671–679 vs. 680.

680 vs. 745.5 Manufacture of products for specific uses vs. Handicrafts

Class handicrafts as a routine way of making secondary and final products in 680. Class handicrafts emphasizing artistic aspects in 745.5. If in doubt, prefer 680.

See also 745.5.

681.11 **[Manufacture of] Instruments for measuring time.**

See 529.78 vs. 681.11.

681.2 [Manufacture of] Testing and measuring instruments

Class simple tools used for measuring, e.g., folding rulers, at 621.994.

688.1 [Manufacture of] Models and miniatures

Class artistic models and miniatures in 745.5928.

688.4 Smokers' supplies

Including tobacco substitutes.

688.6 Nonmotor land vehicles

See 629.046 vs. 385–388.

688.8 Packaging technology

Class management aspects of packaging at 658.564, artistic aspects of containers in 700, e.g., vases 738.382.

690 Buildings

Class comprehensive works on architectural acoustics at 729.29.

690 vs. 624 **Buildings vs. Civil engineering**

To be classed in 690, the work must limit its discussion to habitable structures (buildings). If other structures are discussed, the work is classed in 624 Civil engineering. For example, a work entitled "Building," which includes discussions not only on buildings but also on dams and bridges, is classed at 624, not 690. If in doubt, prefer 624.

696 Utilities

Class here comprehensive works on energy and environmental engineering of buildings. Class a specific aspect of energy and environmental engineering with the aspect, e.g., ventilation 697.92.

697.1 Heating with open fires (Radiative heating)

Class fireplace-like stoves that have visible fires but which are actually convective heaters in 697.2.

697.54 District heating

Class comprehensive works on district heating at 697.03.

Class hot-water district heating, the typical kind in Europe, at 697.4.

697.78 Solar heating

Class the building of solar houses at 690.869.

700 The arts   Fine and decorative arts

SUMMARY

700 is one of the most inconsistent of the main classes. Therefore, the classifier should be even more circumspect in the application of this class than is ordinarily required in working with the Dewey Decimal Classification.

See also 246–247 vs. 700.

Artists

Note carefully the instructions in Edition 19 at each major area for the classification of artists. Even within one division, the 730s, the treatment varies: 730.924 for a sculptor, 739.22724 for a goldsmith, 730.0924 for a sculptor who has also worked in one or more of the other plastic arts.

Financial patronage of the arts

Class public or private patronage with the subject in art adding s.s. 079 if applicable. For example, The National Council on the Arts listing of available grants, scholarships, and fellowships, and how to apply for them is classed at 700.79; patronage of sculpture 730.79.

The administrative report of a government department or agency administering financial support is classed in 352–354 (*see 350*). The same type of report from a private agency is classed with the specific subject in art plus s.s. 06.

A report on the results of the patronage, e.g., projects made possible by grants, is classed with the subject without s.s. 079.

Standard subdivision 0222 Pictures, charts, designs

Be extremely cautious in the use of this standard subdivision throughout the fine arts schedule. It is usually redundant.

Standard subdivision 028 Techniques, procedures, apparatus, equipment, materials

Do not use this standard subdivision if the class number already implies technique, as is frequently the case. For example, in 747 techniques of interior decoration are implicit; therefore, the use of s.s. 028 is redundant.

Standard subdivision 074 Museums, collections, exhibits

Standard subdivision 074 for collections or exhibitions is never added to the work of an individual artist whether the work falls in s.s. 0924 (e.g., an exhibition of the work of a French sculptor 730.924) or in the number for the individual artist's country (e.g., an exhibition of the work of a Canadian painter 759.11). However, it may be added to s.s. 09 when the latter has been used to denote historical period or place of origin, e.g., an exhibition in New York City of the nude in French art 704.942109440741471. (Note that the area notation for New York City is taken from 708.1–708.9, not from Table 2 Areas.)

The rule of approximating the whole applies here as elsewhere in the Classification. Therefore, do not add s.s. 074 if the period or place of origin does not approximate the full period or area expressed by the notation used for the subject being exhibited.

Standard subdivision 075 Collecting objects

Standard subdivision 075 Collecting objects is closely allied to s.s. 074, and the same rules of application apply. However, use caution when indicating historical or geographical treatment; do not indicate historical or geographical treatment unless the author makes a strong point that the collecting is being done in a specific place, e.g., collecting English glass in Australia 748.2920750994, but a price guide (given in pounds) to English glass 748.292075, since the guide may well be used in other countries.

Standard subdivision 092 Persons associated with the subject

This standard subdivision takes on an additional meaning in the art schedule in that it may be added where applicable to designate the works themselves of an artist or artists, not just critical appraisal and description of the works. Works of an artist or artists are designated in one of two ways, either by the use of s.s. 092 as in sculpture, or by period or place as in drawing 741.92–741.99.

700   The arts

Generally the word "arts," used without a qualifier, is a signal that the area covered is broader than the fine and decorative arts. Literature, music, and the performing arts are the other kinds of arts most often included. A quick check each time that "art" or "arts" is used should establish the area covered.

700.1–.9   Standard subdivisions of the arts

Use this standard subdivision span for material that includes two or more of the fine and decorative arts and one or more of the other arts, e.g., a work about a painter who is also a sculptor and a poet 700.924. If only one fine or decorative art and one of the other arts is involved, class in the number coming first in the schedule, e.g., a U.S. painter and poet 759.13.

701.1   Appreciative aspects [of fine and decorative arts]

Class here general works on art appreciation. Art appreciation may include some theory, some history, and some technique, since "understanding" is the essential point.

Class history of art in 709.

701.17   Aesthetics

Class interdisciplinary works on aesthetics, the study of beauty, at 111.85.

701.8   Inherent features [of the fine and decorative arts]

Class here comprehensive works on color. In practice most material about color will be confined to color in painting 752.

702.81   [Techniques, procedures, apparatus, equipment, materials of] Mixed-media and composites

Class finished works produced by the techniques spelled out in this number and its subdivisions in 709 rather than in narrower classes, such as painting or sculpture, even if these finished works are called painting or sculpture.

702.87–.89   [Techniques of reproduction, execution, identification, conservation, preservation, restoration, routine maintenance and repair]

Class here works in which the emphasis is on the techniques listed. Class works discussing the role of the museum in these activities in 069.51–069.54. If in doubt, prefer 702.87–702.89.

704.03–.87   [**Treatment of the fine and decorative arts with respect to groups of persons**]

Use the following table of precedence. Note that the first and last facets fall outside this span:

(1) Nonliterate peoples	709.011 plus s.s. 093–099 for place
(2) Treatment with respect to groups of specific kinds of persons other than racial, ethnic, national	704.04–.87
(3) Racial, ethnic, national groups	704.03, adding as instructed, only for a group nondominant in its area
(4) Place (includes racial, ethnic, national groups dominant in their respective areas)	709.1, 709.3–709.9

Examples: Jewish art in the U.S. 704.039240973; art of black Americans 704.0396073; art of the Mayan empire 709.7281; women artists and their work 704.042; women artists and their work in the United States 704.0420973.

704.9   **Iconography**

Iconography takes precedence over historical and geographical treatment, e.g., a general work on Romanesque art 709.021, Romanesque art of Normandy 709.442, but The Virgin Mary in Romanesque art of Normandy 704.9485509442. However, care should be taken in classifying works in certain areas such as early Christian, Byzantine, and Romanesque art. Class in 704.9 only if a point is made that iconography or one of its aspects is the focus of the work.

Standard subdivision 09 plus area notation is added to show the nationality of the artists rather than the location of the subject, e.g., British portraits of British royal children 704.94250941. Note that area number 41 stands for the British artists, not the British royal children.

Generally in any use of the iconography numbers, the rule of approximating the whole is waived. There are two exceptions: 704.9432 Animals and 704.9434 Plants. If a work covers only dogs in art, for instance, a standard subdivision should not be added. The rule of approximating the whole *does* apply to numbers from Table 2. Therefore, if s.s. 09 has been added for place of origin, do not add s.s. 074 unless the area covered by the work being classed approximates the whole of the area indicated by the first standard subdivision.

704.942   **[Iconography of] Human figures and their parts**

In the case of portraiture, when s.s. 092 is added, it means the artist or artists doing the work, not the person portrayed.

704.9432–   **[Iconography of animals and plants]**
   .9434
Class works on the symbolism of animals or plants at 704.946.

704.945   [Iconography of] Abstractions

Abstraction is rarely treated as a subject in iconography. Abstractionism is usually treated as a school or style and is classed at 709.04052 if not limited by country.

706   Organizations and management of fine and decorative arts

The biography of an art dealer, formerly 706.5, is now classed at 380.1457.

707.4   Temporary and traveling collections and exhibits

A permanent collection on tour and a temporary exhibit of a private collection are classed here. The location of the temporary exhibition may be shown by continuing to add as shown at s.s. 07401–07409 in Table 1 of Edition 19.

When a temporary exhibition travels from place to place, use the area number that encompasses all the places visited. If only two places are involved, class in the number coming first in Table 2.

Class here also auction or sales catalogs in which an exhibition is involved.

708   Galleries, museums, private collections of fine and decorative arts

Class here only establishments housing general art collections. If the institution's collections are limited to a specific medium, place, or time of origin, class with the medium, place, or time, using s.s. 074 plus notation for place if applicable, e.g., the catalog of a museum limited to textile arts and located in New York City 746.07401471.

Annual reports dealing with acquisitions, activities, programs, and projects are classed here, e.g., the annual report of the Metropolitan Museum of Art in New York City 708.1471. *See 700: Financial patronage of the arts for administrative reports.*

709   Historical and geographical treatment of fine and decorative arts

Class here only if the work covers a broad spectrum of the fine and decorative arts, e.g., several graphic arts and at least one of the plastic arts. Class here also experimental and mixed-media art that does not fit easily into a recognized medium.

See also 760.

709.01–.05   Periods of development [of fine and decorative arts]

European art is classed here if limited to period, school, or style. (*See 709.3–.9 in Edition 19.*) Class art of other continents in 709.3–709.9.

709.011   [Fine and decorative arts of] Nonliterate peoples

Standard subdivision 09 plus area numbers may be added to 709.011 and its subdivisions. Note, however, that many contemporary nonliterate peoples are achieving literacy. Use of this number, therefore, is restricted to nonliterate peoples of the past and nonliterate peoples clearly not a part of contemporary modern society. For instance, the art of prehistoric Ethiopia is classed at 709.011093978, but the art of contemporary Africa (including the work of nonliterate peoples) is classed at 709.6.

See also 704.03–.87.

709.22   Collected artists

Including works of artists from several geographic areas except Western artists limited to a specific period of development. Class works of artists so limited in 709.01–709.05.

In addition to works on the artists themselves, class here also works on art historiographers and art patrons. Class collectors of specific art forms with the form, using s.s. 075092, e.g., collectors of modern art 709.040075092. *For works on art dealers, see note at 706.*

710 Civic and landscape art

711   **Area planning (Civic art)**

The comprehensive number for city planning is 307.12. Works classed in 711 must focus on the presentation and analysis of the physical plans even if historical and social background material is included. However, if these elements predominate, class in 307.12.

Area planning 711 and Architecture 720 are often treated together. If there is no predominance, class the work at 720.

711.551 |Area planning of| Civic, administrative, governmental |areas|

Treat civic, administrative, governmental as a unitary term.

711.74   Pedestrian transport facilities

Including pedestrian malls.

711.75 |Area planning of| Railroad transport facilities

Including rapid transit facilities.

712   Landscape design (Landscape architecture)

Landscape design, landscape architecture, and landscape planning are terms used interchangeably and are all classed here.

Class engineering aspects of landscape architecture in 624.

717   Structures in landscape design

Including design of pedestrian facilities and street furniture; garden ornaments and furniture when not treated as sculpture.

719.32   Public parks and natural monuments

Treat public parks and natural monuments as a unitary term.

720 Architecture

SUMMARY

721   **Architectural construction**
722   **Ancient and Oriental architecture**
723   **Medieval architecture, ca. 300–1399**
724   **Modern architecture, 1400–**
725   **Public structures**
726   **Buildings for religious and related purposes**
727   **School buildings and other buildings for educational and research purposes**
728   **Residential buildings (Domestic architecture)**
729   **Design and decoration of structures and accessories**

Class here comprehensive works that include not only architecture in general but all or one or more of the following: architectural construction 721, building construction 690, area planning 711, or landscape design 712.

720.222   Pictures, charts, designs

Class here the architectural drawings of an individual architect or the collected drawings of more than one architect.

Class a collection of architectural drawings for one structure or a specific type of structure in 725–728, using s.s. 0222.

720.288   Conservation, preservation, restoration

Class here works on conservation, preservation, and restoration that are focused on architectural techniques and procedures even though historical and sociological background material is included. The comprehensive number for this subject, if architecture is of only minor importance, is 363.69.

720.42–.43   [Architecture of buildings for use by the handicapped, the aged, the infirm]

See s.s. 088.

720.9   **Historical and geographical treatment [of architecture]**

Class Oriental schools and styles in 722.1–722.5. This directive refers to modern, as well as to ancient and medieval schools and styles, and is interpreted as meaning also architecture in a geographical area, not just a school or style.

720.9 vs. **Historical and geographical treatment [of architecture] vs. Specific types**
725–728 **of structures**

Important instructions appear at both 720.9 and 722–724 in Edition 19 regarding the choice between these alternatives. General works of an individual architect are classed at 720.924, an individual's work on one structure or one type of structure is classed in 725–728 using s.s. 0924 if applicable, e.g., 726.50924 for an architect and a church designed by him.

720.9 vs. **Historical and geograhical treatment [of architecture] vs. General history**
930–990 **[of specific areas]**

It has been the policy of the Decimal Classification Division to class many works about the history of buildings in 930–990 because they contain material illustrating the civilization of a period or place. However, do not use 930–990 unless the emphasis is on general history, e.g., life in and social aspects of a place or period. Arrangement by architectural style, inclusion of architectural plans, and details of design and construction point to classification in the history of architecture.

Class guidebooks and informational books of the type intended to be used by visitors to the site of a historic building in 914–919, since these are considered to be essentially travel guides.

See also 914–919: Historic buildings and houses.

722.7 Roman [architecture]

Since this number is used for comprehensive works on Roman architecture, it is redundant to add s.s. 0937. However, s.s. 0937 can be added to bring out Roman architecture in a specific place, e.g., 722.709377 for the architecture of Pompeii (Southern Italy).

722.8 Greek (Hellenic) [architecture]

The principle at 722.7 applies here also to the use of s.s. 0938.

723 **Medieval architecture, ca. 300–1399**

Class here schools and styles of architecture not limited to one country. European or Western architecture is included, as is that of the Middle Eastern tradition if part of the Western heritage, e.g., Muslim architecture in the medieval Mediterranean world 723.3.

Class schools and styles of architecture limited to a specific country in 720.9 or 722.

724 **Modern architecture, 1400–**

The principles given at 723 apply here also.

725–728   **Specific types of structures**

Class in these numbers comprehensive works on the architecture of a specific kind of structure, its exterior as well as its interior decoration, and its furnishings—in other words, the building and its contents.

Class structures being rehabilitated to a new use with the new use, e.g., warehouses being converted to housing 728.31, not 725.35. If, however, the structures are being converted to many uses, class with the original use.

See also 720.9 vs. 725–728.

725.1   **[Architecture of] Government buildings**

Class here buildings of the United Nations and similar organizations; civic center buildings.

725.21   [Architecture of buildings for] Retail trade (Stores and shops)

Treat stores and shops as a unitary term.

725.23   [Architecture of] Office [buildings]

Add standard subdivisions only for multipurpose office buildings.

725.31   [Architecture of] Railroad passenger station [buildings]

Including rapid transit stations.

725.33   [Architecture of] Railroad accessory [buildings]

Including rapid transit buildings.

725.4   [Architecture of] Industrial buildings

Including aquaculture stations.

725.8042   **[Architecture of] Multipurpose complexes [for recreation]**

Class here cultural centers that include educational and research facilities normally classed separately in 727.6–727.8, e.g., Centre Pompidou 725.80420944361.

725.822   [Architecture of] Theater and opera buildings

Treat theater and opera as a unitary term.

725.83   [Architecture of] Auditorium buildings

Class here performing arts centers.

725.9   Other public structures

Including convention centers.

725.96   [Architecture of] Arches, gateways, walls

Treat arches, gateways, and walls as a unitary term.

726.1 **[Architecture of] Temples and shrines**

Treat temples and shrines as a unitary term.

Be as specific as possible in building the number, e.g., a Hinayana Buddhist temple in Thailand 726.1439109593. If the branch or sect is not clear, add from 292–299 only as far as the information warrants, e.g., Buddhist temples in Java (sect not specified) 726.143095982; temple forms in southern India (religion not identified) 726.1409548.

726.2 [Architecture of] Mosques and minarets

Treat mosques and minarets as a unitary term.

726.5 **[Architecture of] Christian church buildings**

Note that geographical location takes precedence over denomination for churches 726.5, cathedrals 726.6, and Christian monastic buildings 726.77, e.g., Lutheran church buildings in the United States 726.50973, not 726.58410973.

726.6 **[Architecture of] Cathedral church buildings**

See 726.5.

726.77 **[Architecture of monastic buildings] Of specific Christian orders**

See 726.5.

726.8 [Architecture of] Mortuary chapels and tombs

Treat mortuary chapels and tombs as a unitary term.

727.6–.8 **[Architecture of museum, art gallery, and library buildings]**

See 725.8042.

728.82 [Architecture of] Palaces and chateaux

Treat palaces and chateaux as a unitary term.

728.83 [Architecture of] Mansions and manor houses

Treat mansions and manor houses as a unitary term.

728.9 [Architecture of] Accessory domestic structures

Also including summer houses, pavilions, playhouses, tree houses, housing for pets, dovecotes.

729   **Design and decoration of structures and accessories**

Class here comprehensive works on interior design, a broader concept than interior decoration, which is a part of it. Class interior decoration in 747.

More material is taken out of 729 by notes than is left in. Class in 729 only those general works in which the focus is specifically architectural design. Design and construction treated together are classed in 721. Construction alone is classed in 690. Decoration is classed in 729 only when the subject is being treated as an aspect of architectural decoration rather than as an art object in itself. For example: *The Hidden World of* (French) *Misericords* is classed at 730.944 rather that at 729.5 or 726.525 because the interest in them is as works of sculpture rather than as parts of various structures. If the subject is how medieval French churches were decoratd in relief, then 726.525 is correct.

729.9   **Built-in ecclesiastical furniture**

Class built-in ecclesiastical furniture or parts of it (e.g., pew ends) in a specific medium with the medium if not treated in an architectural context. For example, class carved pew ends in 730, altarpieces and retables with built-in furniture at 749.4.

730 Plastic arts   Sculpture

SUMMARY

731   **Processes and representations of sculptures**
732   **Nonliterate, ancient, Oriental sculpture**
733   **Greek, Etruscan, Roman sculpture**
734   **Medieval sculpture, ca. 500–1399**
735   **Modern sculpture, 1400–**
736   **Carving and carvings**
737   **Numismatics and sigillography**
738   **Ceramic arts**
739   **Art metalwork**

Class sound sculpture (in which the sound is as basic as the visual work) at 702.8 if the work deals with technique or in 709 if it deals with products. Class kinetic sculpture, mixed media and composites, assemblages, constructions, and land art in these numbers also.

Use 730.01–730.09 for standard subdivisions of two or more of the plastic arts. For instance, prefer 730.01–730.09 for any work combining sculpture and one of the other plastic arts in 736–739, or for any combination of those other plastic arts whether or not sculpture is included.

730.924   Individual sculptors

Class individual sculptors here regardless of process, representation, school, or style. Class an individual sculptor who also does carving or any of the other plastic arts at 730.0924.

731–735   Sculpture

See 736–739 vs. 731–735.

731   Processes and representations of sculpture

Class works on medieval and modern Western schools limited to a specific country or locality in 730.9 plus notation for geographic area. Class works not so limited in 732–735. In other words, 731.5 Forms, 731.7 Sculpture in the round, and 731.8 Iconography cannot be used unless the subject is being treated universally, unlimited by time, place, or person.

731.5   Forms [of sculpture]

See 731.

731.7   Sculpture in the round

See 731.

731.8   Iconography

See 731.

732.2   [Sculpture of] Nonliterate [societies]

If material is limited by place and includes the work of both nonliterate and modern societies, class the sculpture of the West and Africa in 730.9 plus area notation, specific styles and schools in the appropriate numbers in 732.3–732.9. If another plastic art is included, e.g., carving, class in 730.09 plus area notation. *See also 709.011.*

733   Greek, Etruscan, Roman sculpture

Class here works covering both Greek and Roman sculpture.

The principle at 722.7 applies here also to the addition of s.s. 09 plus area to each subdivision.

735.21   Early modern [sculpture], 1400–1799

Including rococo.

736–739   Other plastic arts

See note at 730 for works combining one or more plastic arts with sculpture.

736–739 vs. **Other plastic arts vs. Sculpture**
731–735
The plastic arts in 736–739 are often difficult to separate from sculpture; prefer 731–735 Sculpture if in doubt, e.g., bronze figures are classed in sculpture, but a bronze figurine is classed at 739.512 if it was a part (such as a finial or handle) of a larger decorative work.

736.22   Specific forms |of precious and semiprecious stones|

Including carved figurines of precious and semiprecious stones, e.g., those by Fabergé.

736.4   Wood |carving and carvings|

If in doubt as to whether a work about wood deals with carving or sculpture, prefer 731–735 Sculpture. If the work treats both subjects, it is classed in Plastic arts 730–730.09.

736.5   Stone |carving and carvings|

Including sepulchral slabs, incised effigial slabs.

736.98   Paper cutting and folding

Including silhouettes if produced solely by cutting, Chinese paper cutting.

Class comprehensive works on silhouettes and silhouettes produced by drawing only at 741.7.

737.3   Counters and tokens

Treat counters and tokens as a unitary term.

737.49 |Coins| Of various specific countries

Class coins by the place in which they were minted, not by the political jurisdiction issuing them, e.g., Roman coins minted in Alexandria, Egypt 737.4932, not 737.4937.

Examples: U.S. coins 737.4973; coins of countries in Europe in 737.494.

738   Ceramic arts

Class here comprehensive works that include 738.2 Porcelain, 738.3 Earthenware and stoneware, 738.4–738.8 Specialized products (usually 738.6 Ornamental bricks and tiles, or 738.8 Other products, or both). Glass may also be included. Add standard subdivisions to 738 for this combination, especially s.s. 09 plus area numbers, if applicable.

Class a combination of porcelain and earthenware or stoneware not including specialized products in 738.2.

738.092   [**Persons associated with ceramic arts**]

Class here all potters regardless of type of ceramic used or type of product made. This includes biographical, descriptive, and critical material on the potter or on the potter and his works. Works of an individual potter, including exhibitions, are also classed here. An exhibition of the works of more than one potter is classed in 738 or the appropriate subdivision of it plus s.s. 09 with additions for country or period, plus s.s. 074 for an exhibition if applicable.

Class enamelers in 739.4092, mosaic artists in 738.5092.

738.1   **Techniques, procedures, apparatus, equipment, materials [of ceramic arts]**

Class here works on techniques that include treatment of materials, apparatus, and equipment in themselves and not just as applied to the techniques.

738.14   **Techniques and procedures [in the ceramic arts]**

Class here works on technique in which materials, apparatus, and equipment are discussed only in relation to the techniques involved.

738.2   **Pottery (China)   Porcelain**

If Specialized products 738.4–738.8 are included, the combination of pottery and special products is classed at 738, not 738.2.

738.23   Specific varieties and brands of pottery

Class here works that include tableware, vases, or other containers of earthenware and stoneware as well as porcelain.

738.24   Specific products of pottery

Note that certain specific pottery products are classed in 738.4–738.8, e.g., porcelain and earthenware tiles 738.6.

738.28   Specific products of porcelain

Note that certain specific porcelain products are classed in 738.4–738.8, e.g., porcelain figurines 738.82.

738.38   Specific products

Note that certain specific earthenware and stoneware products are classed in 738.4–738.8, e.g., earthenware and stoneware figurines 738.82.

738.383   Other containers

Examples: pots, pot lids, jugs, mugs. Do not add standard subdivisions for one type of container.

738.8   Other products

Including lamps.

739.22–.24   Art metalwork in specific metals

If the work covers both Goldsmithing 739.22 and Silversmithing 739.23, consider it to be comprehensive and class it at 739.2, e.g., a biography of an individual artist working in both gold and silver 739.20924. The first of two rule does not apply in this case.

739.228   Various specific products [of gold and gold plate]

Treat gold and gold plate as a unitary term.

739.2283   [Gold] Tableware

For the purpose of this schedule, tableware is considered to consist of utensils used for setting a table or serving food and drink. It includes flatware and hollow ware, such as bowls.

739.23   Silversmithing

Be wary of historical and geographical treatment. The numbers for such treatment are derived from the add note at 739.2271–739.2279. Do not use 739.2309. For example, silversmiths of London are classed at 739.23722, Baltimore silver at 739.2377526, but London hallmarks at 739.230278.

739.3   Watch- and clockcases

The number is limited to the art metalwork of the cases alone. If the mechanism of the watches or clocks is included, class the work in manufacturing, i.e., 681.113 for clocks and 681.114 for watches.

739.4   Ironwork

Treat wrought iron and cast iron as a unitary term.

739.512   Bronze

This number comprises the treatment of work in bronze as a decorative art. Class bronze sculpture in 731–735. For example, class a bronze figure or figurine with sculpture unless the figurine was part of a larger decorative work. Therefore, small statues of Krishna are classed in 732.44 as Indic bronze sculpture rather than here.

739.7   Arms and armor

Class here decorative treatment of shapes, handles, grips, metalwork, and other features. Class manufacturing in 623.44, interdisciplinary works on small firearms (civilian as well as military) in 683.4, interdisciplinary works on knives at 621.932.

739.722   Swords and sabers

Treat swords and sabers as a unitary term.

740 Drawing, and decorative and minor arts

SUMMARY

741   **Drawing and drawings**
742   **Perspective**
743   **Drawing and drawings by subject**
745   **Decorative and minor arts**
746   **Textile arts and handicrafts**
747   **Interior decoration**
748   **Glass**
749   **Furniture and accessories**

741.092 |Drawing| Artists

Class here a comprehensive combination of the works of an artist known for his drawing, description and critical appraisal of the drawings, and biography. However, class the catalog of an exhibition in 741.92 Historical periods or 741.93–.99 Specific continents, countries, localities even if some critical or biographical material is included.

741.5–.7   Special applications |of drawing|

Only drawing artists are classed in 741.092. Description, critical appraisal, biography, and works of artists working in other media as well as drawing are classed with the special applications in 741.5–741.7, using s.s. 092 if applicable, e.g., Norman Rockwell's covers for the *Saturday Evening Post* 741.6520924. However, class an exhibition of the original oil paintings for those covers at 759.13 for Norman Rockwell as an American painter.

Class comprehensive works at 741.6, not 741. (The second note at 741.5–741.7 in Edition 19 has been changed; *see DC&,* Vol. 4, No. 2, p. 31).

741.5   Cartoons, caricatures, comics

Class a collection of cartoons or caricatures on a specific subject intended to entertain or amuse in 741.59. However, if the purpose is to inform or persuade, class the work with the subject, e.g., political cartoons by Herblock in appropriate numbers in 320 or 973.

741.58   Animated cartoons

Material classed here is confined to drawing techniques, description, and critical appraisal only. Class collections of cartoons in 741.59, techniques of photography of animated cartoons at 778.5347. Comprehensive works including drawing, photography, and production are classed in 791.43. If there is an emphasis on any one element, class the work with that element.

741.6   Graphic design, illustration, commercial art

See 769.5.

741.7   Silhouettes

Class cut-out silhouettes at 736.98.

741.9   Collections of drawings

Class here exhibition catalogs. *See also the note at 741.93–.99.*

Class a combination of drawing and painting with the one that predominates. If neither predominates or if in doubt, prefer 750 Painting.

Class preliminary drawings with the finished work unless they are treated as works of art in their own right.

Consider watercolors to be paintings unless the use of watercolor is confined to a one-color wash highlighting the drawing.

741.93–.99   [Collections of drawings from] Specific continents, countries, localities

Do not add s.s. 074 to the area number for an exhibition of the work of an individual artist, e.g., drawings of a single United States artist on exhibition 741.943, but an exhibition in Detroit of the drawings of more than one United States artist 741.973074017434.

745   Decorative and minor arts

Although Edition 19 says to class folk art here, works calling themselves "folk art" may include sculpture and painting, especially portraiture; in such cases prefer 709.

Add standard subdivisions both for the main-heading concept and for folk art if applicable, e.g., decorative arts of the 19th century 745.09034, folk art of Pennsylvania 745.09748.

745.1 **Antiques**

Class a specific type of antique with the subject in art if a number is provided, e.g., gold coins 737.43, antique New England furniture 749.214.

If there is no available number in 700–779, use the appropriate number in 600–699, e.g., antique passenger automobiles 629.222. If there is a separate technology number for the use of the object in question as opposed to the number for manufacture of it, prefer the use number, e.g., thimbles 646.19 rather than 687.8.

If antiques and collectibles fit in neither the art nor the technology numbers, class with the subject with which they are most closely associated, e.g., Shirley Temple collectibles 791.430280924.

745.5 **Handicrafts**

The term handicrafts has a limited meaning in the Dewey Decimal Classification. Here it means artistic work only, and includes those crafts spelled out in this number and its subdivisions. In general usage the term crafts may be used for country crafts, and cottage industries and trades, such as those of the farrier, the cooper, and the thatcher. Crafts in this sense, and handicrafts as the routine way of manufacturing secondary and final products are classed in 680 or with a more specific technology. *See also 680 vs. 745.5.*

745.51 [Handicrafts] In woods

Class general works on cabinetmaking in 684.08, works limited to wooden furniture in 684.104, works on antique furniture (reproduction, restoration, and repair) in 749.1, works on treenware (woodenware) at 674.88.

745.53 **[Handicrafts] In leathers and furs**

Class the construction of clothing in leathers and furs at 646.1.

745.56 [Handicrafts] In metals

Including handicrafts using aluminum foil, tin cans, and wire.

745.592 **[Making] Toys, models, miniatures, related objects**

Class works including both manufactured and handmade toys and models in 688.

745.5928 [Making] Models and miniatures

Class here interdisciplinary works on handcrafted miniatures and models.

Class handcrafted miniatures and models of a specific subject as follows:

(1) Class in 700–779:

(a) if there is a specific number for the model, e.g., paper airplanes 745.592;

(b) if there is a specific number for the subject illustrated by the model, e.g., handcrafted miniature furniture 749.0228. Note that in this case s.s. 0228 is used to indicate the model;

(c) if there is no number for the model or the subject illustrated in 600–699. In this case the most specific number possible is chosen. *But see 3 immediately below.*

(2) Class in 600–699 if there is no specific number in 700–779, and

(a) if there is a specific number in 600–699 for the model, e.g., handcrafted model airplanes 629.133134;

(b) if there is a specific number for the subject illustrated by the model, e.g., handcrafted miniature reciprocating steam engines 621.1640228. In this case s.s. 0228 is used to indicate the model.

See also 1 c immediately above.

(3) Regardless of the above, class miniature and model educational exhibits, models for technical and professional use with the subject illustrated, e.g., handcrafted miniature anthropological exhibits 573.074. If no exhibit is involved use s.s. 0228.

Class assembly-line or mechanized manufacture of models and miniatures at 688.1.

745.61 **Decorative lettering**

Class penmanship at 652.1, typography in 686.22.

Treat calligraphy and artistic lettering as a unitary term.

745.67 **Illumination of manuscripts and books**

Illumination includes not only the manuscripts and books produced in medieval Europe, but Egyptian and Roman survivals from antiquity. In addition, Persian, Mogul, and Indian illuminations often labeled "miniatures" are considered painted illustrations or illuminations and are classed here rather than in 751.77.

Treat manuscripts and books as a unitary term.

Use s.s. 028 freely for techniques, procedures, apparatus, equipment, and materials, e.g., Persian techniques 745.67028.

745.924 Fruit and vegetable arrangements

Including carving of vegetables to produce artificial flowers.

746.04 **Specific materials [in textile arts and handicrafts]**

Class works here only if the emphasis is on the material being used and a wide range of products is being discussed.

Designing pictures with string is classed in 746.3 because a specific product results.

746.1–.9 **Products and processes [in the textile arts and handicrafts]**

Note that in the table of precedence here in Edition 19, product is preferred to process whether the product or the process of making it is being described. The number for a specific process is used only for general works on the process or if the process is being applied to a quite comprehensive group of products.

746.43 Knitting, crocheting, tatting

Class here comprehensive works on knitting and crocheting; do not follow the rule for first of two.

746.46 Patchwork and quilting

Class quilts at 746.97.

746.75 **[Rugs and carpets] Woven with pile**

This is the comprehensive number for Oriental rugs, and standard subdivisions (except s.s. 091–099) may be added for them; however, do not add standard subdivisions for rugs woven with a pile that are not Oriental, e.g., Finnish pile rugs 746.75.

746.94–.98 **Interior [textile] furnishings**

Treat each single product in this span as though it approximated the whole of the number in which it is classed, e.g., quilt patterns 746.97041, New England quilts on exhibition in New York City 746.97097407401471.

747   **Interior decoration**

Class here comprehensive works on interior decoration of residential buildings. Class interior decoration of specific types of residential buildings in 747.88, e.g., decorating for apartment living 747.88314.

Class works on interior design, broader than 747, in 729.

747.2   **Historical and geographical treatment |of interior decoration|**

Such treatment often is not explicit. For example, a work might be titled "Contemporary Interior Decoration," but if all the examples are British and the suggested sources for advice or buying are British, class at 747.22.

747.7   **Decoration of specific rooms of residential buildings**

All of the terms in the headings of the subdivisions of 747.7 may be considered unitary terms.

748.2   **Glassware**

Do not try to distinguish among blown, pressed, moulded, cast, or decorated glass. Treat these terms as unitary, e.g., a book on New Jersey pressed glass for collectors 748.29149075.

Class here glassware products of a specific company. Such a work may contain information about the company for the collector. However, if the focus of the book is on the organization and production of the company, it is classed at 338.76661.

748.5   **Stained, painted, leaded, mosaic glass**

Treat stained, painted, and leaded as a unitary term. Do not add standard subdivisions other than s.s. 028 as spelled out at 748.5 in Edition 19 for mosaic glass alone.

748.6   Methods of decoration |of glass|

Class artists using the methods in 748.29, e.g., English glass engravers 748.292.

748.82 |Glass| Bottles

Including bottles of interest to collectors regardless of original use. Class manufacture of glass bottles at 666.192.

749.21–.29   **Geographical treatment |of furniture and accessories|**

An individual furniture maker is classed according to his country only; but the work of a whole family or of a firm or school is classed by locality, e.g., the life and work of Thomas Chippendale 749.22, but Zoar (Ohio) furniture 749.217166.

749.4 Built-in furniture

See 729.9.

749.62 Heating [fixtures and furniture]

Including stoves.

749.63 Lighting [fixtures and furniture]

Class here comprehensive works on lighting fixtures and furniture, and works on glass lighting fixtures and furniture.

Class lighting fixtures and furniture (lamps and candlesticks) made of a specific material other than glass with the material, e.g., silver candlesticks 739.238.

750 Painting and paintings

SUMMARY

751 **Processes and forms**
752 **Color**
753 **Abstractions, symbolism, allegory, mythology, legend**
754 **Subjects of everyday life (Genre paintings)**
755 **Religion and religious symbolism**
756 **Historical events**
757 **Human figures and their parts**
758 **Other subjects**
759 **Historical and geographical treatment**

Class glass underpainting here unless the treatment is limited to decorative work. If so limited, class at 748.6.

Class at 750, using s.s. 0740 plus area notation, comprehensive exhibitions of paintings not limited geographically or by period of development, e.g., a comprehensive exhibition of paintings in Washington, D.C. 750.740153.

Observe the following table of precedence, e.g., the work of a single American landscape painter 759.13, but American landscape painting 758.10973:

Individual painters and their work	759.1–759.9
Collected painters and their works:	
Techniques, procedures, apparatus, equipment, materials	751.2–751.6
Iconography	753–758
Specific forms	751.7
Geographical treatment (except for comprehensive works on European art and Western art; in these cases prefer period)	759.1–759.9
Periods of development	759.01–759.07

751.77   [Painting] Miniatures

Class miniatures done as illuminations (illustrations) in manuscripts and books in 745.67.

752   Color

The technology of color is classed in 667. *See also discussion at 701.8.*

753–758   **Iconography**

See notes at 704.9 concerning the use of s.s. 07 and s.s. 09.

754   Subjects of everyday life (Genre paintings)

Limit the use of this number to works that are labeled "genre painting."

759   Historical and geographical treatment [of painting]

Class an exhibition of paintings not limited by place, period, or subject in 750.740 plus the area notation for the place of exhibition.

759.011 **[Painting by] Nonliterate peoples**

Add s.s. 091–099 for place to 759.011 and its subdivisions. If the work covers the painting of both nonliterate and modern cultures, class in 759.1–759.9.

See related discussion at 709.11.

759.02–.07 **[Treatment of painting by period]**

Class a work involving two periods in European painting with the first of the two periods. If more than two periods are covered, class the work at 759.94.

Class schools of painting associated with a specific locality in 759.1–759.9, e.g., the Florentine School of Italian painting 759.551. In the same manner, indicate painting being done in a specific situation, e.g., an exhibit in New York City of paintings by faculty and students of the Philadelphia College of Art 759.1481107401471.

759.2 [Painting of] British Isles   [Painting of] England

Note that for the purposes of classification, England, Scotland, and Northern Ireland are considered to be separate countries, and therefore the notation for an individual painter may be carried to this level. Wales may also be specifically shown. For example, Scottish painters are classed at 759.2911; English painters at 759.2; painters from Wales at 759.2929; from Northern Ireland at 759.2916.

760 Graphic arts   Printmaking and prints

SUMMARY

761   **Relief processes (Block printing)**
763   **Lithographic (Planographic) processes**
764   **Chromolithography and serigraphy**
765   **Metal engraving**
766   **Mezzotinting, aquatinting, related processes**
767   **Etching and drypoint**
769   **Prints**

For the purposes of the Dewey Decimal Classification, graphic arts is taken to mean any and all nonplastic representations on flat surfaces. Painting, drawing, prints, and photographs are included. Class here comprehensive works on the graphic arts so defined.

Including typewriter art, typographical designs, copy art made with photoduplication equipment.

Class here any combination of three or more of the graphic arts, e.g., paintings, drawings, and prints; paintings, drawings, and photographs.

Class here combinations of prints and at least one of the other graphic arts, e.g., painting and prints. Note that in combinations of two forms, one of them must be prints to be classed here. *For painting and drawing, see 741.9.*

Class a combination of graphic arts and sculpture or other plastic arts at 709.

760.75 |Collecting prints|

Do not use. Class collecting prints at 769.12.

761–767 **Printmaking**

Class works on commercial (manufacturing) use of these processes in 686.2.

761 Relief processes (Block printing)

Including rubber-stamp printing, raw potato printing.

764.8 Serigraphy (Silk-screen printing)

Serigraphy is screen process printing or screen printing and may be done in other ways than with silkscreen.

769.5 **Various specific forms of prints**

Class here the finished printed product only. Works on specific forms of prints treated as a medium of commercial art are classed in 741.6.

769.567 Postmarks, cancellations, cachets

Standard subdivisions may be added for any of these terms when treated separately.

769.92 Printmakers

Class here a printmaker who copies other artists, and the artist copied (if the emphasis is on him) if only prints made from this work are being discussed, e.g., prints after Gainsborough 769.924.

769.922 Collected printmakers

The first note at 769.922 in Edition 19 applies only when the printmakers are also from more than one period. Class a collection of works of printmakers from several geographic areas, but from one period in 769.901–769.905, e.g., 18th-century printmakers 769.9033. Note that "several geographic areas" in this note must be taken to mean "not limited by continent, country or locality."

770 Photography and photographs

SUMMARY

771 **Apparatus, equipment, materials**
772 **Metallic salt processes**
773 **Pigment processes of printing**
774 **Holography**
778 **Specific fields and special kinds of photography, and related activities**
779 **Photographs**

770.92 Photographers

Note that television and motion-picture photographers are not included. Class here a comprehensive combination of description, critical appraisal, biography, and the works themselves of a photographer. However, class the catalog of an exhibition in 779 (adding as instructed in Edition 19) even if some biographical and critical material is included.

Class cinematographers in 778.53092; television photographers in 778.59092; persons known for both cinematography and television photography in 778.5092.

771.31 Specific makes (brands) of cameras

Description and use.

Class a collection of various specific makes (brands) at 771.3.

772–774 **Special processes**

Most of these processes are of historical interest only, although there has been some recent revival of interest in them.

778.3 vs. **Special kinds of photography vs. Technological photography and photo-**
621.367 **optics**

Class in 778.3 works that emphasize techniques of producing the picture as an end in itself. Works that emphasize the engineering technology underlying the photography, or that emphasize application to scientific uses, are classed in 621.367. Class application to a specific field of science with the subject, e.g., to astronomy 522.63. If in doubt, prefer 778.3.

778.53 **Motion-picture photography (Cinematography) and editing**

Comprehensive works combining material on the techniques of motion-picture production (791.43) and cinematography (778.53) are classed in 791.43.

778.8   Special effects and trick photography

Further examples: techniques of composite photography and photomontage.

If a collage or montage combines photographs with other media, consider 702.812 techniques of collage.

778.9   **Photography of specific subjects**

Class here comprehensive works combining techniques of photographing, photographs of, and photographers of a specific subject, e.g., a history of fashion photography 778.99391. Class biography and critical appraisal of photographers in 770.92.

779   **Photographs**

The Decimal Classification Division adds both s.s. 0922 and s.s. 0924 directly to 779 and its subdivisions for collections of works. Class biographies of photographers in 770.92.

Add s.s. 091–099 to a general exhibition of photographs by artists from a specific place and to the result add s.s. 0740 plus area number from 708.1–708.9 in Edition 19 for the place where the exhibition is held.

780 Music

SUMMARY

781   **General principles and considerations**
782   **Dramatic music and production of musical drama**
783   **Sacred music**
784   **Voice and vocal music**
785   **Instrumental ensembles and their music**
786   **Keyboard instruments and their music**
787   **String instruments and their music**
788   **Wind instruments and their music**
789   **Percussion, mechanical, electrical instruments**

At all headings marked by an asterisk (*), the instructions are to be applied both to the entire heading and to the individual terms in the heading, e.g., at 788.62 *Clarinet and basset horn, apply the instruction to works discussing both the clarinet and the basset horn, the clarinet alone, and the basset horn alone.

Class all forms of incidental film, radio, and television music in 782.85–782.87, e.g., jazz film music 782.85, not 785.42.

780.08 vs. 790.2 |Music in| Relation to literature and other arts vs. The performing arts

Music is one of the performing arts. Class the performing arts as a whole at 790.2. To be classed at 780.08 the work must focus on music and its relation to the other arts. If in doubt, prefer 780.08.

780.42 Popular music

Most works on popular music are basically about popular songs and are classed in 784.5.

780.43 Art ("Classical") music

Most works purporting to be about "music" are really about "classical" music. Therefore, class here only works discussing why certain music is "classical." Class general works on art ("classical") music at 780.

780.729 **Historical and geographical treatment |of schools and courses|**

Period and area notations may be added for either secondary or higher education alone.

780.739 **Programs**

Here, programs means the actual programs given at concerts.

780.81–.84 |Scores and parts|

Class here only the scores and parts themselves. Class critical appraisal and description in 780.9.

Class scores and parts of a specific type of music with the type of music plus the notation for scores and parts (if any), e.g., the score of Georg Friedrich Händel's *The Messiah* (a sacred oratorio) 783.354.

Class the analysis of the scores and parts of a specific type of music with the type of music, plus s.s. 0924 if by an individual composer, e.g., the analysis of the score of *The Messiah* 783.30924. Note that 783.30924 is also the number for a work discussing Händel as the composer of the *The Messiah*.

See also 781.96.

780.901–.905 Periods of development of music, of European music

Even though the periods are those of Western music, this does not limit the use of these numbers to Western or European music only. Any time period of any music transcending ethnic or country limitations is classed here.

780.924   [Individual persons associated with music]

Class here thematic catalogs of individual composers. Class thematic catalogs in general at 780.216.

780.93–.99   Treatment [of music] by specific continents, countries, localities

The second note in Edition 19 requires that a distinction be made between music performed in a country and music composed or improvised in a country, e.g., 780.942 is used for music performed in England which may include such combinations as German, French, American, and English music; 781.742 is used for English music. English music performed in England is classed at 781.742.

781.5   Musical forms

A distinction must be made between a form of music and the music itself, e.g., the sonata as a form of music is classed at 781.52, a piano sonata at 786.41.

781.57 vs.   **Jazz and related [musical] forms** vs. Jazz [music]
   785.42

Class jazz as a form of music in 781.57. Class comprehensive works on jazz music in 785.42. If in doubt, prefer 785.42.

781.7   Music of ethnic groups and various specific countries and localities

Standard subdivisions may be added for folk music alone.

781.91   Musical instruments

Class here comprehensive works on instruments alone. Class specific instruments and their music in 786–789, specific kinds of music for the instruments with the kind of music, e.g., sacred music 783.

781.96   Words to be sung or recited with music

The words must be discussed in a musical context. Thus, if the words are presented as literature, folklore, religious text, class the work in 800, 398, 200 respectively.

Class here collections of words from several types of vocal music, analysis of these collections, or both.

Class the words for a specific type of vocal music, their analysis, or both, with the type of music plus the notation for words (if any), e.g., the libretto of Georg Friedrich Händel's *The Messiah*, a sacred oratorio, and its analysis 783.32. However, class works about the person or persons responsible for the words with the type of music plus s.s. 0924, e.g., works discussing Charles Jennens, Jr., as the arranger of the text of the Bible for *The Messiah* 783.30924.

Class the words and scores of a specific type of vocal music with the type of music plus the notation for scores and parts (if any), e.g., *The Messiah* (both libretto and score) 783.354.

Class the analysis of the words and scores, in general, of a specific type of vocal music with the type of music plus s.s. 09, e.g., English sacred oratorios 783.30942; the analysis of the works and scores by and works about the composer of a specific type of vocal music with the type of music plus s.s. 0924, e.g., the analysis of *The Messiah* (both libretto and score) and works discussing Georg Friedrich Händel as the composer of *The Messiah* 783.30924.

782   **Dramatic music and production of musical drama**

See 784.

782.028   Composition [of dramatic music]

The rhetoric of librettos and scenarios is classed at 808.06678. However, class here the fitting of librettos and scenarios to the music.

782.07   **Study, teaching, production, productions [of dramatic music]**

All aspects of the production of dramatic music, e.g., designing of costumes, are classed at 782.07, not in 791–792.

782.081–.082 Scores and parts [of dramatic music]

See 780.81–.84.

782.085   Librettos [of dramatic music]

See 781.96.

782.1   **Opera**

Class ballad operas in 782.81.

782.1092   **Persons associated with opera**

Class here biographies of singers known equally well as opera and recital singers. Class biographies of singers known primarily as recital singers in 784.3092.

Class here biographies of conductors known primarily as opera conductors. Class biographies of conductors known equally well for conducting operas and orchestral music in 785.092.

782.1094   [European opera]

Use this number for works that stress that they are discussing European opera in contrast to opera from all other sources.

782.12   Librettos [of operas]

Class the story and plot of the opera and analysis of the libretto at 782.13. *See also 781.96.*

782.15   Scores and parts [of operas]

See 780.81–.84.

782.8   **Theater music**

Class analysis of librettos with stories and plots using notation 3, e.g., analysis of the libretto of *The Mikado* (a Gilbert and Sullivan operetta) 782.813, not 782.812. *See also 780.81–.84, and 781.96.*

782.81   **Musical shows**

Class here television musicals, ballad operas.

Add as instructed under 782.8 in Edition 19 for operettas, musical comedies, revues, and film musicals even if only one form is discussed, e.g., the libretto of *My Fair Lady* 782.812.

782.832   [Librettos of incidental dramatic music]

The words of incidental dramatic music are classed here only if in a musical context. Otherwise, they are classed in 800.

782.85–.87   [Incidental film, radio, television music]

To be classed here, the music must be background or mood music.

See also 780.

782.85   Incidental film music

Class sound synchronization and scoring of motion pictures at 778.5344.

782.87	Incidental television music

Class sound synchronization and scoring of television programs at 778.59.

783   **Sacred music**

"Church music" usually means Christian church music and is classed in 783.026.

See also 784.

783.2   **Liturgical and ritualistic music**

Class texts used by a specific religion with the religion, e.g., liturgy and ritual of a Christian church 264. *See also 780.81–.84, and 781.96.*

783.21	Mass (Communion service)

After 1350 the composer usually wrote music only for the Common of the Mass; thus, masses written from 1350 to today are usually classed in 783.22. The major exception is the requiem mass, which is classed in 783.21.

783.3   **[Sacred] Oratorios**

Class comprehensive works on oratorios in 782.82.

See also 780.81–.84, and 781.96.

783.4   **Nonliturgical choral works**

Class here sacred cantatas. Class comprehensive works on cantatas in 782.82.

The subdivisions apply to individual forms, e.g., the libretto of an anthem 783.42. *See also 780.81–.84, and 781.96.*

783.5   **Nonliturgical chants**

The subdivisions may be added to individual forms, e.g., the score of an Anglican chant 783.554. *See also 780.81–.84, and 781.96.*

783.6	[Sacred] Songs

Apply the following criteria:

> If the song is called a carol, class it as a carol in 783.62–783.65.
>
> If the song is called a hymn, class it as a hymn in 783.9.
>
> Otherwise, class it as a song in 783.67.

See also 780.81–.84, and 781.96.

783.9	Hymns

See 783.6.

784   **Voice and vocal music**

Class here comprehensive works on vocal music. Class vocal dramatic music in 782, vocal sacred music in 783.

784.06 vs.   [Organizations and management of voice and vocal music] vs. [Col-
784.0922   lected persons associated with voice and vocal music]

Class an organizational history of a group of singers in 784.06. Class collective biography at 784.0922. If in doubt, prefer 784.0922.

784.0922   [Collected persons associated with voice and vocal music]

See 784.06 vs. 784.0922.

784.1–.7   **Specific kinds of vocal music**

See 780.81–.84, and 781.96.

784.3   **Songs for from one to nine parts**

The types of songs that are classed here are usually those types sung at recitals.

Class here lieder.

784.3092   **[Persons associated with songs for from one to nine parts]**

Class here biographies of singers known primarily as recital singers. Class biographies of singers known equally well as opera and recital singers in 782.1092.

784.68   [Songs] On specific subjects (Topical songs)

Class comprehensive works on protest songs at 784.6836123. Class protest songs on a specific topic with the topic in music, e.g., antiwar protest songs 784.6830366.

785.092   [Persons associated with instrumental ensembles and their music]

Class here biographies of conductors known equally well for conducting operas and orchestral music. Class biographies of conductors known primarily as opera conductors in 782.1092.

785.1–.8   **Specific kinds of [instrumental] music**

See 780.81–.84.

785.42   Jazz [music]

Class here comprehensive works on jazz.

Class a specific kind of jazz with the kind, e.g., jazz piano music 786.46.

See also 781.57 vs. 785.42.

785.420924 [Individual persons associated with jazz]

> Class here a band leader, a composer of all types of jazz, or both, e.g., Duke Ellington, composer and band leader, and Charlie Mingus, composer.
>
> Class here a musician associated with only one instrument but who is also a band leader, a composer of all types of jazz, or both, e.g., Jelly Roll Morton, a pianist, composer, and band leader.
>
> Class a musician associated with only one instrument (playing, composing for it, or both) with the instrument, e.g., Louis Armstrong (a trumpeter) 788.10924; John Coltrane (a saxophonist) 788.660924; Eddie Condon (a guitarist) 787.610924.

785.6 **Concertos**

> Standard subdivisions may be added for any of the three types of concertos, i.e., concerti grossi, concertos for solo instrument or instruments with orchestra or band, and concertos for orchestra.

785.66–.69 **Scores and parts [of concertos]**

> A peculiarity of the add note at this number should be taken into consideration. Following the first clause (directing the addition to 785.6 of the numbers following 78 in 786–789) is a second clause directing the addition of 0 plus the numbers following 5 in the table under 785.1–785.8. In 786–789, from which the digits to be added in the first clause are taken, there are also instructions for further addition. In this case the instructions in 786–789 are to be ignored, and the directions for further addition at 785.66–785.69 are to be used instead.

785.7 Chamber music

> Class here music for ensembles with only one instrument per part.
>
> Apply the following criteria:
>
>> If all of the instruments are the same kind, class the work with the instrument in 786–789, e.g., Brahms' *Sonata for two pianos in F Minor* 786.4957.
>>
>> If one of the instruments in the mixed ensemble is used for accompaniment only, class the work with the major instrument in 786–789, e.g., Bartok's *Violin Sonata* (in which a piano is used as accompaniment) 787.1542.
>>
>> If all of the instruments in the mixed ensemble are of equal importance, class the work in 785.7, e.g., Bartok's *First Sonata, violin and piano* 785.7271, Beethoven's *String Quartet in E Flat, No. 12* (for two violins, one viola, and one cello) 785.7471.

786–789 **Specific instruments and their music**

The headings for each instrument should be read as the instrument and its music, e.g., 788.2 should be read as Trombone and its music, and at 788.5 the note should be read as Including ocarina and its music. 786.2–786.223 and 786.6 are exceptions.

Add subdivisions for either the instrument or its modification by electronic means, e.g., at 787.61 the instruction may be applied if the work discusses the guitar or the electric guitar.

Apply the following criteria for classing the music of instruments and its analysis:

Class in 786–789 comprehensive works on music for an individual instrument or type of instrument, e.g., wind instruments and music written only for wind instruments 788.

Class the music for an individual instrument or type of instrument forming part of a work involving voice, other instruments, or both, with the complete work, e.g., music for the flute in Beethoven's *Symphony No. 5* 785.1154, the music for the solo clarinet in Mozart's *Clarinet Concerto* 785.686204. *See 785.7 for an exception.*

Apply the following criteria for classing musicians:

Class musicians associated with an instrument and its music, or with the music for the instrument, in the number for the instrument and its music plus s.s. 0924 (if possible), e.g., Isaac Stern (a violinist) 787.10924.

Class persons interested only in the instrument as such in the number for the instrument alone plus s.s. 0924 (if possible), e.g., Antonio Stradivari (a violin maker) 787.120924.

See also 780.81–.84.

787.01 Bowed instruments

Class chamber music in 785.7.

787.42 Viols and vielle

Class here viola da gamba.

790 Recreational and performing arts

SUMMARY

791 **Public performances**
792 **Theater (Stage presentations)**
793 **Indoor games and amusements**
794 **Indoor games of skill**
795 **Games of chance**
796 **Athletic and outdoor sports and games**
797 **Aquatic and air sports**
798 **Equestrian sports and animal racing**
799 **Fishing, hunting, shooting**

The original heading for 790 was Amusements. There are two ways of being amused: One can be entertained by others (791 and 792) or one can amuse oneself (793–799). The settings where one can be amused are two: indoors (793–795) and outdoors (796–799). As Dewey made the first number of each span the general number for the activity (i.e., 791, 793, 796), the classifier can usually expect to find in these numbers a broader spectrum of forms of entertainment or amusement.

During the past century participatory amusements have become entertainments as well. Where once golfers were accompanied by only a few individuals who wished to witness this novel recreation, now millions watch them in person or on television. The same is true of most sports. And some outdoor amusements, such as American football, are now played indoors occasionally. Consequently, technology and social values have so altered over the past century that while the location of a subject within the 790s is predictable and reasonable with respect to the original structure of the class, it is neither predictable nor reasonable in the light of modern practices and concepts.

Class here interdisciplinary works on recreation.

Class the sociology of recreation at 306.48.

790.068 Recreation centers

Class here general use. Performances at recreation centers are classed at 790.2.

The notation 068 is also used under specific sports in 793–799 for playing fields, courts, and similar facilities. These numbers are restricted to physical description only. Use is scattered throughout the specific topics under each sport.

790.133   Play with mechanical and scientific toys

Including electric trains, racing car sets, Erector® sets.

Class play with a specific mechanical or scientific toy with the toy, e.g., model airplanes 796.15.

790.134   Participation in contests

Including works on how to participate in and increase one's chances of winning in contests.

Class advertising by means of contests and lotteries at 659.17.

790.2   The performing arts

See 780.08 vs. 790.2.

791   **Public performances**

Broad works that include material in 791 (e.g., motion pictures, television, radio), 792 (stage), and 793 (indoor games and amusements) are classed here. Works that deal with the subjects of 791, 792, 793, 780 (music), and 796 (athletic and outdoor sports and games) are classed at 790.2.

Class the biography of a performer with the activity with which his career is chiefly identified, e.g., the biography of an opera singer 782.10924. If the person's career involves more than one kind of public performance with no particular predominance, class the biography with the activity that comes first in the following table of precedence:

music	780
dancing	793.3
stage other than musical	792
motion pictures	791.43
television	791.45
radio	791.44

For example, class the biography of a stage actor who has also done considerable work in television at 792.0280924. Activities listed in the table above take precedence over all other activities listed in 791.

Class here public performances given at fairs.

791.43 **Motion pictures**

Class here film censorship through editing. Class at 363.31 Censorship and control of information the type of censorship exercised after the film has been released; at 303.376 theories of censorship and sociological studies of film censorship.

Class here and in the appropriate subordinate numbers works combining subjects from 791.43 Motion pictures and 778.53 Motion picture photography unless the latter predominates.

While works describing or criticizing films are generally classed in 791.4372 and 791.4375, works in which the author's intent is to focus on some particular aspect of the film are classed in a number that expresses the aspect through the use of 791.430909 in accordance with the instructions at 791.4301–791.4309 in Edition 19, e.g., a work on westerns 791.4309093278.

Class motion-picture film as a physical medium of communication at 001.5532, motion-picture documentaries at 070.1.

791.433 Types of [motion-picture] presentation

Including puppet films. Class animation of puppet films at 741.58, photography of puppet films at 778.5347.

791.435 **Kinds of motion pictures**

Class here works on how a film is made if the work covers the whole production, not just the photography, which is classed separately in 778.5, or the direction, which is classed at 791.430233.

791.437 Description, critical appraisal, production scripts [of motion-picture films]

Apply the criteria given at 792.9.

791.4372– **[Description, critical appraisal, production scripts of single films and of**
.4375 **two or more films]**

Class here collections of film reviews. Note, however, that works about an actor, director, producer, or other persons associated with motion pictures, that contain descriptions or critical appraisals of the films with which the artist was involved, are classed in the biography number for the artist, e.g., the biography of a motion-picture photographer 778.50924.

Apply the criteria given at 792.9.

791.4375 [Description, critical appraisal, production scripts of] Two or more films

Apply the criteria given at 791.43.

791.44 **Radio**

Class here comprehensive works on radio and television, censorship through editing. Apply the criteria given at 791.43.

791.445 Kinds of [radio] programs

Including disc jockey programs.

791.447 Description, critical appraisal, production scripts [of radio programs]

Apply the criteria given at 792.9.

791.4475 [Description, critical appraisal, production scripts of] Two or more [radio] programs

Apply the criteria given at 791.43.

791.457 Description, critical appraisal, production scripts [of television programs]

Apply the criteria given at 792.9.

791.4575 [Description, critical appraisal, production scripts of] Two or more [television] programs

Apply the criteria given at 791.43.

791.53 **Puppetry**

Class puppet films at 791.433.

791.64 Cheerleading

Cheerleading here is defined as part of pageantry. This topic is divisible by type of sport, e.g., cheerleading for American professional football teams 791.64264.

791.8 **Animal performances**

Class here performing animals and all animal performances except those in circuses and sports.

792 **Theater (Stage presentations)**

Apply the criteria on censorship given at 791.43.

792.23 Comedy

Class comedy as an element in a specific kind of entertainment with the kind of entertainment, e.g., comedy in vaudeville 792.7.

792.7 Vaudeville, music hall, variety, cabaret, night club presentations

Including burlesque.

Standard subdivisions may be added for each topic in the heading.

792.80148 [Abbreviations and symbols for ballet]

Including choreology (Labanotation, Benesh).

792.9 **Description, critical appraisal, production scripts (stage guides) | of dramatic performances |**

The text of a play is classed in the appropriate number in literature, e.g., the text of Thornton Wilder's *Our Town* 812.52. A production script of *Our Town* is classed at 792.92. A production script is distinguished from a literary text in that it contains directions about the way the work is to be performed, i.e., where the furniture is to be placed, where the actors are to stand, and so on.

793.3 Dancing

Including belly, disco, and jazz dancing.

793.32 Theatrical dancing

Including modern dance.

Class here dance reviews.

793.73 **Puzzles and puzzle games**

Class puzzles as formal instructional devices for the teaching of a specific subject with the subject, using s.s. 07 as appropriate, e.g., puzzles teaching the use of the Bible 220.07.

793.735 Riddles

See 398.6.

793.9 Other indoor diversions

Including war games as recreation. Class war games for the purposes of training and development of military understanding at 355.48.

795.2 Roulette and other wheel and top games

Including pinball games and slot machines.

795.3 Games dependent on drawing numbers or counters

Including bingo.

795.4 **Card games**

Class here cardsharping.

Class gambling as a crime at 364.172.

795.41 |Card| Games based chiefly on skill

Including cribbage.

796 **Athletic and outdoor sports and games**

Class biography of sports personnel in the general number for the specific sport regardless of position played or type of game, e.g., a quarterback in American professional football 796.3320924, not 796.332250924 or 796.332640924.

796.15	Play with kites and similar devices
	Including flying model airplanes.
	Class play with other mechanical and scientific toys, e.g., electric trains, at 790.133.
796.2	Active games requiring equipment
	Including flying discs (Frisbees®), Yo-Yos®.
	Class play with building blocks at 793.9.
796.21	Roller skating
	Including skateboarding.
796.3	**Ball games**
	Class a semiprofessional sport with the professional sport, e.g., baseball 796.35764.
796.3527	Various specific [golf] games and matches
	Including masters tournaments.
796.41	Calisthenics
	Class acrobatics, tumbling, trampolining, and contortion at 796.47.
796.48	Olympic games
	Class paralympics and special olympics at 796.0196.
796.5	**Outdoor life**
	Class here works that include topics found under 797, 798, and 799; but class a specific activity with the subject, e.g., fishing 799.1.
	Class here orienteering.
796.51	Walking
	Class here walkers' guides if route details only are given. When description is given of things en route, class in 914–919.
796.522	[Walking and exploring in] Mountains, hills, rocks
	Standard subdivisions may be added for mountaineering alone.
796.54	Camping
	Including snow camping.
796.72	Automobile racing
	Class toy car racing at 790.133.
796.8	Combat sports
	Including stick fighting.

796.812   Wrestling

Including arm wrestling.

796.9   Ice and snow sports

Class snow camping in 796.54.

796.9627   Various specific [ice hockey] games

Class here the Stanley Cup playoffs.

797   Aquatic and air sports

Class comprehensive works on water safety in sports at 797.200289.

797.1   Boating

Including houseboating for recreation.

Class houseboats as dwellings at 643.2, seamanship for houseboats in 623.88.

797.14   Boat racing and regattas

Standard subdivisions may be added for any type of racing, e.g., yacht racing in Britain 791.140941.

797.200289   [Safety measures in swimming and diving]

Class here comprehensive works on the technical aspects of safety in water sports. Class technical aspects of boating safety at 797.10289, interdisciplinary works on water safety at 363.14.

797.5   Air sports

Including ballooning.

797.54   Stunt flying

Class here display aerobatics, e.g., the Blue Angels of the U.S. Navy 797.540973.

797.55   Gliding and soaring

Class here hang gliding.

798.2   **Horsemanship**

The cross reference in Edition 19 at 798.2 *"For horse racing, see 798.4"* means that horse racing is considered to be a part of 798.2 Horsemanship. Therefore, only works that discuss both riding and racing are classed here. Many works having "horsemanship" in their titles do not cover racing and are classed at 798.23.

798.23   Riding

Class here training of both horse and rider. Class training of the horse alone at 636.10888.

798.23079 |Riding competitions and awards|

      Do not use; class riding competitions at 798.24.

798.24   Riding exhibitions

      Class here riding competitions, e.g., three-day event.

799   **Fishing, hunting, shooting**

      Class the manufacture of both mass-produced and handcrafted equipment for sport fishing, hunting, and shooting in 688.79, e.g., artificial flies 688.7912.

799.1   **Fishing**

      Class here fishing for sport only.

      Class interdisciplinary works on fishing in 639.2.

799.2   **Hunting**

      Class here hunting for sport alone.

      Class interdisciplinary works on hunting in 639.1.

800 Literature (Belles-lettres)

In the following discussion, whenever application of principles to various specific literatures is being discussed, notations from Table 3 will be used. Thus —1 will be used to discuss poetry in specific literatures rather than making use of locutions like "811, 841, etc." or "811 and cognate numbers," or confusing devices like "8X1." In —8 Miscellaneous writings a difficulty arises in that notation for the literary period involved intervenes between —8 and its various subdivisions. When reference is made to this form it will be expressed as —8 + the notation for the subdivision, e.g., diaries —8 + 03.

Class interdisciplinary works on language and literature in 400; comprehensive works on the fine arts in 700.

Language

Literature always involves the use of language, and in the Dewey Decimal Classification, language is the basic facet for building numbers in 800.

Literary works are classed by language, not by country of origin. A major exception to this rule is that works in English originating in countries of the Western Hemisphere are classed in 810 and not in 820 with the rest of English literature.*

Class literary works in the language in which they were originally written. An English translation of a work originally written in Spanish is classed with Spanish literature in 860, not with English literature in 820.

Literature of two or more languages. Works embodying literature of two or more languages are usually collections of works of criticism. If two languages are involved, class the work in the number coming first in 810–890. If more than two languages are involved, class the work in the most specific number that will contain them all. For instance, class a work including English, German, and Dutch in 830 since these are all Germanic languages. Class a work involving English, French, and Russian in 808 for collections or 809 for criticism.

If any one language is strongly predominant, class with the language that predominates.

---

*Note that in certain instances country of origin can be indicated through the use of Table 3–A. *See Table 3–A: 93–99, and 800: Number building.*

Form

The second facet to be applied in literature is form. In literature there are two basic modes of expression: poetic and prosaic. The several forms of literature may be in one or the other of these modes:

—1 Poetry
—2 Drama
—3 Fiction
—4 Essays   } May be either prose or poetry
—5 Speeches
—6 Letters
—8 Miscellaneous writings: The epigram, even when poetic, is found here. All else is prose or nonliterary categories, such as diaries, journals, anecdotes.
—7 Satire and humor: Satire and humor are neither form nor mode, but rather categories of writing, marked, in the case of satire by ridicule and derision, in the case of humor by a manner of expression that makes a point amusingly. Literary works in a particular form (—1 to —8 above) exhibiting such qualities are always classed with the form.

Each of the major forms has subforms of various kinds. For instance, we have dramatic poetry, lyric poetry, and narrative poetry. In drama we have tragedy, comedy, and melodrama. In fiction we have science fiction, westerns, gothics, and historical fiction. For the purpose of this manual, these subforms will be designated by the word *kinds.*

Some kinds are further subdivided, e.g., among the kinds of lyric poetry are sonnets, odes, and ballads. These will be represented by the word *varieties.*

Forms are also divided in other ways. In drama we have divisions based on length, e.g., one-act plays, or number of characters, e.g., monologues. In fiction we have short stories, novellas, and novels. Such division will be designated by the word *scope.*

In drama there is a further complication: plays may be written for the stage, screen, television, or radio. This kind of division will be indicated by the word *media.*

The Dewey Decimal Classification holds that there is no mode or form of literature that cannot be hitched to the plow and made to perform useful work. This is most likely to be true of such forms as essays, speeches, letters, and diaries. Letters and diaries, if biographical in nature, are classed as biography; letters, speeches, and essays on a specific subject are classed with the subject, e.g., Jonathan Swift's *The Drapier's Letters* 332.49415, Lewis Thomas's *The Medusa and the Snail* 574.

Class as literature letters compiled from several authors to be read for enjoyment and for their literary value. Class a collection of the letters of individual authors as literature only if the collection has been published for a specific nonbiographical purpose, e.g., to exhibit the literary style of the writer. (Essays, speeches, and letters dealing with literary criticism are, of course, classed with the subject in literature.)

Less frequently, poetry, drama, and fiction also are used as vehicles for conveying factual information. Biographies have been written in verse, fiction has been employed to teach the fundamentals of mathematics. When so used these forms *may* be classed, not as literature, but with the subject with which they deal. Prefer 800 for poetry, drama, and fiction unless the form is purely incidental to the explanation of a specific subject, e.g., Harvey's *Circulation of the Blood* (written in Latin verse) 612.13, not 871.04.

However, an established literary work is classed as literature regardless of the content of the work, e.g., Hesiod's *Works and Days* is classed in 881.01, not 631, even though it deals with practical agriculture. (This is a "grandfather" provision, however. Henceforth (1981), newly established literary works whose major purpose is to inform will be classed with the subject treated.)

The nonfiction novel ("faction") is the classifier's platypus. This kind of novel uses the techiques of fiction writing to tell the story of actual people and actual events. Is such a work to be classed as fact or fiction? The following is suggested only as a guideline in the resolution of the question: Class an account of a true event or series of events using the names of the people involved, and not distorting facts to enhance an intended artistic effect, in the discipline appropriate to the nature of the facts described. Truman Capote's *In Cold Blood*, a true account of a multiple murder, has not been assigned a fiction number, but is classed at 364.1523, the criminology number for murder. If, however, the author uses conversations, reveals the feelings, thoughts, or states of mind of the people he is writing about, then he is actually treating them as fictional persons, and the work should be classed as fiction, e.g., Norman Mailer's *The Executioner's Song* 813.54.

Literary period

The third facet to be applied in literature is literary period. Period tables are supplied under the literature of every language where their use is recommended. They are to be used for the literature of the language in general and for the literature of the traditional homeland of that language. For instance, French poetry of the later 19th century and French poetry of France of the later 19th century are both 841.8.* The same periods are to be used for affiliated literatures (literatures in the same language, but from countries other than the traditional or principal user) if the affiliated literature emanates from the same continent. Thus Swiss French poetry of the later 19th century is also classed at 841.8.* Period is usually omitted if the literature emanates from a country on another continent, e.g., Canadian French poetry of the same period 841.† (Periods are sometimes provided for use with such a country if and when some special device is used to set such literature apart from the literature in general. *See options in Edition 19.*) Exceptions to this rule appear in the table below:

Use literary period	*Do not use literary period*
810 American English	
(Literature in English from the Western Hemisphere)	
Puerto Rico: U.S. periods	All other countries in the
Canada: Canadian periods 4 and 5	Western Hemisphere
820 English	
(Literature in English from the Eastern Hemisphere)	
Ireland: Great Britain periods	All other countries in the
Scotland: Great Britain periods	Eastern Hemisphere
Wales: Great Britain periods	

---

*Note that when more than one author is involved, s.s. 08 or 09 may be added plus notations 93–99 from Table 3–A to indicate national origin of affiliated literatures. *See Table 3–A 93–99.*

†Note that if more than one author is involved and there is no indication of period, s.s. 08 or 09 may be added plus notation 93–99 from Table 3–A to indicate national origin of affiliated literatures. *See Table 3–A 93–99.*

Other elements

Other elements that may be added where indicated are criticism, collections, and the various components listed in Table 3–A in Edition 19.

Authors

Language. Class an author with the language in which he writes.

Class an author who writes in more than one language with the language which he used last, e.g., Samuel Beckett 840. However, if another language is strongly predominant, class with that language. Individual works of such an author are classed with the language in which they were originally written.

An author who continues to write in the same language, but who changes his place of residence or national affiliation to a country using a different language is classed with the language in which he writes. For example, a novel in Russian by Solzhenitsyn is classed at 891.7344, even if the novel was written while the author was living in the United States.

An author who changes his national affiliation to a country using the same language as that in which he has been writing is classed as an author of the country of which he is now a citizen. Thus, T. S. Eliot is classed as a British author.

An author who changes his place of residence, but not his national affiliation, to another country using the same language as that in which he has been writing, continues to be classed as an author of his original country. Thus, a New Zealand author living in London, but still retaining New Zealand citizenship, is classed as a New Zealand author.

If information about these subtleties is not readily available in the work being classed, or in standard reference works, class the work according to the author's country of origin.

Form. Class an author with the form with which he is chiefly identified, e.g., Jane Austen 823.7. If the author is not chiefly identified with one specific form, use form —8 Miscellaneous writings from Table 3 in Edition 19 plus literary period plus notation 09 from the Table at —81–89. Thus an author who is equally famous as novelist, dramatist, and poet is classed (supposing him to be a late 20th-century English author) in 828.91409. (*See also 800: Form.*) An individual work of such an author, of course, is to be classed with the form exemplified by the work.

Literary periods. An author's literary period is determined in accordance with scholarly consensus about when an author flourished. In the absence of such consensus, and in those instances in which the classifier himself cannot determine when an author flourished, the date of the earliest publication, disregard magazine contributions, the mines the period number for his literary works. In ascertaining the date of the earliest publication, disregard magazine contributions, the isolated work of the author when a student, and juvenilia in general.

Biography. The number for the biography or autobiography of an author is determined by following the criteria given under Language, Form, and Literary periods immediately above. It is to be noted that s.s. 092 is not used in literature. Class literary reminiscences in —8 plus period plus subdivision 03, e.g., Hemingway's *A Moveable Feast* 818.5203.

Literary criticism

As used here the term "literary criticism" includes textual criticism.

The chief rule to be observed in classing criticism is that criticism is always classed with the work being criticized. Follow all the criteria given above for classing the original literary works.

Standard subdivision 09 History, description, critical appraisal is added to the number thus derived for criticism of all kinds of literature except criticism of the works of individual authors.

Thus, the criticism of a specific work is classed with the work, e.g., a critical analysis of Hemingway's *For Whom the Bell Tolls* is classed at 813.52, which is the same number as that assigned to the work itself.

A criticism of the work of an author in general is classed in the comprehensive number for the author in question, e.g., a criticism of Hemingway 813.52.

A criticism of fiction of the United States in general is classed at 813.009. Standard subdivision 09 has been added since more than one author is involved. A criticism of early 20th-century American fiction is classed at 813.5209.

A criticism of literature of the United States in general is classed at 810.9, a criticism of fiction from several literatures at 809.3, a criticism of several literatures as a whole at 809.

Criticism of criticism is classed with the criticism being criticized and hence with the original subject of criticism. A criticism of Hemingway is classed at 813.52. If a third person writes a criticism of the criticism of Hemingway, this also is classed at 813.52.

In the same way, if an author writes a criticism of American literature in general, this is classed at 810.9. If another author writes a criticism of this criticism, this also is classed at 810.9.

Class criticism of literature in a specific form from more than one literature in 809.1–809.7. Class in 801.95 the theory and technique of literary criticism. Class in these numbers also critical works in which the emphasis is on the various forms of literature as such, not on the various authors and literatures that may be used as examples. If in doubt between 801.95 and 809.1–809.7, prefer 809.1–809.7.

Works about critics are treated in much the same manner as works about other authors, i.e., the critic is classed with the kind and type of literature that he chiefly criticizes. Thus, a man who devoted the major part of his life to criticizing the works of Hemingway is classed at 813.52. A critic of Spanish literature is classed at 860.9.

It should be noted that criticism and critics are classed with the language of the literature they are criticizing, not with the language in which the criticism is written. For example, a French writer writing in French but criticizing American literature is classed in 810.

Appreciation of literature is classed in the same manner as other criticism.

Number building

The following flow charts are offered as an aid to building numbers and as a supplement to the detailed directions in Edition 19 at both 810–890 and at Table 3.

Flow chart for literature

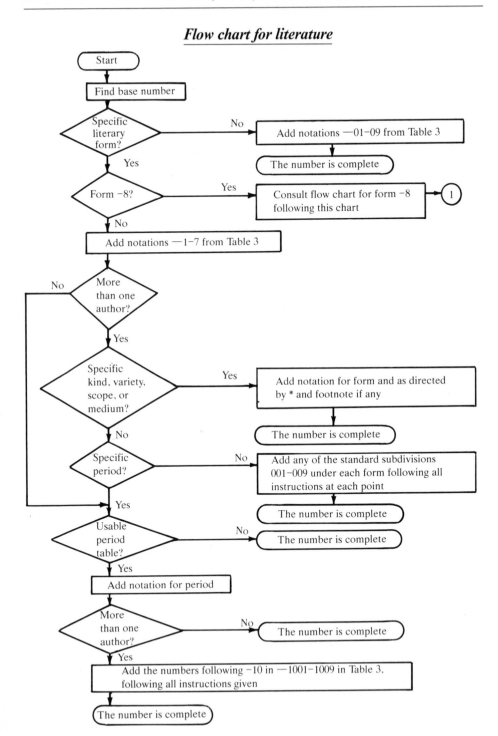

Flow chart for form –8

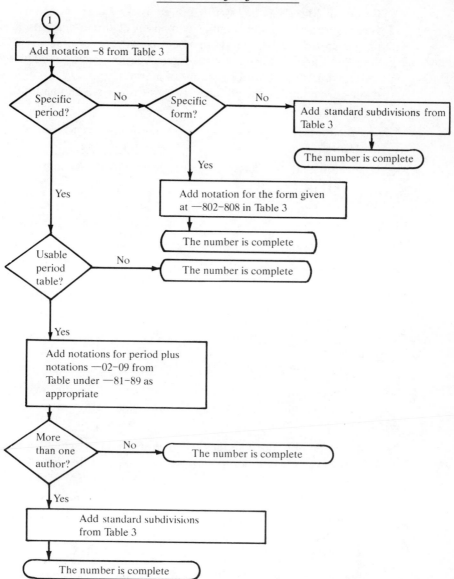

Examples of collections of two or more authors

Except in Miscellaneous writings —8, works by or about an individual author receive a number composed of three elements: base number, form number, period number. (However, authors from affiliated literatures are usually not assigned period numbers.) The following examples are for collections of literature.

(Note that numbers for criticism of these various combinations are parallel.)

One Literature (American),
One Form (Poetry)

1. Specific kind: Sonnets
   811.04208

2. Period: Later 20th century
   811.5408

   a. Specific themes and subjects: Later 20th-century poetry on urban life
   811.54080321732

   b. Specific elements: Narrative techniques in contemporary poetry
   811.5408023

   c. Specific qualities: Mythic motifs in contemporary poetry
   811.5408015

   d. For and by specific kinds of persons: Contemporary women poets
   811.540809287

3. Specific themes and subjects: Chivalry
   811.0080353

4. Specific elements: Description
   811.008022

5. Specific qualities: Romanticism
   811.0080145

6. For and by specific kinds of persons: Illinois poets
   811.00809773

Two or More Literatures,
One Form (Poetry)

1. Specific kind: Sonnets
   808.8142

2. Period: 18th century
   808.81033

   a. Specific themes and subjects: 18th-century poetry on urban life
   808.81932173209033

   b. Specific elements: Narrative techniques in 18th-century poetry
   808.8192309033

   c. Specific qualities: Mythic motifs in 18th-century poetry
   808.81915

   d. For and by specific kinds of persons: 18th-century women poets
   808.819928709033

3. Specific themes and subjects: Chivalry
   808.819353

4. Specific elements: Description
   808.81922

5. Specific qualities: Romanticism
   808.819145

6. For and by specific kinds of persons: Boy poets
   808.81992826

One Literature (American), *Two or More Forms*	*Two or More Literatures,* *Two or More Forms*
1. Specific themes and subjects: Seasons 810.8033	1. Specific themes and subjects: Seasons 808.8033
2. Specific elements: Plot 810.8024	2. Specific elements: Plot 808.8024
3. Specific qualities: Romanticism 810.80145	3. Specific qualities: Romanticism 808.80145
4. For and by specific kinds of persons: Children 810.809282	4. For and by specific kinds of persons: Children 808.899282
5. Period: Mid-19th century 810.8003	5. Period: 18th century 808.80033

Special problems

Folk literature. Folk literature consists of brief works in the oral tradition and is classed in 398.2. Whatever literary individuality the folk literature may once have had has been lost to the anonymity that the passage of time brings. Anonymous classics, however, are not considered to be folk literature. Despite the fact that their authorship is unknown, such works have a recognized literary merit, are almost always lengthy, and form a part of the literary canon. Therefore, they are classed in 800, e.g., *Chanson de Roland* 841.1, *Cantar del mio Cid* 861.1. Folk themes used in original works follow the general rules and are classed in literature, e.g., Mary Stewart's Merlin trilogy 823.914. *See also 398.2 vs. 800.*

Works about animals. Works about animals that constitute a contribution to the body of knowledge of some discipline other than literature are classed in the relevant discipline. Class animal stories in which the author's emphasis is on the habits and behavior of the animal in 590, on the care and training of the animal in 636. Class folklore of animals in 398.245.

Literary accounts of animals are classed with the appropriate form in literature, e.g., poetry. Such accounts may be either fictional or true. A book about animals is certainly fiction if it contains conversations or thoughts of animals. True accounts of animals are often in the form of anecdotes or personal reminiscences. Such accounts are usually accommodated in —8 Miscellaneous writings. They are to be classed, as appropriate, at —8 + 02 anecdotes, at —8 + 03 reminiscences, diaries, journals; or, if the mode of narration is so amorphous as not to allow the choice of a form or basic mode, at —8 + 07 Experimental and nonformalized works.

Adaptations. An adaptation may alter the form of a work or modify the content to such an extent in language, scope, or level of presentation that it can no longer be considered a version of the original. An adaptation is classed in the number appropriate to the adaptation, e.g., Lamb's *Tales from Shakespeare* 823.7. *For translations, see 800: Language.*

Note, however, that a prose translation of poetry (which is merely a change in mode) is not treated as an adaptation, e.g., Dante's *Divine Comedy* translated into German prose 851.1.

Visual novels. Visual novels (cartoon or comic strip novels) are classed in 741.5, if the story is coherent and obvious through the cartoons and is merely enhanced by the text. If the text is coherent without the illustrations, class the work in literature. If in doubt, prefer 741.5.

Illustrations. Class the illustrations of a work with the art form represented by the illustrations. If the illustrations merely accompany or enhance the text, class with the text.

Excerpts. Treat a collection of excerpts as a collection. However, if the collection is meant to serve as a model for studying another discipline, class with the discipline illustrated. For instance, class a collection meant to answer the question "What is a community?" at 307.

Nonliterary works. A literary study of nonliterary works is classed in 809, e.g., religious works as literature 809.9352, the Bible as literature 809.93522.

808.001–	**[Rhetoric]**
808.7	

Class textbooks for learning the fundamentals of the use of a language in 400, using lang. sub. 8 from Table 4. Class in 808 the application of these fundamentals to written and oral communication for the achievement of clarity and aesthetic pleasure. If in doubt as to the choice between the language number and 808, prefer 808.

Three elements combine to produce the finished piece of writing: composition, manuscript, and publishing:

(1) Composition (the putting of words together either in the author's head or on a more permanent record) 808.

How to write plays	808.2
How to write about music	808.06678
How to write about economics	808.06633

(2) Manuscript (the proper making of an organized record) 808.02.

(3) Publishing (disposal of the manuscript) 070.52. Class in 070.52 works limited to securing agents, submitting manuscripts, the relations of authors and publishers.

Works combining (2) and (3) are classed in 808.02 unless heavily weighted toward the publishing end:

How to make money in freelance writing	808.02
Where to market your manuscript	070.52

808.00141 [Literary aspects of communication]

See 001.51.

808.02 **Authorship and editorial techniques**

Class here style manuals.

808.0427 Study of rhetoric through critical reading

Readers used in the study of composition are classed here. Readers limited to a particular literary form are classed in the rhetoric number for the form, e.g., short stories 808.31. College readers in a subject field are classed with the subject.

808.04275 has been discontinued.

808.066   **Professional, technical, expository literature**

Note that language notations are added to the numbers for specific subjects to express how to write about a specific subject in a specific language. This does not mean the language in which the book in hand has been written. A book in any language on the subject of technical writing will usually be telling the user how to write on technical subjects. The number will be 808.0666. However, a book written in Spanish telling Spanish-speaking readers how to do technical writing in English is classed at 808.0666021.

808.1   Rhetoric of poetry

Because many studies of prosody are concerned with how to write poetry, general studies of literary prosody are classed here. However, works on the study of the prosody (for poetry) of a particular language are classed in the history and criticism number for the literature of that language or for the appropriate literature, e.g., a study of the use of language by American poets 811.009, by Japanese poets 895.61009. Studies of rhythm in the prose of literary writers is classed in —8 plus the period for the author.

Prosodic studies of a particular language as a whole from the linguist's point of view are classed at intonation for the specific language, e.g., 451.6 for prosodic studies of the Italian language. Linguistic studies of prosody across several languages and from the linguist's point of view are classed at 410.

808.5   **Rhetoric of speech**

Class here the art or technique of oral expression, including choice of words, rhythm, tone and pitch, inflection, and gesture.

808.83935213 [Collections of fiction about witches]

Class accounts of witches that are clearly not 398.22 folklore or 800 literature at 133.43.

808.839375   [Collections of fiction about ghosts]

Class accounts of ghosts that are clearly not 398.25 folklore or 800 literature at 133.1.

810   **American literature in English**

As English literature is the parent literature, works treating American and English literature equally are classed in 820.

900 General geography and history and their auxiliaries

History is a record of events, their causes and effects, and of the contemporary conditions that clarify and enrich these events. When a work is the story of events that have transpired or an account of the conditions that have prevailed in a particular place or region, it is classed in 900. When it is the history of a specific subject, it is classed in the appropriate discipline, e.g., a history of political developments (such as internal developments in government) without respect to their effect upon the larger society and place where they occur 320.9; of economic events in France 330.944; of warfare 355.009; of clocks 681.11309; of baseball 796.35709.

General history is the description and analysis of general developments in an area, region, or place such as a city, nation, continent, physical region (mountains), or socioeconomic region. Political history is a strong component of general history because it affects the whole of a particular society. But the history of political developments as they affect the internal activity of parties or other political groups is classed in 320.9 or in the 324 numbers for parties, campaigns, and election history. *See also 320.9 vs. 900.*

Until Edition 19 history was considered only retrospectively. Now it has been extended into the present (situation and conditions), but not the future (projected events). Class projected events at 303.49 Social forecasts.

Class interdisciplinary works on the geography and history of specific places in 930–990. The disciplines of geography and history have been separated in the Classification from its inception, even though in either discipline the focus is the place, whether continent, country, state, province, county, city, or town. In Edition 19 History 930–990 has taken to itself what had been parts of Geography 910, namely, archaeology and civilization, the latter being indicated in Edition 18 by 91 plus the area number for the place discussed plus 03 for civilization plus period. What remains in geography are historical geography, atlases and maps, physical geography, travel, and travel descriptions associated with particular places.

Note that position on the map rather than political affiliation usually determines the number assigned to the history or the geography of a particular place, for while political affiliation may change, position on the earth's surface does not.

Citation order

The citation order in the 900s, when all conditions are met, is straightforward:

> *History:* 9 + place + period + standard subdivision, e.g., a dictionary of the history of Jalisco state (Mexico) during the 20th century: 972.350803.

> *Geography:* 91 + place + type of geography (physical, travel, or regional) + period + standard subdivision, e.g., a dictionary of travel in Italy today: 914.50492803.

Classification of specific events

Specific events are usually classed with the history of the discipline to which they relate. The history of a transportation accident is classed in 363, e.g., the sinking of the Titanic 363.123091631. The history of a crime is classed in 364, e.g., the Whitechapel murders committed by Jack the Ripper 364.1523. A sporting accident is classed in 796–799, e.g., a fatal accident during an automobile race 796.72.

(It should be noted that the disciplines to which specific events are related are usually the social sciences. Events are seldom technological in nature.)

If the specific event was important enough to affect the general social life and history of the place where it occurred, it is classed with the history of that place regardless of any other discipline involved. The sinking of the Lusitania is classed at 940.4514, the assassination of Abraham Lincoln at 973.7, the San Francisco earthquake at 979.461051.

In applying any of the above, the classifier should take into account the author's purpose or point of view. For instance, a work about the assassination of John F. Kennedy that is focused on the modus operandi of the crime, the detective work involved in solving it, or both, is classed at 364.1524 and not at 973.922.

If safety factors are stressed, the work is classed in 363.1 or 363.3 and their subdivisions and not with any other discipline involved. A study of the wreck of the Andrea Doria to determine what the causes of the accident were, what preventive measures might be mandated by the incident, is classed at 363.12365.

Collected accounts of events are treated in the same manner, provided that they all pertain to one discipline. Class collected events without such focus in 904. *See also the discussion at 910.453.*

904   **Collected accounts of specific events**

Class here collections of events not connected with a specific subject.

Class collections of such events related to a specific period but not limited to a specific area or region in 909.07–909.08 and 909.1–909.83.

Class collections of such events in specific areas in 930–990.

See also 900: Classification of specific events.

904.7   Events induced by human activity

Including collections of mutinies, and pirates' expeditions when not limited to a specific area or region. Class in 909.09 a work about one or more such events in a specific region as found under area notation 16 in Table 2.

907.202   **Historians and historiographers**

For historians and historiographers do not follow the directions under standard subdivisions 07201–09 in Table 1 that state ". . . however, class persons in −092." Class the biography of an individual historiographer writing on world history, no matter where he lives, at 907.2024, not 909.2, which has been preempted for other uses. Class collected biographies of historiographers at 907.2022. Class biographies of historiographers writing on a specific area, not limited to one historical period, in 930–990, using s.s. 07202, e.g., the biography of a historiographer writing about U.S. history 973.072024. But if a historical period is added, use s.s. 092 as instructed in Table 1 at s.s. 07201–09, e.g., the biography of a historiographer writing on the U.S. Revolutionary War, 1775–1789 973.30924, not 973.3072024.

Class the biography of other persons in the appropriate subdivisions of 909.09 or 930–990.

909   **General world history**

Class here a chronological series of events.

Class collected accounts of specific events not limited by a specific period, area, or region or by a specific subject in 904.

See also 910 vs. 909 and 930–990.

909.07–.08   **[General world history ca. 500–   ]**

Class here general histories, covering more than two continents (or more than two countries if not on the same continent), during the historical periods of 500–1450/1500 and 1450/1500 to the present time.

Class specific periods in 909.1–909.8. Class the Crusades at 909.07. Class history of Europe during the period of the Crusades in 940.18.

909.09   [General world history of] Areas, regions, places in general

See 909.

909.1–.8   **[General world history by period]**

Class here works about world's fairs that provide exhibits from many countries and that are not confined to any one subject or discipline. Class fairs covering a specific area with the specific area, using s.s. 074 exhibits from Table 1 if applicable. If the work is about fairs whose exhibits are related to a specific discipline, class with the specific discipline, using s.s. 074 if applicable. Class technology exhibits in 607.34.

910 General geography   Travel

SUMMARY

911 Historical geography
912 Graphic representations of surface of earth
     and of extraterrestrial worlds
913 Geography of and travel in ancient world
914 Geography of and travel in Europe
915 Geography of and travel in Asia
916 Geography of and travel in Africa
917 Geography of and travel in North America
918 Geography of and travel in South America
919 Geography of and travel in other parts of
     world and extraterrestrial worlds

In geography are included the description and analysis of the earth's surface not limited to a single discipline or subject, and, by extension, the description and analysis of other worlds. Class geographical treatment of a specific discipline or subject with the discipline or subject, e.g., religion 200.9, geomorphology 551.409, the fine arts 709.

**910 vs.
909 and
930–990**

[**General geography and travel**] **vs.** [**General history**]

If a work deals with both physical geography or travel, and civilization, class it in 909 or 930–990, unless the treatment of physical geography or travel is predominant. If in doubt whether to class a work in 910 or either 909 or 930–990, prefer 909 or 930–990. If the work deals with the description of the physical earth only, class it in 910.02 or in 913–919, using notation 02 from the tables at 913.1–913.9 and 914–919 in Edition 19.

910.014

Languages (Terminology) [**of general geography**]

Class here works containing geographical place names as such, i.e., dealing with the origin, history, meaning of the names.

For geographical dictionaries, see 910.3.

910.02

The earth (Physical geography)

For a discussion of the distinction between physical geography and geology, see 551 vs. 910.02.

910.091636

[**Geography of and travel in Southwest Atlantic**]

Class the Bermuda Triangle mystery at 001.94.

910.202   World travel guides

Class here guide books and tour books providing tourists updated information about places in many areas of the globe: how to travel, what to see, where to stay, how to plan a vacation.

Class guides to areas, regions, or places in general in 910.09, to specific continents, countries, and localities in 913–919, using notation 04 from the tables at 913.1–913.9 and 914–919 in Edition 19.

910.222   Pictures and designs [in general geography]

Including aerial photographs not limited to one specific area or region.

910.3   **Dictionaries, encyclopedias, concordances, gazetteers**

Class here works containing geographical names in alphabetical order, giving geographical information about each place, e.g., *Webster's Geographical Dictionary* 910.321. Such works commonly contain some historical material. If the historical material predominates, class in 909, 930–990.

Class similar works not arranged in alphabetical order at 910; works discussing various place names as names at 910.014.

910.4   **Accounts of travel**

Class travel in areas, regions, or places in general in 910.09, travel in specific areas in 913–919, using notation 04 from the tables at 913.1–913.9 and 914–919 in Edition 19; collections of ocean trips in 910.45. Class guides as instructed at 910.202. Class travel accounts that emphasize the analysis or description of the civilization of the country visited in 930–990, e.g., travels of Marco Polo 950.2.

Standard subdivisions 0922–0924 from Table 1 can be added to 910.4–910.45 for works dealing with description, biography, or autobiography of travelers. Class in 910.922 and 910.924 works about geographers or explorers whose trips were intended to enlarge geographic knowledge.

Do not use s.s. 092 for first person accounts of travel.

910.41   Trips around the world

Including ocean and sea trips around the world.

910.45   Ocean travel and seafaring life

Class ocean trips around the world in 910.41.

910.453   Collected voyages of adventure

This number should be used with extreme caution. If in any doubt whatever whether the event in question is an adventure, class it elsewhere, e.g., shipwrecks 363.123.

910.92   Geographers, travelers, explorers regardless of country of origin

Works classed here must deal with the growth of geographic knowledge and not be limited to any one specific area or region. Class biographies of those who travel for pleasure in 910.4–910.45, using s.s. 092.

910.93–.99   Discovery and exploration by specific countries

Examples: exploration by the United States in general 910.973; exploration by the United States in tropical regions 910.0913; exploration by the United States in Antarctica 919.8904; British explorations in Africa in 19th century 916.0423; British explorations in North America (considered as part of the history of North America) 970.017.

911   Historical geography

Class here maps explaining wars.

See also 320.12 vs. 911.

912.1   [Graphic representations of] Specific subjects, and regions in general

Class maps explaining wars in 911.

912.1001–   [Graphic representations of] Specific subjects
.1899

Note that here subject takes precedence over location, i.e., use these numbers before 912.19 or 912.3–912.9, e.g., maps of fine arts centers in France 912.17084, not 912.44.

Do not class tax and real estate maps, land atlases of counties here. Class these in 912.3–912.9. *See 912.3–.9.*

Do not class tidal atlases here. Treat them as nautical charts and class them in 623.89209.

Class soil surveys in 631.47.

912.122   [Graphic representations of Biblical areas]

Class general geography of Biblical areas in 220.91.

912.3–.9 [Graphic representations of] Specific continents, countries, localities; extraterrestrial worlds

> Class here tax and real estate maps, and land atlases of counties, e.g., *Tax Maps of Du Page County, Illinois* 912.77324; *Dolph's Land Atlas of Broward County, Florida* 912.75935; *Atlas of Delaware County, Pennsylvania, Containing Nineteen Maps Exhibiting the Early Grants and Patents* 912.74814.

913 **Geography of and travel in ancient world**

> *See 914–919: Add table.* Meaning of the subdivisions is substantially the same as those of the zero subdivisions of 913.

913.1–.9 **[Geography of and travel in specific] Continents, countries, localities [in ancient world]**

Add table

> *See 914–919: Add table. The meaning of the subdivisions is substantially the same.*

914–919 **Geography of and travel in specific continents, countries, localities in modern world; extraterrestrial worlds**

> Class here photographs limited by place.

> Class description and portrayal of man's situation, way of life, culture, civilization, and total customs in a given place in 930–990. Class a specific aspect with the subject, e.g., marriage customs in Japan 392.50952, travel in Arizona to gather geological data 557.91. *See also 910.*

Historic buildings and houses

Except as discussed below, class here works describing historic houses and other historic buildings (and parts thereof) designed for the use of visitors to the sites whether or not the works are designated specifically as guides. Do not use subdivision 04 from the add table for such guides if they do not approximate the whole of the area in which they are located.

Class historic buildings that have become museums in one of the following ways:

(1) If the museum is associated with the life of an individual, class the guide in the biography number for that person, e.g., the home of Thomas Wolfe in Asheville, North Carolina 813.52.

(2) If the museum is associated with the history of a place, class with the appropriate number in 940–990, using s.s. 074 if applicable, e.g., a museum of Canadian history in Windsor, Ontario 971.0074011332.

(3) If the building is still in use for a specific purpose, class guides to it with the subject, e.g., a guide to the New York Stock Exchange building 332.64273. Churches do not follow this rule but are classed in 914–919.

Class architecture in 720, interior decoration in 747.

Add table

s.s. 0014   **[Languages (Terminology)]**

Class here place names. Apply to specific areas the principles stated at 910.014.

s.s. 003   **[Dictionaries, encyclopedias, concordances, gazetteers]**

Apply to specific areas the principles stated at 910.3.

s.s. 0092   **[Persons connected with general geography]**

Do not use. Class in base number. *See 919–914: Add table 04: Biography.*

02   The earth (Physical geography)

Physical geography is the description of the earth, its land, air, water, and whatever lives on or in them; but not people and their civilization.

See also 551 vs. 910.02.

04   Travel

Use this subdivision for accounts of travel. Such accounts should contain such things as events of the trip, places stopped at, accommodations, modes of transportation. If the work is purely a description of the area visited, with none, or very few, of these accompaniments, use subdivision 02 for physical geography, or class the work in 930–990 for civilization and social conditions of the place visited, as the case may be. Works of a person who has lived for several years in the area described are usually classed in 930–990.

Travel does not normally cover the whole of any given area. Class accounts according to the widest span covered, e.g., travel from New York to San Francisco 917.304, from Marseilles to Paris 914.404, from New York City to Buffalo, New York 917.4704. Standard subdivisions may be added to such numbers.

Class accounts of modern travelers traveling through ancient areas in the corresponding modern area numbers in 914–919, e.g., modern travels through Bible lands 915.6904.

Discovery and exploration

Use 04 for works describing excursions into previously unknown or little known areas, e.g., the Lewis and Clark expedition 917.8042, Byrd's expedition to the South Pole 919.8904. However, if the initial exploration of a place forms an important part of its early history, class the work in 930–990, e.g., early exploration of North America 970.01.

Class accounts of archaeological expeditions in 930.1.

Guidebooks

Guidebooks are books providing tourists and travelers with detailed information about the area through which they travel, telling them what to see, where to stay, and where to dine. However, if the lodging and dining are the only topics treated in the guidebook, class it in 647.94–647.95.

Class contemporary guidebooks to ancient areas in 913, e.g., Pausanias' guide to Attica 913.85049. Class modern guidebooks to ancient areas in the corresponding modern area numbers in 914–919, e.g., 1982 Fodor's guide to the ruins of Rome 914.563204928.

Class guidebooks emphasizing a specific subject in 914–919, not with the subject, e.g., a guidebook to holy places in Spain 914.604, not 263.042.

Class a guide for persons moving to another country on a permanent basis in 940–990.

See also 914–919: Historic buildings and houses.

Biography

Standard subdivision 092 is added to subdivision 04 for biographies of discoverers, explorers, and travelers, but not for general geographers nor for first-person accounts of travel. Class biographies of general geographers in the base number for the area without further subdivision. Add 04 for first-person accounts of travel, but not 0924.

920 General biography, genealogy, insignia

929.1   Genealogy

This is the comprehensive number for works providing information about genealogy itself: what it is, where to go to find genealogical records, what to look for, what sources to use, how to obtain these sources, how to trace family trees.

Class family histories at 929.2, the genealogical sources themselves in 929.3.

929.1028   [Techniques, procedures, apparatus, equipment, materials of genealogy]

Do not use. Class genealogical techniques and procedures in base number or in 929.1072. (*See 929.1072.*) Class equipment, apparatus, and materials, insofar as these are applicable to genealogy, in 929.3.

929.1072   [Research in genealogy]

Class here the techniques and procedures involved in doing genealogical research only if it is necessary to bring out the special features of doing research in genealogy in a specific area. Add area notations as instructed at s.s. 07201–09 in Edition 19, e.g., doing genealogical research in Virginia 929.10720755.

Class comprehensive works on genealogical research at 929.1 without further subdivision.

929.1094–   [Historical and geographical treatment of genealogy in specific con-
.1099   tinents, countries, localities in modern world]

Do not use. Class treatment of genealogy by area in 929.1072. *See 929.1072.*

929.2   Family histories

Inasmuch as families move around and disperse, the area number selected for a family history should not be too specific. Use s.s. 09 plus area notation for the country in which the family lives, but not for a specific state, province, area, or locality. For example, class the history of a Florida family at 929.20973, not 929.209759.

Class a family history with the country in which the family presently lives, not with the country from which the family's ancestors came. For example, class the Duponts, a U.S. family of French origin, at 929.20973, not 929.20944.

Class a family history emphasizing the contributions of its members to a specific occupation with the subject, e.g., the Rothschilds as a family of bankers 332.10922.

Class the history of a royal family in 929.7.

Class the family history of a prominent person that contains material about the person's life with the biography number for the person, e.g., the forebears, family, and life of Winston Churchill 941.0820924.

Class a history of the families in a specific area with the history of the area if the work also gives some historical information about the area itself, e.g., prominent families in New York City 974.71.

Class the techniques of compiling a family history at 929.1.

929.3   **Genealogical sources**

Class here the sources themselves as listed in the first note at 929.3 in Edition 19 and guides to them. However, if the work consists largely of instructions on the use of the sources, class it at 929.1.

Class here census material published by a genealogical agency or by an individual person. Class census material published by an agency of government in 312.

Standard subdivisions and areas may be added for any source considered separately, e.g., wills of Orange County, North Carolina 929.3756565.

929.44   Forenames

Including lists of names for the newborn.

Class names of ships, houses, and pets at 929.97.

929.6   Heraldry

Class at this number works dealing with family coats of arms.

Class other coats of arms at 929.82.

929.7   **Royal houses, peerage, gentry, orders of knighthood**

Class here the history and genealogy of royal families. However, if the work includes general historical events or biographies of members of the royal families, class the work in 930–990.

Class other family histories here only if they emphasize the tracing of rank. If in doubt, class family history at 929.2.

Class here works emphasizing lineage or descent with respect to royalty, the peerage, or gentry, e.g., *Burke's Peerage* 929.72, *Virginians of Gentle Birth* 929.7999755; genealogies tracing or establishing a particular title.

929.81   Awards, orders, decorations

Standard subdivisions may be added for either orders or decorations considered alone.

929.82   Armorial bearings

Class at this number armorial bearings that are not used by families, i.e., coats of arms that are used by such organizations as church groups, fraternities and sororities, and by some countries (such as the Great Seal of the United States).

Standard subdivisions may be added to this number for works treating coats of arms, crests, or seals separately.

930–990　　　**General history of ancient world, of specific continents, countries, localities; of extraterrestrial worlds**

Follow the directions for the addition of historical periods found under centered entry 930–990 for areas that are part of a larger jurisdiction, even though the historical periods are not spelled out in the history schedule for the smaller areas, e.g., Ulster during the reign of the Tudors 941.605, not 941.6. Add historical periods to specific areas only if the area was part of the larger jurisdiction during the period covered, e.g., Gibraltar 1550–1600 946.8904; but Gibraltar 1950–1970 946.89, not 946.89082.

When adding standard subdivisions to the historical periods in 01–09 use the notations found in Table 1, not those in 001–009 under 930–990.

Note that s.s. 009 takes precedence over period, e.g., rural regions of England in the 19th century 942.009734, not 942.081.

Class historians and historiographers (s.s. 007202) as instructed at 907.202.

See also 720.9 vs. 930–990, 910 vs. 909, and 930–990.

Historic preservation

Class comprehensive works on historic preservation and lists of preservation projects to be undertaken at 363.69. However, if such a list is primarily devoted to inventorying or describing the sites, class in the appropriate number in 930–990, or, if primarily a description of buildings at the site, class in 720.

Class administrative annual reports of an agency in charge of the preservation of historical sites at 351.859 and cognate numbers in 353–354 or, if local, at 352.9459.

Class historic preservation in an architectural context at 720.288 and at numbers throughout 721–729 marked by an asterisk, adding s.s. 0288.

Racial, ethnic, national groups

Class general history of a racial, ethnic, or national group in 909.04, e.g., a world history of black people of African origin 909.0496.

Class the general history of an ethnic group in a specific place with the history of the place using the notation 004 plus the number for the ethnic group in Table 5 as spelled out at centered entry 930–990 in Edition 19. Do not use the history period notations at 01–09 when 004 is used, e.g., general history of Afro-Americans in North Carolina, 1830–1855 975.600496073, not 975.6030496073.

DO NOT ADD S.S. 089 TO ANY NUMBERS IN 930–990.

Note that these instructions apply only to general history. Works on an ethnic group in relation to a specific subject are classed with the subject, e.g., sociological studies of Afro-American life styles 305.896073, not 973.0496073. If the work is on the relation of the state to a specific ethnic group, class it in 323.11, e.g., the relation of the state to Afro-Americans in Louisiana 323.11960730763.

For history and civilization of American native races, see 970: Native races.

Wars

In most instances, class the history of a war with the history of the country in which most of the fighting took place, e.g., the Vietnam War 959.7043. Class specific battles or actions in a war in the number for the war, not with the place where the action occurred, e.g., air raids on Tokyo in World War 2 940.5425, not 952.135033.

The Spanish-American War is an exception to the above rule. Class a battle occurring in the Philippines during this war at 973.8937, not 959.9031.

Wars extending over more than one continent (the Crusades, for example), are classed in 909. However, since it is often impossible to know at the beginning of a war where most of the fighting will take place, or how many countries will be involved, incorrect numbers have been assigned to some wars that began in the lifetime of the DDC. For example, World Wars 1 and 2 are classed in 940 instead of 909.

Class history of a subordinate area of a country during a war with the number for the area, not with the war, e.g., history of Maryland during the Civil War 975.203, not 973.709752. However, class the area's participation in the war with the war, e.g., Maryland's participation in the Civil War 973.709752, not 975.203.

Military history as it affects the place in which the military action took place is classed with the history of the place.

Class collected accounts of battles from various wars and places at 904.7.

Class the sociology of war at 303.66, the sociology of military institutions at 306.27, social factors affecting war at 355.022, social causes of war at 355.0274.

See also 355.009 vs. 900.

Prison, internment, and concentration camps. Class prisoner-of-war camps and internment camps in World War 1 in 940.472, in World War 2 in 940.5472. To be classed in these numbers the camps must be connected with the course and conduct of the war. Note that area notations are to be added for the country maintaining the camp, not for the area in which the camp was located. However, a second set of area notations may be added to each of these numbers through the use of s.s. 09 to express the area in which the camp was located. For example, Japanese camps in the Philippines are classed at 940.54725209599. Do not add the second standard subdivision for a camp maintained by a country in its own territory, e.g., United States camps in the United States 940.547273, not 940.5472730973.

Class interdisciplinary works on concentration camps at 365.45. Class at this number also camps used by a country for the internment of certain of its own citizens, e.g., internment camps maintained by the United States for Japanese Americans in World War 2 365.450973.

Class concentration camps maintained by Germany during World War 2 for the extermination of Jews and other ethnic groups at 940.531503924.

Occupied countries. The history of the occupation of a country during time of war is classed in the appropriate subdivision of the number for the war, e.g., occupation of countries in World War 2 940.5336. Military administration of the government of an occupied country during or following the war is classed at 355.49. International law with respect to occupation is classed at 341.66.

History of specific units in a war. Class history of specific military units in a war in the numbers for military units under history of the particular war, e.g., military units in World War 1 940.412–940.413. If there is no specific number for military units, class a work on military units in the number for military operations, e.g., military units in the Vietnam War 959.70434.

Class comprehensive works on military units and military units in peacetime at 355.31 and cognate numbers in 355–359.

Personal narratives. Class the personal narratives of participants in a war in the appropriate subdivision of the history numbers for the specific war, e.g., personal narratives of American soldiers in World War 2 940.548173. Class narratives that focus on a specific campaign, battle, or other subject with the subject, e.g., a personal account of the Battle of Berlin 940.5421, of Axis intelligence operations in World War 2 940.5487.

The narrative of a person's experiences during the time of a war, if it does not focus on the war as such, is classed as biography and not in the number for the war.

930 General history of ancient world to ca. 499

930.1   **Archaeology**

Class here interdisciplinary works on archaeology. Class industrial archaeology in 609, archaeology of specific areas in 931–999.

Class works dealing primarily with the artistic values of archaeological objects in 700.

931–939   **[General history of] Specific places [in ancient world]**

Class here archaeology of specific places in the ancient world, i.e., archaeology of those places and areas listed in area 3 from Table 2. Class archaeology of ancient places that do not have such numbers in 940–999, e.g., archaeology of ancient North America 970.01, of ancient Australia 994.01.

See also —3 vs. —4–9 in Table 2. Areas.

940 General history of Europe   Western Europe

940.541   [Military] Operations [in World War 2]

Class here operations in three or more theaters; do not class in 940.542.

940.542   Campaigns and battles [of World War 2] by theater

See 940.541.

941   [History of the] British Isles

Class here works on the United Kingdom (England, Wales, Scotland, and Northern Ireland), a political entity, and on Great Britain (England, Wales, and Scotland), a geographical entity. Class in 942 only works dealing with England alone, or with England and Wales. Histories of the period since 1603 (or including this period) will seldom deal with England or England and Wales alone. Histories of the period before 1603 may deal with England or England and Wales alone. Books on the civilization of this area may deal with any combination. The following combinations of two areas will be classed in 941: England and Scotland, England and Ireland, Ireland and Wales.

970 General history of North America

Native races

The principal fact to keep in mind in assigning class numbers to works on the various native American races is that the various tribes and groups of tribes have moved in the course of time from place to place and that these places are often widely scattered.

Therefore, in general, a work on a specific tribe or group of tribes is classed in 970.00497, no attempt being made to assign a more specific location. Examples follow:

Cherokee Indians	970.00497
Algonquin Indians	970.00497
Sioux Indians	970.00497
Plains Indians	970.00497

If, however, the focus of the work is clearly on the Indians in a specific place, use the number for the specific area plus 00497:

Native races of Canada	971.00497
Cherokee Indians in North Carolina	975.600497
Native races of the Great Plains	978.00497

If a prehistoric period is involved, class the work with the period and do not use 00497:

Mayas of Middle America before 1500	972.01
Native tribes of United States before 1492	973.1
Native tribes of North America before 1492	970.01

Class a work on American native races in a specific war with the history of the war, e.g., the Sioux War of 1876 973.82.

Class biography with the tribe or group of tribes to which the person or persons belong.

973.36   Celebrations, commemorations, memorials [of the American Revolution]

Class the American Revolution bicentennial celebration at this number, using s.s. 09 for the celebration in a specific place. Class the administrative annual report of an agency in charge of a bicentennial celebration at 353.00859 and cognate numbers under 353.9.

980 General history of South America

Native races

The same principles apply to classing works on the native races of South America as to classing the native races of North America, except that area 98 and notation 00498 are used instead of area 97 and notation 00497. *See 970 General history of North America: Native races.*

990 General history of other parts of world, of extraterrestrial worlds Pacific Ocean islands (Oceania)

999   Extraterrestrial worlds

Class here speculation on and the search for intelligent life on other worlds.

Indexes

Indexes

The *Manual* has two indexes:

(1) The numerical index. This consists of a list of numbers given in the order of the tables and schedules, beginning with Tables 1–7 and proceeding to class numbers from 000 to 999. Indented under each number is a further set of one or more numbers. The latter set indicates the passages in the *Manual* where the superior numbers are discussed or mentioned. For example, under 700 the following entries appear: **246–247 vs. 700, 300 vs. 600:** Biography & company history, 688.8, **800, 930.1.** This means that at **246–247 vs. 700,** at **300 vs. 600:** Biography & company history, at 688.8, at **800,** and at **930.1** in the text of the *Manual* there is discussion of, mention of, or reference to 700 that may be helpful to the classifier in determining exactly how to use 700. Discussion of a number at the number itself has not been indexed.

(2) The alphabetical index. Bear in mind that the numbers following a term indicate the locations where that topic is discussed in the *Manual,* not necessarily those where it may be classed in the Decimal Classification. The alphabetical index is an index to the *Manual,* not to Edition 19.

With few exceptions, proper names (e.g., Universal Serials and Book Exchange) and classes of persons (e.g., nurses) have not been indexed, nor have numbers and topics used as examples in the text of the *Manual.*

Numbers are printed in boldface in the index if they are so printed in the text of the *Manual.* When a number is in boldface, that is an indication that whatever is said of the number applies as well to its subdivisions. What is said of a lightface number applies only to the number, not to its subdivisions.

Tables: A number preceded by "*s.s.*" is found in Table 1, by "*areas*" in Table 2, by "*lit. sub.*" in Table 3, by "*lang. sub.*" in Table 4, by "*r.e.n.*" in Table 5, by "*lang.*" in Table 6, and by "*pers.*" in Table 7.

Abbreviations Used in the Index

admin.	administration(s)
&	and
econ.	economic(s)
econ. geol.	economic geology
ed.	education(al)
eng.	engineering, engineers
ftn.	footnote
govt.	government(s), governmental
internat.	international
lang.	*language* (Table 6)
lang. sub.	*language subdivision* (Table 4)
lit.	literary, literature(s)
lit. sub.	*literature subdivision* (Table 3)
lit. sub. (Table 3–A)	*literature subdivision* Table 3–A
med.	medical, medicine
mfg.	manufactures, manufacturing
mil.	military
pers.	*persons* (Table 7)
pol.	political, politics
pol. sci.	political science
psych.	psychological, psychology
pub.	public
r.e.n.	*racial, ethnic, national groups* (Table 5)
s.a.	*see also*
sci.	science(s), scientific
soc.	social, socialization, sociology
s.s.	*standard subdivision* (Table 1)
tech.	technical, technique, technological, technology
trmt.	treatment
U.K.	United Kingdom
U.S.	United States

Numerical Index

Table 1. Standard Subdivisions

S.s. 01
100
340.1
520
530.1
539.01

S.s. 014
lang. sub. 864
400

S.s. 015
001.9

S.s. 0151
539.01

S.s. 019
150
158.3
158.4
158.7 vs. 650
370.15

S.s. 0212
310

S.s. 0218
362–363: Add table

S.s. 0222
700
720.222

S.s. 0228
745.5928

S.s. 024
340.024

S.s. 024613
610.73

S.s. 025
s.s. **06**
338.76

S.s. 028
s.s. **072 vs.** *s.s.* **028**
520
621.3678
700
745.67
748.5

S.s. 0287
152.8
628.161

S.s. 0288
930–990: Historic preservation

S.s. 0289
363.1

S.s. 0294
s.s. **025**
380.141–.145
384–388

S.s. 03
s.s. **014**
000

S.s. 04
  Table 1. Standard Subdivisions
S.s. 05
  Table 1. Standard Subdivisions
  000
S.s. 06
  000
  351.0006
  364.106
  367
  384
  385–388
  700: Financial patronage of the arts

S.s. 068
  s.s. 0289
  254
  262.136
  338.09
  362.1
  363.1
  658 and *s.s.* 068
  658.11
  658.809
  658.838
  658.89
  790.068

S.s. 0681–0688
  262.136

S.s. 0681
  351.7232
  362–363: Add table: **8**
  658 and *s.s.* 068: (1) Financial
    management
  658 and *s.s.* 068: (5) Management
    of materials
  658.11

S.s. 0682
  647.96–.99 vs. 658.2 and *s.s.* 0682
  658 and *s.s.* 068: (2) Plant
    management

S.s. 0683
  158.7 vs. 650
  658 and *s.s.* 068: (3) Personnel
    management

S.s. 0684
  658 vs. 658.4: ftn.

S.s. 0685
  658 and *s.s.* 068: (4) Production
    management

S.s. 0687
  346.02
  658 and *s.s.* 068: (5) Management
    of materials

S.s. 0688
  658 and *s.s.* 068: (6) Marketing
    management
  658.809
  658.838
  658.89

S.s. 07
  s.s. 077
  355.5
  370
  370.113
  370.71
  370.733
  373.246
  379.158
  793.73

S.s. 071
  378.3
  379.11

S.s. 0711
  355.00711
  378.4–.9

S.s. 072
  s.s. 0287
  s.s. 0723
  001.4
  001.9
  152.8
  511.5

S.s. 07201–07209
  907.202
  929.1072

S.s. 07202
  907.202

S.s. 0723
  388.41314

S.s. 0724
  001.64
  152

S.s. 074
  010
  700
  704.9
  708
  738.092
  741.93–.99
  909.1–.8
  914–919: Historic buildings
    and houses

S.s. 0740
  750
  779

S.s. 07401–07409
  707.4

S.s. 075
  700

S.s. 075092
  709.22

S.s. 076
  s.s. 0287
  153.94
  351.3
  371.26

S.s. 077
  ***s.s.* 07**

S.s. 079
  001.44
  700: Financial patronage of the arts

S.s. 08
  153.94
  362
  362.16
  363.59
  800: Literary period: ftn.

S.s. 088
  ***s.s.* 08**
  ***s.s.* 08 vs. *s.s.* 09**
  306.7
  362–363: Add table

S.s. 08804–08808
  ***s.s.* 088**

S.s. 088041–088042
  305.3

S.s. 0880565
  s.s. 088056

S.s. 089
  ***s.s.* 08**
  ***s.s.* 08 vs. *s.s.* 09**
  Table 5. Racial, Ethnic, National Groups
  340: Law & aboriginal groups
  930–990: Racial, ethnic, national
    groups

S.s. 09
Table 1. Standard subdivisions
s.s. **074 &** *s.s.* **075**
s.s. **08 vs.** *s.s.* **09**
s.s. **092**
areas **2**
133.43
180–190
312
312.6
314–319
338.372
350
351.2
355.031
355.0332–.0335
355.347
355.5
355.7
358.403
359.03
363.3493809
370.1965
370.732
384
385–388
388.41314
500.5
509
551.4
700
704.9
709.011
733
738
738.092
781.96
800: Literary period: ftn.
800: Literary criticism
929.2
930–990: Wars: Prison, internment, & concentration camps
973.36

S.s. 091–099
746.75
759.011
779

S.s. 091
areas **2 vs.** *areas* **1,** *areas* **3–9**

S.s. 092
s.s. **01**
s.s. **025**
s.s. **06**
areas **2 vs.** *areas* **1,** *areas* **3–9**
180–190
232
291
297.4
297.61
364.1
700
704.942
741.5–.7
800: Authors: Biography
907.202
910.4
910.92
914–919: Add table: 04: Biography

S.s. 0922–0924
910.4

S.s. 0922
s.s. **08 vs.** *s.s.* **09**
s.s. **092**
s.s. 0926
271
779

S.s. 0924
s.s. 08 vs. s.s. 09
s.s. 092
s.s. 0922
s.s. 0926
150.195
171
271
362.1–.4
700
706
720.9 vs. 725–728
779
780. 81–.84
781.96
786–789
914–919: Add table: 04: Biography

S.s. 0926
362.1–.4

S.s. 093–099
areas 2 vs. areas 1, areas 3–9
340.59
704.03–.87

S.s. 0937
722.7

S.s. 0938
722.8

Table 2. Areas

Table 2. Areas
700
704.9

Areas 1–9
271

Areas 1
areas 2 vs. areas 1, areas 3–9
areas 3–9

Areas 167
areas 163–165

Areas 182
areas 163–165 vs. areas 182

Areas 2
s.s. 092

Areas 22
271

Areas 24
271

Areas 3
areas 4–9
931–939

Areas 3–9
areas 163–165 vs. areas 182
areas 2 vs. areas 1, areas 3–9
133.43

Areas 4–9
areas 3 vs. areas 4–9

Areas 41–42
areas 4–9: Cities, towns,
villages

Areas 42
areas 41 vs. areas 42

Areas 5
areas 1821

Areas 66
areas 3–9

Areas 7
areas 1812

Areas 74799
areas 71339

Areas 753
340: Use of area number for
capital districts

Areas 947
340: Use of area number for
capital districts

Areas 98
980

Areas 99
areas 19 vs. **99**
500.5

Table 3. Subdivisions of Individual Literatures

Table 3. Subdivisions of Individual
   Literatures
800

Lit. sub. 1
   800: Form
   lit. sub. 807 and 8 + 07

Lit. sub. 107
   lit. sub. 108

Lit. sub. 2
   800: Form

Lit. sub. 3
   800: Form

Lit. sub. 4
   800: Form

Lit. sub. 5
   800: Form

Lit. sub. 6
   800: Form

Lit. sub. 7
   lit. sub. (Table 3–A) 17
   800: Form

Lit. sub. 8
   636.0887
   800
   800: Form
   800: Authors: Form
   800: Examples of collections of two
      or more authors
   800: Special problems: Works
      about animals
   808.1

Lit. sub. 8 + 02
   lit. sub. 807 and 8 + 07
   800: Special problems: Works
      about animals

Lit. sub. 8 + 03
   800: Authors: Biography
   800: Special problems: Works
      about animals

Lit. sub. 8 + 07
   800: Special problems: Works
      about animals

Lit. sub. 802
   lit. sub. 807 and 8 + 07

Lit. sub. 803
   636.0887

Lit. sub. 81–89: Table: 09
   800: Authors: Form

Table 3–A
   800: Language: ftn.
   800: Other facets

Lit. sub. (Table 3–A) 351
   lit. sub. (Table 3–A) 382

Lit. sub. (Table 3–A) 382
   lit. sub. (Table 3–A) 372

Lit. sub. (Table 3–A) 93–99
   800: Literary period: ftn.

Table 4. Subdivisions of Individual Languages

Table 4. Subdivisions of Individual
   Languages
400
411–418

Lang. sub. 15
   lang. sub. 5

Lang. sub. 152
   lang. sub. 81

010

010
  s.s. 016
  000
011.31
  090
011.34
  050
011.35
  070
011.42
  093
011.44
  090
011.7
  013
  050
016
  050
016.34
  348.028
017–019
  050

020–090

020
  000
021.83
  351.852
025.002854
  022.9
025.52
  025.04
025.56
  021
027
  020.9
  021.2
027.65
  327.73
027.8
  371.3078

028.12
  011.02
030
  000
  001.93
050
  000
051–059
  371.805
060
  000
069
  000
069.13
  069.56
069.51–.54
  702.87–.89
069.56
  069.13
070
  000
070.1–.4
  070.1
070.1
  791.43
070.50294
  010
070.52
  808.001–808.7
070.92
  070.4
080
  000
  001.543
090
  000

100

100
  190
101.41
  001.51

152.10287	153.93
152.1	150.287
152.322	153.0287
150.194	153.40287
152.4	153.90287
155.232	153.9323
152.5	153.9333
153.8	153.9324
152.8	153.9334
152.0287	153.9333
152.0723	153.9323
155.4120287	153.9334
152.80287	153.9324
150.287	153.94
153	**155**
121	**155.28**
152.33	**155.5**
153.4	**158**
155	158.6
153.3	158.60287
154.3	371.264
153.43	154.3
160	153
153.46	155
153.43	**150.8**
153.6	155.25
001.51	**155.5**
152.384	155.0287
400	**155.28**
651.7	155.2
153.7	**155**
152.1	155.418
152.1423	**158**
153.8	155.20287
152.5	**155.28**
155.232	155.232
153.85	**152.4**
155.25	158.3
153.852	155.28
302.24	150.287
153.9	**155**
153.4	155.0287
158.6	155.20287
	157.92

155.925
150
155.93
155.9
155.94
150 vs. 302–307
155.9
155.92
307
155.95
155.9
155.96
155.9
157
150 vs. 616.89
616.890019
157.2–.8
157
158
155.2
158.1
646.7
158.2
155.92
158.1
158.25
150
158.9
158.1
159
150

160–190

160
100
153.43
170
100
171
395
170.44
170.202

172–179
100
172.1
355.224
174.3
340.112
174.9097
070.1
174.915
150.287
150.724
176
306.7
179.1–.4
179
180–190
140
171
180
100
101
140
190
100
100

200

200
100 vs. 200
170
181.04–.09
210
326
361.38
366
781.96
209
270
209.2
280
210–269
209.2
212.1
113

232.94
226
232.954–.955
226.7–.8
232.955
231.73
263.042
232.98
229.8–.9
234.3
232.3
236
234.2
236.3
232.6
236.9
232.7

240

241
209.2
261.8 vs. 241
291
241.3–.4
241.6
241.4
234.2
241.698–.699
241.6
242
291
242.8
264.13
245
291
246–247
291
248
291
248.2
209.2
248.22
209.2

248.22092
248
248.32
264.1
248.5
269.2

250

250
291
251
220.6
252
220.6
252.3
269.2
253
209.2
253.2
253
255
209.2
254
271
255.1–.9
255.01–.09
255.91–.98
255.901–.909

260

260
254
261
209.2
261.1
291
261.2–.8
261.1
261.55–.56
215
261.7
261.8
322.1 vs. **200**

287
287.83
289.9
299

290

290
210
291
200
200.9
290
299
291.092
291
291.17
291
291.8
291.175
215
291.177
322.1 vs. **200**
291.2
210
291
291.8
291.211
212.1
291.213
133.9
291.24
213
291.22
291.3
291
291.34
291.38
291.4
291
291.5
291
291.8

291.6
291
291.61–.64
291
291.63
291
291.64
291
291.65
291
291.7
291
291.8
291
291.9
291
292–299
133.9
212.1
213
215
291
322.1 vs. **200**
726.1
292.13
398.2 vs. 291.13
293.13
398.2 vs. 291.13
294.3423
294.35
294.363
294.3421
294.385
294.382
294.3923
299.54
294.523
294.548
294.543
181.45
294.59
294.544
181.45

294.595
294.592
296.142
296.19
296.155
221.44
296.16
135.4
296.3
220
296.33
220.15
296.42
220.6
296.437
296.142
296.19
296.8
296.65
296.82
296.71
296.833
296.71
297.1–.7
297.4
297.24
297.61
297.65
299
133 vs. 200
292–293
299.1–.9

300

300
s.s. 0289
150
307
301–307
300
306
320
361
361.1

301
301–307
301–306 vs. 361–365
306
301.7
335.02
302–307
150
155.92
156
363
302
150
156
301–307
301.019
302.2
001.51
153.6
651.7
302.3
158.2
302.34
150
364.1066
302.54
155.232
303
301–307
303.376
791.43
303.482
327
303.483
600
303.49
900
303.623
322.4
303.625
364.1
303.64
322.42

303.66
930–990: Wars
304
301–307
304.2
363
363.7
508
304.6
312
304.8
325
305–306
306
305
301–307
306
305.567
326
306
301–307
305
306.089
306
306.09
306
306.1
362.293
306.2
320
306.27
930–990: Wars
306.3
339.47
306.36
331
306.48
790
306.7–.8
305.3
306.7019
150 vs. 302–307
155.3
155.34

306.9
616.078
307
150 vs. 302–307
301–307
361
361.8
307.12
711
307.2
325
307.336
306.3
307.72
630
307.77
334.683
335.9

310

310
300
312
304.6
310
929.3
312.26
614.40212
312.3
312.2
312.6
362.1–.4
362.19
614.40212
616.00212
312.4
312.2
363.1
312.6
573.6

328.306
  350: Branches of govt.
328.331
  350: Branches of govt.
328.3453
  351.0036
328.37
  348.3–.9
328.4–.9
  s.s. **092**
  328.33
328.4–.9: Add table: 07453
  351.0036
328.4–.9: Add table: 0761
  328.361

330

330
  300
  380
330.028
  330.0151
330.1543
  330.0151
331–333
  330
  338.14
331
  320
  330
  331.119 vs. 331.7
  371.1
  658.3 vs. 331
331.1
  331
331.11
  331.12
331.117
  331.11
331.118
  331.11
331.12
  331.11

331.123
  331.12
331.124
  331.12
331.125
  331.12
331.13
  331.12
331.133
  370.19342
  371.1
331.14
  331.12
331.2
  331
331.21
  658.322
331.252
  331.255
  351.5
  368
331.2529
  331.255
331.255
  368
331.25922
  370.113
331.2596
  371.14
331.3–.6
  331
  331.133
  331.137804
  331.702
331.4
  305.43
331.621–.629
  331.6209
331.7
  331
  331.119 vs. 331.7
331.702
  355.1154
  370.113

335.42
335
335.43
321.92
335
335.434
335.430947
335.434
335.5
335
335.6
321.94
335.95694
334.683
335.9
336
330
339
336.2
343.04
351.724
336.2009
336.201
336.207
658.153
336.3435
332.45
337
330
382.9
338
330
363.5, 363.6, and 363.8
600
338.01
331–333
338.09
338.6042
658.11
338.1–.4
332.0415
338.5212
600

338.1
630
338.19
363.8
338.2
333.8
338.371
338.372
338.3727
338.372
338.4734701
347.013
338.47355
355.0213
338.5
330
338.6–.9
338.1–.4
338.6–.8
338.76
338.6041
332.0415
338.7–.8
338.1–.4 vs. 338.7–.8
338.7
300 vs. 600: Biography and company
history
338.70924
338.76
338.76
620.0092
338.76191
332.3
338.763
334.683
335.9
338.76661
748.2
338.8
343.072
338.9
361
500: Relation to other disciplines

342–347: *s.s.* 0269
  340: Terminology: Law enforcement
  346.048
  347.01
  347.05
  347.07
342–344
  340: Terminology: Civil law
342
  342.03
342.023
  342.035
342.042
  340.9
  342.09
342.062
  347.01
342.07
  324.6 vs. 342.07
342.083
  342.085
342.085
  326
  343.012
  344.035643
  344.079
342.0858
  342.066
  343.04
342.087
  326
  342.085
342.09
  340: Terminology: Municipal law
342.7305
  342.05
  342.068
343.0143
  345.01
343.032
  344.091
343.034
  343.04

343.04–.06
  336.2
  351.724
343.04
  330
  343.043
  343.05
  343.052
343.042
  343.04
343.043
  343.04
343.05–.06
  343.04
343.0523
  343.04
343.053
  346.052
343.056
  343.087
343.0560269
  343.056
343.068
  658.153
343.07
  343.08
343.0742
  346.074
  346.086
343.076
  343.083
343.07660887
  344.049
343.0786591
  343.082
343.07869
  346.045
343.078791
  344.097
343.087
  343.056
343.0932
  343.087

346.066
   342.09
   346.0652
346.0666
   346.092
346.07
   338.09
   341.752
   346.066
346.074
   346.072
   346.092
346.086092
   343.0944
346.0862
   343.093
346.086364
   343.011
347
   320
   342–347: *s.s.* 0262
   345
   350: Branches of govt.
347.0068
   350: Branches of govt.
347.01
   350: Levels of govt.
347.013
   350: Branches of govt.
347.017
   344.031–.032
   345.01
347.0504
   340.023
347.06
   347.067
347.7328
   343.056
   346.0486
348
   340
   349

349
   340
   340.092
   348

350

350–354
   300
   320
   342–347: *s.s.* 0262
   342.0664
   350
   350: Branches of govt.
   350: Public admin.
   351.0006
   351.2
   363
   385–388
   658 and *s.s.* **068:** ftn.
350
   331.255
   351.093
350.001–.996
   350
350.1
   331
350.851
   340: Terminology: Law enforcement
351–354
   346.02
   355.028
   362–363: Add table: **8**
351
   350
   350: Levels of govt.
   350: Jurisdictions
   350: Citation order of spec. topics
   351.004
   351.093
   351.2
   352
   353–354

351.0001–.0009
  350: Citation order of spec. topics
351.0006
  350.0005
  352
351.001–.009
  350: Citation order of spec. topics
351.001–.004
  350: Citation order of spec. topics
351.00372
  328.375
351.004
  351.01–.08
351.007
  350: Citation order of spec. topics
  351.7
351.0076
  352
351.009
  350: Citation order of spec. topics
  352
351.01–.09
  350: Citation order of spec. topics
351.01–.08
  350: Citation order of spec. topics
351.06
  355.6
351.09
  350: Citation order of spec. topics
351.1–.9
  350: Citation order of spec. topics
351.1–.6
  351.7
351.1
  344.0189041
  352
351.1234
  368
351.2
  352
351.3
  352
351.4
  352

351.5
  352
  368
351.6
  352
351.7–.8
  343.07
351.71–.72
  351.7
  352
351.71
  352
351.7122–.7123
  352
351.72
  352
351.722
  343.034
  352
351.72236
  342–347: *s.s.* 0262
351.7232
  352
351.724
  330
  336.2
  352
351.74–.89
  351.01–.08
  351.1–.72
351.74–.78
  351.7
351.74
  352
351.761–.765
  352
351.7782
  352
351.782
  363.37809
351.783
  363.1
351.8
  352

351.819
352
351.82
500: Relation to other disciplines
351.824
352
351.829
363.5, 363.6, and 363.8
351.835
368
351.841043
362.1
351.8429
351.761–.765
351.8495
350: Public admin.
351.851
350: Public admin.
351.0092
370.196
351.852
352
351.855
500: Relation to other disciplines
351.859
930–990: Historic preservation
351.873
383.4
351.875
350: Public admin.
351.89
350: Citation order of spec. topics
351.892
327.2
351.2
351.99
352
351.993
351.0036
351.996
363.31

352–354
336.2
340: Terminology: Law enforcement
350: Public admin.
351.0006
700: Financial patronage of the arts
352
344.0189041
350: Levels of govt.
350: Local govt.
352.0006
352
352.002–.009
352.03–.09
352.002
352
352.00476
352
352.0051
352
352.0052
352
352.0053
352
352.0054
352
352.0055
352
352.0056
352
352.009
352
352.1–.9
352.03–.09
352.1
352
352.12–.13
352
352.12
352
352.13
352
352.16
352

352.1622–.1623
352
352.17
352
352.172
352
352.2
352
352.3
363.1
363.37809
352.4
352
352.5–.9
352
352.9361–.9365
352
352.9419
352
352.9424
352
352.9452
352
352.9459
930–990: Historic preservation
353–354
s.s. **092**
328.375
342–347: *s.s.* 0262
343.034
344.0189041
350: Jurisdictions
350: Local govt.
351.2
355.6
500: Relation to other disciplines
930–990: Historic preservation
353
350
350: Jurisdictions
350: Citation order of spec. topics
353.001–.009
350: Citation order of spec. topics

353.0074
359.97
353.00819
070.595
353.00859
973.36
353.0089
350: Citation order of spec. topics
353.01–.09
350: Citation order of spec. topics
353.1–.8
350: Citation order of spec. topics
353–354
353.9
350: Jurisdictions
350: Citation order of spec. topics
973.36
353.901–.909
350: Citation order of spec. topics
353.91–.93
350: Citation order of spec. topics
353.911–.919
350: Citation order of spec. topics
353.921–.929
350: Citation order of spec. topics
353.931–.939
350: Citation order of spec. topics
353.97–.99
350: Jurisdictions
350: Citation order of spec. topics
353.97–.99: Add table: 0001–0009
350: Citation order of spec. topics
353.97–.99: Add table: 001–009
350: Citation order of spec. topics
353.97–.99: Add table: 01–09
350: Citation order of spec. topics
353.97–.99: Add table: 1–9
350: Citation order of spec. topics
354
325.31 vs. 325.33–.39
350
350: Jurisdictions
350: Citation order of spec. topics

354.1
  341.2
  353–354
354.3–.9
  350: Citation order of spec. topics
354.3–.9: Add table: 0001–0009
  350: Citation order of spec. topics
354.3–.9: Add table: 001–009
  350: Citation order of spec. topics
354.3–.9: Add table: 01–04
  350: Citation order of spec. topics
354.3–.9: Add table: 061–068
  350: Citation order of spec. topics
354.3–.9: Add table: 07
  350: Citation order of spec. topics
354.3–.9: Add table: 08
  350: Citation order of spec. topics
354.3–.9: Add table: 09
  350: Citation order of spec. topics
355–359
  300
  342–347: *s.s.* 0262
  350
  355
  355.009 vs. 900
  930–990: Wars: History of spec. units
    in a war
355
  355.00711
355.007
  355.55
355.009
  355.332
355.02–.88
  355.009
355.021
  355.43
355.021309
  355.009
355.0217
  358.39
355.02184
  355.425

355.022
  930–990: Wars
355.0274
  930–990: Wars
355.03
  327.174
355.03209
  355.032
355.03301–.03309
  355.009
  355.0332–.0335
355.07
  355.8
355.1
  390.4355
355.115
  331.255
  362.86
355.1151
  331.255
  368
355.1296
  365.45
  365.48
355.13323
  355.34
355.14
  355.1342
  391.04355
355.17
  394.4
355.2232
  355.37
  355.5
355.22363
  355.224
355.309
  355.009
355.31
  930–990: Wars: History of spec. units
    in a war
355.343
  327.12

355.350944
  355.352
355.37
  355.351
355.43
  355.021 vs. 355.43
355.48
  793.9
355.49
  355.028
  930–990: Wars: Occupied countries
355.6
  355.341
355.622
  342–347: *s.s.* 0262
  343.01
355.67
  355.621
355.69
  355.34
  383.145
355.709
  355.45
355.71
  365.45
  365.48
355.81–.88
  355.8
355.81
  355.14 vs. 355.81
355.82
  327.174
356–359
  355.82–.83
356.184
  355.547–.548
358.1
  357.1
358.3
  355.26
358.403
  355.0332–.0335
358.45
  355.413

359.03
  355.0332–.0335
359.413
  355.413
359.83
  359.32

360

360
  300
  610 vs. 362.1
361–365
  301–306 vs. 361–365
  303.484
361–363
  157.9
361
  360
  361.25
  362–363: Add table: 5
  363.1
361.2
  322.0425
361.25
  363.35
361.32
  158.3
361.6
  361.02–.06
  361.25
361.615
  361.7
361.7
  361.02–.06
  361.25
  361.76
361.75–.76
  361.76
361.763
  361.77
361.765
  658.153

361.77
  361.763
361.8
  361.9
361.9
  361.25
361.91–.99
  361.6
362–363
  364.1 vs. 362–363
  614.5 vs. 362–363
362–363: Add table
  362–363
  363.34
362–363: Add table: 1–7
  363.72
362–363: Add table: 5
  361 vs. 362
  362–363: Add table: **6–8**
  362–363: Add table: **8**
362–363: Add table: 56
  363.5, 363.6, and 363.8
362–363: Add table: 6–8
  362–363: Add table: **5**
362–363: Add table: 6
  363.1
  363.98
362–363: Add table: 62
  362–363: Add table
  362–363: Add table: **6 vs. 7**
362–363: Add table: 63
  362–363: Add table: **6 vs. 7**
362–363: Add table: 64
  362–363: Add table: **6 vs. 7**
362–363: Add table: 65
  362–363: Add table: **6 vs. 7**
362–363: Add table: 7
  362–363: Add table: **6 vs. 7**
362–363: Add table: 8
  363.348
  363.58
362–363: Add table: 81
  363.348

362–363: Add table: 86
  158.3
362
  355.115
  361 vs. 362
  361.02–.06
  361.1
  362.1–.4
  362.82
  363.1
  363.23
  613–614 vs. 362.1
362.042
  361.1 vs. **362.042**
362.1–.4
  266
362.1
  362.108
  610 vs. 362.1
  613–614 vs. 362.1
  614.40212
362.1042520973
  368.42
362.109
  610.9
362.10973
  368.42
362.16
  363.59
362.175
  362.17
362.19
  616.1–.9: Add table: 071
362.1968
  362.4
362.196855
  362.42
362.2
  157.94
  362.3
362.20425
  362.2

363.252–.256
  363.258
363.256–.258
  363.24
363.2565
  137
363.2860973
  359.97
363.289
  363.2
363.3
  363.1
363.31
  791.43
363.347
  363.35
363.348
  363.232
363.3495
  551.2
363.37
  363.349
  628
363.377
  363.179
363.4
  306.7
  363.23
363.51
  363.55
363.55
  363.51
363.59
  362.61
  363.508
363.61
  363.17
  363.7394
  628
363.69
  069.53
  720.288
  930–990: Historic preservation

363.7
  363
  363.73
  628
363.70525
  304.2
363.728
  363.17
  363.61
  363.737
363.7291–.7299
  363.729
363.73
  574.5222
  658.408
363.735
  363.738
363.73525
  304.28
363.738
  363.17
  363.728
363.73922
  553.9
  628.53
363.7394
  628.168 vs. 363.7394
363.73942
  553.7
363.7394209
  628.1686
363.73945
  628.1688
363.739463
  363.61
363.739472
  363.61
363.74
  363.73
363.882
  362.58
  363.8

368.43
  331.252
  331.255
  368
  368.4
369
  360

370

370
  157.9
  300
  350: Public admin.
370.112
  375.88
370.113
  373.246
370.15
  153.15
370.19
  371.207
  372.21
370.196
  303.482
370.71
  371.12
370.73
  370.711
370.9
  370.195 vs. **370.9**
  379.4–.9 vs. 370.9
371
  370
371.01–.02
  370
371.01
  370
371.02
  370
371.1
  379.157
371.1024
  370.15

371.207
  370.19
371.26
  153.93
371. 27
  371.26 vs. 371.271
371.271
  371.26 vs. 371.271
371.28
  371.218
371.3
  370
371.332
  372.66
371.38
  370.113
371.4
  158.3
371.42
  371.26
371.425
  370.113
371.58
  371.295
371.59
  371.207
371.8
  370
  370.1934
371.81
  370.1934
371.83
  s.s. **06**
371.9
  370
371.9046
  371.9
371.91
  371.9
371.911
  371.9
371.912
  362.42
  371.9

380

380–388
  384–388
380–382
  300
  338.47
  338.76
  380.1
  658.83
380
  300
  330
  380.141–.145
  384–388
380.1–.5
  380
380.1
  380
380.141–.145
  380.106
380.144
  326
380.1457
  706
380.3
  380
380.5
  380
381–382
  339.47
  380
  380.106
  380.141–.145
381
  326
  380
382
  326
  337.1
  380
382.09
  382.5

382.1
  382.9
383–384
  001.51
  300
  380
383
  380
383.14–.18
  383.12
383.183
  383.145
383.4
  383.06
384
  380
  380.3
385–388
  300
  380
  629.046 vs. 385–388
385
  350: Public admin.
388
  385
389.16
  658.4062

390

390
  300
391.04355
  355.14 vs. 355.81
392.6
  306.7
394.1
  362.293
394.15
  394.12
394.16
  394.12
394.26
  394.5

511.3	**520**
160	
512.1	520
510	**500**
512.2–.5	**500:** Dominant subdivisions
512.02	**500.5**
512.5	**530**
510	521–522
512.55	**520**
512.2	521
512.9	**520**
510	521.582
512	**523.1**
512.92–.93	522
513.2–.4	**520**
513	523
510	**500:** Dominant subdivisions
513.0212	**520**
513.92	**521.5 vs. 523**
513.1	**523.1**
510	523.1
515	**523.8**
515.3–.4	523.101
515.1	**521.5 vs. 523**
510	**523.1**
515.35	523.112
515.62	**523.1**
515.62	523.12–.19
515.35	**521.5 vs. 523**
515.83	523.1
515	525.6
515.9	551.4708
515.8	526
516	**500:** Relation to other disciplines
514	**526–529**
516.2	526.1
510	**526–529**
516	526.3
516.24	**526–529**
510	526.7
519.5	531.14
001.4225	526.9
519.2	**333.009**
519.53	**526–529**
519.24	

541
  546 vs. 541
  548 vs. 549
541.22
  539.12 vs. **541.22**
543.08
  543 vs. 544–545
544–545
  543 vs. 544–545
546
  540
  548 vs. 549
546.24
  546
546.3
  546 vs. 541
546.7
  546 vs. 541
547
  500
  546.6812
547.01–.08
  546
547.7
  547.84
548
  541
  549.13–.18
549
  546 vs. 549
  548 vs. 549
  552
549.1
  549.13–.18

550

550
  500
  500: Dominant subdivisions
  500.5
  523
  551

551–559
  551.093–.099
551
  500: Dominant subdivisions
  550
551.136
  551.4
  551.41 vs. 551.136
551.2
  551.4
551.31
  551.46–.49
551.353
  551.3
551.36
  551.4708
551.4
  551 vs. 910.02
  551.3
  551.46–.49
551.41
  551.4
  551.46084
551.4608
  551.09162
551.46084
  551.4
551.461–.469
  551.4609
551.4708
  525.6
551.48
  551.46–.49
551.489
  551.5773
  551.64
551.514
  551.513–.514
551.5252
  551.52509
551.542
  551.5409
  551.543

570

570–590
 363
570
 500
 500: Dominant subdivisions
572–573
 500: Dominant subdivisions
572
 306
572.2
 573.3
573
 301–307
 306
 572.3
573.3
 569.9
 573.2
574–599
 570–590 vs. 600
 574
 612.1–.8
574
 500: Dominant subdivisions
 508
 570
574–574.5
 574.8
574.1
 574.4
 574.6
574.192
 547
 574.133
 574.88
574.2
 574.6
574.24
 363.17
 574.5222
574.3
 599.03

574.32
 574.8
 574.87322
574.5222
 363.17
 574.24
574.52642
 582.1605
574.52643
 584.9045
574.543
 509
574.599
 570–590 vs. 600
574.8762
 574.8
574.9
 508
574.909–.929
 574.526
574.92
 551.46
575
 560 vs. 575
 573.2
 616.01
575.1
 573.2
 575.2
576
 547
 574.24
 589
576.175
 616.01
578–579
 574.028

580

580–590
 547
 574.24
 574.6

580
  500
  500: Dominant subdivisions
  574
580.744
  580.742
581
  500: Dominant subdivisions
  580
582–589: Add table: 04
  574.166
  582–589
582
  581
582.0467
  582.0332
582.13
  581
583
  581
589
  616.01
589.46
  589.9
589.9504133
  581.133

590

590
  500
  500: Dominant subdivisions
  591.29 vs. 616–618
  800: Special problems: Works about
    animals
591–599
  600
  619
591
  500: Dominant subdivisions
  590
591.1
  591.4

591.11–.18
  591.1
591.29
  591.113
  591.295
591.293
  591.292
  591.295
591.295
  576.64
591.3
  591.1
591.51
  156
591.59
  001.51
592–599: Add table: 04
  574.166
593.1
  616.01
594.0471
  574
599
  591
599.02
  591
599.745
  599.5
599.9
  500: Relation to other disciplines

600

600
  338.1–.4
  355.8
  363
  363.1065
  380
  500: Relation to other disciplines
  570–590 vs. 600
  610
  658 and *s.s.* **068**
  745.1
  745.5928

602.75
  s.s. 0275
604.201516
  516.6
604.7
  363.176 vs. 604.7
606.8
  658 and *s.s.* **068**
607.34
  909.1–.8
609
  608
  930.1

610

610
  157.94
  362.1–.4
  362.1023
  362.17
  570–590
  615.533
  615.534
  615.882
  616
  616.01
610.65
  362.17
610.69
  616.0023
610.695
  266
610.696
  362.1
610.724
  610
610.73–619.98
  616
610.9
  615.8809
610.924
  615.53

611–612
  500: Relation to other disciplines
  619
611
  573.6 vs. 611
  610
611.018
  611 vs. 612
  612
611.0184
  611.41
611.1–.8
  612.1–.8
612
  591.1
  610
  611 vs. 612
612.0145
  612.0144
612.01522
  612.3923
612.04
  612.76
612.1–.8
  591.1
612.3
  613.2
612.491
  612.41
  612.75
612.63–.68
  591.1
  599.03
612.8
  150
  152 vs. 612.8
612.821
  154.6 vs. 612.821
613
  610
  613–614 vs. 362.1
613.07
  371.7

615.882
  610.9
  615.8809
615.88209
  615.8809
615.899
  610.9
  615.8809
615.89909
  615.8809
615.9
  363.17
  615.7 vs. 615.9
615.907
  363.1763
  615.900287
615.954
  615.902
616–619
  574
616–618
  154.7
  362–363
  362.1–.4
  362.108
  573.8
  591
  591.29 vs. 616–618
  610
  610.736
  615.53
  615.7 vs. 616–618
  616
616
  610
  614.5
  616.001–.009
  616.07
  617 vs. 616
  617.4
  617.5
  618.92
616.0019
  616.08

616.01–.99
  616
616.047
  616.072
  616.08
  616.1–.9: Add table: 072
616.07
  612 vs. 616
616.075
  615.907
  616
  616.00287
  616.072
616.07572
  616.0757
616.078
  155.937
  612.67
616.079
  591.29 vs. 616–618
616.1–.9: Add table
  616.61
616.1–.9: Add table: 01
  616.1–.9: Add table: 071
616.1–.9: Add table: 05
  616.8605
616.1–.9: Add table: 06
  616.892–.898
616.1–.9: Add table: 0651
  616.892–.898
616.1–.9: Add table: 06512
  154.7
616.1–.9: Add table: 07
  616.1–.9: Add table: 06
616.1–.9: Add table: 08
  616.89
616.1–.9: Add table: 09
  362.1–.4
616.1–.8
  612.1–.8
  617.5
616.1–.7
  616.08

617.412059
  616.12806
617.4120645
  616.12806
617.461059
  616.61
617.463
  613.942
617.5−.8
  617: Add table: **06**
617.5
  617.3
617.58
  616.837
617.6−.8
  617.5
617.6
  617.522 vs. 617.6
617.63
  616.31
617.645
  618.92097
617.9
  617.307 vs. **617.9**
618
  610
618.1−.8: Add table: 06512
  154.7
618.1
  613.942
618.178059
  618.8
618.2
  612.63
618.24
  618.2052
619
  610

620

620−690
  338
  363

620
  500: Relation to other disciplines
  658 and *s.s.* **068**
620.0068
  658 and *s.s.* **068**
620.11
  620.112
620.11228
  620.1121
620.11296
  620.1121
620.12−.19
  620.18
620.4162
  551.46
  627
621.367
  778.3 vs. 621.367
621.38195
  001.644
621.4023
  628.53
621.462
  621.31042
621.48
  662.2
621.8672
  629.049
621.932
  739.7
622.1828
  622.18282
622.19
  622.12−.17
622.29
  627.98
622.338
  622.3382
622.4
  622.2
  622.31−.32
622.6
  622.2
  622.31−.32

628.44
  628.1
  628.54
628.5
  363
  574.5222
  620.85
  658.408
628.53
  628.532
  628.54
628.532
  621.4023
  628.53
628.54
  628.1
  628.168
  628.1683
  628.44
628.55
  628.54
628.7
  628.1
628.92
  363.37
628.96
  363.78
629
  629.046 vs. 385–388
629.13255
  363.12465
629.14
  629.132523
  629.13333
629.2272
  629.2275
629.25
  629.287
629.2826
  363.12565
  363.2332
629.450092
  629.4092
629.891
  629.892

630

630
  570–590
  574
  574.6
631
  631.3
631.47
  912.1001–.1899
631.5
  631.57
631.64
  622.31
631.7
  631.587 vs. 631.7
632–638
  363
632
  363.78
633–635
  631.57
633.1
  633–635
633.119427
  632.4
633.2
  636.01
633.202
  636.01
633.25
  633–635
633.3–.4
  633–635
633.5
  633–635
635
  633–635
635.9
  582.1 vs. 635.9
635.97
  582.1 vs. 635.9
636–639
  591

636
    800: Special problems: Works about
      animals
636.084
    636.01   .
636.088
    636.089
636.089
    610
636.0891–.0892
    574
    591
636.1
    798.23
636.2142
    637.12
637.14
    637.12
    637.13 vs. 637.14
637.141
    637.13 vs. 637.14
637.142–.147
    637.13 vs. 637.14
638
    639.3
639.1
    799.2
639.2
    799.1
639.4–.7
    639.3
639.4
    639.2
639.9
    363.7

640

640
    640.202
641.1
    613.2
641.3
    570–590 vs. 600

641.5–.8
    642.1–.5
641.5636
    641.6
641.578
    641.5784
641.5784
    641.76
641.76
    641.5784
643.12
    643.3–.7
643.2
    797.1
646.1
    745.53
646.2
    646.21
646.4
    646.21
647.94–.95
    914–919: Add table: 04: Guidebooks
647.943–.949
    647.94
647.95
    642.4 vs. **647.95**
649.57
    613.71
649.7
    207
    370.114
649.8
    610

650

650.1
    646.7
    658.409
651.8
    658.05
651.934
    340.024

652–653
  651.374
652
  001.543
  411
652.1
  745.61
657
  651.374
657.1
  657 vs. **658.1511–.1512**
657.32
  657 vs. **658.1511–.1512**
657.8
  658 and s.s. 068: (1) Financial
    management
658
  331.255
  363.1
  380.1 vs. 658.8
658.02
  658 and s.s. 068
658.04
  658 and s.s. 068
  658.402
658.05
  658 vs. 658.4
658.11
  338.09
  338.6042
  658.21
658.114
  658.402
658.15
  332.0415
  658 and s.s. 068: (1) Financial
    management
658.151–.155
  658.159
658.1511
  657 vs. **658.1511–.1512**
658.1512
  657 vs. **658.1511–.1512**

658.15242
  658 and s.s. 068: (2) Plant management
658.2
  647.96–.99 vs. 658.2 and s.s. 0682
  658 and s.s. 068: (2) Plant management
658.3
  331
  658 and s.s. 068: (3) Personnel
    management
658.3112
  137
658.3253
  351.5
  368
658.3254
  368
658.4
  658 vs. 658.4
  658.42
658.4038
  658.455
658.45
  651.7
658.4563
  060.42
658.5
  658 and s.s. 068: (4) Production
    management
658.564
  658.823
  688.8
658.7
  658 and s.s. 068: (5) Management of
    materials
658.8
  658 and s.s. 068: (6) Marketing
    management
659.1
  343.082
659.17
  790.134

680

680
  671–679 vs. 680
  745.5
681.11
  529.78 vs. **681.11**
681.113
  739.3
681.114
  739.3
681.763
  631.3
682
  680
683
  680
683.4
  739.7
684
  680
684.08
  745.51
684.104
  745.51
685
  676.2845
  680
686
  680
686.2
  761–767
686.22
  745.61
686.3
  095
687
  680
688
  745.592
688.1
  745.5928
688.4
  679.7

688.6
  629.046 vs. 385–388
688.79
  799

690

690
  643.12
  720
  729
690.869
  697.78
697
  621.402
697.03
  697.54
697.2
  697.1
697.4
  697.54

700

700
  246–247 vs. 700
  300 vs. 600: Biography & company
    history
  688.8
  800
  930.1
700–779
  745.1
  745.5928
702.8
  730
702.812
  778.8
704.03
  704.03–.87
704.04–.87
  704.03–.87
704.9432
  704.9

731.5
731
731.7
731
731.8
731
732–735
731
732.3–.9
732.2
736–739
729.9
736.98
741.7
738
738.092
738.2
738.2
738
738.3
738
738.4–.8
738
738.2
738.24
738.28
738.38
738.5092
738.092
738.6
738
738.8
738
739.2
739.22–.24
739.22
739.22–.24
739.2271–.2279
739.23
739.23
739.22–.24
739.2309
739.23

739.4092
738.092
739.7
623.44

740

741
741.5–.7
741.092
741.5–.7
741.5
800: Special problems:
Visual novels
741.58
791.433
741.59
741.5
741.58
741.6
741.5–.7
769.5
741.7
736.98
741.92–.99
700
741.92
741.092
741.93–.99
741.092
745.5
680 vs. 745.5
745.5928
623.8201
688.1
745.67
091
751.77
746.3
746.04
746.92
646.21
746.94–.98
646.21

746.97
746.46
747
645
729
914–919: Historic buildings and houses
747.88
747
748.29
748.6
748.6
750
749
645
749.1
745.51

750–760

750
741.9
750.740
759
751.2–.6
750
751.7
750
751.77
745.67
752
701.8
753–758
750
759.01–.07
750
759.1–.9
750
759.011
759.02–.07
759.13
741.5–.7
759.94
759.02–.07

769.12
760.75
769.56
383
769.901–.905
769.922

770

770.92
778.9
779
771.3
771.31
778.5
791.435
778.5092
770.92
778.53
791.43
778.53092
770.92
778.5344
782.85
778.5347
741.58
791.433
778.59
621.388
782.87
778.59092
770.92
779
770.92

780

780
780.43
791
780.216
780.924
780.9
780.81–.84

782
784
782.1092
784.3092
785.092
782.13
782.12
782.8
782.81
782.81
782.1
782.82
783.3
783.4
782.85–.87
780
783
784
783.026
783
783.22
783.21
783.62–.65
783.6
783.67
783.6
783.9
783.6
784.0922
784.06 vs. 784.0922
784.3092
782.1092
784.5
780.42
784.6836123
784.68
785.09
782.1092
785.1–.8: Add table: 5
785.66–.69
785.42
781.57 vs. 785.42
785.7
787.01

786–789
781.91
785.66–.69
785.7
786.2–786.223
786–789
786.6
786–789

790

790.133
796.15
796.72
790.2
780.08 vs. 790.2
790.068
791
791–792
782.07
791
790
791.43
741.58
778.53
791
791.4301–.4309
791.43
791.430233
791.435
791.430909
791.43
791.433
791.53
791.4372
791.43
791.4375
791.43
791.44
384.5443
791
791.45
384.55443
791

792
790
791
792.07
  371.332
793–799
790
  790.068
793–795
790
793
790
791
793.3
791
793.735
  398.6
793.9
  355.48
  796.2
796–799
790
796
790
791
796.0196
  796.48
796.47
  796.41
796.54
  796.9
797
796.5
797.10289
  797.200289
797.200289
  797
798
  636.10888
796.5
798.23
798.2
798.24
  798.23079

798.4
798.2
799
796.5

800

800
  s.s. **08**
  001.543
  133.1
  133.43
  242
  371.332
  398.2 vs. 800
  398.22
  398.25
  591
  636.0887
  781.96
  782.832
  808.83935213
  808.839375
801.95
  800: Literary criticism
808
  001.543
  808.001–.7
808.00141
  001.51
808.02
  808.001–.7
808.025
  808.001–.7
808.04275
  808.0427
808.06634
  340: Legal writing
808.066651
  651.7
808.06678
  782.028
808.5
  lang. sub. 152

808.819382
  242
808.88
  080
808.883
  636.0887
809–899
  242
809
  800: Special problems:
    Nonliterary works
809.1–.7
  800: Literary criticism
809. 933
  398.2 vs. 800

810–890

810–890
  Table 6. Languages
  080
810
  800: Language
  800: Literary period
820–890
  800: Language: Literature of two or
    more languages
820
  800: Language
  800: Literary period
  810

900

900
  lit. sub. 803 & 8 + 03
  297.65
  300
  303.6
  305.8
  306
  307 vs. 900
  320
  320.9 vs. 900
  355.009 vs. 900
  364.1
  400
  609
  630
904
  322.4
  363.34
  900: Classification of spec. events
  909
904.5
  551.2
904.7
  363.1
  930–990: Wars
907.202
  930–990
907.2022
  907.202
907.2024
  907.202
909
  001.9
  306
  322.42
  910 vs. 909 and 930–990
  910.3
  930–990: Wars
909.04
  930–990: Racial, ethnic, national
    groups

909.07–.08
904
909.07
909.07–.08
909.09
904.7
907.202
909.1–.8
909.07–.08
909.1–.83
904
909.2
907.202

910

910–919
551 vs. 910.02
551.4
910
508
647.94
900
910.3
910.014
910.3
914–919: Add table: *s.s.* 0014
910.02
551 vs. 910.02
910 vs. 909 and 930–990
910.09
910.202
910.4
910.202
910.4
910.3
914–919: Add table: 003
910.4–.45
910.4
910.92
910.41
910.45
910.45
910.4

910.922
910.4
910.924
910.4
911
320.12 vs. **911**
912.1
912.155
551.0222
912.19
912.1001–.1899
912.3–.9
912.1001–.1899
913
914–919: Add table: 04: Guidebooks
913.1–.9
areas **4–9:** Physiographic regions and features
913.1–.9: Add table: 02
910 vs. 909 and 930–990
913.1–.9: Add table: 04
551 vs. 910.02
910.202
910.4
914–919: Add table: 04: Guidebooks
914–919
areas **4–9:** Physiographic regions and features
720.9 vs. 930–990
796.51
914–919: Add table: 04
914–919: Add table: 04: Guidebooks
914–919: Add table: 02
914–919: Add table: 04
914–919: Add table: 04
551 vs. 910.02
910.202
910.4
914–919: Historic buildings and houses
917
areas 1812

920

929.1
  929.1072
929.2
929.3
929.1072
  929.1028
929.1094–.1099
929.2
  s.s. **092**
929.1
  929.7
929.3
  312
929.1
  929.1028
929.7
  929.2
929.81
  s.s. 079
  001.44
929.82
  929.6
929.9
  s.s. 0275
  602.75
929.97
  929.44

930

930–990
  s.s. **092**
  areas **4–9**: Physiographic regions and
    features
  001.543
  001.9
  001.95
  306
  322.4
  322.42
  361
  551.2
  720.9 vs. 930–990
  900
  904
  907.202
  910 vs. 909 and 930–990
  910.3
  910.4
  914–919
  914–919: Add table: 04
  **914–919: Add table: 04: Discovery
    and exploration**
  929.7
930–990: Add table: 001–009
  930–990
930–990: Add table: 004
  **930–990: Racial, ethnic, national
    groups**
930–990: Add table: 007202
  930–990
930–990: Add table: 009
  930–990
930–990: Add table: 01–09
  930–990
  **930–990: Racial, ethnic, national
    groups**
930.1
  **914–919: Add table: 04: Discovery
    and exploration**
930.1028
  622.19

931–999
930.1
931–939
areas **3** vs. *areas* **4–9**
933
220.9

940–990

940–990
  914–919: Historic buildings and
    houses
  914–919: Add table: 04: Guidebooks
  931–939
940.18
  909.07–.08
940.472
  930–990: Wars: Prison, internment,
    and concentration camps
940.531503924
  930–990: Wars: Prison, internment,
    and concentration camps

940.542
  940.541
940.5472
  930–990: Wars: Prison, internment,
    and concentration camps
942
941
956.94001
  320.54
970
  areas 1812
970.00497
  970
971–979: 00497 (in note)
  970
973.711
  326
981–989: 00498 (in note)
  980

Alphabetical Index

Advertising		Alcohol	
law	343.082	sale	
Aerial photographs	910.222	pub. admin.	351.761–.765
Aerobatics	797.54	Alcoholics	
Aerospace physiology	612.0144	soc. services	
Aesthetics	111.85	mil. forces	355.345
	701.17	pub. admin.	351.761–.765
Affiliated literatures	*lit. sub.*	Alcoholism	362.292
	(Table 3–A)	Algebra	**510**
	93–99	Allergies	**616.97**
	800: Literary	Allocation of resources	**363.5, 363.6,**
	period		**and 363.8**
Affirmative action			**363.6**
education	370.19342	Allopathy	615.531
teachers	371.1	Alloys	
Aggression	155.232	chemistry	**546**
Aggressive feelings	**152.4**	engineering	**620.18**
	155.232	metal mfg.	**669.2–.7**
Agrapha	**229.8–.9**	Aluminum foil	
Agricultural		handicrafts	745.56
animals	**574**	Alumni	**378.4–.9**
	591	Ambulatory services	
equipment	**631.3**	health care	362.12
methods	**631**	Amendments	
pests	**574.6**	constitutional law	**342.03**
plants	**574**	Amerindians	**970**
	581	Ammunition	
Air		small arms	623.451
accidents		Anarchist communities	335.9
investigation	363.12465	Anatomy	574.4
econ. geol.	553.9	animals	591.4
forces		human	**611 vs. 612**
mil. sci.	**358.4**		**612**
pollution	**628.53**	Ancient	
	628.532	ethical systems	**171**
pressure	551.5409	philosophy	**140**
	551.543	world	*areas* **3 vs.**
quality studies	**628.53**		*areas* **4–9**
temperatures		Angiosperms	**581**
meteorology	551.52509		
Aircraft			
mil. forces	358.4183		

Art
  appreciation **701.1**
  Christian religious
    use **246–247 vs. 700**
  galleries **708**
  history **701.1**
    709
  museums **708**
  music 780.43
  techniques **700**
    702.81
Artificial recharge
  water eng. 628.114
Asphalt concrete 666.893
Assemblages
  sculpture **730**
Assignment of debts
  law 346.077
Astrology 133.4
    133.58
Athletics
  law 344.099
Atman 126
Atmospheric pressure 551.5409
    551.543
Atomic
  spectra **539.7**
  spectrometry **539.7**
Attention 153.733
Attitude change 153.85
Attractiveness 155.232
Auction catalogs
  art works **707.4**
Audits
  govt. agencies 351.7232
Aura 612.0142
Authorizations **342–347:**
    s.s. 0262
Autistic students **371.928**
Autoimmune diseases **616.079**
Automata 629.892
Auxiliaries
  mil. forces 355.35

Average factory wages **331.287**
Avesta 295.82
Avot 296.123
Awards *s.s.* 079
    001.44
  military **355.134092**
    355.1342
Ayurveda ("Hindu
    medicine") **615.53**

B

B cells 591.293
Background music 782.85–.87
Ballad operas **782.81**
Ballooning 797.5
Bankruptcy
  law 346.078
    estates 346.056
Barbarians *lit. sub.*
    (Table 3–A)
    352
Barbecuing 641.5784
    641.76
Battles **930–990: Wars**
Bayonet practice
  mil. sci. **355.547–.548**
Behavior modification 153.85
    370.15
Belly dancing 793.3
Beneficial organisms **574.6**
Benesh 792.80148
Bermuda Triangle
  mystery 910.091636
Bible
  lands
    geography 912.122
  translations 220.5
    220.5209
Biblical
  criticism **220.6**
  exegesis **220.6**
  interpretation **220.6**
  theology **220**

Bibliographies	**010**	Blood-forming system	611.41
directories	**050**		612.41
incunabula	093	Boat racing	797.14
manuscripts	**090**	Boating safety	
newspapers	070	sports	797.200289
rare books	**090**	Body	
serials	**050**	language	153.6
Bicentennial			**400**
U.S.	973.36	mechanics	612.76
Bilingual dictionaries	*lang. sub.* **32–39**	Bon (pre-Buddhist	
Bilingualism	*lang. sub.* **042**	religion)	299.54
	371.97	Bone marrow	611.41
	404.2		612.41
Bills			612.75
law	**342–347:**	Book binding	095
	s.s. 0262	Botanic medicine	615.537
Bingo	795.3	Botanical gardens	**580.74**
Biobibliographies	016	Botany	**500**
Biochemicals	**547**		580
Biography	*s.s.* **092**	Bottles	
	s.s. 0922	art	748.82
	180–190	Braille	411
	300 vs. 600	Brain drain	331.12791
	800: Authors	Branches of	
Biological processes	**574**	government	**350: Branches**
animals	**591**		of
plants	**581**		government
Biology	**500**	Brazing	**671.56**
	570	Briefs	**340: Legal**
Biometrics	**574.072**		writing
Biosociology	156	British Isles	*areas* **41 vs.**
Biostatistics	**574.072**		*areas* **42**
Birth control	613.94	Broadsides	**090**
soc. services	362.58	Bronze metalwork	739.512
Bisexual relations	155.34	Bruderhof Communities	289.73
Bisexuality	155.334	Buddha	294.3421
Black		Budgets	
arts	133.4	law	343.034
holes	**523**	pub. admin.	**351.722**
Methodist churches	287.83		
Bleaching materials			
manufacture	667.14		
Blood flow	612.1181		

Building	
blocks	
recreation	796.2
codes	343.07869
	346.045
construction	**690 vs. 624**
Buildings	
heating	621.402
Bunts	
crop disease	**632.4**
Burlesque	792.7
Business	
directories	**338.76**
law	**346.07**
location	**332.6732**
	338.09
	338.6042
meetings	060.42
success	646.7
Busing	
law	344.0798
Byzantine rite	281.5

C

Cabala	296.16
Cabalistic literature	296.16
Cabinet departments	**351.01–.08**
Cabinetmaking	745.51
Cabinets	
pub. admin.	351.004
Calculus of finite	
differences	**515.62**
Caliphate	297.65
Cameras	771.31
Camps	
mil. forces	**355.7**
Cancer	**616.992 vs.**
	616.994
Cans	
handicrafts	745.56
Cantatas	**783.4**

Capital	
districts	
law	**340**
Capital formation	
(econ.)	**332.0415**
Carbon	
compounds	546.6812
dioxide	546.6812
halides	546.6812
oxides	546.6812
Carbonates	546.6812
Cardsharping	**795.4**
Careers	
mil. forces	355.0023
Caricatures	**741.5**
Carols	783.6
Carriers	
law	**343.093**
Cartoon novels	**800: Special**
	problems:
	Visual
	novels
Cartoons	**741.5**
Case studies	
illness	**362.1–.4:**
	Biographies
Casebooks	**342–347:**
	s.s. 0264
Cases	
internat. law	**341.026**
	341.0268
Casting	
metal mfg.	669.1413
Catalogs	**010**
Catering	642.4 vs. **647.95**
Catholic Traditionalist	
Movement	**282**
Catholics of the	
Byzantine rite	281.5
Cellular	
biology	**574.8**
immunity	**591.29**

Claims	
adjustment	341.55
courts	347.04
Classical	
economics	330.153
education	375.88
literature	
education	375.88
mechanics	**530.12**
music	780.43
Cleaning materials	
manufacture	667.12
Clergy	**253**
Climate zones	551.69
Climatology	**551.5 vs. 551.6**
Clinical	
chemistry	**616.0756**
medicine	**616**
	616.075
psychology	**157.9**
Clockcases	**739.3**
Close air support	358.4142
Clothing construction	
home econ.	646.21
Clubs	**367**
Coast guards	
law	343.01997
Coastal pools	551.4609
Coats of arms	929.6
	929.82
Codes	
model	**342–347:**
	s.s. 02632
Cognition	**153.4**
	153.93
Coins	737.49
Cold War	327.14
Collage	778.8
Collectibles	**745.1**
Collecting	
arts	**700**
Collections	*s.s.* **08**
	080

College	
choice of	378.198
Colonial troops	
mil. forces	355.352
Colonies	341.28
Colonization	**325**
	325.3
	325.31 vs.
	325.33–.39
Color	
art	701.8
	752
Combustible materials	363.377
Combustion	
pollution source	621.4023
Comedy	*lit. sub.*
	(Table 3–A)
	17
entertainment	792.23
sketches	*lit. sub.* 2057
Comic strip novels	**800: Special**
	problems:
	Visual novels
Commemorative	
coins	343.032
	344.091
medals	343.032
	344.091
Communes (Soviet)	334.683
Communicable	
diseases	**616.01**
Communication	001.51
office practice	**651.7**
psychology	**150 vs. 302–307**
	153.4
	153.6
Communication-	
handicapped	
people	362.42
Communications	**380.3**
Communism	321.92
	335
	335.434
Communities	**307**
psychology	**307**

Content analysis	*s.s.* 0141	Costume design	646.21
Contests		Council of Europe	341.242
recreation	790.134	Councils of state	351.004
Context analysis	401.41	Counseling	158.3
Continental		Counterfactuals	**160**
shelves	**333.917**	Country life	**630**
	551.4	County charters	**342.02**
slopes	551.41	Courts	**347**
terraces	551.41		347.01
Continents	551.41 vs.		347.012
	551.136		347.013
Continuing education	**374**		**347.02**
Continuum			347.04
mechanics	**530.12**	Craft unions	331.8832
physics	530.14	Creation	213
Contortion	796.41		291.22
Contraception	613.94	Credit unions	
Contracts		law	346.0668
law	**346.02**	Credits	
Control		education	371.218
soc. problems	**362–363:** Add	Creep	
	table: **6 vs. 7**	geology	**551.3**
Controversies	001.9	Cribbage	795.41
	130	Crime	
Convention centers		prevention	**364.4**
architecture	725.9	victims	
Conversation		soc. services	**364**
ethics	**177**	Crimes	**364.1**
psychology	**150 vs. 302–307**		**364.1** vs.
Cookery	**642.1–.5**		**362–363**
Copy art	**760**	statistics	312.2
Coronary care	616.123028		**312.4**
Corporations		without victims	**364.1**
law	342.09	Criminal	
	346.066	investigation	363.25
Corruption			**364.1**
govt. service	**351.99**	justice	345.05
Cosmological			**364**
argument	113	offenses	**364.1**
Cosmology	**523.1**		**364.1** vs.
Cost control			**362–363**
soc. services	**362–363:** Add	Criminology	**301–306** vs.
	table: **8**		**361–365**

Departments of		Digital electronics	**621.3815**
government	351.01–.08	Diplomacy	327.2
Dependent		Diplomatic	
jurisdictions		history	**327.09**
law	**340:** Jurisdic-	personnel	**351.2**
	tion in time		351.892
Dermatological		Directories	*s.s.* 025
allergies	**616.973**	of bibliographies	011.7
Descriptive		Disability	
astronomy	**520**	soc. problem	**362.1–.4**
	521.5 vs. 523	Disarmament	327.174
geometry	516.6	Disasters	**363.34**
grammar	*lang. sub.* **8**		**363.349**
research	*s.s.* 0723	Disc jockey programs	791.445
Desertification	333.7313	Disciplines	
Design		treatment of	*s.s.* **09**
architecture	**729**	Disco dancing	793.3
Detergents	667.13	Discovery	**910.93–.99**
Determinism	*lit sub.*		**914–919:** Add
	(Table 3–A)		table: 04:
	12		Discovery &
Development banks	332.2		exploration
Developmental		Discrimination	
psychology	155.25	labor econ.	331.133
Developmentally		Diseases	**591**
handicapped			**613 vs. 614**
persons	**362.4**		614.40212
Devotional literature	**242**		**614.5 vs.**
Diagnosis			**362–363**
psychiatric disorders	157.92		**616**
Dialectical materialism	146.32		616.001–.009
	335.4112		616.00212
Dialogues	*lit. sub.* 2	history	610.9
Diaries	*lit. sub.* 803	incidence	**362.19**
	800: Form	Disorienting drugs	**615.78**
Dicotyledons	**581**	Displaced standard	
Dictionaries	*s.s.* **032–039**	subdivisions	**Table 1.**
Dietetics	**613.2**		**Standard**
	613.7		**Subdivisions**
Dietotherapy	615.854	Dissent	361.25
Differential		Dissenters	280.4
equations	**515.35**	Dissertations	011.7
psychology	**155**	District heating	697.54
Digestive system		Divination	**133.3**
allergies	**616.975**		133.4

Divinatory arts	**133.3**	Drug	
Documentary films	**791.43**	addiction	362.293
Dog pounds	363.78	addicts	
Dominance		soc. services	
psychology	**158.2**	mil. forces	355.345
Donations		pub. admin.	351.761–.765
management	658.153	allergies	**615.704**
Double		culture	306.1
jeopardy		reactions	615.704
law	345.04	resistance	
taxation	**341.75**	of microorganisms	**616.01**
Doubles	*lit. sub.*	therapy	615
	(Table 3–A)	trade	
	27	pub. admin.	351.761–.765
Doubling the cube	516.204	treatment	**615.7 vs.**
Dovecotes			**616–618**
architecture	728.9	Drugs	615
Draft resistance	355.224		**615.7 vs.**
Dragoons	**357.1**		**616–618**
Drama	**800:** Form	Dukhobors	289.9
elementary ed.	372.66	Dune stabilization	631.6
teaching method	371.332		
Dramatic music		E	
production	782.07		
Drawing rights	**332.45**	EEC	341.2422
Drawings	**741.9**	Earthenware	
	741.93–.99	art	738
Dreams			738.38
lit. trmt.	*lit. sub.*	Earthquakes	**551.2**
	(Table 3–A)	Eating	
	35	customs	**394.12**
psychology	**154.6** vs.	Ecclesiastical furniture	**729.9**
	612.821	Ecology	**574.526**
	154.63	sociology	**304.2**
Drilling platforms	622.29	Econometrics	330.0151
Drinking		Economic	
customs	**394.12**	conditions	**330.9**
Drives	153.8	geology	550
			551
			553
		Ecumenicalism	262.0011

Educational	
anthropology	**370.19**
exchanges	370.196
finance	**379.11**
guidance	371.422
planning	371.207
policy	**370.19**
psychology	**153.15**
	370.15
sociology	**370.19**
	370.1934
testing	*s.s.* 0287
Effigial slabs	736.5
Elections	**324.6 vs. 342.07**
Electric	
motors	621.31042
trains	
recreation	790.133
Electrochemistry	**621.31242**
Electrodialysis	541.372
Electrolytic balance	
human physiology	612.3923
Electromagnetic	
fields	530.141
waves	530.141
Electronic funds	
transfer systems	332.1028
Electrophoresis	541.37
Elementary functions	**515**
Embryo transplant	618.178059
Emotions	**152.4**
Encyclopedias	*s.s.* **032–039**
Endocrine gynecology	618.1
Endowed schools	373.222
Energy	
engineering	
bldg. construction	696
from wastes	662.8
management	**658 &** *s.s.* **068**
resources	621.042
Engineering mechanics	620.1
England	941

Entertaining	
ethics	**177**
Enuresis	616.63
	616.89
Environmental	
engineering	
bldg. construction	696
policy	**304.2**
problems	**363.7**
psychology	**155.9**
	155.92
toxicology	615.902
Epic poetry	*lit. sub.* 103
Epidemiology	**614.4**
Equal	
educational	
opportunity	**370.1934**
employment	
opportunity	
teachers	371.1
Equilibrium	
macroeconomics	**339.5**
Erector® sets	790.133
Eschatology	
Judaism	296.33
Escrows	346.0436
Espionage	327.12
Essays	**800:** Form
Estate planning	346.052
Estates	
probate law	346.052
Estuaries	551.4609
Ethical	
education	370.114
systems	**171**
Ethics	**100**
law	340.112

Factory	
law	**344.01**
wages	**331.287**
Faculties	
universities	**378.4–.9**
Fairs	**607.34**
Families	306.85
soc. services	**362.82**
Family	
histories	*s.s.* **092**
	929.2
	929.7
planning	613.94
welfare	**362.82**
Fantasies	154.3
Farces	*lit. sub.* 20523
Farm machinery	**631.3**
Fascism	321.94
Fatigue	**616.89**
Faults	
ethics	179.8–.9
Features	
journalism	070.44
Federal countries	
law	**340:** Law of
	countries
	with federal
	governments
Feeds	664.6
Feelings	**152.4**
Fees	
law	**344.01**
Felts	
manufacture	**677.63**
Femininity	
psychology	**155.33**
Feminism	305.42
Feral children	155.4567
Ferryboats	623.8243
Fertilizers	**631.8**
Few bodies problem	530.14
Fiction	**800:** Form
Field crops	**633–635**

Figurines	736.22
Finance	
public ed.	**379.11**
Financial	
management	**658 &** *s.s.* **068:**
	(1) Financial
	management
	658.159
patronage	
arts	**700**
support	
education	*s.s.* **07**
Fine arts	**800**
Fire	
companies	**363.37809**
fighting	363.37
prevention	363.377
resistance	
safety eng.	628.922
safety	363.37
Fiscal law	
international	341.751
Fish	
and game laws	**346.046954**
culture	639.2
	639.3
economics	338.372
Fisheries	639.2
Fishing	
economics	**338.372**
sports	**799.1**
equipment	**799**
Flag code	344.09
Flammability studies	628.922
Flammable materials	363.179
Flood	
control	363.34936
	627.4
forecasting	551.64
relief	**363.3493809**
Flower language	001.56
Flowers	**582.1 vs. 635.9**

Gametogenesis	**574.8**
Gangs	364.1066
Garden	
crops	**633–635**
ornaments	
landscape design	717
Gathas	295.82
Gauge fields	530.143
Gematria	220.68
Genealogical sources	**929.3**
Genealogy	929.1
	929.1094–.1099
research	**929.1072**
Generative grammar	415
Genetic	
diseases	**616.1–.9: Add**
	table: 042
psychology	**155**
Genetics	**573.2**
Genre paintings	754
Gentlemen	*lit. sub.*
	(Table 3–A)
	352
Gentry	
genealogy	**929.7**
Geochemistry	551.9
Geological	
maps	551.0222
stratifications	551.81
surveys	**554–559**
Geology	**551**
Geometry	**510**
	516
Geophysics	**551 vs. 910.02**
Geriatric	
dentistry	618.977
specialties	618.977
surgery	618.977
Ghosts	133.1
	133.8
folklore	398.25
lit. trmt.	808.839375

Gibbs' phase rule	
equation	541.363
Glass underpainting	**750**
Glassware	**748.2**
Gnosticism	299.932
Gospel stories	225.9505
	226.09505
Government	
agencies	
management	**658 & *s.s.* 068**
audits	351.7232
corporations	
pub. admin.	351.0092
reports	**361–365**
services	**350: Public**
	adminis-
	tration:
	Executive
	branch of
	government
Governments	**320.2–.4**
	320.3
	320.4 vs. 320.9
Grade crossings	
railroads	625.7
Grading	
food tech.	664.07
Graffiti	001.543
Graphology	137
	155.282
Graphs	511.5
Grasslands	584.9045
Gravity	531.14
	531.5
geology	**551.3**
Great	
Britain	*areas* **41** vs.
	areas **42**
	941
White Brotherhood	299.93
Greek	
architecture	722.8
sculpture	**733**

Ground waters	553.78–.79	Hang		
Group		gliders	629.14	
practice		gliding	629.14	
health services	362.17	sports	797.55	
therapy		Haridasas	294.5512	
psychiatry	**616.892–.898**	Harmful		
Groups	***s.s.* 08**	microorganisms	**616.01**	
	***s.s.* 08 vs. *s.s.* 09**	organisms	**574.6**	
Groups (mathematics)	512.2	Hazardous materials	**363.17**	
Guarantees	343.08		363.176 vs.	
Guerrilla warfare	355.425		604.7	
Guidebooks	**720.9 vs.**		363.1763	
	930–990	Headaches	616.0472	
	910.202	Headstart	**372.21**	
	914–919: Add	Health		
	table: 04:	insurance	362.10425	
	Guidebooks		**368.382**	
	914–919:		368.42	
	Guidebooks	occupations	362.1023	
	914–919:	services	**610 vs. 362.1**	
	Historic		**613–614 vs.**	
	buildings		**362.1**	
	and houses	mil. forces	355.345	
Gun control	363.33	Hearing examiners		
	363.33 vs.	(law)	342.0664	
	363.179	Hearings		
Guru Granth	294.682	law	**342–347:**	
			***s.s.* 0262**	
H		Heart pacers	616.12806	
		Heating		
Habits	**152.33**	buildings	**621.402**	
Haiku	*lit. sub.* 104	Helpfulness	158.3	
Halakah	296.18	Helping behavior	158.3	
Halfway homes	362.74	Hematopoietic system	611.41	
	365.34		612.41	
Handicapped persons	**362.4**	Hemopoietic system	611.41	
Handicaps			612.41	
statistics	**312.3047**	Hemorrheology	612.1181	
Handicrafts	**680 vs. 745.5**	Herbariums	**580.74**	
	745.5		580.742	
Handwriting analysis	137	Heroes	*lit. sub.*	
			(Table 3–A)	
			352	

Inorganic		Interior	
chemistry	540	decoration	**645**
compounds	**546**		**729**
Input			**747**
data processing	001.644		**747.2**
Insects			**914–919:**
culture	639.3		Historic
In-service training			buildings &
museums	069.63		houses
Institutional		design	**729**
care		Interludes	*lit. sub.* 2052
older adults	362.61	Internal revenue code	**343.04**
housekeeping	**646.96–.99 vs.**	International	
	658.2 and	economics	337
	***s.s.* 0682**		337.1
		law	**341**
Institutionalized			**341 vs. 327**
children	155.446	monetary systems	**332.45**
Institutions		organizations	**341 vs. 327**
sociology	**306**	soc. services	**361.77**
Instructional		relations	327
materials centers	371.3078		**341 vs. 327**
media centers	021.2	unions	**331.88091**
Insurance	**368**	Internment camps	**930–990:** Wars:
management	658.153		Prison,
Insurgent governments	341.68		internment,
Intellectual history	001		& concentra-
Intelligence	**153.4**		tion camps
tests	**153.93**		
	153.932	Interpersonal relations	**158.2**
	153.9323	Interpretation of Bible	**220.6**
	153.9324	Interstate compacts	342.042
	153.933	Interstellar	
	153.9333	communication	001.510999
	153.9334	Intimacy	**158.2**
Intentionality	**153.8**	Intonation	*lang. sub.* 5
Intercultural education	303.482	Introversion	155.232
Interdenominational		Inventions	**608**
churches	289.9	Invertebrates	
councils	262.5	culture	639.2
Interferons	576.64		639.3
	591.29		

Lamps		Legal		
art	738.8	aid		
Lancers	**357.1**	law		345.01
Land				347.017
art	**730**	assistants		**340.023**
atlases	912.3–.9	counseling		361.38
forms	**551.4**	practice		**340.02**
ownership	**333.1–.5 vs.**			347.0504
	346.043	writing		**340:** Legal
redistribution	**333.31**			writing
reform	**333.31**	Legislative		
surveys	**333.009**	councils		328.361
trusts	346.068	powers		
Landscape		foreign rel.		328.346
architecture	712	Lending collections		
design	712	museums		069.13
planning	712	Letter writing		
Landslides		office practice		**651.7**
geology	**551.3**	Letters (alphabets)		
Language	**800:** Authors:	history		411
	Language	Letters (lit. form)		**800:** Form
	800: Language	Levels of government		**350:** Levels of
law	344.09			government
Last Judgment	232.7	Lexicography		*lang. sub.* 3028
Latin		Liability		
Old	**470**	insurance		368.1
Vulgar	**470**	of public officials		342.068
Law		of states		341.26
enforcement	**340:**	Library finance		
	Terminology	pub. admin.		351.852
reports	**340:** Legal	Librettos		782.028
	writing			782.12
Laws of Manu	294.5926	Licensing		
Leaders		law		
religious	**291.61–.65**	international		341.753
Christian church	**262.1**	municipal		**343.07**
Leadership	158.4			**344.01**
Learning	**153.15**	Lieder		**784.3**
	370.15	Liens		
Leather clothing		law		346.074
arts	**745.53**	Life		
		after death		133.9013
		sciences		**500**

Lighter-than-air	
aircraft	
mil. patrols	358.45
Lighting fixtures	
art	749.63
Lightships	623.828
Lingayats	294.55
Linguistically	
handicapped	
persons	362.42
students	**371.97**
Liquid wastes	**628.168**
	628.54
Literary	
criticism	**800: Literary criticism**
forms	**800: Authors: Form**
	800: Form
notebooks	*lit. sub.* 803
periods	**800: Authors: Literary periods**
	800: Literary periods
Lobbying	328.38
law	342.05
Local	
government	320.8
law	342.09
pub. admin.	**350: Levels of government**
	350: Local government
law	**340: Terminology: Municipal law**
	340: Law of countries with federal governments
	342.09

Locating businesses	658.11
	658.21
Logic	**153.43**
Loneliness	**158.2**
Lord's Supper	264.36
Lotteries	
recreation	790.134

M

Macroeconomics	**338.9**
Macromolecules	**547.84**
Madhyamika	294.392
Magnetism	
biophysics	574.191
Magnetosphere	551.513–.514
Mahasamghika	294.391
Mainstreaming	
education	**371.9**
library service	027.663
Malacology	**594**
Maladjusted students	371.94
Malpractice	346.032
Management	**658 & *s.s.* 068**
	658 vs. 658.4
Manicheism	299.932
Manuals	*s.s.* 0202
Manufactures	**620**
Manuscripts	
bibliographies	**090**
Manusmrti	294.5926
Many bodies problem	530.14
Maps	**911**
	912.1001–.1899
	912.3–.9
Mariculture	639.09162
Marine	
biology	**551.46**
carnivores	**599.5**
mammals	**599.5**
science	**551.46**
Market research	
management	658.83
	658.838
	658.89

Marketing	
management	**658 & *s.s.* 068:**
	(6)
	Marketing
	management
	658.809
Marxism	**335**
Masculinity	**155.33**
Masks	
headgear	391.43
Mass media	
law	**343.099**
Mass (physics)	**531.5**
spectrometry	**539.6028**
Mass (religion)	264.36
music	783.21
Masters tournaments	
golf	796.3527
Materials	
management	**658 & *s.s.* 068:**
	(5)
	Management
	of materials
properties of	
engineering	620.112
Mathematical	
economics	330.0151
linguistics	401.51
physics	**530.15**
Maturity	
psychology	155.25
Meadows	584.9045
Meals	
planning	**642.1–.5**
service	**642.1–.5**
Measurement	**389.1**
Measuring tools	621.994
Mechanics	**530.12**
Mechanics' liens	346.024
Medals	
law	343.032
	344.091

Medical	
evidence	347.067
folk lit.	615.882
history	610.9
jurisprudence	347.067
microbiology	**616.01**
missions	**266**
personnel	**616.1–.9: Add**
	table: **023**
	617.023
research	
animals	**574**
plants	**574**
sciences	**150**
technology	**616.1–.9: Add**
	table: **023**
	617. 023
Medieval	
architecture	**723**
ethical systems	**171**
philosophy	**140**
Meiosis	574.87322
Memberships	
directories	
legislatures	328.33
lists	*s.s.* 025
	s.s. **06**
Membrane processes	
water trmt.	628.164
Memory	**153.4**
cells	591.293
ed. psych.	**370.15**
physiology	**612.82**
Men	
prisons for	365.44
Mental	
illnesses	
health services	**362.2**
retardation	
soc. services	362.3
	362.36

Military-industrial		Modality	**160**
complex	355.0213	Model	
Milk production	**637.12**	airplanes	
	637.13 vs.	recreation	796.15
	637.14	codes	**342–347:**
Mill			*s.s.* 02632
econ. school	330.153	Models	688.1
Millennium	232.6		**745.592**
Mind	153		745.5928
Mind-body problem	153	Modern	
Mine		architecture	**724**
environments		dance	793.32
technology	**622.2**	mathematics	**372.73**
	622.31–.32	philosophy	**140**
reclamation	622.31		**190**
transport	**622.2**		**199**
	622.31–.32	Molecular	
Mineralogy	**546 vs. 549**	biology	**574.8**
	548 vs. 549		574.88
Minerals	**546 vs. 549**	spectra	
	549.13–.18	physics	539.6
	552	structure	
	552.09	biology	539.12 vs.
	553.6		**541.22**
prospecting for	**622.18**	Montessori system	371.392
Miniatures	688.1	Monuments	069.53
	745.5928	Mood music	782.85–.87
	745.67	Moon	
	751.77	astrology	133.53
Minibikes	629.2275	Mopeds	629.2272
Minimum wage	331.23	Moral	
Ministerial counseling	361.38	development	
Miracles	**226.7–.8**	psychology	155.418
	231.73	education	370.114
	232.917	judgment	
	235.2	psychology	153.46
Missiology	266.001	reasoning	
Mixed-media		psychology	153.46
arts	**702.81**	theology	**261.8 vs. 241**
sculpture	**730**	Morphology	574.4
Mobile homes		animals	591.4
law	346.043	human	**611 vs. 612**
	346.047		

Natural	
history	**508**
	570–590
religion	**100 vs. 200**
Nautical	
charts	623.8920222
craft	623.8207
maps	623.8920222
Negation	**160**
Negative income tax	336.242
Neurolinguistics	401.9
Newborn infants	
names for	929.44
News media	070.1
Newspapers	
bibliographies	070
Niagara Falls	*areas* 71339
Nitrogen fixation	**589.9504133**
Noh plays	*lit. sub.* 2051
Non-Christian religions	290
	291
Noncombat services	
mil. forces	**355.34**
Noncommissioned	
officers' clubs	355.346
Nonconformist	
(British context)	280.4
Nondenominational	
churches	289.9
Nonexplosive agents	
ordnance	**623.459**
Nonfiction novel	**800: Form**
Nonlinguistic	
communication	*s.s.* 0147
Nonliterary works	**800: Special**
	problems:
	Nonliterary
	works
Nonliturgical	
chants	**783.5**
choral works	**783.4**
Normal schools	**370.73**
Normative ethics	170.202

Nuclear	
deterrence	355.0217
explosives	662.2
forces	
mil. sci.	358.39
medicine	616.07575
test bans	358.39
warfare	358.39
Nuclei	539.723
Number building	
literature	**800: Number**
	building
Nursing	**610.73**
	610.736
Nutrition	**613.2**

O

Observation	
psychology	153.733
Occident	*areas* **1821**
Occupation	
mil. sci.	355.028
Occupations	
licensing	**344.01**
Occupied countries	**930–990: Wars:**
	Occupied
	countries
government	341.66
Ocean	
basins	*areas* **163–165**
	vs. *areas* **182**
trips	**910.4**
	910.41
Oceanographic	
engineering	**551.46**
Oceans	*areas* **163–165**
engineering	620.4162
	627
Offenses	
criminology	**364.1**
	364.1 vs.
	362–363

P

Paleozoology	590
Palmistry	138
Pan movements	320.54
Papal	
administration	262.136
opinions	262.91
Par value modification	346.0926
Parables	**226.7–.8**
Parades	394.5
Paralympics	796.48
Paraplegia	**616.837**
Parchment	
manufacture	676.2845
Parishes	
administration	**254**
Park	
police	363.28
services	363.68
Parks	
law	344.094
Parole	364.62
Particle interactions	539.754
Particles (nuclear)	539.754
Parts	
music	780.81–.84
Passover Haggadah	296.437
Pastoral literature	*lit. sub.* (Table 3–A) 14
Pathogenic organisms	**616.01**
Pathology	
human	**612**
	612 vs. 616
	616.07
Patient	
compliance	**615.5**
education	**615.5**
Patronage	
arts	700
Pattern perception	152.1423
Pavilions	
architecture	728.9
Pavlovian conditioning	153.152

Pedestrian	
facilities	
landscape design	717
malls	711.74
Pediatric	
dentistry	618.92097
diseases	**618.92**
specialties	618.92097
surgery	618.92097
Peer review	
medical services	**362.1**
Peerage	
genealogy	**929.7**
Penal colonies	365.34
Penances	291.34
Penmanship	**745.61**
Pension trusts	
tax law	343.064
Pensions	
government	331.255
	351.5
Pentecostal movement	**270.82**
Peoples Temple	289.9
Perception	**153.4**
ed. psych.	**370.15**
Perceptrons	001.534
Perfection of believers	234
Performing	
animals	791.8
arts	780.08 vs. 790.2
centers	725.83
law	344.097
Periodical indexes	**050**
Personal	
analysis	**158.1**
improvement	**158.1**
income	**339.32**
liability	
pub. officials	342.068
life	646.7
names	929.44
property	
law	346.047

Planation		Politicians	*s.s.* **092**
geology	**551.3**	Politics	
Planning		sociology	**320:** The
education	371.207		relationships
Plant			of political
location	658.21		science to the
management	**658 & *s.s.* 068:**		other social
	(2) Plant		sciences
	management	Pollution	304.28
Plasma cells	591.293		363.73
Plastic arts	**736–739 vs.**		363.737
	731–735		**363.738**
Play (activity)	155.418	biology	574.5222
Playhouses		damage	
architecture	728.9	law	346.038
Playing fields	790.068	engineering	620.85
Plea bargaining	345.072	prevention	
Plots		by management	658.408
operas	**782.8**	toxicology	615.902
Plymouth Brethren	289.9	Poor people	305.569
Poetry	**800:** Form	Popular music	780.42
	808.1	Population	**304.6**
Points		control	304.66
mechanics of	531		363.98
Police		law	344.048
corruption		problems	**363.9**
criminology	364.1323		363.91
files	363.24		363.92
manuals	**345.052**	projections	
services	**363.2**	statistics	312.8
	363.23	Porcelain	
Political		art	738
affairs			738.28
Christian view	**261.8**	Portraiture	**704.942**
conditions	**320.9**	Postal	
history	**320.9**	management	383.06
	320.9 vs. 900		**383.4**
	900	offenses	343.0992
institutions	**320:** The	organization	383.06
	relationships	services	
	of political	mil. forces	**355.34**
	science to the	Postdoctoral work	378.1553
	other social	Potato printing	761
	sciences		

Pottery	**738.2**	Preservation	
	738.23	art	702.87–.89
Poultry			720.288
food tech.	**664.931–.939**	historic	**920–990:**
Poverty			Historic
soc. services	362.57		preservation
	362.58	Pressure (dynamics)	531.11
Power		Pressure groups	322.43–.44
resources	**333.79**	Prevention	
supply	363.62	soc. problems	**362–363:** Add
Practice			table: **6 vs. 7**
law	**340.023**		
	347.0504	Price supports	
teaching	*s.s.* **07**	law	343.083
	370.733	Primitive	
Prairies	584.9045	art	709.011
Prayer	264.1	painting	**759.011**
	264.13	sculpture	732.2
Precalculus	512.1	Primitivism	*lit. sub.*
	515		(Table 3–A) 1
Precipitation		Printmaking	**761–767**
meteorology	551.5773	Prints	**769.5**
Preemption		Prison reform	**365**
law		Prisoner-of-war camps	365.48
international	341.754		**930–990:** Wars:
municipal	343.025		Prison,
Pregnancy	**599.03**		internment,
	612.63		& concentra-
			tion camps
Prehistoric man	573.3	Prisoners	
Preliminary materials		rights of	
law	**342–347:**	law	344.035643
	s.s. 0262–	Prisons	**930–990:** Wars:
	s.s. 0263		Prison,
	342–347:		internment,
	s.s. 0262		& concentra-
	348.01		tion camps
Presbyterian Church		Private	
of Wales	285.23	housing	
Preschool children		law	**344.063635**
psychology	155.423	international law	**340.9**
Prescriptive grammar	*lang. sub.* **8**		**341**
		schools	371.02

Privateering	
abolition	341.63
Prize law	341.63
	343.096
Probabilities	**519.2**
	519.24
Problem solving	**153.43**
Procaryotic organisms	**589.9**
Procedure	
law	347.05
Procedures	*s.s.* **072 vs.**
	s.s. **028**
Process metallurgy	**669**
Processions	394.5
Product	
hazards	**363.19**
recall	
law	**343.0944**
Production	
economics	**338**
agriculture	**630**
management	**658 & *s.s.* 068:**
	(4)
	Production
	management
scripts	**792.9**
Products	
lists of	**338.1–.4**
	380.141–.145
	381.382
Professional writing	**808.066**
Programmed texts	*s.s.* 077
Promotion	
mil. service	
law	343.013
Pronunciation	*lang. sub.* 152
	lang. sub. 81
Proofs of God	212.1
Propaganda	327.14
Properties of materials	620.112
Property insurance	368.1
Prophecy	220.15

Proposed legislation	**350: Public administration: Executive branch of government**
Prose literature	*lit. sub.* 808
Prosody	808.1
Prosthetic devices	**617.9**
Protest	361.25
songs	784.68
Protests	322.43–.44
Protists	589
Provincial	
governments	**350: Levels of government**
Provisional courts	342.062
Pseudepigrapha	221.44
	229.8–.9
Pseudo gospels	**229.8–.9**
Psionic medicine	**615.53**
Psychiatric disorders	**150**
	150 vs. 616.89
	616.89
	616.890019
Psychiatry	**150 vs. 616.89**
	150.195
Psychoanalysis	616.890019
	616.8917019
	616.8917092
	616.892–.898
Psychoanalytic systems	**150 vs. 616.89**
	150.195
Psychodiagnoses	157.92
Psycholinguistics	153.6
	401.9
Psychological	
systems	150.19
warfare	327.14
Psychology	**130**
education	**370.15**
experimental	150.724
	152
schools of	150.19

Psychophysiology	**152 vs. 612.8**
	612.8
Psychosomatic	
medicine	616.08
	616.63
	616.8048
	616.84
Psychotherapy	**616.892–.898**
Public	
administration	**350:** Public ad-
	ministration
administrators	*s.s.* **092**
corporations	351.0092
health	**362.1–.4**
	613–614 vs.
	362.1
	613 vs. 614
lending rights	**346.048**
performance	**791**
relations	
libraries	021.7
safety	**363.1**
schools	371.01
finance	**379.11**
schools (U.K.)	373.222
utilities	**363.5, 363.6,**
	& 363.8
	363.6 vs. 333.7
Publishers	**070.5**
Punch and Judy shows	*lit. sub.* 2057
Puppet films	791.433
Puzzles	
recreation	793.73

Q

Q document	**226.06**
Qualitative chemistry	**543 vs. 544–545**
Quantitative chemistry	**543 vs. 544–545**
Quantitative	
psychology	155.4120287
Quantum	**530.12**
Questions	
logic	**160**
Quilts	746.46

R

ROTC	
law	343.012
Racial	
differences	572.3
groups	*s.s.* **08**
	s.s. **08 vs.** *s.s.* **09**
history	**930–990:**
	Racial,
	ethnic,
	national
	groups
psychology	**155.8 vs. 155.89**
sociology	**305.8**
Racing car sets	790.133
Radiation poisoning	615.92
Radical writing	*lit. sub.*
	(Table 3–A) 1
Radiesthesia	615.845
Radio programs	
commerce	384.5443
recreation	**791.44**
	791.447
	791.4475
Radiology	616.0757
	616.07572
Radionics	615.845
Radiopharmacy	615.2
Railroad transportation	**385**
Ranches	636.01
Rank	
mil. service	
law	343.013
Rapid transit facilities	
architecture	711.75
	725.31
	725.33
Rapture	236
Rare books	
bibliographies	**090**
Ras Tafari movement	299.67
Rat abatement	
programs	363.78

Rationing	**363.5, 363.6,**	Reform	
	& 363.8	movements	303.84
	363.856		322.43–.44
pub. admin.	351.829	soc. action	361.25
Raw potato printing	761	Regional	
Readers (books)	*lang. sub.* 864	medicine	**617.5**
	808.0427	sociology	**301.09**
Reading	*lang. sub.* 86	surgery	**617.5**
Real		Regions	*areas* **1**
estate		Registers	
investment trusts	346.0437	govt. personnel	**351.2**
maps	912.3–.9	Rehabilitation	157.94
property		of criminals	346.013
govt. ownership	351.7122–.7123	Religion	**100 vs. 200**
law	346.0436		**133 vs. 200**
variables	**515.8**		**170**
Reasoning		and state	322.1 vs. **200**
psychology	**153.4**	in education	**377**
	153.43	elementary	372.8
Rebels	*lit. sub.* (Table	Religious	
	3–A) 352	associations	366
Recall	153.152	instruction	
Recitations	*lit. sub.* 504	Christian	**207**
Records	**001.55**	orders	**255**
management			**255.01–.09**
law			**255.901–.909**
business	346.065	philosophy	**181.04–.09**
government	342.066	Remedial measures	
privacy of		soc. problems	**362–363:**
law	342.0858		Add table: **8**
Recreation		Remote sensing	
centers	790.068	technology	621.3678
on Sunday	263.4	Rental collections	
services	363.68	museums	069.13
Red meats		Reorganization	
food tech.	**664.921–.929**	executive depts.	
Redemption		law	342.064
Christian	232.3	Repair	
Redistribution of land	**333.31**	household	**643.3–.7**
Reference (reasoning)	**160**	Repealed laws	**348.3–.9**
Reflexes	**150.194**		

Rules of order	060.42
Rural	
civilization	**630**
communities	307.72
conditions	**630**

S

Sabbatical year	
Judaism	296.43
Sacramentaries	264.023
Sacrifices	291.34
Safety	*s.s.* 0289
	363.1
	900:
	Classifica-
	tion of
	specific
	events
management	**658 & *s.s.* 068**
Saints	
miracles by	235.2
Salaries management	**658.322**
Sales catalogs	
art works	707.4
Salt-water lagoons	551.4609
Salvage operations	363.348
Sanitary engineering	**628**
Sanitation services	
mil. forces	355.345
Sarvastivada	294.391
Satire	*lit. sub.* 7
Sautrantika	294.391
Scarcity School	
economics	330.153
Scenarios	
musical	782.028

School	
algebra	512.9
children	
psychology	155.424
health	**371.7**
libraries	371.3078
mathematics	**510**
policy	**371**
resource centers	371.3078
safety	**371.7**
	371.77
Schools of philosophy	101
Schrödinger	
representation	530.124
	530.124 vs.
	531.1133
Science	
and religion	**215**
policy	**338.9**
	500
Scientific photography	**778.3 vs.**
	621.367
Scores	
music	780.81–.84
Scoring	
motion pictures	782.85
television programs	782.87
Scotland	941
Screening programs	
health care	362.17
Sculpture	**736–739 vs.**
	731–735
	736.4
Sea	
basins	*areas* **163–165**
	vs. *areas* **182**
trips	**910.4**
	910.41
Seafood	
food tech.	**664.941–.949**
Second Coming of	
Christ	232.6
Secondary schools	*s.s.* 0712

Sleep	**154.6** vs.		Social (continued)	
	612.821		security	**368.4**
disturbances	**616.89**		law	
Slot machines			international	341.76
recreation	795.2		municipal	344.023
Small arms			taxes (U.S.)	343.05
ammunition	623.451		services	**361–365**
practice				**362–363**
mil. sci.	**355.547–.548**			**362–363:**
Snacks				Add table: **8**
food tech.	664.6			**363**
Snow camping	796.54		stratification	**305**
Soaps	667.13		structure	**305**
Sociability			theology	**261**
ethics	**177**			**261.8** vs. **241**
Social			welfare	**361** vs. **362**
action	361.25			**361.02–.06**
	361.6			**362**
	361.7		Socialism	**335**
	362–363:		Socialist communities	335.9
	Add table: **5**		Sociobiology	156
	362.0425		Socioeconomic	
change	**303.4**		affairs	
environment			Christian view	**261.8**
psychology	**155.92**		planning	**361**
institutions	**306**			**361.6**
insurance	**343.078**		regions	*areas* 172
pathology	301–306 vs.		Sociological	
	361–365		jurisprudence	340.115
problems	**361–365**		Sociology	**301–307**
	361		of education	**370.19**
	361.1			**370.1934**
	361.1 vs.		of politics	**320:** The
	362.042			relationships
	362–363			of political
	363			science to
psychology	**150**			other social
	150 vs. **302–307**			sciences
relations				
ethics	**177**			
sciences	**150**			

Soil		Spelling	*lang. sub.* 81
conditioners	**631.8**	Spermatophytes	**581**
conservation	333.7316	Spiritualism	*lit. sub.* (Table
management			3–A) 37
on farms	636.01		133.8
pollution	**628.54**		133.9
surveys	**631.47 vs.**	Sports *see* Athletics	
	631.49	Squaring the circle	516.204
	912.1001–.1899	Squatters' rights	
Soils	**631.4**	property law	346.0432
reclamation	631.6	Standardization	
Solar houses	697.78	law	343.075
Soldering	671.56	Stars	**523.8**
Solid wastes	628.1	Starting businesses	658.11
	628.44	State and religion	322.1 vs. **200**
pub. admin.	**351.824**	States	**320.1**
Songs	783.6	liability of	341.26
	784.3	States of matter	**530.4**
Soto	294.3927	Statesmen	*s.s.* **092**
Souls	129	Statistical	
Sound		analysis	001.4225
sculpture	**730**		**310**
synchronization		mechanics	**530.13**
motion pictures	782.85	method	*s.s.* 0723
television		physics	**530.13**
programs	782.87	Statistics	*s.s.* 0212
Sources of water	628.11		**519.2**
Space	*areas* **19 vs.**		**519.5 vs.**
	areas **99**		**001.422**
colonies	629.442	Status offenders	364.36
physiology	612.0144	Steel	
sciences	500.5	engineering	620.17
Special		Stenography	**651.374**
delivery	383.145	Stick fighting	796.8
education	**371.9**	Stoneware	
olympics	796.48	art	738
Spectra	539.6		738.38
	539.7	Stony materials	
Speculative philosophy	**110**	econ. geol.	**553.5 vs. 552**
Speech	**808.5**		**553.6**
perception	401.9	petrology	552.03
training	*lang. sub.* 152	Storage	
Speeches	**800:** Form	data processing	001.644

Stoves	
art	749.62
Strategy	
mil. sci.	**355.021 vs.**
	355.43
	355.43
Stratifications	
geology	551.81
Street furniture	
landscape design	717
Strength of materials	**620.1121–.1126**
Stress incontinence	616.63
Student	
finance	**378.3**
organizations	*s.s.* **06**
participation	
school discipline	371.207
periodicals	371.805
Students	
law	344.079
sociology of	**370.1934**
Study and teaching	**370**
spec. subj.	370.113
Study-release courses	
(U.S.)	374.29
Style manuals	**808.02**
Subject	
bibliographies	016
catalogs	016
Submarine	
geology	551.4608
geomorphology	**551.4**
physiology	612.014415
Subsidence	
geology	**551.3**
Subsurface	
mining	**622.2**
resources	**333.8**
Suburban	
transportation	**388.4**
Subversion	327.12
Success in business	646.7
Sufism	**297.4**

Summer houses	
architecture	728.9
Summonses	345.072
Sun (astrology)	133.53
Sunday	
observance	263.4
recreation	263.4
work	263.4
Superstitions	001.96
Surface	
mining	**622.31–.32**
waters	553.78–.79
Surgery	**617**
Surgical	
appliances	617.9
technology	617.023
therapy	**617:** Add
	table: **059**
	617: Add
	table: **06**
	617.4
Surrealism	*lit. sub.*
	(Table 3–A) 1
Surveys	*s.s.* 0723
	507.23
Swimming pools	
law	346.043
Symbolic logic	**160**
Symbolism	
art	**704.9432–.9434**
astrology	133.53
Sympathy	179.9
Symptomatology	616.072
	616.1–.9: Add
	table: **072**
Synagogue dedication	296.44
Synagogues	296.65
Synchronization of	
sound	
motion pictures	782.85
television programs	782.87
Syncretistic religions	**299**

Synopses	*s.s.* 0202	Teachers	371.1
Synoptic meteorology	551.69		**371.12**
Synthetic		education of	370.71
meat			**371.12**
food tech.	664.64	selection	379.157
petroleum	665.5	Teachers' colleges	**370.73**
Systems	620.7	Teaching methods	**371.12**
analysis	001.61	Technical	
of law	340.5	innovations	
		economics	338.06

T

		reports	**300 vs. 600**
T cells	**591.29**	writing	**808.066**
Tableware		Techniques	*s.s.* **072 vs.**
pottery	738.23		*s.s.* **028**
Tariff		Technological	
law	343.056	photography	**778.3 vs.**
Tax			**621.367**
law	**343.04**	Technology	**300 vs. 600**
	343.042		**500**
	343.043		**621 vs. 530**
	343.05	transfer	**338.9**
	343.052	Telecommunication	
	343.0523	companies	**384**
	343.056	Telephone counseling	361.323
	343.064	Television	
	343.066	musicals	**782.81**
management	658.153	photography	621.388
maps	912.3–.9	programs	
shelters	343.0523	commerce	384.55443
Taxation		recreation	791.457
internat. law	**341.75**		791.4575
Taxes	**336.2**	Temperature	
	336.201	geology	**551.3**
pub. admin.	**351.724**	Temples	
Tax-exempt		architecture	**726.1**
organizations		Temporary exhibitions	
tax law	**343.066**	art	**707.4**
Teacher		Tender offers	
centers	370.72	law	346.0666
certification	379.157	Tenure	
corps	**371.967**	teachers	371.14
training	*s.s.* **07**	Terminal care	
		health services	362.17

Terminology	*s.s.* **014**	Therapies	**615.8**
Territory of states	320.12 vs. **911**		615.856
Terrorism	322.42		**616.892–.898**
	364.1		**617:** Add
Terrorist groups	322.42		table: **059**
Testing	*s.s.* **0287**		**617:** Add
	150.287		table: **06**
	152.1		**617.4**
	152.8	Therapy	**613 vs. 615.8**
	153.0287		**615.53**
	153.90287		**615.8809**
	153.93		**616.1–.9:** Add
	155.0287		table: **06**
	155.28	Thermal properties	
	155.4120287	eng. materials	**620.1121**
	155.4180287	Thinking	**153.4**
Tests	**155**		**612.82**
	155.28	Thirteen Articles	
education	**371.26**	of Faith	**296.3**
	371.26 vs.	Thought	**153.4**
	371.271	Tibetan Buddhism	299.54
	372.3–.8	Tidal atlases	**912.1001–.1899**
Test-tube babies	618.178059	Tides	**525.6**
Textbooks	*s.s.* **07**		551.4708
	s.s. 077	Time	
	371.32	measurement	529.78 vs.
	372.3–.8		**681.11**
Textile		sharing	
arts	**746.1–.9**	real property	333.3234
furnishings	**746.94–.98**	Tin cans	
Textiles	**746.04**	handicrafts	745.56
Texts		Tipitika	294.382
liturgical music	**783.2**	Tissue biology	**574.8**
Thematic catalogs	780.924	human	**611 vs. 612**
Theoretical astronomy	**521.5 vs. 523**	Tobacco substitutes	688.4
Theory	*s.s.* **01**	Top management	**658.42**
Therapeutic systems	**615.53**	Topological algebras	512.2
Therapeutics	615		512.22
		Topology	514
		Torts	**345.02**
		Tour books	910.202

U

Ulama	297.6
Ultimatums	341.58
Undercover work	
police services	363.232
Underwater mining	627.98
Unification Church	289.9
Uniforms	
military	355.14 vs.
	355.81
	355.1409
Union lists	
of legal materials	348.028
Unions	331.8832
	331.8833
	331.8834
	331.886
mil. personnel	355.338
United Kingdom	*areas* **41** vs.
	areas **42**
	941
Universal priesthood	
of believers	234
University faculties	**378.4–.9**
Urban heat islands	551.5252
Ureters	
diseases	616.63
surgery	617.461
Usury	
law	346.073
Utopian socialism	335.02

V

Vaibhasika	294.391
Valued functions	**515.7**
Variation	
genetics	**575.2**
	575.28
Vases	
art	738.23
Vegetable carving	745.924

Vegetarian cookery	**641.6**
Vegetation	
geology	**551.3**
Vehicles	**629.046 vs.**
	385–388
law	**343.0944**
Vehicular accidents	
investigations	363.12565
Verb tables	*lang. sub.* **82**
Veterans'	
benefits	
mil. sci.	**355.115**
insurance	343.011
Veterinary	
medicine	**610**
sciences	**636.089**
Vetos	328.375
Vibrational spectra	539.6
Vices	
ethics	179.8–.9
Victimology	362.88
Victims	
of crime	
soc. services	**364**
of war	
internat. law	341.67
Vigilance	
psychology	153.733
Vijnanavada	294.392
Villages	*areas* **4–9:**
	Cities,
	towns,
	villages
	307.72
	307.762
Viola da gamba	787.42
Violent crimes	
statistics	312.2
	312.4
Virgin birth	232.921
Virtues	
ethics	179.8–.9
	179.9

Water		Welfare services	**361 vs. 362**
analysis	628.161		**361.02–.06**
conservation	333.7316		**362**
	628.11	law	**343.078**
management			**344.031–.032**
agriculture	636.01	veterans	
pollution		internat. law	341.766
engineering	**628.168** vs.	Well digging	628.114
	363.7394	Welsh Calvinistic	
	628.168 vs.	Methodist Church	285.23
	628.162	Western	
	628.1683	Hemisphere	*areas* **1812**
	628.1686	philosophy	**140**
	628.1688		**190**
	628.746	White magic	*lit. sub.* (Table
soc. measures	363.7394		3–A) 37
quality	363.61	Whole milk	
	553.7	processing	**637.13 vs.**
requirements	628.17		**637.14**
safety		Wife beating	362.83
sports	797		364.1555
	797.200289	Wildings	155.4567
sources	628.11	Winemaking	663.2
supply		Wire	
engineering	628.1	handicrafts	745.56
	628.10287	Wiretapping	
	628.161	law	**345.052**
	628.162	Witchcraft	*lit. sub.* (Table
soc. services	363.61		3–A) 37
treatment			133.43
sanitary eng.	**628.746**	Witches	133.43
use	628.17		398.22
Watercolors	**741.9**		808.83935213
Wave mechanics	530.124	Wolf children	155.4567
	530.124 vs.	Women	305.42
	531.1133		305.43
Waves	530.124	Wood carving	736.4
	530.124 vs.	Woodlands	582.1605
	531.1133	Word lists	*s.s.* **014**
Weather	**551.5 vs. 551.6**	Words	
belts	551.69	for music	781.96
			782.832
			783.2